ZAGATSURVEY®

2006/07

AMERICA'S TOP GOLF COURSES

Golf Editors: Joseph Passov, Craig Better and Tom Mackin

Editor: Betsy Andrews

Published and distributed by
ZAGAT SURVEY, LLC
4 Columbus Circle
New York, New York 10019
Tel: 212 977 6000
E-mail: golf@zagat.com
Web site: www.zagat.com

Acknowledgments

We thank ESPN Golf Schools, Sara Kalish, Nick Nicholas and Betsy Ryan Passov. We are also grateful to our senior associate editor, Shelley Gallagher, and editorial assistant, Leah Hochbaum, as well as the following members of our staff: Reni Chin, Larry Cohn, Schuyler Frazier, Jeff Freier, Natalie Lebert, Mike Liao, Dave Makulec, Robert Poole, Josh Rogers, Thomas Sheehan, Joshua Siegel, Erinn Stivala and Sharon Yates.

Contents

About This Survey

Here are the results of our *2006/07 America's Top Golf Courses Survey* covering 1,095 top courses in the USA, including the Virgin Islands and Puerto Rico.

This marks the 26th year that Zagat Survey has reported on the shared experiences of diners, travelers and, more recently, golfers. What started in 1979 as a hobby involving 200 of our friends rating local NYC restaurants has come a long way. Today we have over 250,000 active surveyors and now cover entertaining, hotels, resorts, spas, movies, music, nightlife, restaurants, shopping and tourist attractions. All of these guides are based on consumer surveys. Our guides are also available on PDAs, cell phones and by subscription at zagat.com, where you can vote and shop as well.

By regularly surveying large numbers of avid customers, we hope to have achieved a uniquely current and reliable guide. Thanks to our nearly 6,000 reviewers who play an impressive annual total of 552,000 rounds, you have the benefit of your fellow golfers' experiences at virtually every course. Of our surveyors, 83% are men, 17% women; the breakdown by age is 7% in their 20s; 26%, 30s; 24%, 40s; 28%, 50s; and 15%, 60s and above. Our editors have done their best to synopsize our surveyors' opinions, with their comments shown in quotation marks. We sincerely thank each of these people; this book is really "theirs."

We are especially grateful to our editors, Joseph Passov, author of *The Unofficial Guide to Golf Vacations in the Eastern U.S.*; Craig Better, contributing writer to *Golf Magazine*, *Travel + Leisure Golf* and editor of *Pub Links Golfer – NJ/PA*; and Tom Mackin, former associate editor of *Golf Magazine*.

To help you find the right course, we have prepared a number of handy lists – see Most Popular (page 9) and Top Ratings (pages 10–18) – and 45 indexes, plus information on urban driving ranges and 100 leading private courses.

To vote in any of our upcoming *Surveys*, just register at zagat.com. Each participant will receive a free copy of the resulting guide (or a comparable reward). Your comments and even criticisms of this guide are also solicited. There is always room for improvement with your help. Just contact us at golf@zagat.com.

New York, NY
September 22, 2005

Nina and Tim Zagat

What's New

Move over, baseball – as Zagat's *2006/07 America's Top Golf Courses* indicates, golf is fast becoming a favorite American pastime. And golfers no longer play close to home only. Over 85% of our surveyors plan at least one golf vacation in the next year. Course owners are ready for them, with the best of new and traditional approaches.

The Grass Is Greener: Venerable properties like Arizona's Grayhawk, Hawaii's Kapalua and Florida's Walt Disney World tore up their Pro Tour greens in 2005 and replaced them with innovative grasses that stay healthier longer. As turf science advances, look for more layouts to follow suit.

Arizona Innovations: Arizona outfits are rolling out new wheels. Single swingers buzz about Kierland in the sporty, roofless Segway GT, the Vespa of golf carts, which shortens playing time and is gentler on the green stuff. Hot shots there and at Whirlwind cool off on air-conditioned rides, while in winter they crank up the heat, courtesy of Scottsdale-based Coolwell's climate-control system.

These Cleats Were Made for Walkin': For purists, there's nothing better than to walk with a caddie toting your bag. Neo-traditionalists embrace a caddie comeback at top spots like Oregon's Bandon Dunes and Wisconsin's Whistling Straits and newcomers like South Carolina's May River at Palmetto Bluff and Wynn Las Vegas. Even old favorites, like Barton Creek's Fazio Foothills in Texas and the Champ at Florida's PGA National, are getting back to basics.

Weather Woes: Duffer-destination states California and Florida were hit hard by natural disasters. DeBary, Hunter's Creek and Amelia Island's Oak Marsh rebuilt fairways and greens following four Florida hurricanes. Others like Lost Key will be in rehab for a while. As the song says, "It never rains in California . . . It pours. Man, it pours." Cimarrón and Rustic Canyon, two of the courses washed out by 2005's desert deluge, have cleaned up better than ever.

Mackdaddy Tracks: High-profile tracks pamper high-rolling hacks at new casino clubs like Wynn Las Vegas with a layout by Tom Fazio, who also works his voodoo at Louisiana's L'Auberge du Lac, where Contraband Bayou unveils later in 2005. And though it's still being tweaked at press time, Trump National Golf Club, perched above the Pacific in California's Rancho Palos Verdes, will be ready, The Donald promises, for its fall 2005 debut at the LPGA's Office Depot Championship.

Pony Up for Putts: With fees ranging from $20 for Kansas' Buffalo Dunes to a walloping Wynn-priced $500, there are putts for every pocket. Most swingers are spenders, though, with more than half saying they are willing to shell out at least $200 for a top-ranked round.

Phoenix, AZ   Joseph Passov
September 22, 2005

Golf Travel Tips

Leave Your Sticks at Home: That's right, leave 'em in the garage. Consider using rental sets for trips with fewer than three rounds. Rental quality has improved markedly in recent years, "borrowed-club syndrome" suggests you'll play better with someone else's clubs, and you'll save yourself heavy lifting. If you must bring your clubs but don't trust the airlines, consider a club-shipping service.

Get the Best Rates: It's all about the discounts. Check into special rates via corporate affiliations, affinity groups, senior citizenship and frequent-flier clubs. With resorts, when a rate is quoted, always ask: "Is this the lowest price you have?" Usually, calling resorts directly rather than a chain's toll-free number can score you lower rates.

Research Online: The Internet can be your best friend when it comes to getting the lowdown on the links. More and more courses have their own Web sites providing descriptions, photos and course maps, as well as online-only bargains. Throughout this guide, we've provided these Web site addresses.

Go Against the Grain: Oftentimes following the crowd will cost you. If you go to Palm Springs or Scottsdale on a winter weekend, you'll pay top dollar, wait to play or face other booking restrictions. On the other hand, you'll get better value and easier access during shoulder seasons and weekdays, especially if you try some less well-known destinations. Many of these are wonderful to play and are listed herein. And anywhere you go, look for twilight and replay discounts.

Don't Count On a Career Round: You shouldn't expect to score well your first time on any course. GPS, yardage books and pin position sheets can only do so much. Consider planning two rounds at a track you're excited about, or if you're with a group, try a scramble format or a betting game that keeps everyone interested. Remember, golf is supposed to be fun, especially when you're on vacation!

Flash a Little Green: Sometimes, to be treated like a king you need to show the money. Golf isn't a high-paying industry unless your name is Tiger or Jack, so a few bucks' tip can often make a big difference in how you're treated.

Tap-Ins – A Few Final Thoughts: Don't forget the rain gear. Getting stuck on the back nine during a downpour without a jacket can ruin any round. Also, pack an extra pair of golf shoes if you're playing more than three rounds. A good travel planner can also make your life easier. So will calling the course a few days in advance to double-check your tee time, make sure the greens aren't being aerated that day and so on. Lastly, and we can't stress this enough – leave a little time to get lost, and enjoy yourself no matter how you play. After all, it sure beats working!

Ratings & Symbols

Name, Address, Phone Number, Web Site, Yardage, USGA Rating, Slope

Caddies/Forecaddies, Carts Only, Guests Only, Restricted Tee Times

Zagat Ratings

		C	F	S	V	$
Tim & Nina's Hole-in-One, Swamp	🏃🛒⚴🕐	▽ 17	19	15	18	$195

4 Columbus Circle; 212-977-6000; www.zagat.com; 6100/5000; 65.7/63.4; 119/105

"It ain't Pebble Beach", but "play is kinda rocky" anyway at this "rodent-infested" urban course near "scenic" Central Park, where "hackers" and "aging caddies" "duck errant balls"; since "its best hole is the 19th", golfers who gush over "gorgeous links" aren't referring to the "weedy greens" so much as the "killer hot dogs" from the "snack carts that are always in the way."

Review, with surveyors' comments in quotes

Properties throughout Tops lists are followed by nearest major city/area. The alphabetical index at the back of the book lists their page numbers.

Top Spots: Courses with the highest overall ratings, popularity and importance are listed in BLOCK CAPITAL LETTERS.

🏃 Caddies/Forecaddies
🛒 Carts Only
⚴ Guests Only
🕐 Restricted Tee Times (call ahead for public hours)

Ratings are on a scale of **0** to **30** as follows:

C Course	F Facilities	S Service	V Value
17	19	15	18

0–9 poor to fair	**20–25** very good to excellent
10–15 fair to good	**26–30** extraordinary to perfection
16–19 good to very good	▽ low response/less reliable

Price ($) is the cost per non-member or non-guest to play 18 holes on a weekend in high season (excluding the extra cost of a cart), **i.e. the highest possible price of play.**

Most Popular

Each of our surveyors has been asked to name his or her five favorite courses. The following list reflects their choices.

1. Pebble Beach, *Monterey Peninsula, CA*
2. Bethpage, Black, *Long Island, NY*
3. Spyglass Hill, *Monterey Peninsula, CA*
4. Kapalua, Plantation, *Maui, HI*
5. Spanish Bay, *Monterey Peninsula, CA*
6. Kiawah Island, Ocean, *Charleston, SC*
7. Torrey Pines, South, *San Diego, CA*
8. TPC at Sawgrass, Stadium, *Jacksonville, FL*
9. Bandon Dunes, Bandon Dunes Course, *Coos Bay, OR*
10. Pinehurst Resort, No. 2, *Pinehurst, NC*
11. Bandon Dunes, Pacific Dunes, *Coos Bay, OR*
12. Whistling Straits, Straits, *Kohler, WI*
13. Montauk Downs, *Long Island, NY*
14. Sea Pines, Harbour Town Golf Links, *Hilton Head, SC*
15. Troon North, Monument, *Scottsdale, AZ*
16. Pasatiempo, *Santa Cruz, CA*
17. Poppy Hills, *Monterey Peninsula, CA*
18. Half Moon Bay, Ocean, *San Francisco Bay Area, CA*
19. Bethpage, Red, *Long Island, NY*
20. Crystal Springs, Ballyowen, *NYC Metro*
21. Pine Hill, *Cherry Hill, NJ*
22. Caledonia Golf & Fish Club, *Pawleys Island, SC*
23. Pelican Hill, Ocean North, *Orange County, CA*
24. Torrey Pines, North, *San Diego, CA**
25. Doral, Blue Monster, *Miami, FL*
26. Grayhawk, Raptor, *Scottsdale, AZ*
27. Aviara, *San Diego, CA*
28. Harbor Pines, *Atlantic City, NJ*
29. Cog Hill, No. 4 (Dubsdread), *Chicago, IL*
30. Hominy Hill, *Freehold, NJ*
31. World Woods, Pine Barrens, *Tampa, FL*
32. We-Ko-Pa, *Scottsdale, AZ*
33. Boulders, North, *Scottsdale, AZ*
34. Experience at Koele, *Lanai, HI*
35. Princeville, Prince, *Kauai, HI**
36. Harding Park, *San Francisco Bay Area, CA*
37. Harbor Links, *Long Island, NY*
38. Troon North, Pinnacle, *Scottsdale, AZ**
39. Pelican Hill, Ocean South, *Orange County, CA*
40. Centennial, *NYC Metro*
41. Bulle Rock, *Baltimore, MD*
42. Challenge at Manele, *Lanai, HI*
43. Blackwolf Run, River, *Kohler, WI*
44. Bethpage, Blue, *Long Island, NY*
45. Long Island National, *Long Island, NY*
46. Arnold Palmer's Bay Hill, *Orlando, FL*
47. Architects, *Trenton, NJ*
48. Bethpage, Green, *Long Island, NY**
49. Kapalua, Bay, *Maui, HI*
50. Whiskey Creek, *Frederick, MD*

* Indicates a tie with course above

Top Ratings

Excluding courses with low voting.

Top-Rated Courses

30 Whistling Straits, Straits, *Kohler, WI*
29 Bandon Dunes, Bandon Dunes Course, *Coos Bay, OR*
    Bethpage, Black, *Long Island, NY*
    Pebble Beach, *Monterey Peninsula, CA*
    TPC at Sawgrass, Stadium, *Jacksonville, FL*
    Bandon Dunes, Pacific Dunes, *Coos Bay, OR*
    Arcadia Bluffs, *Traverse City, MI*
    Kiawah Island, Ocean, *Charleston, SC*
    Blackwolf Run, River, *Kohler, WI*
    Bulle Rock, *Baltimore, MD*
    Madden's on Gull Lake, Classic, *Brainerd, MN*
    Longaberger, *Columbus, OH*
    Spyglass Hill, *Monterey Peninsula, CA*
    Sunriver, Crosswater, *Bend, OR*
28 Paa-Ko Ridge, *Albuquerque, NM*
    Kapalua, Plantation, *Maui, HI*
    Pinehurst Resort, No. 2, *Pinehurst, NC*
    We-Ko-Pa, *Scottsdale, AZ*
    Sugarloaf, *Central ME*
    Ocean Hammock, *Daytona Beach, FL*
    Cog Hill, No. 4 (Dubsdread), *Chicago, IL*
    World Woods, Pine Barrens, *Tampa, FL*
    Pole Creek, *Denver, CO*
    Troon North, Monument, *Scottsdale, AZ*
    Shadow Creek, *Las Vegas, NV*
    Links at Lighthouse Sound, *Ocean City, MD*
    Gold Canyon, Dinosaur Mountain, *Phoenix, AZ*
    Arnold Palmer's Bay Hill, *Orlando, FL*
    Caledonia Golf & Fish Club, *Pawleys Island, SC*
    Karsten Creek, *Stillwater, OK*
    Barton Creek, Fazio Canyons, *Austin, TX*
    Lakewood Shores, Gailes, *Bay City, MI*
    Reflection Bay at Lake Las Vegas, *Las Vegas, NV*
    Wolf Creek, *Las Vegas, NV*
    Coral Canyon, *St. George, UT*
    Grossinger, Big G, *Catskills, NY*
    Grand View Lodge, Deacon's Lodge, *Brainerd, MN*
    Princeville, Prince, *Kauai, HI*
    Challenge at Manele, *Lanai, HI*
    Coyote Moon, *Lake Tahoe, CA*
27 Cambrian Ridge, *Montgomery, AL*
    Troon North, Pinnacle, *Scottsdale, AZ*
    Ventana Canyon, Mountain, *Tucson, AZ*
    Sea Pines, Harbour Town Golf Links, *Hilton Head, SC*
    Belgrade Lakes, *Central ME*
    Sandestin, Raven, *Panhandle, FL**
    Stonewall, *Leesburg, VA*
    Boyne Highlands, Arthur Hills, *Petoskey, MI*
    Capitol Hill, Judge, *Montgomery, AL**
    Shanty Creek, The Legend, *Traverse City, MI**

Top Courses by Region

Arizona
28 We-Ko-Pa, *Scottsdale*
   Troon North, Monument, *Scottsdale*
   Gold Canyon, Dinosaur Mountain, *Phoenix*
27 Troon North, Pinnacle, *Scottsdale*
   Ventana Canyon, Mountain, *Tucson*
   Boulders, North, *Scottsdale*
   Grayhawk, Raptor, *Scottsdale*
26 Ventana Canyon, Canyon, *Tucson*
   Vistoso, *Tucson*
   Boulders, South, *Scottsdale*

California
29 Pebble Beach, *Monterey Peninsula*
   Spyglass Hill, *Monterey Peninsula*
28 Coyote Moon, *Lake Tahoe*
27 CordeValle, *San Francisco Bay Area*
   Pasatiempo, *Santa Cruz*
   La Purisima, *Santa Barbara*
   Maderas, *San Diego*
26 Dragon at Gold Mountain, *Lake Tahoe*
   Torrey Pines, South, *San Diego*
   Pelican Hill, Ocean North, *Orange County*

Florida
29 TPC at Sawgrass, Stadium, *Jacksonville*
28 Ocean Hammock, *Daytona Beach*
   World Woods, Pine Barrens, *Tampa*
   Arnold Palmer's Bay Hill, *Orlando*
27 Sandestin, Raven, *Panhandle*
   Westin Innisbrook, Copperhead, *Tampa*
26 Walt Disney World, Osprey Ridge, *Orlando*
   Orange County National, Panther Lake, *Orlando*
   LPGA International, Legends, *Daytona Beach*
   Doral, Blue Monster, *Miami*

Hawaii
28 Kapalua, Plantation, *Maui*
   Princeville, Prince, *Kauai*
   Challenge at Manele, *Lanai*
27 Kauai Lagoons, Kiele, *Kauai*
   Mauna Kea, Mauna Kea Course, *Big Island*
   Mauna Lani, South, *Big Island*
   Experience at Koele, *Lanai*
26 Hualalai, *Big Island*
   Poipu Bay, *Kauai*
   Mauna Lani, North, *Big Island*

Mid-Atlantic (DC, DE, MD, PA, VA, WV)
29 Bulle Rock, *Baltimore, MD*
28 Links at Lighthouse Sound, *Ocean City, MD*
27 Stonewall, *Leesburg, VA*
   Nemacolin Woodlands, Mystic Rock, *Pittsburgh, PA*
   Golden Horseshoe, Gold, *Williamsburg, VA*
   Homestead, Cascades, *Roanoke, VA*
   Augustine, *DC Metro Area*
26 Royal New Kent, *Williamsburg, VA*
   Whiskey Creek, *Frederick, MD*
   Baywood Greens, *Rehoboth Beach, DE*

Midwest (IA, IL, IN, KS, MI, MN, MO, ND, NE, OH, OK, SD, WI)
30 Whistling Straits, Straits, *Kohler, WI*
29 Arcadia Bluffs, *Traverse City, MI*
Blackwolf Run, River, *Kohler, WI*
Madden's on Gull Lake, Classic, *Brainerd, MN*
Longaberger, *Columbus, OH*
28 Cog Hill, No. 4 (Dubsdread), *Chicago, IL*
Karsten Creek, *Stillwater, OK*
Lakewood Shores, Gailes, *Bay City, MI*
Grand View Lodge, Deacon's Lodge, *Brainerd, MN*
27 Boyne Highlands, Arthur Hills, *Petoskey, MI*
Shanty Creek, The Legend, *Traverse City, MI**

New England (MA, ME, NH, RI, VT)
28 Sugarloaf, *Central ME*
27 Belgrade Lakes, *Central ME*
Ranch, *Berkshires, MA*
Taconic, *Berkshires, MA*
Crumpin-Fox, *Berkshires, MA*
Farm Neck, *Martha's Vineyard, MA*
26 Pinehills, Jones, *Boston, MA*
Pinehills, Nicklaus, *Boston, MA*
Dunegrass, *Southern ME*
Red Tail, *Worcester, MA*

New York & Environs (CT, NJ, NY)
29 Bethpage, Black, *Long Island, NY*
28 Grossinger, Big G, *Catskills, NY*
27 Crystal Springs, Ballyowen, *NYC Metro*
Seven Oaks, *Finger Lakes, NY*
Pine Hill, *Cherry Hill, NJ*
26 Richter Park, *Danbury, CT*
Hominy Hill, *Freehold, NJ*
Twisted Dune, *Atlantic City, NJ*
25 Architects, *Trenton, NJ*
Turning Stone, Shenendoah, *Finger Lakes, NY*

Pacific Northwest (OR, WA)
29 Bandon Dunes, Bandon Dunes Course, *Coos Bay, OR*
Bandon Dunes, Pacific Dunes, *Coos Bay, OR*
Sunriver, Crosswater, *Bend, OR*
27 Pumpkin Ridge, Ghost Creek, *Portland, OR*
Gold Mountain, Olympic, *Bremerton, WA*
26 Port Ludlow, *Bremerton, WA*
25 Desert Canyon, *Wenatchee, WA*
Trophy Lake, *Bremerton, WA*
Golf Club at Newcastle, Coal Creek, *Seattle, WA*
McCormick Woods, *Bremerton, WA*

Rocky Mountains (CO, ID, MT, NV, UT, WY)
28 Pole Creek, *Denver, CO*
Shadow Creek, *Las Vegas, NV*
Reflection Bay at Lake Las Vegas, *Las Vegas, NV*
Wolf Creek, *Las Vegas, NV*
Coral Canyon, *St. George, UT*
27 Bear's Best Las Vegas, *Las Vegas, NV*
Broadmoor, East, *Colorado Springs, CO*
Redlands Mesa, *Grand Junction, CO*
Coeur d'Alene Resort, *Coeur d'Alene, ID*
Raven at Three Peaks, *Vail, CO*

Southeast (AL, AR, GA, KY, LA, MS, NC, SC, TN)
29 Kiawah Island, Ocean, *Charleston, SC*
28 Pinehurst Resort, No. 2, *Pinehurst, NC*
Caledonia Golf & Fish Club, *Pawleys Island, SC*
27 Cambrian Ridge, *Montgomery, AL*
Sea Pines, Harbour Town Golf Links, *Hilton Head, SC*
Capitol Hill, Judge, *Montgomery, AL*
Pinehurst Resort, No. 8, *Pinehurst, NC*
Barefoot Resort, Fazio, *Myrtle Beach, SC*
Pine Needles Lodge, Pine Needles, *Pinehurst, NC*
Grand National, Lake, *Auburn, AL*
Sea Island, Seaside, *Lowcountry, GA**

Southwest (NM, TX)
28 Paa-Ko Ridge, *Albuquerque, NM*
Barton Creek, Fazio Canyons, *Austin, TX*
27 Pine Dunes, *Tyler, TX*
Tribute, *Dallas, TX*
26 La Cantera, Resort, *San Antonio, TX*
Cowboys, *Dallas, TX*
La Cantera, Palmer, *San Antonio, TX*
Texas Star, *Dallas, TX*
25 Horseshoe Bay, Ram Rock, *Austin, TX*
Univ. of NM Championship Course, *Albuquerque, NM*

Top Courses by Special Feature

In some categories, clubs with more than one course are listed once, with their highest Course rating.

Budget ($40 and under)
26 Riverdale, Dunes, *Denver, CO*
25 Bethpage, Red, *Long Island, NY*
Granville, *Columbus, OH*
24 Wasatch Mountain, Mountain, *Salt Lake City, UT*
Mariana Butte, *Boulder, CO*
Alvamar Public, *Kansas City, KS*
22 Bethpage, Blue, *Long Island, NY*
Memorial Park, *Houston, TX*

Conditioning
30 Whistling Straits, Straits, *Kohler, WI*
29 Bandon Dunes, Bandon Dunes Course, *Coos Bay, OR*
Bethpage, Black, *Long Island, NY*
TPC at Sawgrass, Stadium, *Jacksonville, FL*
Kiawah Island, Ocean, *Charleston, SC*
Blackwolf Run, River, *Kohler, WI*
Longaberger, *Columbus, OH*
28 We-Ko-Pa, *Scottsdale, AZ*

Environmentally Friendly
29 TPC at Sawgrass, *Jacksonville, FL*
Kiawah Island, *Charleston, SC*
28 Barton Creek, *Austin, TX*
27 Thunderhawk, *Chicago, IL*
Broadmoor, *Colorado Springs, CO*
26 Desert Willow, *Palm Springs, CA*
Spanish Bay, *Monterey Peninsula, CA*
25 PGA Golf Club, *Port St. Lucie, FL*

Expense Account ($200 and over)

30 Whistling Straits, Straits, *Kohler, WI*
29 Bandon Dunes, Bandon Dunes Course, *Coos Bay, OR*
Pebble Beach, *Monterey Peninsula, CA*
TPC at Sawgrass, Stadium, *Jacksonville, FL*
Bandon Dunes, Pacific Dunes, *Coos Bay, OR*
Kiawah Island, Ocean, *Charleston, SC*
Spyglass Hill, *Monterey Peninsula, CA*
28 Kapalua, Plantation, *Maui, HI*

Fine Food Too

29 Pebble Beach, *Monterey Peninsula, CA*
27 Sea Island, *Lowcountry, GA*
25 TPC of Scottsdale, *Scottsdale, AZ*
Grand Cypress, *Orlando, FL*
24 Keystone Ranch, *Vail, CO*
Wente Vineyards, *San Francisco Bay Area, CA*
22 Phoenician, *Scottsdale, AZ*
21 Bali Hai, *Las Vegas, NV*

Instruction

27 Westin Innisbrook, *Tampa, FL*
Treetops, *Gaylord, MI*
Pine Needles Lodge, *Pinehurst, NC*
Grayhawk, *Scottsdale, AZ*
26 Doral, *Miami, FL*
25 Rio Secco, *Las Vegas, NV*
Grand Cypress, *Orlando, FL*
23 ChampionsGate, *Orlando, FL*

Newcomers/Rated

23 Angeles National, *Los Angeles, CA*
22 Hudson Hills, *NYC Metro*
Arroyo Trabuco, *Orange County, CA*
21 Moorpark, *Los Angeles, CA*
20 Gillette Ridge, *Hartford, CT*

Newcomers/Unrated

Bandon Dunes, Bandon Trails, *Coos Bay, OR*
May River at Palmetto Bluff, *Hilton Head, SC*
Neshanic Valley, *Bridgewater, NJ*
Vineyard Golf at Renault, *Atlantic City, NJ*
Wynn Las Vegas, *Las Vegas, NV*

19th Holes

29 Pebble Beach, *Monterey Peninsula, CA*
TPC at Sawgrass, *Jacksonville, FL*
28 Arnold Palmer's Bay Hill, *Orlando, FL*
27 Grayhawk, *Scottsdale, AZ*
Homestead, *Roanoke, VA*
26 Pelican Hill, *Orange County, CA*
Spanish Bay, *Monterey Peninsula, CA*
25 Half Moon Bay, *San Francisco Bay Area, CA*

Outstanding Accommodations

30 Whistling Straits/Blackwolf Run, *Kohler, WI*
29 Pebble Beach, *Monterey Peninsula, CA*
Kiawah Island, *Charleston, SC*
28 Troon North, *Scottsdale, AZ*
Shadow Creek, *Las Vegas, NV*
Reflection Bay/Falls at Lake Las Vegas, *Las Vegas, NV*
Princeville, *Kauai, HI*
Challenge at Manele, *Lanai, HI*

Practice Facilities

29 TPC at Sawgrass, *Jacksonville, FL*
Longaberger, *Columbus, OH*
28 Pinehurst Resort, *Pinehurst, NC*
World Woods, *Tampa, FL*
27 Grayhawk, *Scottsdale, AZ*
26 PGA West, *Palm Springs, CA*
25 PGA Golf Club, *Port St. Lucie, FL*
24 Four Seasons at Las Colinas, *Dallas, TX*

Pro Shops

29 Bandon Dunes, *Coos Bay, OR*
Pebble Beach, *Monterey Peninsula, CA*
TPC at Sawgrass, *Jacksonville, FL*
28 Pinehurst Resort, *Pinehurst, NC*
Troon North, *Scottsdale, AZ*
27 Grayhawk, *Scottsdale, AZ*
Broadmoor, *Colorado Springs, CO*
25 Grand Cypress, *Orlando, FL*

Resort

30 Whistling Straits, *Kohler, WI*
29 Bandon Dunes, *Coos Bay, OR*
Pebble Beach, *Monterey Peninsula, CA*
TPC at Sawgrass, *Jacksonville, FL*
Kiawah Island, *Charleston, SC*
Madden's on Gull Lake, *Brainerd, MN*
Sunriver, *Bend, OR*
28 Kapalua, *Maui, HI*

Scenic

30 Whistling Straits, Straits, *Kohler, WI*
29 Bandon Dunes, Bandon Dunes Course, *Coos Bay, OR*
Pebble Beach, *Monterey Peninsula, CA*
Arcadia Bluffs, *Traverse City, MI*
Kiawah Island, Ocean, *Charleston, SC*
28 Paa-Ko Ridge, *Albuquerque, NM*
Shadow Creek, *Las Vegas, NV*
Gold Canyon, Dinosaur Mountain, *Phoenix, AZ*

Women-Friendly

27 Pine Needles Lodge, Pine Needles, *Pinehurst, NC*
Broadmoor, East, *Colorado Springs, CO*
Coeur d'Alene Resort, *Coeur d'Alene, ID*
26 Greenbrier, Old White, *White Sulphur Springs, WV*
24 Keystone Ranch, River, *Vail, CO*
LPGA International, Champions, *Daytona Beach, FL*
23 Amelia Island Plantation, Ocean Links, *Jacksonville, FL*
22 Phoenician, *Scottsdale, AZ*

Top-Rated Facilities

Facilities include clubhouses, pro shops, practice areas, restaurants and, at resorts, lodging and other amenities. Clubs with more than one course are listed once, with their highest rating.

29 Sea Island, *Lowcountry, GA*
Whistling Straits, *Kohler, WI*
Greenbrier, *White Sulphur Springs, WV*
Pinehurst Resort, *Pinehurst, NC*

28 Hualalai, *Big Island, HI*
Blackwolf Run, *Kohler, WI*
Reynolds Plantation, *Lake Oconee, GA*
Golf Club at Newcastle, *Seattle, WA*
Dragon at Gold Mountain, *Lake Tahoe, CA*
Shadow Creek, *Las Vegas, NV*

27 Nemacolin Woodlands, *Pittsburgh, PA*
TPC at Sawgrass, *Jacksonville, FL*
Broadmoor, *Colorado Springs, CO*
Bay Harbor, *Petoskey, MI*
Kingsmill, *Williamsburg, VA*
ChampionsGate, *Orlando, FL*
Coeur d'Alene Resort, *Coeur d'Alene, ID*
CordeValle, *San Francisco Bay Area, CA*
Bandon Dunes, *Coos Bay, OR*
Boulders, *Scottsdale, AZ*
Troon North, *Scottsdale, AZ*
Longaberger, *Columbus, OH*
Pebble Beach, *Monterey Peninsula, CA*
Four Seasons at Las Colinas, *Dallas, TX*
Arcadia Bluffs, *Traverse City, MI*
Aviara, *San Diego, CA**
Ritz-Carlton Orlando, *Orlando, FL*
La Cantera, *San Antonio, TX*
Grand Cypress, *Orlando, FL*
Kapalua, *Maui, HI*
Bulle Rock, *Baltimore, MD*
Challenge at Manele, *Lanai, HI*

26 Capitol Hill, *Montgomery, AL*
Turning Stone, *Finger Lakes, NY**
Capitol Hill, *Montgomery, AL*
Pinehills, *Boston, MA*
Tiburón, *Naples, FL*
Keswick Club, *Charlottesville, VA*
Glen Club, *Chicago, IL*
Mauna Lani, *Big Island, HI*
Spanish Bay, *Monterey Peninsula, CA*
TPC of Louisiana, *New Orleans, LA*
Phoenician, *Scottsdale, AZ*
Reflection Bay at Lake Las Vegas, *Las Vegas, NV*
Treetops, *Gaylord, MI*
Grayhawk, *Scottsdale, AZ*
Ventana Canyon, *Tucson, AZ*
Boyne Highlands, *Petoskey, MI*
Kiawah Island, *Charleston, SC*
Cowboys, *Dallas, TX*
Sunriver, *Bend, OR**

Top-Rated Service

Clubs with more than one course are listed once, with their highest rating.

29 Hualalai, *Big Island, HI*
Coeur d'Alene Resort, *Coeur d'Alene, ID*
Greenbrier, *White Sulphur Springs, WV*
Whistling Straits, *Kohler, WI*
Sea Island, *Lowcountry, GA*
28 Blackwolf Run, *Kohler, WI*
Ritz-Carlton Orlando, *Orlando, FL*
Bandon Dunes, *Coos Bay, OR*
Shadow Creek, *Las Vegas, NV*
Reynolds Plantation, *Lake Oconee, GA*
Pine Lakes International, *Myrtle Beach, SC*
Longaberger, *Columbus, OH*
CordeValle, *San Francisco Bay Area, CA*
27 Pinehurst Resort, *Pinehurst, NC*
Boyne Highlands, *Petoskey, MI*
Arcadia Bluffs, *Traverse City, MI*
Golf Club at Newcastle, *Seattle, WA*
Pebble Beach, *Monterey Peninsula, CA*
Bay Harbor, *Petoskey, MI*
Broadmoor, *Colorado Springs, CO**
Tiburón, *Naples, FL*
Challenge at Manele, *Lanai, HI*
Spanish Bay, *Monterey Peninsula, CA*
26 Bulle Rock, *Baltimore, MD*
Aviara, *San Diego, CA*
Kiawah Island, *Charleston, SC*
Troon North, *Scottsdale, AZ*
Four Seasons at Las Colinas, *Dallas, TX*
Mauna Lani, *Big Island, HI*
Madden's on Gull Lake, *Brainerd, MN*
Cowboys, *Dallas, TX*
Bear's Best Las Vegas, *Las Vegas, NV*
Whitehawk Ranch, *Lake Tahoe, CA*
TPC of Louisiana, *New Orleans, LA*
Grayhawk, *Scottsdale, AZ*
Arnold Palmer's Bay Hill, *Orlando, FL*
Experience at Koele, *Lanai, HI*
Barton Creek, *Austin, TX*
Barnsley Gardens, *Atlanta, GA*
Nemacolin Woodlands, *Pittsburgh, PA*
Ventana Canyon, *Tucson, AZ*
TPC at Sawgrass, *Jacksonville, FL*
Pinehills, *Boston, MA*
25 Phoenician, *Scottsdale, AZ*
Walt Disney World, *Orlando, FL*
La Cantera, *San Antonio, TX*
Reflection Bay at Lake Las Vegas, *Las Vegas, NV**
Caledonia Golf & Fish Club, *Pawleys Island, SC*
Treetops, *Gaylord, MI*
Raven at South Mountain, *Phoenix, AZ*

Top-Rated Values

28 Bethpage, Black, *Long Island, NY*
Wasatch Mountain, Mountain, *Salt Lake City, UT*
Grand National, Links, *Auburn, AL*
Cambrian Ridge, *Montgomery, AL*
Bethpage, Red, *Long Island, NY*
Grand National, Lake, *Auburn, AL*
27 Wasatch Mountain, Lakes, *Salt Lake City, UT*
Gold Mountain, Olympic, *Bremerton, WA*
Capitol Hill, Judge, *Montgomery, AL*
Forest Akers MSU, West, *Lansing, MI*
Pacific Grove Municipal, *Monterey Peninsula, CA*
Bandon Dunes, Pacific Dunes, *Coos Bay, OR*
Bethpage, Green, *Long Island, NY*
26 Bethpage, Blue, *Long Island, NY*
Capitol Hill, Legislator, *Montgomery, AL*
World Woods, Pine Barrens, *Tampa, FL*
Walking Stick, *Colorado Springs, CO*
Riverdale, Dunes, *Denver, CO*
Capitol Hill, Senator, *Montgomery, AL*
Pine Dunes, *Tyler, TX*
Willinger's, *Minneapolis, MN**
Eaglesticks, *Columbus, OH*
Rustic Canyon, *Los Angeles, CA*
Redlands Mesa, *Grand Junction, CO*
World Woods, Rolling Oaks, *Tampa, FL*
Conklin Players Club, *Finger Lakes, NY*
Oak Valley, *San Bernardino, CA*
Paa-Ko Ridge, *Albuquerque, NM*
Bandon Dunes, Bandon Dunes Course, *Coos Bay, OR*
La Purisima, *Santa Barbara, CA*
Papago Municipal, *Phoenix, AZ*
25 Montauk Downs, *Long Island, NY*
Hominy Hill, *Freehold, NJ*
Greystone, *Baltimore, MD*
Arroyo Trabuco, *Orange County, CA*
Mariana Butte, *Boulder, CO*
Seven Oaks, *Finger Lakes, NY**
Vineyard, *Cincinnati, OH**
Wailua, *Kauai, HI**
Craft Farms, The Woodlands, *Mobile, AL**
Oxmoor Valley, Ridge, *Birmingham, AL**
Poppy Ridge, *San Francisco Bay Area, CA*
Elk Ridge, *Gaylord, MI*
Univ. of NM Championship Course, *Albuquerque, NM*
Hunter Ranch, *San Luis Obispo, CA*
University Ridge, *Madison, WI*
Coral Canyon, *St. George, UT*
Ravines, *Jacksonville, FL*
PGA Golf Club, South, *Port St. Lucie, FL*
24 Primm Valley, Lakes, *Las Vegas, NV*
Orchard Valley, *Chicago, IL*
Lakewood Shores, Gailes, *Bay City, MI*
Beachtree, *Aberdeen, MD*
Heritage Bluffs, *Chicago, IL*
Forest Akers MSU, East, *Lansing, MI*
Oasis Golf Club, Oasis, *Las Vegas, NV**

Course Directory

Alabama

Anniston

Silver Lakes
▽ 26 | 25 | 25 | 25 | $65 |

1 Sunbelt Pkwy., Glencoe; 256-892-3268; www.rtjgolf.com
Backbreaker/Heartbreaker: 7674/4907; 77.7/68.8; 151/124
Heartbreaker/Mindbreaker: 7407/4865; 76.6/68.3; 148/122
Mindbreaker/Backbreaker: 7425/4686; 76.1/67.5; 155/118

"Mind the names" warn crushed combatants, as they're "indicative of the challenge you'll meet" at this RTJ Trail 27-holer northeast of Birmingham, where the "tough" nines are so demanding that deflated duffers have "renamed them all Ballbreaker"; still, given "unbelievable prices", it's "well worth a visit" for the "chance to be toyed with by a master architect", particularly on the noteworthy opening and closing holes.

Auburn

Grand National, Lake
27 | 25 | 24 | 28 | $57 |

3000 Sunbelt Pkwy., Opelika; 334-749-9042; 800-949-4444;
www.rtjgolf.com; 7149/4910; 74.9/68.7; 138/117

"Wet and wild!" gush golfers sloshing across this "awesome" RTJ Trailster "with a ton of water" on 13 holes, including No. 15, an "island par-3 that's impossible in the wind"; "bring your A game" because it's "hard, hard, hard", though even high-handicappers hail it as "deserving all the praise it has gotten" for resort "golf the way it should be" with a "fantastic course", a "gorgeous lodge, great service" and "inexpensive fees."

Grand National, Links
26 | 26 | 25 | 28 | $57 |

3000 Sunbelt Pkwy., Opelika; 334-749-9042; 800-949-4444;
www.rtjgolf.com; 7311/4843; 74.9/69.6; 141/113

"Positively beautiful", "this course has everything one could want", including a "terrific layout, a great staff, a wonderful practice facility" and an enjoyable "clubhouse lunch", which all add up to a "great bang for the buck" at the No. 1 Value in Alabama; swingers stuck on semantics say it's "not links but more woodlands" with "open, undulating fairways" and "more target golf" than its sister.

Birmingham

Limestone Springs
▽ 25 | 23 | 23 | 21 | $78 |

3000 Colonial Dr., Oneonta; 205-274-4653; www.limestonesprings.com;
6987/5042; 74.2/69.6; 139/128

"It's worth the drive" 30 miles north of Birmingham to this tree-lined 1999 Jerry Pate design "in a beautiful setting" of water-laced limestone; it was "built with members in mind, not pros", and indeed, the general population of players praises the "great service and conditioning"; with a superb par-4 closer and practice facilities carved into Sand Mountain, it's a "memorable experience."

Oxmoor Valley, Ridge
25 | 24 | 23 | 25 | $57 |

100 Sunbelt Pkwy.; 205-942-1177; 800-949-4444; www.rtjgolf.com;
7055/4974; 73.5/69.1; 140/122

"Don't even think about walking" this "serious test" with "lots of elevation changes" squawk easy riders careening their carts around a "pristine" spread that offers "incredible views with solitude, no roads or houses and few parallel fairways"; pooped players pout about "lots of chances to have a 60-ft. putt with six breaks", but experts exalt a layout that "tempts better players to try shots that get them into trouble", and everyone agrees it's a "super value" for "country club golf at a public course price!"

Oxmoor Valley, Valley   24 | 25 | 23 | 24 | $57

100 Sunbelt Pkwy.; 205-942-1177; 800-949-4444; www.rtjgolf.com; 7292/4899; 74.6/69.4; 130/122

Paradox-minded pin-seekers purport that, "contrary to its name, this course offers substantial elevation changes at the beginning and end"; though some assert "I like the Ridge better", others opine that this "challenging" sister is "your best bet" on "this part of the RTJ Trail"; though you might be surprised when it rolls out "lots of hills", you'll flat out agree that it's a "great course for the money."

Huntsville

Hampton Cove, Highlands   ▽ 19 | 22 | 21 | 23 | $50

450 Old Hwy. 431, Owens Cross Roads; 256-551-1818; 800-949-4444; www.rtjgolf.com; 7262/4765; 75.7/68.3; 136/113

So it's "not in the same league with Grand National or Capitol Hill" – this "tough" if "predictable" spread is still a "great place for a trip"; "another enjoyable stop on the Robert Trent Jones Trail", it's a "terrific value" for golf amid Japanese black pines, crepe myrtles and yawning bunkers, with a handsome pro shop to boot.

Hampton Cove, River   ▽ 22 | 20 | 20 | 23 | $50

450 Old Hwy. 431, Owens Cross Roads; 256-551-1818; 800-949-4444; www.rtjgolf.com; 7667/5278; 77.8/70.4; 136/119

Swingers sing 'take me to the River' for a "unique-style course", a bunkerless links laced with water hazards, towering oaks and massive elevated greens that form a "different type of challenge"; sightseers sigh over "great views on several holes", though there may be too much time to look, since play can be "a bit slow."

Mobile

Craft Farms, Cotton Creek 🏌   ▽ 19 | 22 | 24 | 22 | $79

3840 Cotton Creek Circle, Gulf Shores; 251-968-7500; 800-327-2657; www.craftfarms.com; 7028/5175; 73.3/70.9; 133/122

Fastidious flag-seekers fawn over this "crisp, clean layout with good customer service and a pleasant environment" on the Gulf of Mexico; Arnold Palmer crafted a design with wide, rolling fairways and undulating greens, but coin-counting critics conclude "there are better courses for the money in the area."

Craft Farms, The Woodlands   22 | 20 | 24 | 25 | $69

19995 Oak Rd. W., Gulf Shores; 251-968-7500; 800-327-2657; www.craftfarms.com; 6500/5002; 70.8/67.9; 123/109

"If you want your money's worth, this is the one to play" wax wallet-watchers who are welcomed with open arms by the "best people" at the most "interesting and challenging" of the Craft Farms courses; it's "short" but "scenic" and "well laid-out" to "reward good shots", plus as its name suggests, it sports "more mature pine trees than most tracks in the area, providing a bit more shade."

Kiva Dunes 25 | 23 | 21 | 22 | $94

815 Plantation Dr., Gulf Shores; 251-540-7000; 888-833-5482;
www.kivadunes.com; 7092/5006; 73.9/68.5; 132/115

"One of Jerry Pate's best designs" is a "sweet track" "in excellent
condition" with "top-notch greens" in a "great setting" on a
peninsula between Mobile Bay and the Gulf of Mexico; "bring
plenty of ammo if you play from the back tees", and "watch out
when it blows": it has "tons of water" and sand, and the "first three
holes play dead into the wind", making this seasider "enjoyable"
but possibly "too hard for your average vacation golfer."

Peninsula Golf & Racquet 🏠 24 | 24 | 25 | 23 | $87

20 Peninsula Blvd., Gulf Shores; 251-968-8009;
www.peninsulagolfclub.com
Cypress/Lakes: 7055/4978; 74/69.6; 131/121
Lakes/Marsh: 7026/5072; 73.8/68.7; 130/115
Marsh/Cypress: 7179/5080; 74.7/70.1; 133/120

"Twenty-seven holes of variety, spice and playability" please
"bunches of old duffers" dawdling on the "easy, wide fairways"
of this "well-groomed" "gem" perched on the shores of Mobile
Bay; a "staff that's the best anywhere" garners the Top spot for
Service in Alabama with "iced towels and apples" that "make
you feel as good as a country club member"; some of the locals
might not be quite as hospitable, including the "snakes and
coyotes that have been sighted" occasionally at the adjacent
Bon Secour Wildlife Preserve.

Rock Creek ▽ 26 | 26 | 23 | 25 | $66

140 Clubhouse Dr., Fairhope; 251-928-4223; www.rockcreekgolf.com;
6920/5831; 72.2/67.3; 129/119

Set amid Mobile Bay's woods and wetlands, TimberCreek's near
neighbor is "darn close" to "almost as good as it gets" say
roundsmen rocking par on this "fun and fair course for all levels"
and ages; says one pair of putting parents, the "great sandwiches
in the restaurant" help make it a "favorite for our boys' golf trip."

TimberCreek ▽ 22 | 23 | 21 | 24 | $55

9650 Timbercreek Blvd., Daphne; 251-621-9900; 877-621-9900;
www.golftimbercreek.com
Dogwood/Magnolia: 7062/4885; 72.2/66.7; 130/106
Magnolia/Pines: 7090/4990; 72.2/67.8; 126/107
Pines/Dogwood: 6928/4911; 71.8/66.7; 122/105

"Even the course itself treats you with Southern hospitality" at this
hilly 27-holer with an acclaimed clubhouse in the wildlife-filled
forest on Mobile Bay's eastern shore; swinging lumberjacks who
pine to play the Pines' No. 7, a lake-menaced par-4, call all three
combos "very good in all aspects, especially value and variety."

Montgomery

CAMBRIAN RIDGE 27 | 25 | 24 | 28 | $68

101 Sunbelt Pkwy., Greenville; 334-382-9787; www.rtjgolf.com
Canyon/Sherling: 7427/4857; 75.4/68.1; 142/127
Loblolly/Canyon: 7297/4772; 74.6/68.4; 140/126
Sherling/Loblolly: 7232/4785; 73.9/67; 133/119

Warm up on a Stairmaster because "Canyon/Sherling gives
walkers a real workout" thanks to "undulating, varied terrain" with

"significant elevation changes" on the "best secret on the Robert Trent Jones Trail"; while wallet-watchers tab this "outstanding", "scenic", "long and hard" layout "one of the best values in golf", its "middle-of-nowhere location" 40 miles south of Montgomery prompts party animals to pout "do not attempt to look for any nightlife in Greenville."

CAPITOL HILL, JUDGE

27 | 26 | 25 | 27 | $67

2600 Constitution Ave., Prattville; 334-285-1114; 800-949-4444; www.rtjgolf.com; 7794/4955; 77.8/68.3; 144/121

One obsessive trackster testifies "I have a picture on my wall" of "one of the most memorable opening shots around", "a 200-ft. drop from the tee box to the fairway" on this "brutally difficult" and "immaculate" "U.S. Open–caliber course"; "heavily played because of its beauty and reputation", Alabama's Most Popular layout "will truly judge your game", so "bring an extra sleeve and your sense of humor."

Capitol Hill, Legislator

25 | 24 | 24 | 26 | $57

2600 Constitution Ave., Prattville; 334-285-1114; 800-949-4444; www.rtjgolf.com; 7417/5488; 74.1/70; 126/121

Unlike in the United States government, this Legislator is more "mild-mannered" than its sibling, Judge; the "fairest of the three" layouts at Capitol Hill on the RTJ Trail, it's "the only course built for the average player", with "river holes that are very scenic yet playable" at all levels; even though it's "not quite in the same class" as its complex compatriots, most constituents are willing to lobby for its "huge elevation changes", "tight fairways" and "traditional style."

Capitol Hill, Senator

24 | 26 | 24 | 26 | $57

2600 Constitution Ave., Prattville; 334-285-1114; 800-949-4444; www.rtjgolf.com; 7697/5122; 76.6/68.8; 131/112

"It looks like you're on Mars, not in Alabama" at this "incredible links course" with "lots of mounds, high rough" and "narrow, fast greens"; if it's "not as pretty as the other two at Capitol Hill", it's "a good change of pace" for a "challenging" round that might "beat you to death if you're not a five handicap or under"; still, the vote on the floor is unanimous: the state's top-rated track for Facilities is "well worth a round."

Alaska

Anchorage

Eagleglen

– | – | – | – | $40

4414 First St.; 907-552-3821; www.elmendorfservices.com; 6689/5443; 71.6/70.9; 126/119

Globe-trotter Robert Trent Jones Jr. (with a little help from his father) carved out courses in some remote outposts, so it's no surprise that he stopped at Elmendorf Air Force Base in 1973 to lay out a spread that some call the "best in the state of Alaska"; it might get chilly, but the greens are large, the bunkering is ample, the back-to-nature setting along Ship Creek affords numerous moose sightings and tee shots under the midnight sun have late-night lofters loving it – "whenever you can golf in the summer until 11 PM, it's the greatest!"

Arizona

★ **Top Courses in State**
28 We-Ko-Pa, *Scottsdale*
   Troon North, Monument, *Scottsdale*
   Gold Canyon, Dinosaur Mountain, *Phoenix*
27 Troon North, Pinnacle, *Scottsdale*
   Ventana Canyon, Mountain, *Tucson*
   Boulders, North, *Scottsdale*
   Grayhawk, Raptor, *Scottsdale*
26 Ventana Canyon, Canyon, *Tucson*
   Vistoso, *Tucson*
   Boulders, South, *Scottsdale*

Phoenix

Arizona Biltmore, Adobe 🏌   18 | 22 | 22 | 15 |$175
2400 E. Missouri Ave.; 602-955-9655; www.arizonabiltmore.com;
6428/5417; 70.3/70.7; 123/120
"Gorgeous mountain views" and bunkers recently restored to
their 1920s glory are the foundations for "one of the oldest resort
courses in Arizona", one that's "predominantly flat" and "wide
open", which "provides forgiving second shots" and sets up "easy
for first-time players"; still, even hackers huff the "historic" "course
and facilities are not aging as gracefully" as the "lovely homes"
that surround it.

Arizona Biltmore, Links 🏌   20 | 21 | 22 | 15 |$175
2400 E. Missouri Ave.; 602-955-9655; www.arizonabiltmore.com;
6300/4747; 69.7/66.8; 126/110
The "sister course" at the "great" Biltmore resort features "tighter
fairways" and "hillier terrain" than "the more traditional Adobe";
it "wanders around a mountain" where the "dramatically beautiful"
downhill par-3 14th helps make it "the more scenic of the two"
tracks; big ball bashers should "leave your driver at home" for
this relatively "short" spread that some call a "shotmaker's delight",
while bored budgeteers bemoan its "uninteresting" layout and
"too expensive" tabs.

Dove Valley Ranch 🏌   19 | 17 | 18 | 17 |$130
33244 N. Black Mountain Pkwy., Cave Creek; 480-488-0009;
www.dovevalleyranch.com; 7011/5337; 72.7/70.8; 131/120
Schizophrenic swingers embrace this "picturesque" Robert Trent
Jones Jr. track "a little out of the way" "north of town" for its dual
personality; "what you see is what you get" on the "wide-open
front" while "the GPS comes in handy" on the "narrow" "desert-
style back nine" with "blind shots and waste areas running
across the fairways"; some praise the "eager-to-please" staff
and "nice clubhouse", while others say it's "not special enough
to warrant the drive."

Estrella Mountain Ranch   26 | 21 | 22 | 23 |$139
11800 S. Golf Club Dr., Goodyear; 623-386-2600;
www.estrellamountainranch.com; 7139/5124; 73.6/68.2; 136/115
It's "a long way to drive", but the "hours you spend on the course
will not easily be forgotten" say starstruck swingers of this "middle-
of-nowhere" Jack Nicklaus II design that "challenges all levels of

golfer" with "many forced carries over the desert from the tees"; even this far "off the beaten trail", you'll find a clubhouse that offers "top-notch creature comforts" to go with the "can't-be-beat views from the par-3s."

GOLD CANYON, DINOSAUR MOUNTAIN
`28 | 21 | 21 | 22 | $187`

6100 S. Kings Ranch Rd., Gold Canyon; 480-982-9449; 800-827-5281; www.gcgr.com; 6653/4833; 71.3/67.4; 143/115

"If you like drama, this is your course", Ken Kavanaugh's "stunning" group of "green ribbons that stretch across the desert floor" against a "superb" "mountain backdrop"; "lots of elevation changes" "that get your attention on every shot" make it "tough for a duffer", but "this is what desert golf is all about", so "bring your camera" and compass to this "well-kept if hard-to-find" "challenge."

Gold Canyon, Sidewinder
`21 | 22 | 22 | 19 | $102`

6100 S. Kings Ranch Rd., Gold Canyon; 480-982-9449; 800-827-5281; www.gcgr.com; 6509/4426; 71.9/66.5; 130/111

It's a "high-class act here – one not to miss" say swingers winding their way through this "tough but beautiful" Gold Canyon "sister" with "excellent challenges", "great scenery" and "good grounds"; some slicers overlook the "short driving range" and "overpriced" fees for distinctive desert sightings of "deer, snakes, reptiles, jackrabbits and good-looking beverage girls", while tougher tee-totalers hiss it's "a nice second course, but play Dinosaur if you have the choice."

Las Sendas ⌂
`25 | 22 | 22 | 20 | $150`

7555 E. Eagle Crest Dr., Mesa; 480-396-4000; www.lassendas.com; 6874/5100; 72.5/69.9; 145/128

"In the shadows of Red Mountain" lies a "meticulously groomed" "shotmaker's test" designed by Robert Trent Jones Jr.; "greens like glass" might "bring you to your knees" but the rest of the layout is "quite playable – if you choose the right tees" and "hit 'em straight"; its "nice setting" makes for "beautiful views" because the "fairway homes are generally not intrusive."

Legend at Arrowhead, The
`18 | 15 | 15 | 18 | $79`

21027 N. 67th Ave., Glendale; 623-561-0953; www.americangolf.com; 6969/5233; 73.1/70.1; 131/120

Aim toward this "high-handicapper's delight", a Palmer course in northeast Phoenix that scores points for some "challenging holes" with "multi-tiered greens"; an "older public", it's "not inspiring" for scratch players who pout about "homes surrounding many of the fairways", even if their novice friends find it "fun."

Longbow
`▽ 21 | 18 | 17 | 22 | $99`

5601 E. Longbow Pkwy., Mesa; 480-807-5400; www.longbowgolf.com; 7003/5202; 72.2/68.9; 129/120

"One of the better values in the Valley" is this "challenging" but "open, fair" and "walkable" course with imaginative bunkering and a "good balance of risk/reward for all levels of golfer"; in 2003, Ken Kavanaugh redesigned his own 1997 layout to accommodate a business park expansion, but he couldn't eliminate the small airport nearby, so "watch out for private planes falling out of the sky" from the handsome post-round patio.

Los Caballeros ⚬

▽ 22 | 20 | 21 | 23 | $135

1551 S. Vulture Mine Rd., Wickenburg; 928-684-2704;
www.loscaballerosgolf.com; 6962/5264; 73.5/71.2; 138/124
"This consummate Phoenix-area golf course" is a "treat" "worth
the hour drive" "outside the city congestion" for "tree-lined
hillsides overlooking the fairways" and "the neatest set of par-5s"
featuring elevation changes, "blind shots, water and length";
"part of an old Arizona-style resort", it has a "quiet" 'Los Cab' vibe
that "runs to the genteel" – I "felt like I owned my own course"
says one solitude-loving *hombre* who "never saw anyone" but his
own foursome "after leaving the range."

Marriott's Wildfire, Faldo Championship

24 | 24 | 24 | 20 | $205

5350 E. Marriott Dr.; 480-473-0205; 888-705-7775; www.wildfiregolf.com;
6846/5245; 71.6/69.6; 127/120
"Bring your sand wedge!" because there are "beaches in Arizona"
from the looks of this "unique" Nick Faldo/Brian Curley spread, or
at least there are a whole lot of bunkers – 106 in all, "some big
enough to hide a car in"; add "lots of desert to carry on your
drives" toward "super greens", and those "generous" fairways
might be of no help to your score on this "beautifully manicured"
track at a "top-notch facility" "where management rather than
length is the premium."

Marriott's Wildfire, Palmer Signature

23 | 24 | 23 | 19 | $205

5350 E. Marriott Dr.; 480-473-0205; 888-705-7775; www.wildfiregolf.com;
7170/5505; 73.3/70.1; 135/116
We're talkin' "some serious golf holes here", so "you need to
have your A game" advise Arnie's Army recruits who "hit the ball
down the middle of very narrow fairways" onto "fast and tough"
greens at this "challenge" at the "beautiful" Marriott resort; this
"impeccable", "well-marshaled" layout stressing "friendliness"
and "service" sports "breathtaking" views and "more of a desert
feel" than brother Faldo, so "watch for rattlers!"

Ocotillo

23 | 19 | 21 | 20 | $155

3751 S. Clubhouse Dr., Chandler; 480-917-6660; 888-624-8899;
www.ocotillogolf.com
Gold/Blue: 7016/5128; 72.2/69.6; 133/124
Gold/White: 6804/5124; 71.5/69.3; 128/118
White/Blue: 6782/5134; 71.3/70.2; 130/117
You may need a snorkel at this "beautiful" "Florida-like course",
which features "the most water you'll ever see in Arizona", along
with "hills" and "interesting greens"; wet blankets counsel
"placement, placement, placement" lest your ball receive a
"complimentary sauna", while naturalists needled by "surrounding
houses" huff "they want you to think it's some type of oasis",
but it's "more like 27 holes in the middle of the suburbs"; soothe
your "frustration" with a "deal that can't be beat" via a coupon in
Thursday's *Arizona Republic*.

Papago Municipal

20 | 10 | 11 | 26 | $34

5595 E. Moreland St.; 602-275-8428; 7068/5937; 73.3/72.4; 132/119
"Killer-good muni" public putters proclaim of this "best-kept
secret" "close to the airport", which is convenient "if you have a

long connection" layover; the old-style "parklike" track's "cheap fees = great value" that rates as Arizona's Top deal, but veterans who vent it's "a little rough around the edges" since "maintenance that has gone down lately" wonder, where did Papa-go?

Pointe at Lookout Mountain ⌖ 　22　21　22　20　$144
11111 N. Seventh St.; 602-866-6356; 800-947-9784; www.pointehilton.com; 6535/4557; 71.2/65.3; 135/113

This "wonder in the desert" kept "beautifully conditioned" with "breathtaking par-4s overlooking the Valley" "starts out pleasantly then builds to hilly elevation changes" where "you will use every club in your bag"; though "ice-cold packs for your neck" from a "friendly, helpful staff" may make some dazzled duffers feel like "a movie star", fickle foozlers point out "the course has seen better days" and "some holes are beside the expressway"; look out for the "great restaurant and bar" to finish off your round.

Raven at South Mountain 　　23　23　25　20　$160
3636 E. Baseline Rd.; 602-243-3636; www.ravenatsouthmountain.com; 7078/5800; 73.9/72.9; 133/124

"I felt like a touring pro" rave golfers about this "Eastern parkland" "oasis in the middle of the desert" near the Sky Harbor Airport where "unbelievable service" featuring heat-beating "towels dipped in mango-scented ice water" lightens the blackest birdie-yearning moods; "impeccably maintained" in "old-style" "wall-to-wall grass" complete "with an excellent practice facility", this course "requires really good ability to play in the wind", but it has players of all feathers flocking to it "again and again."

Raven at Verrado 　　　　　　26　25　25　24　$139
4242 N. Golf Dr., Buckeye; 623-388-3000; www.ravenatverrado.com; 7258/5402; 73.8/69.8; 132/118

Birdie hunters fly 30 miles west of Phoenix to land at "one of the best new courses around", deftly designed by John Fought and Tom Lehman amid the foothills of the White Tank Mountains where "conditions are sublime" and "service is off the charts"; while ravenous roundsmen find the all-inclusive golf with "quality meals and beverages before and after the round" "appealing", some Heckle-and-Jekyllers harrumph "the only drawback is the driving distance" from the city.

Superstition Springs ⌖ 　　19　18　16　19　$95
6542 E. Baseline Rd., Mesa; 480-985-5622; www.superstitionspringsgc.com; 7005/5328; 73/66.3; 130/110

"Don't expect royal treatment, just golf" at this "fine little gem" east of Phoenix that's "moderately priced", according to long hitters who hail the "back tees on No. 9 (one of the best in the state)", a par-4 with a lake tucked into its left dogleg; you may want to do a rain dance to freshen up putting surfaces that are "more brown than green", but don't stomp around too much because a "significant downpour" results in "lakes of casual water on the fairways."

Trilogy at Vistancia 　　▽ 25　22　24　22　$99
12575 W. Golf Club Dr., Peoria; 623-328-5100; www.trilogygolfclub.com; 7259/5573; 73.9/72.2; 134/129

A trilogy of cheers for this "immaculate" "secret" "in the middle of nowhere" surrounded by the Twin Buttes and Bradshaw Mountains where, "if you suffer through the slow two-lane drive out, you will be rewarded" with a "friendly staff" and "birdies aplenty"; although it's "nicely laid out", hacking herds huff "take a drop and a penalty stroke" as "any off-line shots roll right into" prairielike "one- to two-ft. native grasses that line the fairways."

Whirlwind, Cattail   26 | 25 | 24 | 24 | $150
5692 W. North Loop Rd., Chandler; 480-940-1500;
www.whirlwindgolf.com; 7218/5383; 73.4/70.8; 132/123
"Give it a try, you won't be disappointed" by this "sweet" and "beautiful", "wide-open" Gary Panks design that's "home of the Nationwide Tour stop each fall"; though it's "not as flashy as some of the Scottsdale courses", "perfect conditions" along with "great atmosphere" and staff make the "best unknown course in the East Valley" purr-fect "for the weekend golfer."

Whirlwind, Devil's Claw   26 | 25 | 24 | 24 | $150
5692 W. North Loop Rd., Chandler; 480-940-1500;
www.whirlwindgolf.com; 7029/5540; 72.6/71.4; 129/121
The jury's out as to which is the better of the Panks "courses run from the same HQ" on the Gila River Indian Community, but with "awesome conditions", "good price performance" and a location "only 15 minutes from the airport", you might run into anyone on either, including local linkster "Alice Cooper"; the "varied terrain", "calm pace of play" and "first-rate staff" lead secretive swingers to say "ssshhh! – don't tell anyone about this" mildly devilish design, while inviting types insist "if you're in the area, it's not to be missed."

Wigwam, Red   19 | 20 | 21 | 19 | $120
451 N. Litchfield Rd., Litchfield Park; 623-935-9414; 800-909-4224;
www.wigwamresort.com; 6865/5808; 72.4/71.8; 126/118
At more than 30 years young, Wigwam's "newest" is no spring chicken, but even if it is "getting a bit tired", this "solid, old-fashioned layout" remains "friendly and playable", with "plentiful risk/reward opportunities" and "exceptional grooming"; plus, it's your only option at the historic resort while the Gold and Blue courses undergo renovations through early fall 2006.

San Carlos

Apache Stronghold ⌂   ▽ 25 | 10 | 15 | 22 | $45
Hwy. 70 (4 mi. east of Hwy. 77); 928-475-7664; 800-272-2438;
www.golfapache.com; 7519/5535; 74.9/70.5; 138/117
Long drivers declare that this "sleeper" "90 miles from Scottsdale" is "worth the trip" with roadside attractions that include an "on-site casino" and an "exceptional layout" by Tom Doak; you can wrestle this "super desert course" at a "great value", though you'd possibly be willing to cough up more wampum if "the management would decide to put some money into its upkeep" and facilities.

Scottsdale

BOULDERS, NORTH   27 | 27 | 27 | 19 | $290
34631 N. Tom Darlington Dr., Carefree; 480-488-9028;
www.thebouldersclub.com; 6811/4900; 72.6/68.5; 137/115
Bring "the corporate credit card" say bowled-over budget busters who rave about the "luxurious" amenities ("they should be for the

price"), "impeccable conditions" and "staff so great" you might "even write the pro expressing your satisfaction" at "one of the great American resorts" where the "world-class spa is an added bonus if your spouse doesn't golf"; Arizona's Top Facilities and Service complement a "wonderful, challenging course" with "majestic rock outcroppings" and a variety of "wildlife" that make it "worth a loop, even for duffers."

Boulders, South ☺ 26 | 27 | 27 | 18 | $290

34631 N. Tom Darlington Dr., Carefree; 480-488-9028; www.theouldersclub.com; 6726/4684; 71.9/68.7; 140/117

The "name says it all" on this "meticulously maintained" course with "Teflon greens" and "natural" "boulder formations" that "make you feel like you're on another planet"; delivering "double-wow!" "desert golf", Jay Morrish's "brutal test" is "not for the faint of heart", but a "first-class" staff that "knows your name before you even get out of your car" helps make it "worth every penny" and all the sweat, so "check into a casita and stay awhile" at the "top-of-the-line" resort.

Camelback, Club 🏌 19 | 21 | 21 | 18 | $125

7847 N. Mockingbird Ln.; 480-596-7050; www.camelbackinn.com; 7014/5808; 72.6/71.5; 122/118

This "forgiving", "female-friendly" layout is "great for novices", particularly if they also like a "beautiful restaurant and clubhouse"; despite mature palms and ample vistas of the namesake mountains, hackers hopping the shuttle from the JW Marriott for "sightseeing" "views of the lovely homes" en route say this spread is "like a Northeastern resort course", albeit one "in need of a face-lift."

Camelback, Resort 🏌 20 | 21 | 21 | 17 | $170

7847 N. Mockingbird Ln.; 480-596-7050; www.camelbackinn.com; 6903/5132; 72.8/68.6; 132/114

"Fun for all levels yet challenging for the more experienced", this is one "cool course in a hot climate", particularly following Arthur Hills' "beautiful makeover", rave resort golfers; area hackers humping across the "overpriced", "ordinary layout" say its "goofy design befuddles locals", though the "nice pro shop with good variety" makes for a "decent" shopping spree.

Eagle Mountain 🏌 24 | 22 | 22 | 20 | $185

14915 E. Eagle Mountain Pkwy., Fountain Hills; 480-816-1234; www.eaglemtn.com; 6802/5065; 71.7/68.2; 139/118

"Wow, wow, wow, did I say 'wow'?" say swingers soaring over the "beautiful vistas" from this "hilly", "well-manicured" layout that sits "literally on the side of a mountain"; "don't drink too much and watch the hairpin turns driving the cart, or you'll be a hawk's dinner", though even "hackers" can eat the course for lunch since the "forgiving fairways all seem to funnel toward the middle"; "the finishing hole is worth every penny" of the "pricey fees", and the "friendliest and most helpful" "service is a birdie experience."

GRAYHAWK, RAPTOR 27 | 26 | 26 | 19 | $230

8620 E. Thompson Peak Pkwy.; 480-502-1800; 800-472-9429; www.grayhawkgolf.com; 7135/5309; 74.1/71.3; 143/127

"What a place" "to be really impressed" gush golfers on this Tom Fazio–designed, "first-class desert course", a "monument in the

Scottsdale area" that dishes out "fairways like carpet", "difficult greens", "gut-wrenching par-3s" and the "deepest sand traps ever", not to mention a "super pro shop" and "great food"; with a staff that "actually comes to talk and clean your clubs while hitting at the range", "service is so good" that it "almost makes you forget how expensive it is to play there."

Grayhawk, Talon   26 | 26 | 26 | 18 | $230
8620 E. Thompson Peak Pkwy.; 480-502-1800; 800-472-9429; www.grayhawkgolf.com; 6973/5143; 73.6/70; 143/121
"It's fun even when you lose a dozen balls" declare duffers dazzled by this "exceptional" "country club for a day" that's "keeping alive the spirit of golf" in North Scottsdale; given "how perfect the greens" and "gorgeous the fairways" are on this "awesome course", the club's "name should be changed to Greenhawk"; after your round, "slide into Phil's Grill for the best-ever French dip" but go easy on the signature monster margaritas – vacationing city slickers swear "we saw wolves rolling in the first fairway."

Kierland   21 | 24 | 23 | 19 | $180
15636 N. Clubgate Dr.; 480-922-9283; www.kierlandgolf.com
Acacia/Ironwood: 6974/4985; 72.5/67.8; 128/118
Acacia/Mesquite: 6913/4898; 72.2/67.7; 131/116
Ironwood/Mesquite: 7017/5017; 73/68.1; 130/114
In a "perfect" setting adjacent to the Westin Kierland, "the service is the key" to the success of this "challenging but not too penal" 27-holer that features "lots of grass", an "excellent practice area" and "cold, scented towels the marshal brings you"; lured by "lots of wildlife", nature-loving linksters "would go back in a heartbeat", but detractors drone it's "cookie-cutter golf" "surrounded by homes."

Legend Trail   24 | 21 | 22 | 19 | $170
9462 Legendary Ln.; 480-488-7434; www.legendtrailgc.com; 6845/5001; 73.2/68.2; 135/122
Legend has it that it's a "long, long, long" way "from the tips" with "many forced carries over the desert" on this "excellent", "semi-mountainous" course that's "challenging" but "keeps everyone in the game"; though "disappointed" drivers drawl it's too "pricey" for a "manufactured" layout you "can't play without hitting a home", at trail's end, a "friendly staff" and "beautiful scenery" help make the experience "interesting enough to warrant returning."

McCormick Ranch, Palm ⛳   17 | 16 | 18 | 16 | $155
7505 E. McCormick Pkwy.; 480-948-0260; www.mccormickranchgolf.com; 7044/5057; 73.7/68.5; 137/118
The "practice facilities are extensive" and the "people are friendly" enough on this "traditional" layout that, at thirtysomething years old, is the "grandfather of Scottsdale courses"; bellicose "business associates" say "if the company's paying" and you "don't need the challenge", play this "flat, boring" "host of a large number of corporate golf outings" – "otherwise, find another course."

McCormick Ranch, Pine ⛳   17 | 16 | 18 | 17 | $155
7505 E. McCormick Pkwy.; 480-948-0260; www.mccormickranchgolf.com; 7187/5333; 74.4/70; 135/120
"One of the few courses with real trees" in the Scottsdale desert, this "traditional" track is well named; it's a "nice course", but

beyond the occasional arboreal ardor of "fairways that are tighter than on its sister, Palm", not even No. 15's island fairway and green can keep champs from charging it's "not very memorable."

Phoenician, The ⌂
22 26 25 17 $180

6000 E. Camelback Rd.; 480-423-2449; 800-888-8234;
www.thephoenician.com
Canyon/Desert: 6068/4777; 69.4/67.7; 131/114
Desert/Oasis: 6310/5024; 70.3/69.7; 130/113
Oasis/Canyon: 6258/4871; 70.1/67.9; 130/111

"Everyone loves" this "A++" track fawn fans of its "three incredible and different nines" winding through a "lush" landscape "in the shadow of Camelback Mountain" where "breathtaking vistas abound"; while killjoys complain there are "too many holes in too small a space", the majority rules "anyone wanting to disappear for four hours and spoil themselves" can do it here.

Sanctuary at Westworld
20 19 19 20 $119

10690 E. Sheena Dr.; 480-502-8200; www.sanctuarygolf.com;
6624/4926; 71.2/67.8; 139/117

"A find!" cry swinging sleuths who've snooped out this "hidden gem", an Audobon Signature sunk amid "protected wetlands that don't come into play (usually)"; "have your slice straightened out by the time you play" its "fine variety" of "tricky holes", as the "risk/reward, short par-4s" and "tight" "target-golf" shots "require course management" skills; the "power lines overhead" don't quite mar the "beautiful mountain views" available from its "fast" dance floors, while "one of the Valley's best lunch-and-greens fee specials" keeps 'em coming back to the scene.

SunRidge Canyon ⌂
26 22 22 21 $190

13100 N. Sunridge Dr., Fountain Hills; 480-837-5100; 800-562-5178;
www.sunridgegolf.com; 6823/5141; 72.6/68.2; 142/129

It "tends to fly under the radar", so you might not know yet that this "incredibly beautiful" course "winding through Fountain Hills" is "brutal, absolutely brutal"; "a must-play for the masochistic golfer", it's "tough from the tips" with "pretty narrow" holes and "fast, steep" greens that "murder" your putt; despite "too many homes surrounding" it, the "stunning scenery", "one of the best finishes" and "impeccable conditions make it all worthwhile."

Talking Stick, North
22 21 21 19 $170

9998 E. Indian Bend Rd.; 480-860-2221; www.talkingstickgolfclub.com;
7133/5532; 73.8/70; 125/116

Walk softly or take a cart on this "welcome change to standard desert architecture" say smitten sandmen who "love the bunkering and design by Coore and Crenshaw" on a layout that provides "opportunities to use every shot in your bag"; "with not a brown blade of grass to be found", "lots of celebrities" in action and quality "mountain views", a round here is certainly "enjoyable" – just "watch out for the Pony Express across the flat plains fairways."

Talking Stick, South
22 23 22 20 $170

9998 E. Indian Bend Rd.; 480-860-2221; www.talkingstickgolfclub.com;
6833/5428; 72.7/69.1; 129/118

Architects Ben Crenshaw and Bill Coore crafted a different kind of challenge at the North's slightly younger sister, one that exudes "more of the parkland style not seen often in Arizona"; it's a "good setup" in "great condition", but "for the money, the view of the warehouses" at the water plant is "disappointing" – with a fine pro shop, a photogenic clubhouse and serious practice facilities, the foreground provides a more pleasing look-see.

TPC of Scottsdale, Desert   20 | 20 | 21 | 21 | $55
17020 N. Hayden Rd.; 480-585-4334; www.tpc.com;
6423/4612; 69.6/66; 119/109

"A good time is had by all" flaunt foursomes fixated on "precision shot placement" on "tight" fairways on this "challenging little course" where you might recover par with an easy landing on greens that are "slick" but "so big you can't miss them"; though it's "shadowed by the Stadium course", this "awesome value" is "not TPC Lite" but a "fooler" that's "much tougher than it looks" where "distractions" include "coyotes watching you" and the "deafening Gulfstream and Lear parade" overhead.

TPC of Scottsdale, Stadium ⌘   25 | 26 | 23 | 17 | $228
17020 N. Hayden Rd.; 480-585-4334; www.tpc.com;
7216/5567; 74.6/72.9; 138/130

"Play where the pros play!" shout star-struck swingers who can practically "feel the crowd" on "the famous par-3 16th" at this "excellent Weiskopf and Morrish course" that hosts the PGA Tour's FBR Open; "they treat you like a king" – "and they should" at these prices; save some green to enjoy "top-notch facilities", including a grill room with "delicious food" and the luxe Fairmont Princess hotel, which sits "only a few feet away."

TROON NORTH, MONUMENT ⊘   28 | 27 | 26 | 19 | $295
10320 E. Dynamite Blvd.; 480-585-5300; www.troonnorthgolf.com;
7028/5050; 73.3/68.5; 147/117

"No one pampers the golfer and course like the folks" at this "desert mecca", "everything you expect and more" in "one of the best of the West"; canyon crawlers "fending off rattlesnakes and climbing through the cacti to get the errant slice" sigh "I still cry when I think about" the "stunning saguaro-forest" setting for this "pristine", "almost surreal" Weiskopf/Morrish layout; just "bring your A game" and "your Amex" because "t'aint cheap" or easy.

TROON NORTH, PINNACLE ⊘   27 | 27 | 26 | 18 | $295
10320 E. Dynamite Blvd.; 480-585-5300; www.troonnorthgolf.com;
7044/4980; 73.4/68.6; 147/120

"It's not just a clever name" proclaim players "planning trips to Scottsdale around tee times" at this "property with all the whistles", including Four Seasons affiliation; "it's worth risking heat stroke for the off-season rates" on the "good mix of hilly and flat" Tom Weiskopf holes with "lots of doglegs", all kept in "gorgeous" condition, even if critics of its winter "cart-path-only" rule rail "too much time in the desert makes you feel like Lawrence of Arabia" – despite the "overbuilding of houses" nearby.

WE-KO-PA   28 | 25 | 25 | 24 | $195
18200 E. Toh Vee Circle, Fort McDowell; 480-836-9000; www.wekopa.com;
7225/5337; 73/69.1; 136/119

"Two words: GO and NOW" to Arizona's Top Course because this "world-class" "natural beauty" with "no homes or OB (yeah!)"

is "another great example of what desert golf is meant to be"; situated on the Yavapai Indian Nation reservation with "changing elevations" and "fabulous" views of the Four Peaks, its "dual fairways" and "spectacular driving range" are overseen by a "very attentive staff"; even pedal-to-the-metal putters who protest the "cart-path-only rule" concede that it creates "perfect conditions", so "if you're only going to play one round on your trip, do it here."

Sedona

Sedona Golf Resort
23 | 20 | 21 | 21 | $115

35 Ridge Trail Dr.; 928-284-9355; 877-733-9885; www.sedonagolfresort.com; 6646/5059; 70.3/67; 129/114
"If you are in Sedona play this course" rave Red Rock enthusiasts who tee it up "for the view alone" on its "perfectly manicured", "moderately challenging" high-desert layout; despite "recent housing developments that have encroached on some holes", spirits soar over this "paradise on earth" where the "knockout" setting "can offset the worst round" and "courteous, helpful personnel" help make it a "top pick" in the area.

Tempe

ASU Karsten 🏌
20 | 20 | 19 | 22 | $89

1125 E. Rio Salado Pkwy.; 480-921-8070; www.asukarsten.com; 7057/4765; 74.1/67.5; 132/103
"A good place to spot future PGA stars", ASU's "links-style" "university course", the "challenging and tight" home to the "perennial NCAA contender Sun Devils", can sometimes be "just a little too hot to handle"; despite "the constant buzz of jets overhead" and a location "trapped" beneath the "power lines" in "industrial hell", "Pete Dye did a good job with the layout", and the "value is excellent" thanks to "well-maintained" holes, a "good restaurant" and "friendly college students in knickers."

Tucson

Arizona National 🏌
24 | 23 | 22 | 19 | $165

9777 E. Sabino Greens Dr.; 520-749-3636; www.arizonanationalgolfclub.com; 6785/4733; 72.4/67.7; 146/113
Teacher's pets and truants alike warm to the curriculum at the "spectacular" "home to the University of Arizona" Wildcats; the "Tucson-area must-play" offers "great elevation changes" with "views all the way to Mexico", but tutors advise "bring your A game" and study up, as "local knowledge is needed to stay out of trouble" on a "tight course with not a lot of room for error"; luckily, you "can't find better service."

El Conquistador, Conquistador 🏌
20 | 23 | 22 | 21 | $120

10555 N. La Cañada Dr.; 520-544-5000; www.hiltonelconquistador.com; 6781/4821; 72.7/69; 126/121
"Experience the Tucson mountains" at "one of the nicest resorts around" – a "top-drawer facility" with a "well-run course" amid "nice topography" "a bit of a drive" from its affiliated Hilton; the "excellent scenery" includes mesquite stands, cacti, ridges, ravines and some housing on a track that is "very forgiving in certain areas and challenging in others."

La Paloma 🏨 ⚷　　　24 | 25 | 24 | 20 | $195
3660 E. Sunrise Dr.; 520-299-1500; 800-222-1249; www.lapalomacc.com
Canyon/Hill: 6997/5057; 73.1/70.6; 149/126
Hill/Ridge: 7017/4878; 72.3/68.5; 144/123
Ridge/Canyon: 7088/5075; 73.2/70.1; 154/123
Mashie-toting masochists melt for this hilly, cactus-laden "Jack Nicklaus torture track" that represents "target golf at its most extreme", offset by a "friendly staff" and an "excellent practice area and dining"; while it "can be pricey", its "beautiful Westin hotel" and "scenic", "impressive holes, especially on the Canyon" nine, make for "all-around" "user-friendly golf packages" – if you're not a "higher handicap."

San Ignacio 🏨　　　▽ 20 | 14 | 15 | 24 | $65
4201 S. Camino del Sol, Green Valley; 520-648-3468;
6704/5865; 72/70.5; 135/125
Saints alive – 3,000 feet above sea level 20 miles south of Tucson lies a "short and tight" "enjoyable desert experience" designed by Arthur Hills that provides "something for everyone"; although the offerings include majestic views of the Santa Rita Mountains and "one of the best driving/chipping/putting/practice areas in the Tucson area", some sportsters sigh "it's not the best in Green Valley", even if it is "worth the money."

Starr Pass 🏨　　　22 | 21 | 19 | 18 | $185
3645 W. Starr Pass Blvd.; 520-670-0400; 800-503-2898;
www.starrpasstucson.com
Coyote/Rattler: 7002/5262; 73/70.8; 138/125
Coyote/Roadrunner: 6753/4963; 71.7/67.6; 143/120
Rattler/Roadrunner: 6731/5039; 71.7/68.2; 142/120
The former home to the PGA Tour's Tucson Open is a "classic desert layout among the saguaros", now with a new nine accompanying the existing 18, which were spruced up in the redesign by Arnold Palmer; though some Kingmakers say, "with the addition of the Marriott on-site", it "should be a real destination" for "great vistas" and a "fair challenge", others take a pass, citing "tricked-up" holes and "blind shots."

Ventana Canyon, Canyon　　　26 | 26 | 26 | 22 | $209
6200 N. Club House Ln.; 520-577-1400; 6819/4939; 72.6/70.2; 140/119
"Chasing wildlife off the tee box makes you forget all about the office" on Tom Fazio's "wonderful desert course overlooking Tucson" that boasts "beautiful fairways", "stupendous views and atmosphere" and "great practice facilities"; two acclaimed on-site hotels, the Lodge at Ventana Canyon and Loews Ventana Canyon, inspire some to call this the "best resort in Arizona", but if you skip breakfast for golf in winter, "watch out for early morning frost" at this altitude.

VENTANA CANYON, MOUNTAIN　　　27 | 25 | 25 | 20 | $209
6200 N. Club House Ln.; 520-577-1400; 6907/4676; 73/68.3; 147/119
"Breathtaking views, excellent service, great golf" sums up the majority view of this "killer" "natural-desert course" in the shadows of two "first-rate" resorts; a fickle few fuss over "having to compete with club members", but the majority "loves this place" including the "great facilities", the "short par-3" No. 3 "where you must carry a deep ravine to a green guarded by mountain rock" and the

"vista from the 18th tee" that's so "fantastic", you should "plan to finish the round at sunset."

Vistoso　　　　　26 | 22 | 22 | 23 | $159
955 W. Vistoso Highlands Dr.; 520-797-7900; www.vistosogolf.com; 6954/5095; 72.1/68.7; 147/120
It's lucky there's a "nice indoor/outdoor dining room" here, because "this course eats my lunch" say famished foozlers of this "truly rough and tough desert track with long carries, split fairways and too many decisions to make"; aces give kudos to the "immaculate shape" and "variation" on Tom Weiskopf's "target-golf test", while wayward hitters simply wail "bring an extra sleeve of balls."

Arkansas

Fairfield Bay

Mountain Ranch　　　　　– | – | – | – | $49
820 Lost Creek Pkwy.; 501-884-3400; www.mountainranchgolf.com; 6780/5325; 72.8/66.2; 140/126
No wonder this 1983 Edmund Ault design calls Lost Creek Parkway home – it isn't easy to locate; if you're in the neighborhood, 80 miles north of Little Rock, you'll find a handsome layout that traverses hilly Ozark Mountain terrain and dishes out a healthy variety of holes, with several especially memorable par-5s.

California

★ **Top Courses in State**
29 Pebble Beach, *Monterey Peninsula*
　　Spyglass Hill, *Monterey Peninsula*
28 Coyote Moon, *Lake Tahoe*
27 CordeValle, *San Francisco Bay Area*
　　Pasatiempo, *Santa Cruz*
　　La Purisima, *Santa Barbara*
　　Maderas, *San Diego*
26 Dragon at Gold Mountain, *Lake Tahoe*
　　Torrey Pines, South, *San Diego*
　　Pelican Hill, Ocean North, *Orange County*

Lake Tahoe

COYOTE MOON　　　　　28 | 22 | 23 | 20 | $150
10685 Northwoods Blvd., Truckee; 530-587-0886; www.coyotemoongolf.com; 7177/5022; 74.1/68.4; 138/127
"Mountain golf doesn't get any better" howl clubbing coyotes over the moon with this pup of a spread, a "gorgeous", millenial "jewel" "just outside of Truckee" that winds through rolling hills, towering pines and wildflowers; nature lovers lob balls on "spectacular holes" around fly-fishing lakes and "awesome rock formations" on old logging tracts in this "breathtaking" setting.

Dragon at Gold Mountain 於　　26 | 28 | 25 | 21 | $139
3887 County Rd. A-K, Clio; 530-832-4887; 800-368-7786; www.dragongolf.com; 7077/4611; 74.2/66.6; 147/128
This "breathtaking, fire-breathing, exhilarating" "Dragon will slay you if you get too confident", but it will also "leave you wanting

more"; "winding through the mountains" and trees in the "middle of nowhere" not far from Lake Tahoe, this "tough, tough, tough" beast with "borderline unfair" greens is "way too hard for mortals", but it can be "exceptionally fun" – "provided your ego doesn't get in the way"; rest after your battle within the resort's "outstanding facilities" (rated Top in California) including a clubhouse based on a design by Frank Lloyd Wright.

Lake Tahoe Golf Course
18 | 15 | 16 | 18 | $74

2500 Emerald Bay Rd., South Lake Tahoe; 530-577-0788; www.laketahoegc.com; 6741/5654; 70.8/66.7; 126/109
"You can whack the ball a mile in the thin mountain air" at this "nice interlude to gambling" surrounded by the Sierra Nevada Mountains; the "run-of-the-mill" layout is "wide and flat" with "relatively large, fairly slow greens", but the setting is "stunning"; since this spread "doesn't cost an arm and a leg", perhaps it's all those "good-value" hunters "watching out for late snow", "water hazards", "geese and wolves" here that make for "five-hour endurance rounds."

Northstar at Tahoe
18 | 16 | 18 | 16 | $99

168 Basque Dr., Truckee; 530-562-2490; 800-466-6784; www.northstarattahoe.com; 6897/5470; 72.4/70.8; 140/136
"If only the course was as easy as its ski mountain" say alpine aces about this "long, narrow and tough" layout in a "beautiful" "setting in the high Sierras backdropped by Lake Tahoe" with a "tight", "woodsy front" half and a "tricky", "wide-open" back; though "everything flies just a little farther than usual" this high up, some rocket-launching linksters lament that with "burnt fairways", "irregular greens" and a "total disconnect between the two nines", "the only thing that takes your breath away" here "is the altitude."

Resort at Squaw Creek
18 | 22 | 20 | 14 | $125

400 Squaw Creek Rd., Olympic Valley; 530-581-6637; 800-327-3353; www.squawcreek.com; 6931/6010; 72.9/69.3; 143/125
"Start in the sun and end in the snow" on this RTJ Jr. "target-golf" track "nicely settled at the base of Squaw Valley ski resort", where you should so "be ready for any type of weather" during the "short season" from May to October; manicurists mashing the "spotty conditions" might not know that the "grounds crew pulls weeds from the fairways by hand" and "only organic pesticides are used" to protect the "surrounding marsh" "habitat", which makes for "beautiful views" against the peaks but also swallows "slightly errant balls" "for good."

Whitehawk Ranch
25 | 21 | 26 | 21 | $125

768 Whitehawk Dr., Clio; 530-836-0394; 800-332-4295; www.golfwhitehawk.com; 6928/4816; 72.6/62.9; 133/105
"A mountain must", this "exceptionally designed", "gorgeous course" built on former ranchland challenges you "with a succession of great holes" where "conditions are always a 10"; it's "a long drive" to "the middle of nowhere, or near to it", but "if you have just one day in North Tahoe, play" this "atmospheric" spread for its "vistas" and "awesome facilities", including a "driving range that provides Titleist balls."

Los Angeles

Angeles National
23 | 12 | 20 | 18 | $98

9401 Foothill Blvd., Sunland; 818-951-8771; www.angelesnational.com; 7000/6000; 74.4/68.9; 140/116

Celeb sightings include Cy Young winner Eric Gagne and Football-Hall-of-Famer Eric Dickerson at this "fine addition" 30 minutes from Downtown; it sports "beautiful views", "forgiving" fairways, "firm greens" and a "great practice" range; the clubhouse is still a "trailer" with a "glorified snack bar", but when the facilities are completed in 2006, the restaurant will be overseen by *Iron Chef* Sammi Iwasaki – and even now, if the spread is good enough to be "Shigeki Maruyama's home course", it's good enough for you.

Industry Hills, Babe D. Zaharias 🖾
23 | 20 | 17 | 21 | $96

1 Industry Hills Pkwy., City of Industry; 626-810-4653; www.ihgolfclub.com; 6821/5363; 73.9/73.3; 135/129

Don your "patience cap" and "don't let the length fool you": this is a "brutal" "shotmaker's" course with "narrow fairways" and "multi-tiered, fast greens" "requiring every club in your bag", except for your driver ("leave it in the car" with your "testosterone"); although "surprisingly pretty" and "charming" with "one of LA's only covered driving ranges" and a "cute funicular to bring carts back up the hill", it suffers "for its location" say perspiring putters who pout "why does it always seem to be 98 and smoggy here?"

Industry Hills, Eisenhower 🖾
24 | 19 | 17 | 22 | $96

1 Industry Hills Pkwy., City of Industry; 626-810-4653; www.ihgolfclub.com; 7199/5620; 75.4/74.1; 144/139

"Humans shouldn't play the blacks" on Babe's "bruiser" brother, "one of the toughest" layouts in California; be "prepared for blind shots, elevation changes" and "golf's steepest greens" on this "masterpiece", but play it seasonally only, as locals who don't like Ike in summer say "100 degrees combined with horrific smog and the neighboring cow pasture turn this long, mountainous course built on landfill into a sweat pit", even if the associated Pacific Palms resort helps make up for it with post-round pampering.

Lost Canyons, Shadow
24 | 23 | 23 | 18 | $120

3301 Lost Canyon Dr., Simi Valley; 805-522-4653; www.lostcanyons.com; 7005/4795; 75/69.1; 149/125

"Lost Canyons means lost balls", so "don't bite off more than you can chew" on "Pete Dye's typically punishing" "thinking-man's" layout; given "forced carries" over "deep ravines", plus "sidehill lies", "a few blind shots" and "elevated" "slippery greens" "that roll true", it's "not for the faint of heart" "or the beginner", particularly when the "Santa Anas pick up"; it is, however, "unbelievably scenic" with "top-notch facilities" including "the "best driving range around" – but with prices as "steep" as its "plateau" putting surfaces, it "should be good!"

Lost Canyons, Sky
23 | 22 | 22 | 18 | $120

3301 Lost Canyon Dr., Simi Valley; 805-522-4653; www.lostcanyons.com; 7285/4885; 76.1/70; 149/120

"If you like Pete Dye, go", but "bring a ton of balls" – "otherwise, be very afraid" of this "insanely tough", "hilly" layout "where damage control is the order of the day" on "tight landing areas" and "undulating greens" "that require accuracy, or you are dead"; though sometimes "very slow and very crowded", it's "extraordinary in its beauty" and has "good facilities and food" and a staff that's more "friendly" than the layout.

Los Verdes
19 | 12 | 11 | 24 | $28

7000 W. Los Verdes Dr., Rancho Palos Verdes; 310-377-7888;
www.americangolf.com; 6617/5772; 71.7/67.7; 121/113

"Hilly, walkable" and "cheap, cheap, cheap", this "oceanside" muni "on the bluffs" of "posh" Palos Verdes offers "to-die-for" "views of Catalina" at the "best bang for your buck" in town; the panorama is so "spectacular", slicers "sleep in their cars for 5 AM tee-time sign-ups" to "get paired up with fivesomes" for "mind-numbing" "six-hour rounds" and "facilities consistent with the price" – if you "don't mind leisure golf", at least you'll "have plenty of time to get to know the group (or two) ahead of you."

Moorpark 🏌
21 | 20 | 19 | 18 | $95

11800 Championship Dr., Moorpark; 805-532-2834;
www.moorparkcountryclub.com
Canyon Crest/Creekside: 6939/4867; 73.8/69; 136/118
Canyon Crest/Ridgeline: 6902/4839; 73/68.6; 138/116
Creekside/Ridgeline: 6977/4722; 73.8/68.5; 142/118

"Magnificent views, interesting fauna and no freeway or airport noise" are three components that are "hard to beat" on this "young" 27-holer 30 miles from LA – add to that list "greens more manicured than your wife's" (or your) nails, and you've got one "lovely course"; "forget it unless you're a mountain goat" say sore-footed foozlers who find its "many huge canyons" and "required long carries" flat out "difficult", particularly "on windy days!!"

Ojai Valley Inn & Spa
25 | 23 | 24 | 20 | $170

905 Country Club Rd., Ojai; 805-646-2420; 800-422-6524; www.golfojai.com;
6292/5211; 71/70.7; 132/129

You'll find it "hard to believe you're only 90 minutes from LA" on this "fab old-school" "gem" "in a peaceful environment" that is "pure heaven" for those seeking a "great getaway" with "golf, spa and nice restaurants"; the "pretty little course going up and down hills" has been "restored to its original pre-WWII layout", which, when added to the "well-appointed amenities and very gracious staff", gives you a "wonderful place to relax and play."

Palos Verdes Golf Club ⏲
23 | 17 | 18 | 19 | $205

3301 Via Campesina, Palos Verdes Estates; 310-375-2533;
6219/4696; 70.5/68.2; 129/123

It's "not that long", but "with nary a flat lie", it's "a blast to play" – "if you can get on" this "great, old" "semi-private tract" designed in the 1920s by George Thomas of Riviera fame amid "narrow" "eucalyptus"-lined fairways "overlooking the Pacific Ocean"; it's "chilly" "on the Palos Verdes Peninsula", so bring your mackinaw and your money because "they charge like it's Pebble Beach."

Robinson Ranch, Mountain
21 | 22 | 21 | 19 | $117

27734 Sand Canyon Rd., Santa Clarita; 661-252-7666;
www.robinsonranchgolf.com; 6508/5076; 72.3/69.5; 137/121

"Narrow", "perfectly green fairways" kept "in tremendous shape" and "A4 bent-grass greens" that are some of the "truest and fastest in LA County" "look good" contrasted by "very brown rough" at this spread for "target golf at its finest"; "bring a portable fan" and a saddle bag of balls because "stray shots in the desert are goners", disappearing into "environmentally protected areas."

Robinson Ranch, Valley | 24 | 22 | 22 | 18 | $117 |

27734 Sand Canyon Rd., Santa Clarita; 661-252-7666;
www.robinsonranchgolf.com; 6903/5408; 74.4/72.2; 149/126
The "greens are slicker than a freshly done bikini wax" and, accordingly, they're surrounded by "a lot of rough" on this "great design" by ranch namesakes Ted Sr. and Jr.; "long from the tips", it's "crazy hard" on the "bearish Death Row holes", Nos. 13–18, but it's in a "beautiful setting", so as "close as it is to an urban environment", "you feel like you're getting away"; pack your SPF 45 and your sombrero in summer 'cause it's "hotter than Hades", even under the shade of the "joke of a tree" on the left side of the finish.

Rustic Canyon | 24 | 16 | 18 | 26 | $53 |

15100 Happy Camp Canyon Rd., Moorpark; 805-530-0221;
6935/5275; 73.1/69.4; 126/113
"You almost feel like you're in Scotland" at this "fabulous" and "secluded" links that's "like nothing you've played in California"; "routed through washes and environmentally protected areas" with "unbelievable bunker complexes" and "maddening", "deceptive" greens "quicker than W's declaration of war", "this is a course to remember", so even though "there's not much else but the golf" here, for "a world-class round for less than $60", "who cares?"

TPC at Valencia | 19 | 23 | 20 | 12 | $143 |

26550 Heritage View Ln., Valencia; 661-288-1995;
www.tpc.com/private/valencia; 7260/5380; 75.8/67.2; 140/116
This hilly, "tight, tree-lined" layout with "complex greens" can be "difficult" for Valley guys, but the "women's tees are manageable" for Valley girls, who "get around quickly" and then "have a great lunch" served by a "tremendous" staff; though the practice area is "excellent", a few "hokey" holes make you "feel like you have to hit through a windmill" on this "big course for Japanese visitors."

Monterey Peninsula

Bayonet Blackhorse, Bayonet | 25 | 16 | 17 | 23 | $93 |

1 McClure Way, Seaside; 831-899-7271; www.bayonetblackhorse.com;
7117/5763; 75.6/74.3; 136/129
"Just like the artillery engineer who designed it", you need a "military mind" to strategize this "outstanding track" "on the former Fort Ord base"; it's "like the Great Wall of China: loooong and narrow", but with "doglegs that can bring you to your knees" and "cypress trees that eat" your ball on its "wooded coastal" fairways; co-host to the Champions Tour's First Tee Open, this "remarkable value" with Monterey Bay views is "overlooked by many visitors", but "locals like it that way."

Bayonet Blackhorse, Blackhorse | 23 | 16 | 18 | 23 | $97 |

1 McClure Way, Seaside; 831-899-7271; www.bayonetblackhorse.com;
7009/5648; 74.9/73; 137/126
"Easy only in comparison" to its "relentless" pardner, this "long and very challenging" forested layout a few miles from Monterey

"can still kick your butt"; amid "many elevation changes" and "wet" "seaside" conditions, "you're gonna need a lot of club", most of it "straight", or "you'll be pitching/punching out of a forest" and "walking off the course emotionally and physically destroyed"; it's an "incredible bargain" "for the price and view", even if "the marshals sometimes make you feel like it's still an army base."

Carmel Valley Ranch ⌂ ⊕   21 | 22 | 22 | 18 | $190

1 Old Ranch Rd., Carmel; 831-626-2510; 800-488-7695; www.cvrgolf.com; 6234/5187; 70.8/65.4; 138/122

"If you like wildlife, you'll love" the "turkeys and deer" "blending into the breathtaking landscape" of this "hidden gem" designed by Pete Dye; the front nine wanders "partially in the Carmel Valley", but the back climbs through "the hillsides above", so "unless you have the legs of a bighorn sheep, you're advised to ride" it; "weather that's warmer and clearer" "even when the coast is cold and windy" helps make this "tranquil" "resort course" a "great" "couples' golf" "alternative to the $$$ and fog of Pebble."

Del Monte 🏃   17 | 14 | 18 | 17 | $95

1300 Sylvan Rd., Monterey; 831-373-2700; www.delmontegolf.com; 6357/6052; 70.8/69.5; 123/121

"The oldest course west of the Mississippi" "is holding up well, given its 100-plus-year history" profess archival aces who call this "gentle, old-fashioned track" "short" but "deceivingly tough" with "small greens and long par-3s that make it more difficult than it looks"; on the other hand, "tight", oak-lined fairways and "holes so close together" that "it's dangerous" have claustrophobes calling for an "extreme makeover" here.

Pacific Grove Municipal   20 | 11 | 14 | 27 | $38

77 Asilomar Blvd., Pacific Grove; 831-648-5777; 5732/5299; 67.5/70.2; 118/116

Monterey's "biggest surprise" could induce "sticker shock!" – in reverse, because California's Top Value sports "the beautiful vistas and [on-course] ambiance of Pebble Beach" "at one-tenth the price"; locals tell a "tale of two nines" in which the "nondescript front" "takes you through trees" to the "spectacular back" where, while "plunking your ball down in the ice-plant rough", "you hear deer munching, seals barking and the surf crashing" beneath "a great old lighthouse"; overlook the "shabby shape" and "cranky locals in the pro shop", and you'll understand why it's "a jewel."

PEBBLE BEACH 🏃   29 | 27 | 27 | 15 | $425

1700 17-Mile Dr., Pebble Beach; 831-624-3811; 800-654-9300; www.pebblebeach.com; 6737/5198; 73.8/71.9; 142/130

Someday "you'll tell your grandkids" you "wept when you saw the 18th" on this "national monument to golf" where "beauty, majesty and history" "exceed the highest expectations"; the Most Popular "mackdaddy of them all" "gets a lot of play", the "seagulls here could steal food from Fort Knox" and "you can hear 'ka-ching' each time you tee it up", but go ahead and "pay the damn money" because, given "ocean holes that ignite adrenalin off the charts", "value is not an issue here" – after all, "how do you rate artwork?"

POPPY HILLS   26 | 23 | 22 | 24 | $160

3200 Lopez Rd., Pebble Beach; 831-625-1513; www.poppyhillsgolf.com;
6833/5403; 74.2/71.6; 144/131

There are "no ocean distractions, just pure golf" at this "stunning"
and "secluded" neighbor to the "seaside spectacle" of "Pebble,
Spyglass and Spanish Bay"; host to the AT&T Pebble Beach Pro-
Am, it's "carved into a pine forest" with "lush" "fairways like
carpet" "abundant with red foxes and deer" and "large", "sloped",
"soft greens" that "roll fast and true"; it might "feel like you're
dating" the "rock stars'" "less attractive sister", but "by Carmel
standards", it's "the best bang for your buck", which means "you'll
come back again and again (and can afford it)."

Quail Lodge ⌐   20 | 22 | 23 | 18 | $195

8205 Valley Greens Dr., Carmel; 831-620-8808; 888-828-8787;
www.quaillodge.com; 6449/5488; 71.4/72; 128/127

"Take advantage" of this "immaculate" but "rather flat", "high-
handicapper-friendly" formation "set in the valley" along the
Carmel River and "beautifully surrounded" by the Santa Lucia
Mountains; compared to its "expensive oceanside" "neighbors",
this "delightful" "resort course" is "ideal" for a package deal,
including "new, first-rate clubhouse facilities" and a namesake
hotel in a "romantic setting" featuring a "great spa, health club",
"beautifully decorated rooms" and "impeccable service."

SPANISH BAY ⅄   26 | 26 | 27 | 17 | $230

2700 17-Mile Dr., Pebble Beach; 831-647-7500; 800-654-9300;
www.pebblebeach.com; 6821/5332; 74.1/72.1; 146/129

It's "one of my favorite courses on the planet!" swoon swingers
smitten with this "windswept" 18, a "taste of Scotland right down
to the morning mist" in "one of the most beautiful areas in the
world", the 17-Mile Drive; infused with "romance and calm", this
"perfectly maintained", "top-tier" "seasider" also serves up drama
with "people-eating bunkers" and "dunes and does as natural
hazards"; a "bagpiper plays haunting melodies" "along with the
surf" in the late afternoon before you "retire" to a seat by your
"fireplace" at the "stately, well-run" Inn at Spanish Bay.

SPYGLASS HILL ⅄   29 | 21 | 25 | 19 | $290

Spyglass Hill Rd., Pebble Beach; 831-625-8563; 800-654-9300;
www.pebblebeach.com; 6938/5379; 75.5/72.9; 147/133

"Think you're pretty good? – you'll never know until you play" this
"glorious" peninsula "butt-kicker"; it "opens with five of the most
scenic", "ocean-hugging" holes "anywhere on earth", then follows
with 13 "narrow" "bowling alleys" through the "medieval" "Del
Monte Forest", which "echoes with balls banging against trees";
"ice plants meaner than an ex-wife" on "the purest, toughest test
on the Monterey Peninsula" make "Pebble look like a cakewalk" –
"at half the price."

Orange County

Arroyo Trabuco ⌂   22 | 21 | 20 | 25 | $85

26772 Avery Pkwy., Mission Viejo; 949-305-5100;
www.arroyotrabuco.com; 7011/5045; 73.7/59.8; 134/121

A "good layout" with "varied terrain" and "reasonably priced
amenities", including "yummy food", add up to "the absolute

best deal in Orange County" at this "nice new addition to the area", which "all public courses could take a page from"; the "environmentally sensitive spots" ("which you cannot enter!") "are a pain" and perhaps the course "needs to mature", but the majority concludes it's a "first-class experience all around" that "doesn't cost your first born to play."

Coyote Hills   19 | 19 | 20 | 18 | $110

1440 E. Bastanchury Rd., Fullerton; 714-672-6800; www.coyotehillsgc.com; 6510/5142; 72.2/67.6; 135/115
Don't "just grab for the driver" at this "short", hilly, 27-hole muni because where "forced carries and trees challenge accuracy", "placement is more important than length"; the "panoramic vistas" of Catalina Island and LA are "all good, but something" (besides length) "always seems to be missing" howl packs of public putters who put down "funky holes" where "good shots roll off into junk" in a "unique setting among active oil drilling equipment" that garners the gnarly nickname "Coyote Wells."

Monarch Beach   21 | 21 | 22 | 15 | $195

22 Monarch Beach Resort N., Dana Point; 949-240-8247; www.monarchbeachgolf.com; 6601/5050; 72.8/70.4; 138/125
Given its "fab location" next to the luxurious Ritz-Carlton and St. Regis hotels, this "favorite" for "tourists and neighbors with too much money to burn" had better be "smooth as silk"; a "short", "straight" RTJ Jr. layout, it features a few "spectacular seaside holes", but with a mostly "inland" layout "lining million-dollar condos" and "mat-and-net" facilities that "don't cut it" for a practice range, it's "nothing to write home about."

Oak Creek 🏳   21 | 21 | 22 | 18 | $135

1 Golf Club Dr., Irvine; 949-653-7300; www.oakcreekgolfclub.com; 6850/4989; 72.7/69; 132/120
"Except for the commuter train going by", this "fab Fazio track" "seems to be isolated" "in no-man's-land", but "crowds have found it" anyway, lured by the "surprisingly undulating", "wonderfully manicured" layout, a "terrific staff", "some of the best practice facilities" and "truly excellent food in the 19th hole"; still, though you can gobble "maybe the best sandwich you've ever had", you'll have to suffer a "frustrating five-hour round" for it.

PELICAN HILL, OCEAN NORTH 🏳   26 | 25 | 25 | 16 | $250

22651 Pelican Hill Rd. S., Newport Coast; 949-760-0707; www.pelicanhill.com; 6856/4950; 73.3/69.4; 133/124
"Bring an East Coast client here in the winter and you're guaranteed to seal the deal" boast ball-whacking businessmen of Tom Fazio's "breathtaking" design "beautifully routed along the arroyos and canyons of the Newport coast", where you can enjoy "magnificent ocean views" while dining on the "best burger" "prepared by Four Seasons chefs" and brought by a "pleasurable staff"; "fully priced" for "fat cats", this "must-play" is "worth the high ticket."

PELICAN HILL, OCEAN SOUTH 🏳   26 | 25 | 24 | 15 | $250

22651 Pelican Hill Rd. S., Newport Coast; 949-760-0707; www.pelicanhill.com; 6589/4710; 72.1/68.2; 130/119
"You can almost step onto the beach" on this "amazing course with challenging holes, ocean views, canyons and lakes" say boosters

of one of the "most beautiful and well-maintained publics in southern California"; while the "lack of an easily accessible driving range is hassle" enough to have some dusty drivers dishing out "two words: grossly overpriced", the majority "loves" the "Four Seasons food and service", and those "back-to-back par-3s on the ocean"? –"wow!"

Strawberry Farms

20 | 19 | 19 | 15 | $145

11 Strawberry Farms Rd., Irvine; 949-551-1811;
www.strawberryfarmsgolf.com; 6700/4832; 72.7/68.7; 136/114
"Professionals only need apply" declare diva duffers of this "tough" "urban" track with "tight fairways on the front" and reservoir "protected areas on the back" nine, which culminates in a "solid set of finishing holes"; with "no houses lining" the layout, it's "surprisingly serene and pleasant", matched by a "good practice range, pro shop and restaurant", even if swinging size-queens quip that "too much course on not enough land" makes one "gigantic layout for miniature golf."

Talega 🏌

23 | 18 | 21 | 19 | $125

990 Avenida Talega, San Clemente; 949-369-6226;
www.talegagolfclub.com; 6951/5245; 73.6/71.1; 137/121
"Shake a leg to get to this winner", a "well-maintained", "long, tough" track with "pearly white traps" "winding through the hills of San Clemente"; featuring "par-3s over water on the front" and a back nine that overlooks canyons, marshes and lakes, it's "fun and challenging for most golfers", "when played from the proper tees"; someone should tell the "exceptionally nice staff", however, that "a driving range would add a lot to the facilities."

Tijeras Creek

20 | 17 | 16 | 17 | $95

29082 Tijeras Creek, Rancho Santa Margarita; 949-589-9793;
www.tijerascreek.com; 6918/5130; 73.4/69.8; 136/120
"Going from the front to the back is like stepping into another world" on this "course with a finish that is legendary in the OC"; it "plays narrowly through a canyon" filled with oaks, sycamores and native chaparral where the "spectacular par-3s are worth the price of admission"; before the turn, however, "some of the holes are real duds", and the "fees are too high for its mid-level facilities."

Tustin Ranch 🏌

19 | 19 | 19 | 16 | $155

12442 Tustin Ranch Rd., Tustin; 714-730-1611; www.tustinranchgolf.com;
6803/5263; 73.5/71.7; 134/132
In a "convenient location off the 5 Freeway" is "a beautiful sight to see", say local loyalists of this "good urbanite" whose "fun and challenging" layout offers "plenty of thought-provoking shots"; carnivorous club-wielding critics refuse to "throw money at" this "flat" "wimp" "full of luxury autos and cookie-cutter McMansions" that offers "too much eye candy" and "not enough meat."

Palm Springs

Cimarrón

18 | 19 | 21 | 18 | $99

67603 30th Ave., Cathedral City; 760-770-6060; www.cimarrongolf.com;
6858/5127; 72.4/69.7; 123/117
Novices needing a "nice change of pace" for a "quick game before leaving" Palm Springs say their "fave in the desert" is this spread

"close to the airport" that's "playable for the duffer", even "when the wind blows"; chippers who "felt cheated" by "greens fees that didn't come down", even though "much of the course and driving range were eliminated from the rains" at the beginning of 2005, will be happy that the reconstruction has been completed.

Desert Dunes ⛳   21   17   17   21 $100
19300 Palm Dr., Desert Hot Springs; 760-251-5367;
6876/5359; 73.8/70.7; 142/122
Meep, meep! – wily coyotes warn of "roadrunners running around" on RTJ Jr.'s "great links layout", "a pleasure to play for all handicaps" in the Palm Springs area; "though it's great fun digging through cactus for your golf balls", get on "early" as the "winds can really whip" "after 2 PM", "wreaking havoc with your game" on a course that may have "seen better days" when service wasn't so "lacking."

Desert Falls ⛳   20   18   18   19 $165
1111 Desert Falls Pkwy., Palm Desert; 760-340-4653;
www.desert-falls.com; 7084/5273; 74/72.1; 133/125
"The Chihuly chandelier in the lobby is drop-dead gorgeous" gush designer glass–loving golfers, but so is this "fabulous, difficult course" and its "exciting vistas"; "unusual for a desert spread", it's got "lots of water" on holes like the "great finish" that shares a lake-, waterfall- and rock-guarded green with No. 9; "from the tips, it's very, very tough", but the same can't be said about tee times: it's "easy to get on even in season."

Desert Willow, Firecliff ⛳   26   24   23   23 $165
38995 Desert Willow Dr., Palm Desert; 760-346-7060; 800-320-3323;
www.desertwillow.com; 7056/5079; 73.6/69; 138/117
Once featured on the cover of *Smithsonian Magazine*, this boldly bunkered, "stunning", "immaculate" spread "challenges you right from the start" with "tough but not punishing" "target-desert golf" amid "lots of wildlife" and "gorgeous" views; the "first-rate" staff pampers you with "plenty of water and cold towels", so "even if you've been staring too long at the cacti and mountains", "you don't want the round to end" – luckily, there's a "super pro shop" and "very good restaurant" waiting when it does.

Desert Willow, Mountain View ⛳   25   23   23   21 $165
38995 Desert Willow Dr., Palm Desert; 760-346-7060; 800-320-3323;
www.desertwillow.com; 6913/5040; 73.4/68.9; 130/116
"I would go out of my way to play it again" say bogey artists of this "awesome" course that dishes out "lots of water", "meticulous greens" and "soft", "wide fairways" full of "scenery and wildlife"; it's "more generous than sister Firecliff" at this resort with a "friendly staff", "first-rate facilities" and "terrific food", but given "great summer rates" that hardly amount to a hill of beans, this otherwise "outstanding" track gets "overwhelmed" by locals.

Golf Resort at Indian Wells, East ⛳   21   22   22   18 $130
44500 Indian Wells Ln., Indian Wells; 760-346-4653;
www.golfresortatindianwells.com; 6631/5516; 72.1/71.5; 133/118
"A fantastic school and great instructors" lure students of swing to the Hyatt's "typical 1970s resort course" surrounded by "rolling hills and trees" with "lovely views and clubhouse"; since "no homes

line the fairways", "it's just you and the spirits of the natives" on "attractive and expansive" property where "you get a free drop" near the "burial grounds"; though some squawk "it's too hot in summer and expensive in winter", a planned overhaul by John Fought and an in-progress redo on sister West might merit the heated weather and wallet.

Heritage Palms 🏌️⏰   ▽ 21 | 20 | 19 | 21 | $95
44291 Heritage Palms Dr. S., Indio; 760-772-7334;
6727/5577; 71.9/66.6; 124/111
"Could be the slickest greens in Palm Springs" proclaim putting pros of this "completely different desert course" that's "mostly grass" and "fairly easy" with "wide fairways" in a "serene community setting"; with "no trees" to shade the Arthur Hills design, it "gets real toasty in the summer", so "play early or late afternoon" to get a cooler "value for the money."

La Quinta, Dunes 🏌️   22 | 24 | 22 | 17 | $135
50-200 Vista Bonita, La Quinta; 760-564-7610; www.laquintaresort.com;
6682/4930; 72.4/69.3; 136/124
"Call me crazy but it doesn't get much better than playing" a "typical Pete Dye torture chamber" "at the crack of dawn" declare daffy dew-sweepers of this "good second-day course" at a resort in "a beautiful setting at the base of the Santa Rosas"; despite "excellent facilities", however, hackers huff the "concrete arroyos" make the Mountain's "weak sister" "like playing through a drainage ditch", but with "invasive homes and condos" "at every turn."

La Quinta, Mountain 🏌️⏰   26 | 24 | 24 | 18 | $190
50-200 Vista Bonita, La Quinta; 760-564-7610; www.laquintaresort.com;
6756/4894; 72.6/68.9; 135/120
Though Pete Dye "took advantage of its natural features", this "jaw-dropping" "beauty" is so "surreal", it's like "playing on another planet"; winding "dramatically" in and around the "majestic scenery" of the Santa Rosas, the "beautifully manicured" layout boasts a "tough and fun front", an "interesting", "challenging back" and "views as extreme as the breaks on the greens" – or the "silly" "winter rates"; "if you can survive", play it "for a song in the summer" when "you can bake a pizza on the red-hot rocks."

Marriott Desert Springs, Palm 🏌️   20 | 23 | 22 | 18 | $155
74855 Country Club Dr., Palm Desert; 760-341-2211; 800-331-3112;
www.desertspringsresort.com; 6761/5492; 72.1/71.9; 130/125
It's "the total package" exclaim enthusiasts of this "top-flight" resort with "lots of water" ("oh yes, they have it"), "palm trees and hummingbirds" at the foot of the Santa Rosas; this layout "favors accuracy over distance" on fairways that occasionally "crank down on you" as they "weave through condominiums"; "bring a sunblock" and "stay hydrated" harp overheated hackers heckling the "sloooooooooow play" on this – "yawn"! – "leisure course designed not to challenge anyone."

Marriott Desert Springs, Valley 🏌️   21 | 22 | 22 | 17 | $155
74855 Country Club Dr., Palm Desert; 760-341-2211; 800-331-3112;
www.desertspringsresort.com; 6627/5262; 71.5/70.2; 127/118
"Relatively short", "wide-open" and "hillier than the Palm but just as nice", this Marriott track features "great views of the mountains"

and "lots" of "Ted Robinson lagoons" "to play over or around"; though it's "well maintained" with "good off-season" discount specials, the "old-school desert-type" design gets "beaten up by the resort crowd" lament local linksters who call it "not outstanding by Palm Springs standards."

Marriott Shadow Ridge   25 | 25 | 24 | 21 | $145
9002 Shadow Ridge Rd., Palm Desert; 760-674-2700;
www.golfshadowridge.com; 7006/5158; 73.9/69.6; 134/119
"This is one good golf course" with "the best practice facility I have ever seen at a resort" praise prospective pros-in-training about this "spectacular Nick Faldo design" that features "memorable routing", "big, undulating greens", "outstanding" "8-ft.-high bunkers" and "four sets of tees that let you bite off all you can chew"; though "pretty expensive", "it's worth the money" "in spite of its newness" as it's "fun and playable" with a "knowledgeable staff" and "gorgeous" "views, views, views."

PGA West,   25 | 26 | 23 | 17 | $235
Jack Nicklaus Tournament
56-150 PGA Blvd., La Quinta; 760-564-7170; 800-742-9378;
www.pgawest.com; 7204/5023; 74.7/69; 139/121
"You may retrieve some of your pride", but Jack's "spectacular" "layout doesn't take a back seat" easily to sister Stadium – it's "fair" to "the average golfer on vacation", but only if they "know where to hit" to avoid "some of the toughest bunkers in golf"; still, an "excellent staff", "great practice facilities" and "beautiful surroundings" can't keep critics from cracking this "tired" track "overwhelmed by condos" is "less than meets the eye."

PGA West, TPC Stadium   26 | 25 | 23 | 17 | $235
56-150 PGA Blvd., La Quinta; 760-564-7170; 800-742-9378;
www.pgawest.com; 7266/5092; 75.9/70; 150/124
"Holy crap", ya gotta love "Pete Dye at his sadistic best" on this "masterpiece" "nut buster"; "long, strong, mean" and "more fun than *Fear Factor*", it "lulls you then stomps you with metal spikes", fomenting "fits" with "7,400 yards of carry, carry, carry", plus "monster traps" and "lightning-fast greens"; you'll think "only God can play No. 6 from the tips", while the legendary "par-3 17th 'Alcatraz' lurks in your mind" for the "six hours of hell" leading to the finish; it's "hard as nails", but that's "why we play."

Tahquitz Creek, Legend   22 | 19 | 18 | 18 | $80
1885 Golf Club Dr.; 760-328-1956; 800-743-2211; www.tahquitzcreek.com;
6815/5861; 72.3/74.4; 123/122
A "beautiful course", this "old-time gem" from the 1950s has been recently renovated and toughened up with the addition of 60 new bunkers; the mountain views make for "picture opportunities", but don't lose your concentration on the severely sloping greens, particularly on some of the "hardest finishing holes in the desert"; this "true classic" is "well kept", despite being "always crowded."

Trilogy at La Quinta   21 | 21 | 23 | 20 | $139
60-151 Trilogy Pkwy., La Quinta; 760-771-0707; www.trilogygolfclub.com;
7100/4998; 72.9/63.6; 137/103
"Don't let it fool you" – despite "a fair amount of water" and "blind surprises", "you can shoot a very low score" on the "treeless",

"wide-open fairways" and "big greens" at this "user-friendly" Gary Panks "beauty" "tucked away in the back corner of La Quinta"; it's "meticulously groomed" in a "pretty setting", but it "isn't as good as it looks on TV" say swingers "surprised" that a course "too easy [even] for high-handicappers" "hosts the Skins Game."

Westin Mission Hills, Gary Player   24 | 21 | 22 | 20 | $145
70705 Ramon Rd., Rancho Mirage; 760-770-9496; 800-358-2211; www.troongolf.com; 7062/4907; 73.4/68; 131/118
An "amazing example of how good a flat course can be", this "desert" Player design is "more traditional" but "more enjoyable" than the Westin's Dye course; "in beautiful shape" with scenery to match, a "fair", "forgiving" layout and "a bit of a challenge to boot", it's "lots of fun to play" "for golfers at all levels", particularly lady lofters who "like its short tees", even if restless roundsmen rant that "it's getting a bit tired."

Westin Mission Hills, Pete Dye   22 | 23 | 23 | 19 | $145
71501 Dinah Shore Dr., Rancho Mirage; 760-328-3198; 800-358-2211; www.troongolf.com; 6706/4841; 72.2/67.6; 131/117
"Not for the weak or the wild", this "deceptively good", "Pete Dye classic" sports "deep sand traps", "huge grass bunkers", "very good greens", "tough shots over water" where "mistakes are severely penalized" and a "beauty" of an 18th, a par-4 dogleg left wedged between hazards; a staff that keeps the spread "in mint condition" and "treats players as private country club members" helps make this "friendly" resort a "favorite" for Palm Springs weekenders.

Riverside

Moreno Valley Ranch ⛳   21 | 17 | 17 | 21 | $65
28095 John F. Kennedy Dr., Moreno Valley; 951-924-4444; www.mvrgolf.com
Lake/Mountain: 6734/5108; 73.2/69.6; 144/121
Lake/Valley: 6948/5246; 74.4/70.1; 141/122
Mountain/Valley: 6880/5196; 73.6/70.1; 146/122
"Lake/Mountain is a favorite combination" say choosy chippers about this "awfully tough" Pete Dye 27-holer, but the "target golf" track "can eat you alive"; it's "worth the long trip" from LA to score "super golf on a budget" with "fast greens" and mountain views, particularly if you overlook the "slightly degraded conditions in recent years" that make a round on a course "that used to be beautiful" now just "up and down."

Oak Quarry ⛳   25 | 19 | 21 | 21 | $95
7151 Sierra Ave.; 951-685-1440; www.oakquarry.com; 7002/5408; 73.9/71.9; 137/121
Carved out of the historic Jensen Quarry "with incredible elevation changes", huge bunkers and "stunning scenery" that make it like "playin' in the Grand Canyon", this "tough" Schmidt/Curley design features such "exciting holes" as the "signature" par-3 14th, with an all-carry tee shot to a peninsula green; "if you can't manage to hit in the short stuff, bring a lot of ammunition" because the rough is "only rocks and steep drop-offs", and "when there's wind" this "great deal" "will test your skill."

Sacramento

DarkHorse

| 25 | 14 | 19 | 22 | $84 |

13450 Combie Rd., Auburn; 530-269-7900;
www.darkhorsegolf.com; 7203/5058; 75/68.3; 140/122
Keith Foster's "pretty", classically bunkered "challenge" amid
ancient oaks and outcroppings northeast of Sacramento "makes
you play both long and strategically"; in other words, it's "perfect"
for rough riding "carts up" to "elevated tees" to "hit down into the
valley"; horse sense says that "minimal facilities are a deterrent" at
a "new course" that "needs to mature" under "more attention",
but if a "great bargain" for "just golf" makes you hot to trot, you
might want to pony up.

Diablo Grande, Legends West ⏲

| 26 | 21 | 20 | 22 | $125 |

9521 Morton Davis Dr., Patterson; 209-892-4653; www.diablogrande.com;
7112/4905; 74.4/69.3; 147/123
"Not as tough" as brother Ranch, this "outstanding" Jack
Nicklaus/Gene Sarazen course "south of Stockton" is still "a
pleasure to play" for its "challenging holes, which are not
forgiving to those who stray from the fairway" (and neither are
the "rattlesnakes" amid the surrounding vineyards); "well
maintained" and uncrowded with "no homes" near it yet, it's
slated for future residential development, so the "friendly staff"
will tell you to get to it while it's still a "great value."

Diablo Grande, Ranch

| 25 | 23 | 20 | 21 | $85 |

9521 Morton Davis Dr., Patterson; 209-892-4653; www.diablogrande.com;
7246/5026; 75.8/70; 144/124
"It's a long drive from everywhere" say Sunday swingers who make
the two-hour trek from Sacramento to "a great complex" whose
"fun" and "challenging" holes are lined with 400-year-old oaks with
grapevine borders; "don't play from the back tees unless you are
practicing to go on Tour" dish duffers bedeviled by the distance on
the 650-yd. par-5 12th with its greenside views of Mikes Peak, while
even the unimpeded pace of play and top-notch pro shop can't stop
grander golfers from griping it's "nothing particularly special."

San Bernardino

Oak Valley 🏞

| 25 | 19 | 19 | 26 | $85 |

1888 Golf Club Dr., Beaumont; 951-769-7200;
www.oakvalleygolf.com; 7040/5349; 74/71.9; 138/128
"If you like variety", the "best-kept secret in the desert" "is
your cup of tea" savor swingers sweet on this "extremely fair and
entertaining" Schmidt/Curley layout where "no two holes are
even close to being alike"; the "friendly staff" will encourage
you to linger longer on this "great course for the price" to "play
at twilight rates" and soak up the "great sunset view" during a
"challenging but not ridiculous" round.

PGA of Southern California at Oak Valley, Champions

| 25 | 22 | 21 | 24 | $75 |

36211 Champions Dr., Beaumont; 951-845-0014; 877-742-2500;
www.scpgagolf.com; 7377/5274; 76.1/72.4; 139/128
This "must-play on the way to Palm Springs from LA" offers a
"challenging, memorable layout" with "beautiful bunkers" that's

"tough in the wind"; "they did it right here" fawn fans, noting that the "helpful staff" and some of "the nicest facilities" around help make it a "tremendous value", while the wedge-weary whine there's "more sand than Iwo Jima."

PGA of Southern California at Oak Valley, Legends
25 | 24 | 21 | 23 | $75

36211 Champions Dr., Beaumont; 951-845-0014; 877-742-2500; www.scpgagolf.com; 7442/5169; 75.9/70.9; 141/130

It's no myth – this is "one marvelous", "old Californian" with "interesting holes" that "use your entire bag"; its "tight fairways" with "visually intimidating bunkers" can be "difficult the first time through", particularly since the "wind plays a factor", so "bring the long sticks" to "enjoy" a "great track at a great value", but don't leave the kids at home, as they've also got a "fine junior program."

San Diego

AVIARA ⌂
26 | 27 | 26 | 17 | $205

7447 Batiquitos Dr., Carlsbad; 760-603-6900; www.fourseasons.com; 7007/5007; 74.2/69.3; 137/127

"Delicious in every way, from the course itself to the chocolate chip cookies that await" at "the starters' desk", this "favorite weekend getaway" "lives up to the Four Seasons reputation" with "great service", a "beautiful clubhouse", a "superb golf school", a "wonderful hotel" and "floral landscaping so pretty" you might "want to pester them for their designer's number"; all this luxury comes at a "big price", however, leaving pennypinchers pouting it's "a pleasure to play here" – "when someone else is paying."

Barona Creek
24 | 22 | 23 | 22 | $100

1932 Wildcat Canyon Rd., Lakeside; 619-387-7018; 888-722-7662; www.barona.com; 7088/5296; 74.5/66; 140/117

My Barona is "fantastic in every way" rave rockin' roundsmen with a knack for this "jewel" "carved out of the desert" on Indian lands; the "plush", "interesting" layout shines with "lightninglike greens" and lots of sun amid "few trees" where "pace, price and service" help make the day "worth the money"; "if your gambles on the course don't work out", "you can go in the casino, have a great buffet and then hit the tables and slots" to "recoup your losses."

Carlton Oaks
19 | 14 | 15 | 18 | $80

9200 Inwood Dr., Santee; 619-448-4242; 800-831-6757; www.carltonoaksgolf.com; 7225/5044; 75.2/70; 146/125

"Along a freeway" 20 minutes from Downtown, this "enjoyable loop" boasts "challenging holes" with "large waste bunkers" and "really fun" "railroad ties", but it manages to be "playable for the average golfer"; "it is used often for tournaments" and outings, for which it is "very suitable", but service tends to be "nonexistent" and the "old and tired facilities" "need to be updated" from their '70s heyday when Curtis Strange won an NCAA Championship here.

Cross Creek
23 | 18 | 21 | 22 | $89

43860 Glenn Meadows Rd., Temecula; 951-506-3402; www.crosscreekgolfclub.com; 6833/4606; 74.1/63.9; 142/116

"Not your typical grip it–and–rip it course", this "best-kept secret" "tucked away" "in the hills above Temecula" "mixes tricky par-3s, demanding par-4s and risk/reward par-5s" on a "well-maintained", "diverse" layout that goes "from woodlands to prairie and back to woodlands"; a staff in "period-motif" knickers greets you at the bag drop where "Arthur Hills created this beautiful golf experience for you" "away from freeways, airports and barking dogs."

Encinitas Ranch

| 17 | 12 | 15 | 19 | $91 |

1275 Quail Gardens Dr., Encinitas; 760-944-1936; www.jcgolf.com; 6587/4690; 71.2/67.1; 127/110

It's not in Anaheim, but some snobs still call this "easy" muni "Mickey Mouse" for its "short" yardages and "not-too-penal" hazards; still, with "awesome views" of "the Pacific in the distance", a "pleasant" staff and a "relaxed environment", this "confidence booster" is a "terrific course for locals", since they can go home and crack a beer after the round without worrying about the absence of a "permanent clubhouse."

Grand Golf Club

| 24 | 22 | 21 | 17 | $155 |

5300 The Grand Del Mar Way; 858-792-6200; 877-530-0636; www.thegrandgolfclub.com; 7054/4974; 74/68.3; 136/116

"Everything about" this "superior" Fazio formation, formerly Del Mar National, feels like a "private club", and with a luxury hotel being built here, it will only get more "high-end" in 2006; "narrow, winding" and "in super shape" with an "unhurried pace" and "tremendous elevation changes" that make for "scary tee shots over desert barrancas", it's "especially beautiful" "in the early morning as dew still covers the fairways"; its "accessibility" helps make it "heaven on earth", despite the "houses all over the place."

La Costa, North 尺

| 22 | 24 | 23 | 17 | $195 |

2100 Costa Del Mar Rd., Carlsbad; 760-438-9111; 800-854-5000; www.lacosta.com; 7094/5939; 74.9/76.3; 141/137

"Pretend you're a PGA pro" and "get treated like royalty" at this "classic" southern Californian at a luxe resort 30 miles north of San Diego where holes from both spreads are used in the Accenture Match Play Championship; its "tough", "knee-high rough" and "great-test greenside bunkers" are "not for the casual hacker", but the "spa keeps the wife happy" say smitten spouses; just "don't play it in winter" when "flooding" makes it "like slop", and "bring a healthy credit card" 'cuz La Costa will cost ya.

La Costa, South 尺

| 22 | 24 | 23 | 16 | $195 |

2100 Costa Del Mar Rd., Carlsbad; 760-438-9111; 800-854-5000; www.lacosta.com; 7077/5612; 74.8/74.2; 140/134

"Lined by trees" and featuring "well-bunkered", "smallish greens", this "traditional", "well-tended" "beauty" is "worth the price of admission" to go a round "where the pros play", particularly on the final four holes, which in the "afternoon onshore breeze" comprise "the longest mile in golf"; you have to "prepare to open your wallet", but the "service and food are wonderful", and the "facilities are world-class now that new owners have revamped the property."

Maderas 🏌

| 27 | 22 | 25 | 21 | $175 |

17750 Old Coach Rd., Poway; 858-451-8100; www.maderasgolf.com; 7115/4967; 75.6/69.8; 145/127

"In an area that doesn't lack in great golf", this "newer course" "stands out"; the "truly magical" Johnny Miller design "challenges you both mentally and physically" with "natural beauty, ingenuity and variety" across "fantastic elevation changes" and on "hard-as-cement, tricky greens"; "perfect conditioning" and "one of the best practice facilities" around make "you want to come back again and again", even if it is "a little off the beaten path."

Mt. Woodson 🏌

22 | 13 | 17 | 22 | $85

16422 N. Woodson Dr.; 760-788-3555; www.mtwoodson.com; 6004/4842; 69.1/68.1; 134/122

"Like a Disneyland ride", this "beautifully groomed" group of holes "hidden away in inland San Diego" is "a blast" for a "short, target-golf" experience with "elevated and blind tees" and "amazing views" from "awesome wooden bridges that span deep canyons"; there are no "crowds, noise" or "homes on the course", but there's also "no driving range", "no clubhouse" and only "a tiny service bar", making their E-ticket prices "steep" for what you get.

Pala Mesa 🏌

20 | 16 | 18 | 21 | $89

2001 Old Hwy. 395, Fallbrook; 760-728-5881; 800-722-4700; www.palamesa.com; 6502/5632; 72/74; 131/134

This "hidden gem" at a resort that has seen a "modernization" is a "great place to stay and play" thanks to its "well-kept greens", "pretty landscaping", "great practice areas" and "nice bar and restaurant"; though the "tight track sits on a hill" that's "kinda funky with holes right next to houses" and "the freeway", at least the location poses some "interesting" "challenges."

Rancho Bernardo Inn

17 | 21 | 20 | 18 | $115

17550 Bernardo Oaks Dr.; 858-487-1611; www.jcgolf.com; 6631/4949; 72.3/68.5; 133/119

Though this "dated" design might be called "That '70s Golf Course", it is attached to a "lovely" resort with a "friendly and helpful staff" and "outstanding facilities" featuring "a world-class restaurant"; "surprisingly inexpensive" golf packages can "include massages and wonderful meals", but you have to suffer a "boring" spread "situated next to a freeway" and "often congested with the elderly and slow-moving residents of surrounding Rancho Bernardo."

RedHawk 🏌

23 | 16 | 18 | 20 | $80

45100 Redhawk Pkwy., Temecula; 951-302-3850; 800-451-4295; www.redhawkgolfcourse.com; 7095/5515; 75.1/72.1; 145/125

It's so "environmentally pleasant" and "beautifully landscaped" with "fountains, flowers, lush greens and fairways" that, even if it is a "schlep from civilization", you might "want to live on this course" in one of the "homes being built"; just be forewarned that "some holes are set up to drive you crazy" on a "fairly tight" layout that's "very tough from the tips", while "nonexistent facilities", "nothing but framers and nail guns in view" and "workers' radios blasting" might really make you bonkers.

SCGA Golf Course

20 | 16 | 17 | 23 | $78

39500 Robert Trent Jones Pkwy., Murrieta; 951-677-7446; 800-752-9724; www.scgagolfcourse.com; 7036/5355; 74.6/71.7; 137/128

"Get a yardage book" because this "fairly priced", "semi-tough" RTJ Sr. design southeast of LA "requires you to think" your way around "elevated tees and greens" that "challenge all levels" especially in "the afternoon winds"; recently renovated, the course is regularly "in pretty good shape" with a "great practice area", so though it's "backed up" by "five-hour rounds", "it's worth playing", particularly if "you get a discount" with your SCGA membership.

Steele Canyon 🏑   24 | 19 | 20 | 22 | $104

3199 Stonefield Dr., Jamul; 619-441-6900; www.steelecanyon.com
Canyon/Meadow: 6479/4577; 72/67.1; 130/116
Meadow/Ranch: 6834/4790; 73.4/67.9; 141/124
Ranch/Canyon: 6767/4655; 73.1/66.8; 139/118

You "need to be on your game when you play this bad boy!" say Harley-ridin' hackers about this 27-hole Player design, a "hard-to-find", "serious test" east of San Diego; "Meadow is built within the residential area", so for "jaw-dropping vistas" and the "most difficult", "interesting" holes, "play the Canyon and Ranch nines" — with "great elevation drops", the combo "plays shorter than it is", but it's a "challenging" "alternative if you can't get on Torrey Pines."

Sycuan Resort, Oak Glen   17 | 15 | 15 | 20 | $61

3007 Dehesa Rd., El Cajon; 619-442-3425; 800-457-5568;
www.sycuanresort.com; 6489/5549; 71.1/71.4; 128/124

"Nestled among the hills" of an old olive grove "20 miles east of San Diego" is this "very pretty" course with "lots of mature trees" that's "shorter" than sister Willow but plays "long when the wind is blowing"; "you don't have to bomb it off the tees" say better ball launchers, but take a cart, as it's "difficult to walk on and play reasonably well" at the same time.

Sycuan Resort, Willow Glen   17 | 17 | 16 | 21 | $61

3007 Dehesa Rd., El Cajon; 619-442-3425; 800-457-5568;
www.sycuanresort.com; 6605/5585; 72.3/72.5; 129/127

The sister course to Oak Glen is "an oldie but goodie" wax wide-eyed whackers who travel 20 miles east of San Diego to stay and play at the Sycuan Tribe Resort and Casino; the longer of the location's two layouts, this "reliable" track "has some nice", "well-groomed" holes lined with "mature trees" and ending in "excellent greens" that have gamblin' golfers calling it a "great value."

Temecula Creek Inn   20 | 18 | 19 | 21 | $85

44501 Rainbow Canyon Rd., Temecula; 951-694-1000; 877-517-1823;
www.temeculacreekinn.com
Creek/Oaks: 6784/5712; 72.3/72.8; 127/118
Stonehouse/Creek: 6605/5686; 71.6/72.8; 130/120
Stonehouse/Oaks: 6693/5658; 72.2/73.1; 129/123

"Take the time to look at the scenery" around this "very nice 27-hole" "resort course" in lush SoCal wine country; like the local product, the "well-maintained", "sporty" spread "gets better with age", "offering three different levels of play from mountain to flat", all leading to dance floors "tough to hit in regulation"; "it's well worth the drive from San Diego", "especially if you stay at the inn", "eat dinner in the bar and dig the jazz" for "a wonderful weekend of golf/food/relaxation."

TORREY PINES, NORTH   25 | 19 | 18 | 23 | $75

11480 N. Torrey Pines Rd., La Jolla; 858-452-3226; 800-985-4653;
www.torreypinesgolfcourse.com; 6874/6122; 72.1/75.4; 129/134

"Get ready for a surprise: this is much more fun (and more scenic) than the highly touted South" fawn fans of this "outstanding" "oceanside" co-host of the PGA Tour's Buick Invitational; while "not as challenging" as its sib, it's "cheaper and easier to get a tee time on", though the latter is still "almost impossible", so despite "very disappointing practice facilities", "you should be happy just to be" on the "best value" in town "smelling the sea breeze" and watching your "ball roll right toward the Pacific."

TORREY PINES, SOUTH   26 | 18 | 18 | 22 | $135

11480 N. Torrey Pines Rd., La Jolla; 858-452-3226; 800-985-4653; www.torreypinesgolfcourse.com; 7607/5542; 78.1/73.5; 143/128

"Bring the big dog when playing this behemoth" (plus "a machete to hit out of the rough"), and "you can pretend you're Tiger" on the "home of the PGA Tour's Buick Invitational and 2008 U.S. Open", a "breathtaking spread with views of the Pacific and the beautifully twisted Torrey pines"; despite "chewed-up" greens and a "staff and clubhouse that leave a lot to be desired", the "spectacular location" and "wonderfully renovated Lodge" make "the hardest course you've ever played" "worth" every "missed putt, shanked drive and skulled pitch."

San Francisco Bay Area

Bridges, The   20 | 23 | 21 | 16 | $95

9000 S. Gale Ridge Rd., San Ramon; 925-735-4253; www.thebridgesgolf.com; 6965/5229; 75/71.4; 148/123

There are "uneven lies, fast greens and canyons lining the course, but other than that, it's a breeze" wink winded whackers about this "solid, upscale" but "brutally difficult" "confidence buster" that's "simply too penal" for "double-digit handicaps"; true, the "clubhouse is beautiful" and "service is excellent", but "Johnny Miller was mad" when he built "one tough continuous dogleg" "plastered with cookie-cutter houses" and "blind tee shots" growl gruff golfers who are "not big fans of forced layups."

Cinnabar Hills   24 | 22 | 21 | 19 | $100

23600 McKean Rd., San Jose; 408-323-5200; www.cinnabarhills.com
Canyon/Mountain: 6641/4859; 72.5/68.1; 137/118
Lake/Canyon: 6688/4959; 72.9/68.4; 138/121
Mountain/Lake: 6853/5010; 73.6/68.1; 142/120

"Get ready to climb Everest" via the "great elevation changes" on this "awesome test of shotmaking and nerves" with "beautiful views" "in the hills south of San Jose"; there's "variety among" the three nines here, but all are "fantastically well maintained" with "rolling fairways" and "Augusta-speed greens"; it delivers a "country club feel without the price", and "GPS on the carts is great for the techies" of the Silicon Valley, so there's "nothing to complain about" – except that "it's a little out of the way."

CordeValle 🏨 ⛳   27 | 27 | 28 | 17 | $225

1 CordeValle Dr., San Martin; 408-695-4590; 877-255-2626; www.cordevalle.com; 7169/5385; 75.1/71; 138/120

"The course is damn good" but "the jacuzzi after my round is the topper" say pampered putters about "this exclusive resort in the heart of the Silicon Valley" with an "outstanding spa, pool, rooms, dining and bar"; you "need to be a member or stay overnight" in a bungalow or villa to play "one of the most beautiful" layouts "you'll ever see", but California's most "over-the-top" service at this RTJ Jr.–designed "caddie-only club" is so "exceptional", it might be worth the "absurdly expensive" prices.

HALF MOON BAY, OCEAN

25 22 22 18 $170

2 Miramontes Point Rd., Half Moon Bay; 650-726-4438; www.halfmoonbaygolf.com; 6712/5109; 71.8/71.6; 125/119

"The salt, the sea, Titleist and me!" cheer chilly chippers who chide "take a jacket" to these "pristine" "ribbons of green laid on dunes and brush" along "dramatic" Pacific cliffs that are "misty, cool and windy" "reminders of the British Isles"; you can "hobnob and golf with the rich and famous", then "finish up with a drink or high tea" at the Ritz-Carlton to "complete your day" of "perfect resort golf."

Half Moon Bay, Old Course ⌂

23 20 22 17 $170

2 Miramontes Point Rd., Half Moon Bay; 650-726-4438; www.halfmoonbaygolf.com; 7090/5305; 75/73.3; 135/128

On a "rare" clear day it's "as good as it gets" on one of the "most picturesque holes ever", the "water's-edge" 18th on this links with a finish that's "reminiscent" of "old courses in Scotland"; the rest of the "long and difficult" spread is "not quite as spectacular" with "too much surrounding housing" and "not nearly as many ocean-view holes" as on its sibling, but a "redesign fixed drainage problems", and you won't have a problem draining your glass when you "relax at the Ritz-Carlton bar" afterwards.

HARDING PARK

24 – 13 23 $90

99 Harding Rd., San Francisco; 415-661-1865; www.harding-park.com; 6845/5375; 72.8/70.4; 126/116

Once used as a parking lot for the U.S. Open, this former "ugly duckling" "has blossomed into quite the swan" after a "multimillion-dollar" "face-lift"; "framed in beautiful cypress trees", "deep, thick rough" and "unbelievable views" "of the city and the Bay", this muni "stunner" with a brand-new clubhouse is an "outstanding deal for residents", but it's "crowded" and "service is a joke", making it a potential "rip-off for out-of-towners" who might want a whack at the 2005 host of the PGA Tour's American Express Championship.

Paradise Valley

17 17 16 22 $50

3950 Paradise Valley Dr., Fairfield; 707-426-1600; www.fairfieldgolf.com; 6993/5413; 73.9/71.1; 129/119

"Swing away" on the "wide-open fairways" and "fast", "huge greens" at this "nicely maintained", "playable" Bay Area muni; though "it can get very windy", it nevertheless delivers a "pleasant" Monday–Friday round with the additional "advantage of weekday coupons", while on weekends, it's Paradise lost: "prepare to spend your entire day on the links" dealing with the "super-slow" crowds.

Poppy Ridge

22 23 21 25 $78

4280 Greenville Rd., Livermore; 925-447-6779; www.poppyridgegolf.com
Chardonnay/Merlot: 7106/5212; 74.8/70.2; 141/120
Merlot/Zinfandel: 7128/5265; 74.8/70.2; 141/120
Zinfandel/Chardonnay: 7048/5267; 74.8/70.2; 141/120

"As smooth as the wines from the nearby vineyards", this "East Bay gem" by Rees Jones offers 27 holes of "wonderful links-style golf" "with few trees but many challenges" including "fairly narrow fairways, punishing rough and fast greens"; "heavy windmill farms indicate what to expect", but taking into account an "excellent range", "friendly staff" and the fact it "drains well in wet weather", it's "outstanding for the price", even if it does feel "like you're testing a NASA shuttle in a wind tunnel."

Presidio | 19 | 16 | 16 | 18 | $90 |
300 Finley Rd., San Francisco; 415-561-4670; www.presidiogolf.com; 6477/5785; 72.2/69.2; 136/127
Tony Bennett could've been singing about this "very hilly", "beautiful challenge in the heart" of San Francisco, a "standard" featuring "ancient cypress trees" and "stunning views" of the Bay, the Presidio and the Golden Gate Bridge, at least when the fog isn't "thick as pea soup"; veterans of this "former military course" warn of "horrible drainage in winter", advise "play in the morning to avoid the wind" and curse "those damn English daisies" that make it so you "can't find your ball, even when it's in the fairway."

Rancho Solano | 18 | 15 | 17 | 22 | $50 |
3250 Rancho Solano Pkwy., Fairfield; 707-429-4653; www.ci.fairfield.ca.us; 6616/5201; 71.2/69.6; 127/117
The "minimal fees" "can't be beat" for the Bay Area on this women-friendly "good test of golf" "well laid out" "up and down the hillside" "where every hole is different", giving you the "ability to use most clubs in your bag from the blue tees"; "elephants and VW Bugs might be buried" in the "largest greens you will ever come across", so play "can get slow" when "the wind picks up in the afternoon" and the putting gets "brutal."

Rio Vista Golf Club | 17 | 17 | 17 | 19 | $49 |
1000 Summerset Dr., Rio Vista; 707-374-2900; www.riovistagolf.com; 6800/5330; 73.6/72.4; 131/124
"If you like wind, you'll feel like you've died and gone to heaven", but if you don't, "play in the morning" on this "enjoyable" "walking course" "tucked away in a retirement community" near the Sacramento River Delta; this "long, tough" layout that "drains great in the rainy winter months" "doesn't get a lot of play", except by "biting bugs", so expect a little bloodsucking en route to its "nice 18th hole."

Roddy Ranch | 20 | 8 | 14 | 18 | $79 |
1 Tour Way, Antioch; 925-978-4653; www.roddyranch.com; 7024/5390; 74.5/71.7; 136/120
Hold onto your ten-gallon hats, buckaroos, because this here's "another NASA wind tunnel", gasp frazzled foozlers of this "undulating" links "challenge on a cattle ranch" with the "toughest pool tables to putt on in the county"; BYO "food and drink" on your "hike from San Francisco" as there are "no facilities to be found" except a "double-wide" as clubhouse at this "good-value" but "no-frills-at-best" "trailer park in the middle of a cow pasture."

Shadow Lakes | ▽ 21 | 15 | 16 | 15 | $80 |
401 W. Country Club Dr., Brentwood; 925-516-2837; www.shadowlakesgolf.com; 6710/5402; 72/71.4; 136/123
In a "great location" in the East Bay in the shadows of the Mt. Diablo Range, Troon's "very relaxing" newbie is carved through native grasses and natural rock outcroppings; though it's "always in excellent condition" with "tough greens", sculpted bunkers and

water on nine holes, some snobs snipe that it's "pretty pricey" for "another, barren, windswept course."

Sonoma Golf Club ⌂ | 22 | 18 | 20 | 16 | $160 |
17700 Arnold Dr., Sonoma; 707-996-0300; www.sonomagolfclub.com; 7103/5511; 74.1/71.8; 132/125
"Play a round of golf and drink some wine – ahhh, life is good" at the Fairmont Sonoma Mission Inn's "lovely old classic", "lush with black oaks and tough greens" surrounded by vineyards with sweeping views of the Macayamas Mountains; host to the Champions Tour's season-ending Charles Schwab Cup, "this one'll pop your cork" with its "tour pro–quality conditions", even if you find the layout "kind of plain"; when it's finished, the "top-notch" clubhouse certainly won't be plain, but neither are the prices at this guests-only spread.

StoneTree | 21 | 20 | 21 | 15 | $115 |
9 Stone Tree Ln., Novato; 415-209-6090; www.stonetreegolf.com; 6810/5232; 73.3/66.4; 143/127
It "feels like you're golfing in Sherwood Forest" remark merry roundsmen of the "targetlike" hilly back that "cuts through the woods" to "funky" "elevated greens" on this "interesting" if "schizophrenic" course with a "flat", open front; "the best drainage in the San Francisco Bay Area" makes it "playable" even "after torrential rain", while the "beautiful clubhouse" shelters you during the downpour; still, poor flubbing friars tucked onto "too tight" fairways "jammed" between "new homes" with "no driving range" say it just isn't worth robbing from the rich for this "overpriced" round.

Wente Vineyards | 24 | 23 | 22 | 19 | $95 |
5050 Arroyo Rd., Livermore; 925-456-2475; 800-999-2885; www.wentegolf.com; 6956/5007; 74/69.4; 146/122
What an "unbeatable" blend of "golf and wine!" gulp *Sideways*-style swingers sipping in this "beautiful Greg Norman design" that flows through the Wente Vineyards where you can "tee it up among acres and acres of grapes" amid "creative routing", "amazing elevation changes" and "extremely fast" greens; it's "a bit expensive", but the "view from the top of Lombard Street [aka No. 10] is breathtaking", and you can "drown the sorrows of your score in a bottle" at the winery's fine restaurant.

San Luis Obispo

Blacklake | 18 | 14 | 17 | 19 | $65 |
1490 Golf Course Ln., Nipomo; 805-343-1214; www.blacklake.com
Canyon/Lake: 6401/5628; 70.9/72; 123/120
Lake/Oaks: 6185/5161; 69.7/69.7; 121/117
Oaks/Canyon: 6034/5047; 69.3/69.5; 121/116
An "excellent variety" of "sporty" holes are kept in "very good condition" and grouped into "three great nines" that "each offer a different challenge" with "trees, water and hills" – all much appreciated "considering the slim pickin's in the area" a few hours up the coast from LA; just "bring a book to read while waiting for the foursome in front of you", as "play is a little slow" and "those mats on the practice range" aren't a worthy diversion.

Hunter Ranch
| 25 | 20 | 21 | 25 | $70 |

4041 E. Hwy. 46, Paso Robles; 805-237-7444; www.hunterranchgolf.com;
6741/5639; 72.6/72; 136/128

You may to have to hunt for this "hidden treat" of "challenging" "connoisseur's golf" "surrounded by vineyards" in the Santa Lucia foothills; "like good Paso Robles Syrah", it "gets better with age", though unlike the wine, it always comes at an "unbelievable value"; "wide open" with "slick and undulating greens", it's "very playable and walkable", unless you're on it in the "sweltering summer" or when the wind kicks up, making the need for "two or three extra clubs not unusual"; at any time, "good practice, shop and food facilities" help make it a "gem."

Santa Barbara

Glen Annie
| 18 | 18 | 18 | 18 | $85 |

405 Glen Annie Rd.; 805-968-6400; www.glenanniegolf.com;
6420/5036; 71.2/69.4; 130/123

There are "more elevation changes than a roller coaster" on this "fun", "sweet" "sleeper" with "postcard views of the Pacific and Channel Islands" just north of Santa Barbara; you'll have to be patient on a "windy" or "foggy day", as it "might not clear up", and the "short par-4s" plus "numerous blind shots" contribute to "verrrryyyy slow play"; still, in part because they're "always working on improvements to the course, service, pro shop and dining", it's "a tremendous value compared to others in the area."

La Purisima
| 27 | 17 | 19 | 26 | $70 |

3455 State Hwy. 246, Lompoc; 805-735-8395; www.lapurisimagolf.com;
7105/5763; 75.6/75.6; 143/135

It has "scenery like heaven on earth, but it plays like hell" preach purists of this "unbelievable" hilly layout "surrounded by nature" "a little off the beaten path" 45 minutes north of Santa Barbara, where "the early morning fog adds to the magic"; "don't go for the facilities – go for the golf", but ladies, beware: it's "incredibly long and difficult from the women's tees"; one more "word to the wise" is "play in the morning" before the "fierce afternoon winds" roll in "from the nearby coast" to "kick your rear."

Rancho San Marcos 斉
| 23 | 18 | 21 | 17 | $145 |

4600 Hwy. 154; 805-683-6334; 877-766-1804; www.rsm1804.com;
6817/5004; 73.2/69.8; 136/119

"If you love golf and great views, this is the course" for you in a "peaceful, serene" setting along the Santa Ynez River; this RTJ Jr. design may be one of the "prettiest places to play" now that it's back in "immaculate condition" following recovery from a recent drought; "very good practice facilities", a "hospitable staff" and a "caddie program that every golfer should experience" help make it "worth the drive" to its "remote" location.

River Course at Alisal
| 20 | 19 | 20 | 20 | $60 |

150 Alisal Rd., Solvang; 805-688-6042; www.rivercourse.com;
6830/5815; 73.1/73.8; 129/128

"Look for clips in a recent movie" of an oenophilic bent to preview this "fun, woodsy course" "just outside the village of Solvang" where "golf and a little wine tasting" combine; both activities make for a "not-just-kiddie" experience at a "great place for a relaxed day" in an "idyllic setting", say swingers sipping in the "affordable" rates; however, though it's "well laid out with no freeway or airport noise", after "really slow" rounds where "wind is always a factor", some club-wielding winos would "rather end up being *Sideways* at the nearby Hitching Post."

Sandpiper　　　　　　　25 | 16 | 17 | 20 | $130

7925 Hollister Ave., Goleta; 805-968-1541; www.sandpipergolf.com; 7068/5701; 73.9/67.8; 131/115

"Another lovely ocean course with several spectacular holes", this "hidden coastal wonder" "just north of Santa Barbara" and "next door to the new Bacara" Resort is "long, wide open (unless you're next to the Pacific)", "well maintained" and, when "the wind is whipping, one of the toughest layouts" around; though some swingers liken it to "Pebble Beach", others say "the greens fee may remind you a bit" of the luxe club up the coast, "but the resemblance stops there."

Santa Cruz

PASATIEMPO 於 ⊘　　　　27 | 19 | 20 | 21 | $165

18 Clubhouse Rd.; 831-459-9155; www.pasatiempo.com; 6439/5646; 72.5/73.5; 136/133

"Play it for history's sake" but "leave your ego at home" when you dance with this "grande dame", "brilliantly designed" in 1929 by Alister MacKenzie; it "starts with a widescreen view of the Santa Cruz coastline" and continues to "shine on routing, shotmaking and overall fun", but it's "not for the faint of club"; "you'll work hard on your score" on "unforgiving, undulating", tree-lined fairways and "unnerving" "greens as fast as Augusta", attributes that make this a "must-play for aficionados" who "appreciate the thought that goes into a masterful course."

San Juan Oaks　　　　　25 | 23 | 21 | 23 | $80

3825 Union Rd., Hollister; 831-636-6118; 800-453-8337; www.sanjuanoaks.com; 7133/4770; 75.6/64.5; 145/115

"Every visit is a pleasure" swoon swingers of this "remote" but "spectacular" "Freddie Couples gem" near Monterey where "dry grass hills surround a vibrant green oasis that begs you to forget your real life and play another 18"; good thing, then, that "you can always get a tee time" on this "rolling", "perfectly groomed" layout with "penal rough" and "lots of bunkers" where most holes "favor a fade"; "a friendly staff", "excellent facilities" and "reasonable fees" help "make for an extremely enjoyable day of golf."

Santa Rosa

Links at Bodega Harbour　　20 | 16 | 18 | 18 | $75

21301 Heron Dr., Bodega Bay; 707-875-3538; www.bodegaharbourgolf.com; 6253/4751; 71.4/70.1; 127/120

It's "almost like Scotland" – "with perhaps more wind" – on this "mystical" "coastal layout" designed by RTJ Jr. "within a one hour's drive of San Francisco" where you'll be blown away by "stunning" "Pebble Beach–like ocean views", "if you can see them through the fog"; "this course can draw blood" in calm weather, but a "hurricanelike" "breeze" "can make up to a three-club difference", and despite "darned ugly homes that wrap around the fairways", most pea soup–loving putters' "palms are sweating just remembering it."

Sea Ranch
18 | 12 | 16 | 18 | $70

42000 Hwy. 1, Sea Ranch; 707-785-2468; www.888searanch.com; 6634/4795; 73/70.2; 134/118

"Bring a jacket" when you "warm up" for your British Isles golf trip at this "classic California coastal design" "close to Mendocino along the Pacific" where "typical summer" "fog and wind" with "zero pollution" and "splendid views" of "cliffs, water", "country scenery and wildlife" make you "think Pebble, with no crowds and one quarter of the price"; "ratty conditions" and facilities that "define primitive" further differentiate it from that luxe layout.

Windsor Golf Club
19 | 14 | 15 | 22 | $53

1340 19th Hole Dr., Windsor; 707-838-7888; www.windsorgolf.com; 6650/5116; 72/68.6; 134/120

"Silos and barns are part of this" "beautiful rolling" Sonoma "gem"; lined with "large black-oak ball magnets", it's "short but fun" "for every level of golfer" with "consistent conditions from round to round"; despite a "restaurant and staff that need help", this former home of the Nike Tour is such "a great value in the wine country", it's "like getting Chateau Lafite in a box"; needless to say, it "can be crowded" so *Late Show*–loving linksters warn "play early if you want to get home for Letterman."

Stockton

Lockeford Springs
▽ 18 | 16 | 16 | 20 | $45

16360 N. Hwy. 88, Lodi; 209-333-6275; www.lockefordsprings.com; 6861/5542; 73.8/71.6; 130/118

"This course is an outstanding value" bleat budget-conscious ball bashers who drive their cars 35 miles southeast of Sacramento to drive their tee shots on a "tough" test "with very deep rough"; traffic brings "long waits on weekends (plan for five-and-a-half-hour rounds)" and "conditions that can vary", but patient players are prepared to pull out all the stops to persevere at such strong par-5s as the watery 18th, where both fairway and green are shaped like an L, as in Lockeford.

Saddle Creek
24 | 21 | 19 | 20 | $110

1001 Saddle Creek Dr., Copperopolis; 209-785-3700; 888-852-5787; www.saddlecreekgolf.com; 6826/4486; 73.1/66.7; 137/117

Hop in your saddle and make the "monster" "two-hour drive from the Bay Area" to this "wonderful", "thoughtful" Jay Morrish design that "rolls gently through" the "beautiful Sierra foothills"; "finding birdies is as hard as finding gold" here, purport prospecting players, because "you will hit over something on almost every hole" to "smooth, fast greens"; still, with "weather that's always perfect" and "superb views of beautiful '49er Gold Rush country", "you need to check it out."

Stevinson Ranch
24 | 20 | 19 | 23 | $85

2700 N. Van Clief Rd., Stevinson; 209-668-8200; 877-752-9276; www.stevinsonranch.com; 7205/5461; 74.7/71.9; 138/124

"Although it will never match oceanside links or high Sierra gems", this is an "awesome" "challenge", "long" and "well bunkered" with "huge, fast greens" and "grass that will bite you"; thanks to its "isolated" location, "there's not much else around town" but the course, which is "rough going if it rains" and "very hot in the summer" but "worth a trip" if you "bring bug spray" and check into the "great overnight facilities."

Yorba Linda

Black Gold
21 | 19 | 20 | 19 | $84

17681 Lakeview Ave.; 714-961-0060; www.blackgoldgolf.com; 6756/4937; 73.1/69.3; 133/124

Designed by the aptly named Arthur Hills on the old Shell Oil field a half mile from the Richard Nixon Library, this "fun" "in-town muni" is "very steep" with "no flat lies" to its "well-kept", "beautiful greens and fairways"; that's "great" – "if one is a billy goat" whine wearied wallopers who call this "another trumped-up course" built on a "bad piece of land" where "views of the beautiful city of Anaheim" are "not exactly stunning."

Colorado

★ **Top Courses in State**
28 Pole Creek, *Denver*
27 Broadmoor, East, *Colorado Springs*
  Redlands Mesa, *Grand Junction*
  Raven at Three Peaks, *Vail*
26 Riverdale, Dunes, *Denver*

Aspen

Aspen Golf Club
17 | 17 | 19 | 16 | $90

39551 Hwy. 82; 970-925-2145; www.aspenrecreation.com; 7136/5222; 73.7/69.1; 133/119

"A great place to meet tourists" is this "beautifully manicured", "gorgeous course" in a "breathtaking setting at the foot of the Maroon Bells" where sightseers go to salivate over the "great views" of Pyramid Peak, Aspen Highlands and Buttermilk Mountain ski runs; so it is the "flat muni in town" – it's "much harder than it looks", with "lightning quick, quirky greens" to force up your score.

Boulder

Indian Peaks
21 | 18 | 17 | 23 | $44

2300 Indian Peaks Trail, Lafayette; 303-666-4706; www.indianpeaksgolf.com; 7083/5468; 73.9/70.8; 134/122

"Wow . . . wow . . . nice" fawn fans who've fallen for this "pretty straightforward" Hale Irwin design "north of suburban Denver" where native grass and a few trees are backdropped by the Rockies; popular with putting parents who appreciate the "good practice facilities and programs for kids", this "once open" and "excellent walking" muni is now getting "surrounded by homes."

Mariana Butte
24 | 14 | 17 | 25 | $36

701 Clubhouse Dr., Loveland; 970-667-8308; www.marianabutte.com; 6604/5067; 70.8/68.4; 130/117

"Butte-i-ful Colorado golf" goes "up, down and around" on this "sweet" "mountain-type course", which is actually "not in the mountains" but less than an hour south of Denver; "with more elevation changes than distance", "you need to be in shape to walk the back nine" where you should "watch out for prairie dogs", who might get better treatment from the "arrogant clubhouse" staff than you do.

Colorado Springs

Broadmoor, East 🏨 ⚬⚬　　　　| 27 | 27 | 27 | 20 | $180 |

1 Lake Ave.; 719-577-5790; www.broadmoor.com; 7144/5921; 73/72.7; 127/139

"God paid extra-special attention so close to heaven", or at least Donald Ross did, because "every blade of grass is perfect" on this "classic" "mountain course" sporting "history and challenging greens galore"; where "Nicklaus won the 1959 Amateur", "the only thing better than the golf is the beauty and the Service", which – along with the Facilities – ranks Top in Colorado; add "thin mountain air that puts yards on your drive" and you arrive at this breathless conclusion: "the Broadmoor is one of the great spots on earth."

Broadmoor, West 🏨 ⚬⚬　　　　| 24 | 26 | 26 | 21 | $180 |

1 Lake Ave.; 719-577-5790; www.broadmoor.com; 7158/5347; 73.3/70.5; 132/127

"You really should have a caddie to read the putts" on these "hellish" "greased-lightning greens", possibly the "fastest in the West"; if you're slow on the draw with the flatstick, just soak in the "gorgeous setting" at "one of the finest resorts in the country"; while some visiting professors protest that it "requires local knowledge to be fun", the majority calls this "nice companion" to the East "very enjoyable."

Walking Stick, Walking Stick　　| 21 | 15 | 18 | 26 | $30 |
Golf Course

4301 Walking Stick Blvd., Pueblo; 719-584-3400; 7147/5181; 73.5/68.5; 131/121

Collaborating architects Keith Foster and Arthur Hills "did well in Pueblo" with this "terrific layout" that's "worth the drive" "half an hour south of Colorado Springs" for "nice, inexpensive golf" that ranks as the No. 1 Value in the Rocky Mountain State; when "the wind is up", it's a "good test for single-digit handicappers" and long hitters alike, but in any type of weather, this "great" municipal course "you can play year round" is "really fun" – just "watch out for rattlesnakes."

Denver

Arrowhead 🏞　　　　　　　| 24 | 18 | 18 | 16 | $125 |

10850 W. Sundown Trail, Littleton; 303-973-9614; www.arrowheadcolorado.com; 6682/5465; 70.9/71.1; 134/127

"It's all about the scenery" on this "most alien yet beautiful course" where "incredible" 300-million-year-old "jutting red rocks" make a home for deer, foxes, black bears and other "wildlife"; as to "whether to hit the ball or stop and take pictures" on the RTJ Jr. spread, Kodak-carrying clubbers choose the latter, clobbering "slow play", "poor maintenance" and "overpricing" on an "ordinary course in an extraordinary place."

Buffalo Run
21 | 19 | 17 | 24 | $40

15700 E. 112th Ave., Commerce City; 303-289-1500;
www.golfexperience.com/buffalorun; 7411/5227; 74.5/68.8; 129/117
"Welcome to Colorado" where the "wide-open spaces" "without a
tree in sight" "truly give you that 'Home on the Range' feeling" on
this "mile-high links" "on the prairies" designed by Keith Foster; it's
"long from the tips", so "you need to hit the ball true and straight"
and keep in mind that the "wind can make this" "solid" course
"trickier than it looks"; even if the deer and the antelope don't roam
here, "the low flying planes" "en route to Denver International
Airport" do, but "if you can ignore" the noise, "the price is right."

Fossil Trace ♒
22 | 20 | 20 | 19 | $56

3050 Illinois St., Golden; 303-277-8750; www.fossiltrace.com;
6831/4681; 71.8/66.7; 138/121
"This one was like my ex-wife: hard, hard and no forgiveness"
drawl divorced drivers of this "Jim Engh masterpiece" "built
around old mining land" and 64-million-year-old "geological sites"
adjacent to the foothills of the Rocky Mountains; there are "many
opportunities to birdie, bogie or better" on "neat" "canyon holes"
where "rock outcroppings come into play", but a few frustrated
foursomes feel this ball-wallopers' bone yard is "tricked up", both
in its "gimmicky" layout and a reservations policy that makes it
"hard to get on."

Fox Hollow at Lakewood
23 | 20 | 17 | 22 | $49

13410 Morrison Rd., Lakewood; 303-986-7888; www.lakewoodgolf.org
Canyon/Meadow: 6808/4473; 71.7/64.4; 133/112
Links/Canyon: 7030/4802; 72.9/66.7; 132/118
Meadow/Links: 6888/4835; 72/66.5; 131/116
"Not bad" say satisfied swingers who "had a great time" on this
"excellent", women-friendly 27-holer "close to Denver" that serves
up one Scottish links–style nine, a second that runs through a
meadow and ancient cottonwoods along Bear Creek and a third
that climbs up along Coyote Gulch; unfortunately, service "stinks" –
you may "love the course" and its "nice views of the Flatirons", but
the staff can be "rude" "enough to make you play elsewhere."

Green Valley Ranch
▽ 22 | 23 | 20 | 23 | $55

4900 Himalaya Rd.; 303-371-3131; www.gvrgolf.com;
7144/4992; 73.5/68.9; 130/119
Go east, young golfer, to this "very good links-style course"
designed by Perry Dye in a small valley out in DIA territory that
"plays more difficult than it looks" and "will test your game"
"on every hole" as it winds through prairies, natural wetlands
and ancient cottonwoods; not everyone finds this valley so green,
though – the new host to the Colorado Open Championship is "not
real exciting" yawn some yipsters.

Legacy Ridge
23 | 20 | 19 | 23 | $45

10801 Legacy Ridge Pkwy., Westminster; 303-438-8997;
www.ci.westminster.co.us; 7157/5383; 73.4/71.5; 144/127
"Greed will get you writing snowmen on your card" at this "nice
Arthur Hills layout" built around a wildlife sanctuary north of Denver
where "lots of water" and "strategically placed bunkers" make
"you have to think a little to score well"; not only that, but you'd
better "keep out of the rough or you will pay" on this "strong"

"suburban test" where you can expect some "great" and some "goofy" holes – just "don't expect amenities."

Murphy Creek 19 | 18 | 17 | 19 | $40

1700 S. Old Tom Morris Rd., Aurora; 303-361-7300; www.golfaurora.com; 7456/5335; 74.6/69.2; 131/123

Ken Kavanaugh sculpted this fairly priced, "east suburban housing tract track" amid a high prairie landscape that is sprinkled with old farm implements reflecting the property's former tenure as a ranch homestead; with rugged, sprawling bunkers splashed across it, the layout is regarded by some roundsmen as "very good" and "tough, especially when the wind blows"; live wires looking for life beyond the "boringly" bucolic simply invoke "Murphy's Law" to describe it.

POLE CREEK 28 | 20 | 20 | 22 | $68

6827 County Rd. 51, Winter Park; 970-887-9195; 800-511-5076; www.polecreekgolf.com
Meadow/Ranch: 7106/5008; 73.7/69; 145/130
Ranch/Ridge: 7173/5058; 73.8/69.2; 142/128
Ridge/Meadow: 7062/5082; 73.3/67.9; 139/132

On the southwestern edge of the Rocky Mountain National Park just 15 minutes from Winter Park ski area is Colorado's No. 1 Course, "one of the best mountain" layouts anywhere; amid alpine scenery, jaw-dropping elevation changes and "beautiful views" of the Continental Divide, the "tight" and "challenging" track climbs through "plenty of woods" into lodgepole pine country before it descends to flatter ground for a dramatic round that is "reasonably priced for resort" play.

Red Hawk Ridge 21 | 16 | 17 | 19 | $62

2156 Red Hawk Ridge Dr., Castle Rock; 303-663-7150; www.redhawkridge.com; 6942/4636; 71.8/67; 130/107

"Mountain goats will enjoy walking" this "well-designed" and "well-priced" Jim Engh spread nestled in the Rocky Mountain foothills with "lots of elevation changes" all the way through to a handsome, watery finish; despite a few "tricked-up holes", this "wonderful layout" could be a "fun" experience, "but it's hampered by golfers failing to repair divots and pitch marks" rant roundsmen who've mastered the art of courteous play.

Ridge at Castle Pines North, The 25 | 24 | 22 | 18 | $125

1414 Castle Pines Pkwy., Castle Rock; 303-688-0100; www.theridgecpn.com; 7013/5011; 71.8/67.6; 143/123

It's "a Colorado classic" say knights and damsels heralding this "world-class" "toughie" "beautifully laid out" by Tom Weiskopf; there are "lots of homes on some holes, but others are out in the woods", most memorably the 18th with its "long carry over cliffs"; the "good practice facility" and "nice clubhouse and staff" lend a "country-club-for-a-day" vibe to a spread that nickle-and-dime knaves nevertheless call "too pricey."

Riverdale, Dunes 26 | 19 | 18 | 26 | $40

13300 Riverdale Rd., Brighton; 303-659-6700; www.riverdalegolf.com; 7067/4884; 73.3/67.6; 134/123

Hang on to your ten-gallon tam-o'-shanter because this "true Scottish course" northwest of Denver along the South Platte River can be "windy" "like a British Open" links; "challenging from the tips" but "not a grip-and-rip type", it's "playable at the ladies' tees"; just "steer clear" of the "traditional Pete Dye" features ("lots of water and railroad ties") as well as the atypical "prairie dogs", and "stay in the short grass to score" well on this "outstanding value" of a muni.

Saddle Rock
20 | 16 | 16 | 20 | $42

21705 E. Arapahoe Rd., Aurora; 303-699-3939; 7351/5407; 74.7/71.9; 140/126

"One of Colorado's toughest courses", this "gem hidden" in "suburban Denver" winds through natural wetlands with "lots of environmentally sensitive areas" that can eat your ball, so barring "wind barriers", go for accuracy; the former Colorado Open host has lots of elevation changes on "some very good holes and some very bad ones", the latter of which are perhaps responsible for the "slow rounds that can occur."

Grand Junction

Redlands Mesa
27 | 23 | 24 | 26 | $76

2325 W. Ridges Blvd; 970-263-9270; www.redlandsmesa.com; 7007/4916; 71.7/69; 135/115

"What a place" – this "visually spectacular" "Jim Engh must-play" can "overwhelm your senses"; playing beneath rugged buttes "beautifully backdropped" by skyscraping pink and red sandstone, it includes "one of the most dramatic inland holes in golf", the signature par-3 17th that drops 150 feet to a green at the bottom of a rock bowl; though traditionalists might find it "a little gimmicky", it's a "great value", thanks in part to the "friendliest-ever marshals" – and no thanks to the local "real estate development squeeze."

Vail

Beaver Creek ⚑ ⏱
21 | 21 | 22 | 15 | $160

103 Offerson Rd., Beaver Creek; 970-845-5775; www.beavercreek.com; 6784/5088; 71/69.3; 140/131

"You have to love the locale" – it's "exclusive", "ouch, super expensive" and "you may see ex-President Gerald Ford" on this "challenging" Robert Trent Jones Jr. "mountain track" whose "tight fairways" "wind up and down the Beaver Creek Valley"; "the only downside is it took the driver out of my hands" say long-hitters lobbing it on this "shoehorned" spread where the "first three goofy holes" might make you wonder "does Mickey Mouse have a course in Colorado?"

Breckenridge
26 | 19 | 20 | 20 | $95

200 Clubhouse Dr., Breckenridge; 970-453-9104; www.breckenridgegolfclub.com
Bear/Beaver: 7276/5063; 73.3/69.2; 150/124
Beaver/Elk: 7145/4908; 73/68.9; 148/131
Elk/Bear: 7257/5971; 73.5/67.2; 143/121

"There's a view on every hole" of the world's only Jack Nicklaus municipal "masterpiece", "27 fantastic" fairways and "4+ hours of fun" at 9,324 Rocky Mountain feet high where "drives go far but balls can roll far as well (off into the woods!)"; "you need to play" the "perfectly maintained" "original 18 (Bear and Beaver)" as well as the newer Elk's "intermediate-ski-slope" terrain "when you travel to the mountains from Denver" in the warmer months – it's "a great place for a golf outing."

Cordillera, Mountain 材魚⊙   21 24 22 14 $235
650 Club House Dr., Edwards; 970-926-5100; www.cordillera-vail.com;
7413/5226; 74.7/68.9; 145/130

"This is mountain golf!" – in other words, it's "hard golf!"; designed by Hale Irwin in a "superb" setting, these "narrow", "tough holes with blind shots" beg for "U.S. Open Champ accuracy", so get your peepers off the "unreal eye candy early in the fall" and "bring your game" to this luxe resort where the "wonderful service" and "fabulous facilities" match the "breathtaking views"; it might be "crazy expensive" on fairways that some slicers suspect were "contrived to develop more homesites", but it sure is "a pleasant day's outing."

Cordillera, Summit 材魚⊙   23 23 23 17 $235
190 Gore Trail, Edwards; 970-926-5300; www.cordillera-vail.com;
7530/5239; 74.5/68.1; 136/128

"The closest thing to heaven imaginable" just might be "on top of a peak" at Cordillera resort where the Golden Bear has clawed out this "Scotland-in-Colorado" course; you can "hit your nine-iron 170 yards" at this altitude, but "even if you're not playing well, you'll enjoy the incredible views" – "if you can afford" the round; both the shot distances and the pricing have ball whackers blubbering "are you kidding me?"

Eagle Ranch   19 17 19 20 $99
50 Lime Park Dr., Eagle; 970-328-2882; 866-328-3232;
www.eagleranchgolf.com; 7530/5497; 74.8/69.8; 141/126

"It must be the 6,600-ft. altitude", or is it just the King-sized "good times" that makes this Arnold Palmer design playing through Brush Creek Valley so "addictive"?; the "landscaping still needs a few more years to mature", but at a soaring 7,530 yards long, you gotta "love carts with GPS" on the first public track built in Vail Valley since 1975, already "a great alternative to the higher priced courses" in the area.

Eagle Vail   18 15 19 17 $92
431 Eagle Dr., Avon; 970-949-5267; 800-341-8051; www.eaglevail.org;
6819/4856; 71.3/67.4; 131/123

Nestled in the heart of Vail Valley is this "nice" course that winds along the Eagle River and "plays tough", even while it's "fun" to watch "your balls go farther than on any other course"; its "beautiful views" culminate in a "scenic finish", which doesn't impress down-to-earth drivers who dis "yuppy" "condo golf" with "spotty conditions" and "street noise" – "take a mountain hike instead", they suggest.

Keystone Ranch, Ranch   23 20 19 17 $120
1239 Keystone Ranch Rd., Keystone; 970-496-4250;
www.keystonegolf.com; 7090/5582; 72.5/69.9; 137/128

"Wonderful holes" that are "pleasurable" for "all abilities" and set against "soaring vistas of the Gore Range" have some delighted duffers dishing "you'll never play a prettier course" as they work their way across the "steep lies" on this "beautiful high-meadow" links; unfortunately, aesthetes attest, "spotty conditions" have "faded" this "jewel" designed by Robert Trent Jones Jr. on former Indian buffalo hunting grounds.

Keystone Ranch, River　　24 | 21 | 23 | 18 | $145

155 River Course Rd., Keystone; 970-496-4250; www.keystonegolf.com; 6886/4762; 70.8/65.1; 132/123

"If you like elevated tees", there's at least a half dozen of them on this "excellent combination" of "lovely river and valley" holes whose front nine starts out 150 feet above the bluegrass fairway then weaves through the Snake River, crisscrossing hiking and biking trails before it starts climbing; "conditions are ok", but a slew of summit-seeking swingers say "the price is high" on a "goofy", "steep mountain" layout where there must be "a better way to get from point A to point B."

Raven at Three Peaks ☺　　27 | 23 | 25 | 21 | $149

2929 N. Golden Eagle Rd., Silverthorne; 970-262-3636; www.ravenatthreepeaks.com; 7413/5235; 73.4/69; 132/129

The "elevation changes are so dramatic" and the views are so "incredible", "you really need to focus on keeping your head down" on this "magnificent golf course above 9,000 feet" between Vail Valley and the Eisenhower Tunnel; boldly designed by Hurdzan/Fry with pro Tom Lehman, the layout "stays in great shape" and "sustains interest hole after hole", particularly on "downhill No. 9" where "watching your tee shot is like flying."

Red Sky, Fazio 🏌🏾🚶‍♂️🏌️‍♀️　　▽ 22 | 24 | 21 | 14 | $200

376 Red Sky Rd., Wolcott; 970-477-8425; 866-873-3759; www.redskygolfclub.com; 7113/5265; 72/68.2; 135/125

Tom Fazio whipped up this "superb", "inventive" "challenge" on gently sloping fairways that hairpin through sagebrush, juniper and aspen forests set against "fantastic" vistas of Castle Peak and the back bowls of Vail; though the former sheep ranch also offers "unbelievable facilities" and near-"perfect service", some swingers sailing across the "breathtaking" terrain say this Red Sky is no delight, given "too many downhill tee shots", "too severe greens" and "no bargains."

Red Sky, Norman 🚶‍♂️🏌️‍♀️　　▽ 25 | 23 | 23 | 20 | $200

376 Red Sky Rd., Wolcott; 970-477-8400; 866-873-3759; www.redskygolfclub.com; 7580/5269; 74.2/68.5; 144/124

His love for the Rockies beckoned Aussie Greg Norman to design this "fabulous" formation 25 minutes from Vail; separated from brother Fazio by a rocky ridge used by migrating elk and deer, it runs through natural terrain, scrub oak, rugged gulches and wildflower meadows with "amazing views" of peaks and ski runs on the "difficult but very scenic back nine"; all this plus "unbelievably great service" boils down to "wow", which is "the best word for this" "terrific track."

Sonnenalp ☺　　21 | 19 | 22 | 18 | $160

1265 Berry Creek Rd., Edwards; 970-477-5370; www.sonnenalp.com; 7059/5293; 72.3/70; 138/115

Perhaps the "most playable course in the Vail Valley" is this Jay Morrish/Bob Cupp design at a luxury mountain resort inspired by its sister facility in Bavaria; "fun, not hard", it's a "well-conditioned" "walk" amid "gorgeous" mountains, meadows, sagebrush, streams and, unfortunately, development; "why are there so many homes spoiling my view?" ask aces "put to sleep" by the simple layout.

Connecticut

Danbury

Great River
25 | 26 | 23 | 16 | $125

130 Coram Ln., Milford; 203-876-8051; 877-478-7470;
www.greatrivergolfclub.com; 7191/5170; 75.2/68; 150/118

A "gargantuan clubhouse", an "amazingly good restaurant", a "friendly, helpful staff" and "one of the best practice facilities in the nation" support this "beautiful layout" in "mint condition" "overlooking the Housatonic River" where a "man-made waterfall" is "followed by an uphill par-5 that will leave you crying 'serenity now'"; still, for ball hitters on a budget, its "big price tag" makes it a "once-a-year special treat", while high-handicaps huffing over "crazy green locations" simply call it "too damned hard."

H. Smith Richardson
17 | 12 | 12 | 20 | $40

2425 Morehouse Hwy., Fairfield; 203-255-7300;
6676/5764; 72.1/73.9; 126/127

"The Country Club of North Fairfield, as it is fondly referred to by some locals, is a great track with views of Long Island Sound on the back nine" and "well-maintained greens and fairways", but if you can't get "through on the antiquated phone-in system", you'll have to "sleep under the stars" "to get a prime Saturday or Sunday tee time"; given the "average hospitality and facilities" and the "absolutely awful service", you just might choose to sleep in instead.

Lyman Orchards, Gary Player
19 | 19 | 18 | 19 | $59

1 Lyman Rd., Middlefield; 888-995-9626; www.lymangolf.com;
6725/4900; 72.7/68.3; 133/118

"Don't forget to grab an apple pie for the way home!" shout swingers sweet on this "challenging" "shotmaker's venue" that "winds through a pretty large orchard" where "frequent elevation changes" make for "interesting holes"; while some crusty club carriers sour on "too many strange" "blind" shots, "forced carries" and "sidehill lies", the majority calls this a "tremendous value" "with nice practice facilities" overseen by "friendly folks" at a place with "additional activities" that are "great for family outings."

Lyman Orchards, Robert Trent Jones
22 | 19 | 19 | 21 | $45

1 Lyman Rd., Middlefield; 888-995-9626; www.lymangolf.com;
7011/5812; 73.2/72; 129/124

"Set in the countryside of central Connecticut" is a "terrific Robert Trent Jones Sr. layout" that makes "nice use of elevated tees and hills"; while it's "not as fancy as its sister course", it's "meticulously cared for" and "much more playable" from the forward boxes where "beginners" can "enjoy the views"; it's "strong from the tips", however, so if you "play the blues and weep", perhaps the "great sit-down lunch" that the "customer-oriented staff" serves will help you to "not be disappointed."

Richter Park
26 | 14 | 15 | 23 | $62

100 Aunt Hack Rd.; 203-792-2552; www.richterpark.com;
6744/5114; 73.3/69.8; 134/126

"I just wish I were a local" say non-Danbury duffers, because this "rolling, wooded, watery" "bargain" is "the best-kept public course in Connecticut", but if you're from out of town, "tee times are rarer than getting struck by lightning while collecting on a winning lottery ticket"; still, particularly "in the fall when the leaves are turning" on trees surrounding "greens that will keep you honest", it's "worth the drive", the hassle, the "lack of a driving range" and the sass you get from the "surly staff" in the "bare-bones clubhouse."

Ridgefield
18 | 13 | 16 | 20 | $50

545 Ridgebury Rd., Ridgefield; 203-748-7008; www.ridgefieldct.org;
6444/5295; 70.9/70.6; 123/119

"Every town wishes they had a local course this good" boast Ridgefield roundsmen of their "Fazio design" that rings up a "great deal for residents" on "extremely scenic and difficult holes, particularly on the back nine"; ornery out-of-towners opine it's "overpriced for visitors" and dismiss the front as "dull pasture", the "driving range" as "limited" and the staff as folks "who think they own the place."

Sterling Farms
19 | 15 | 15 | 20 | $50

1349 Newfield Ave., Stamford; 203-329-7888; www.sterlingfarmsgc.com;
6327/5495; 71.4/72.8; 126/125

"You get the feeling that if you squint your eyes, you're at a private club" on this "great muni for the money" in a convenient "urban location" a "short distance from NYC"; you'll have to "leave the driver in the bag for all but two or three holes", if you can get on it – "crowds" of "short" shooters make for "five-hour rounds" and tough weekend tee times, while the "very good driving range" and "nice restaurant" can't make up for a "staff that plays favorites."

East Haddam

Fox Hopyard
25 | 23 | 22 | 19 | $95

1 Hopyard Rd.; 860-434-6644; 800-943-1903; www.sandri.com;
6912/5111; 74.1/70.7; 136/123

A stone's throw from Devil's Hopyard State Park is this "beautiful", "wooded, winding course with lots of elevation changes" but with multiple tee boxes and "w-i-d-e fairways" that are "great for all levels of skill"; foxy foozlers freshen up at a "driving range and full teaching facility that could be the best in the state" before hopping over to the "outstanding restaurant" in the clubhouse overseen by an "extremely helpful and friendly staff."

Hartford

Gillette Ridge
20 | 18 | 19 | 15 | $80

1360 Hall Blvd./Rte. 218, Bloomfield; 860-726-1430;
www.gilletteridgegolf.com; 7191/5582; 74.8/67.2; 135/117

Named for Francis Gillette, a local 19th-century reformer, politician and business leader, this new Arnold Palmer design with streams, lakes and mature trees that was built on the CIGNA compound as part of a 600-acre redevelopment project is "long and narrow" with "well-bunkered greens"; because it's "not for the novice player", it

"may keep hackers away", while "burnt-out greens" and "poorly seeded fairways" from "opening too early" may keep everyone else away until conditions improve.

Wintonbury Hills
23 | 17 | 19 | 22 | $75

206 Terry Plains Rd., Bloomfield; 860-242-1401; www.wintonburyhillsgolf.com; 6623/5005; 70.8/68.2; 125/112

"Pete Dye, you da man" gush grateful golfers who "thank him for building this" "sporty, challenging layout" 15 minutes from Hartford in an "extraordinary setting" "that's hard to beat" for its "views of the Connecticut hills"; with "perfect fairways", "fast greens" and "difficult slopes" on "memorable holes", it's a "breath of fresh air on the state's public course scene", and the fact that the architect "charged the town just $1 for his design" makes it "really special."

New London

Shennecossett
21 | 13 | 16 | 22 | $41

93 Plant St., Groton; 860-445-0262; www.town.groton.ct.us; 6562/5671; 71.5/72.4; 122/122

"If you like Donald Ross courses, this is a must-play" huzzah history-minded hackers hoofing across this "wonderful, traditional" "classic", a "stand-out muni" that dishes up "fairway bunkers", "tiny greens", "beautiful waterfront holes" and "the best fish and chips in the world"; a few postmodern putters "hate the tall grass" and "ho-hum front nine", but nearly everyone agrees that, overall, this is an "excellent course for the price."

Delaware

Rehoboth Beach

Baywood Greens
26 | 21 | 22 | 21 | $95

32267 Long Neck Rd., Long Neck; 302-947-9800; 888-844-2254; www.baywoodgreens.com; 6983/5136; 73.2/70.9; 129/124

"Finally a great course near the Delaware beaches!" – but perhaps they should change the name to Baywood Gardens because this "unbelievable beauty" is "gorgeous in spring" as "more flowers than Augusta" "frame a playable layout" where "each hole is more interesting than the next"; a "top-notch practice facility" and a "friendly staff" support a "superbly maintained" spread you can play "at a reasonable price."

Bear Trap Dunes
22 | 20 | 20 | 20 | $120

Central Ave., Ocean View; 302-537-5600; 877-232-7872; www.beartrapdunes.com
Black Bear/Kodiak: 6853/5748; 72.4/69.1; 130/118
Grizzly/Black Bear: 6901/5721; 72.7/69.4; 130/121
Grizzly/Kodiak: 6834/5817; 72.1/69.8; 126/120

"Because of the ability to play three different nines", you might "never get tired of" this "sandy" 27-holer near Bethany Beach; it's "still fairly young" but has "potential" in its "dynamic" layout, as well as its "very nice putting green/chipping area", "friendly staff" and "great crab cakes"; still, for Wilmington and Washington whackers, it's "too far to travel" to suffer "very heavy traffic" on a layout "lacking trees" that's "nice" but "won't leave you with any lasting memories" – yet.

Wilmington

Back Creek   22 | 16 | 19 | 23 | $68

101 Back Creek Dr., Middletown; 302-378-6499; www.backcreekgc.com;
7003/5014; 73.6/69.3; 132/115

"Especially for those of us who tend to spray tee shots", the "wide
fairways" make this a "nice layout", even if "some very nasty
native grasses do manage to eat a ball or two" out of the worst
slicers' sleeves; though "homes crowd the course" and "there's
no clubhouse" but "a trailer", "nor any service to speak of", its
"excellent conditioning", "good price" and mere 20-minute drive
from Wilmington make it "great" for return rounds.

Florida

★ **Top Courses in State**
29 TPC at Sawgrass, Stadium, *Jacksonville*
28 Ocean Hammock, *Daytona Beach*
   World Woods, Pine Barrens, *Tampa*
   Arnold Palmer's Bay Hill, *Orlando*
27 Sandestin, Raven, *Panhandle*
   Westin Innisbrook, Copperhead, *Tampa*
26 Walt Disney World, Osprey Ridge, *Orlando*
   Orange County National, Panther Lake, *Orlando*
   LPGA International, Legends, *Daytona Beach*
   Doral, Blue Monster, *Miami*

Daytona Beach

LPGA International, Champions 🏯   24 | 25 | 22 | 23 | $100

1000 Champions Dr.; 386-274-5742; www.lpgainternational.com;
7088/5131; 74/68.9; 134/122

One of two "well-maintained" tracks amid the "beautiful scenery"
at the LPGA headquarters, this Rees Jones design is "wide open"
yet "challenging" – and "not only for the ladies"; because it offers
"a real deal" with "excellent clubhouse facilities" including a pro
shop peddling some of the "best women's wear, golf accessories
and gear", linksters exclaim that they "can't wait to play it again."

LPGA International, Legends 🏯   26 | 24 | 22 | 23 | $100

1000 Champions Dr.; 386-274-5742; www.lpgainternational.com;
6984/5155; 74.5/70.2; 138/123

This Arthur Hills design is "more difficult" than its sister, Champions,
with "tighter fairways" that are "not for novices" and greens
that some tourists tout as "the best in Florida"; it might seem
"expensive", but its pro shop, acclaimed dining and fine practice
facilities help deliver "great value", particularly on a "combined
ticket" with its sibling, which makes the experience here "simply
as good as it gets."

OCEAN HAMMOCK   28 | 24 | 24 | 21 | $235

105 16th Rd., Palm Coast; 386-447-4611; 888-515-4579;
www.oceanhammock.com; 7201/5115; 77/71.5; 147/131

"Absolutely the bomb", this "spectacular oceanfront course" is
"drop-dead gorgeous", not only because of its "breathtaking
views" but because of its "wonderful layout", a "typical Nicklaus
Signature design, which is no bad thing"; "a true pleasure to play

despite the persistent (and strong) winds", it "requires length in the bag and the wallet", but the "good practice facilities" and "first-rate staff" help make it "worth" the clams.

Victoria Hills ▽ 28 | 21 | 23 | 25 | $95
300 Spalding Way, Deland; 386-738-6000; 866-295-4385;
www.stjoegolf.com; 6989/4852; 73.5/67.2; 142/124
"Better practice your bunker play" before swallowing sand in the Pinehurst-style swales on this "stunning" track 35 miles north of Orlando, "a very different design" for Florida where architect "Ron Garl was inspired" by the rolling terrain of "North Carolina"; best of all, now that the new clubhouse is complete, you don't need to suffer a soda in a semi-wide for such "fun, exciting golf."

Ft. Lauderdale

Club at Emerald Hills, The 🔾 24 | 19 | 18 | 19 | $165
4100 N. Hills Dr., Hollywood; 954-961-4000;
www.theclubatemeraldhills.com; 7280/6249; 76.3/71.2; 146/130
"There are shots to the greens that look like you are climbing the pyramids" say wallopers walking like Egyptians across this "challenging", "un-Florida-like" "risk/reward layout" a five-mile trek south of Ft. Lauderdale; it's "always in spectacular shape", except in summer when it's "a little ragged" though the "price drops dramatically", and if you're used to pharaonic luxury, just note that "the clubhouse is frozen in time" – circa 1970s, not 2500 B.C.

Jacaranda, East 🔾 18 | 16 | 16 | 18 | $99
9200 W. Broward Blvd., Plantation; 954-472-5836;
www.golfjacaranda.com; 7195/5638; 74/72.3; 130/124
"All the challenge you need" can be found on this "bit of a hidden jewel" 15 minutes from Ft. Lauderdale, swoon supporters who claim "you'll love the variety" of the "old-school" holes on its "flat but interesting" layout "with doglegs and water" and fairways that ribbon around rare old trees; "if you're in the area, it's a nice round" concede critics, but "parts" of the place feel "like an average course in Ohio", only with "long rounds" and "lots of airport noise."

Jacaranda, West 🔾 18 | 17 | 17 | 18 | $99
9200 W. Broward Blvd., Plantation; 954-472-5836;
www.golfjacaranda.com; 6729/5314; 72.5/71.1; 132/118
A handful of hackers give "two thumbs up" to this "well-appointed" but "fairly easy" "neighborhood course" surrounded by ficus, banyans and live oaks; there's "lots of sand" and water on 16 holes, but its "wide-open" fairways are "good for moderate and experienced players to have a round side by side"; it's clear that "management appreciates your business", argue aces, which perhaps explains why they "overcrowd" a "nice but not exceptional" track.

TPC at Heron Bay 🔾 17 | 22 | 22 | 15 | $141
11801 Heron Bay Blvd., Coral Springs; 954-796-2000; 800-511-6616;
www.tpcheronbay.com; 7268/4961; 74.9/68.7; 127/113
Though it's not far from the Everglades, nomads note there's "more sand than the Sahara" on this course that once hosted the PGA Tour's Honda Classic; while repetitious roundsmen rip the layout as

"boring" because "too many holes resemble each other", satisfied swingers enjoy the "challenge", its "super range", "beautiful clubhouse" and staff that "treats everyone like a pro."

Jacksonville

Amelia Island Plantation, Long Point ⌂ ⚬

| 24 | 20 | 21 | 20 | $160 |

6800 First Coast Hwy., Amelia Island; 904-277-5908; 888-261-6161; www.aipfl.com; 6775/4927; 73/70.2; 135/123

The long and the short of it is that this "well-maintained" Fazio formation is "the best of Amelia Island"; its "beautiful grounds" incorporate "gorgeous hills, ocean, marsh and wildlife" on "varied terrain"; "few water hazards", "many tee boxes" and not a lot of length "make it accessible to all" players who come to this "great family resort" where "package deals" offer "strong value."

Amelia Island Plantation, Oak Marsh ⌂ ⚬

| 23 | 22 | 22 | 21 | $140 |

6800 First Coast Hwy., Amelia Island; 904-277-5907; 888-261-6161; www.aipfl.com; 6580/4983; 71.7/69.9; 130/124

Although this "natural and peaceful" Pete Dye resort course "lost many trees to the summer '04 hurricanes", "you won't miss them"; "plenty of trouble remains" to eat enough balls to drown a duffer in debt, but "you don't care how many you lose" given "beautiful views with the setting sun over the marshes and channels" during "a tough round that's worth the trip."

Amelia Island Plantation, Ocean Links ⌂ ⚬

| 23 | 21 | 22 | 19 | $140 |

6800 First Coast Hwy., Amelia Island; 904-277-5907; 888-261-6161; www.aipfl.com; 6301/4550; 70.3/66.4; 134/115

You may "think you are at Gullane [Scotland] or Old Head" in Ireland when the "oak trees meet the wide-open Atlantic beaches" for the last three holes on this "tough", "tight" test; "blind shots and ocean wind" can be "brutal" on the "wicked-hard back half", but most of the "wonderful combination of challenging holes" "is about land, not water views" – or "distance" say women who "can be competitive from its forward tees."

Ravines

| 21 | 19 | 19 | 25 | $59 |

2932 Ravines Rd., Middleburg; 904-282-7888; 6733/4817; 72.4/67.4; 133/120

Climb this "very hilly, challenging track" "just south of Jacksonville" offering "opportunities to hit across ravines" from "plenty of elevated tees", and "you will not believe you're in Florida"; it "may be in the best shape in 25 years", so if you crave a "well-kept" course and "friendly service" at "an exceptional value", "head to this" spot – and if you truly want to pretend you're playing "a northern mountain course", just ignore the tanned, "jet-skiing natives who occasionally whiz by the 9th tee" on Black Creek.

TPC AT SAWGRASS, STADIUM ⚬

| 29 | 27 | 25 | 19 | $330 |

110 TPC Blvd., Ponte Vedra Beach; 904-273-3230; www.tpcsawgrass.com; 6954/5000; 75/65.3; 149/125

"Excitement is in the air" at "one of America's landmarks", Florida's Top for Course and Facilities; it "tests the pros", so "steel your nerves" on Pete Dye's "masterpiece of railroad ties and waste bunkers", fairways and greens "manicured with scissors" and "thick, juicy, punishing rough", because if you "avoid a meltdown", "you'll remember what you did for the rest of your life" on the famous "island green" ("viva 17!"); "mortgage the doublewide", "empty the kids' college savings account" and play the "real deal" "once before you die."

TPC at Sawgrass, Valley ⊶   24 | 27 | 26 | 18 | $155

110 TPC Blvd., Ponte Vedra Beach; 904-273-3230; www.tpcsawgrass.com; 6864/5126; 72.8/65; 130/115
A "Cinderella" to the Stadium, this "often overlooked" Pete Dye/ Bobby Weed layout next to the Sawgrass Marriott still charms putting princes with a "challenging" "abundance of water", large greens, a superb opening hole, a "first-rate practice facility" and that "great TPC service and style"; though it's sans "the glam", this "tough" but "nice alternative's" "better pacing and pricing" might just "make your day."

Windsor Parke 🏞   ▽ 19 | 16 | 18 | 22 | $55

13823 Sutton Park Dr. N.; 904-223-4653; www.windsorparke.com; 6765/5206; 72.4/71.5; 136/125
"I can't say enough positives" yap yipping yesmen about this "interesting and demanding" Arthur Hills layout conveniently located between the beaches and Downtown Jacksonville; "wind can make it tough" to avoid the strategic bunkering on its tight, tree-lined fairways, but it's nonetheless "beginner-friendly", both on the putter and the pocket; "budget pricing" or no, claustrophobic club carriers complain "why do people buy houses 200 yards right of a tee box and then complain when balls end up in their yard?"

World Golf Village, King & Bear ⏲   25 | 26 | 24 | 21 | $175

1 King Bear Dr., St. Augustine; 904-940-6200; www.wgv.com; 7279/5119; 75.2/70.1; 141/123
"Arnie & Jack, enough said!" to make swingers storm "the front gate" of "heaven", the only course co-designed by Palmer and Nicklaus whose "terrific collaboration" created "some of the best golf anywhere"; it's "not hugely challenging" but stays "in perfect condition", accompanied by a "top-notch practice range", a "professional staff" and the chance to "visit the World Golf Hall of Fame" or "stop by Bill Murray's Caddyshack" bar – "just be careful about staying" in what creatures of comfort call some of the "worst-run" accommodations around.

World Golf Village, Slammer & Squire ⏲   24 | 26 | 25 | 20 | $150

2 World Golf Pl., St. Augustine; 904-940-6100; www.wgv.com; 6939/4996; 73.8/69.1; 135/116
"Even non-golfers" "can't help but get overcome with nostalgia" when in such "close proximity to the Hall of Fame's" "walk through the history" of the sport; they might even be inspired to go a few holes on this "pristine" spread where the "wide-open" fairways "challenge everyone" with variety and interesting chipping areas – and thanks to a "nice staff" and "facilities that can't be beat", they'll be "very happy" they did, even though they'll pay "prices through the roof."

Miami

Biltmore | 18 | 19 | 19 | 19 | $95 |
1210 Anastasia Ave., Coral Gables; 305-460-5364;
www.biltmorehotel.com; 6667/5292; 72/73.4; 126/124
Recently "upgraded", this "historic" Donald Ross "classic" is still
"too flat and boring" for thrill seekers but can be "lots of fun" for
down-to-earth duffers; after a round amid "beautiful homes and
tall trees", amble over to the "1920s hotel" and "have a drink by
the pool for a great way to finish the day", even if the "course and
conditions don't measure up" to the cocktail.

Crandon Park ⛳ | 25 | 17 | 16 | 22 | $148 |
6700 Crandon Blvd., Key Biscayne; 305-361-9120;
www.miamidade.gov/parks/golf.asp; 7301/5423; 76.2/71.8; 145/130
"Incredibly huge" "iguanas that play around the greens" make this
former Champions Tour host "feel like *Jurassic Park*", but there's
nothing primitive about its "magnificent design and condition" or
its "new, stylish, well-appointed clubhouse" (which some of our
surveyors may not know about); with bunkers everywhere, water on
14 holes and "great views across Biscayne Bay", the course has
"tons of character" – and tons of mosquitoes, so "bring repellent"
to avoid "being devoured"; now if there was only a spray to protect
you from "rangers that are golf idiots."

DORAL, BLUE MONSTER ⛳ | 26 | 25 | 23 | 16 | $275 |
4400 NW 87th Ave.; 305-592-2030; 800-713-6725; www.doralresort.com;
7288/5392; 74.5/73; 130/124
"Is there any sand left on Miami Beach?" grouse wedge-grippers
gasping on this "slamming" "big boy", host to the PGA Tour's
Ford Championship, where your ball might take up residence in a
"bunker larger and deeper than your house"; "'Blue' [also] means
lots of water", but not to drink – instead, "if you aren't scratch,
bring some beers to quell your frustration" over soupy hazards
and "rough you could lose a small child in"; in other words, "the
fanfare" over this "fabulous experience" "is right on the money",
even if the pricing is all wrong: "anything this expensive should
come with a steering wheel."

Doral, Gold ⛳ | 21 | 24 | 22 | 18 | $250 |
4400 NW 87th Ave.; 305-592-2030; 800-713-6725; www.doralresort.com;
6602/5179; 73.3/71.4; 129/123
It's "a keeper" claim club carriers of this "gentle" "classic" that's
"more playable than the Monster" and therefore "very busy"; "well
maintained for her age" with a "great teaching staff" to boot,
this golden girl of "old-school golf" is a "nice alternative" at a
"better value" than brother Blue, but she's "situated directly
under airplanes landing at MIA" and surrounded by "a run-down
residential area" where a "lack of a starters" "leads to afternoon
free-for-alls" that make Miamians moan "skip" it – "you'll never
miss" this "plain Jane."

Doral, Great White ⛳ | 21 | 24 | 21 | 16 | $275 |
4400 NW 87th Ave.; 305-592-2030; 800-713-6725; www.doralresort.com;
7171/5026; 75.1/70.7; 133/130
"Doral runs a class act", and this "artistic" Greg Norman course
is part of the package; introducing "Palm Springs to Miami", this

"unusual" "desertlike" design "will bring you to your knees" with "plenty" of coquina-filled "waste bunkers" and "challenging water"; it's "superbly" maintained and "easier to get on" than its siblings at Doral, so it's "worth a vacation splurge" – that is if you don't mind some "goony" holes and "the sound of landing gear in your backswing" courtesy of jet planes coming into the nearby airport.

Naples

Lely, Flamingo Island 🏌   21 | 21 | 22 | 19 | $149
8004 Lely Resort Blvd.; 239-793-2600; 800-388-4653; www.lely-resort.com; 7171/5377; 75/71.4; 136/123

Dotted with pines, sabal palms, bunkers and "helpful workers" 15 minutes from the Ft. Myers beaches, this "very, very nice" course was designed by Robert Trent Jones Sr. with "excellent greens", multiple tee options and "fairways that look forgiving, but take a hint: appearances can be deceiving"; "it ain't cheap" for a track with "too many houses" surrounding it, but with holes like the stunning water-surrounded 5th, it still offers "a great round of golf."

Lely, Mustang 🏌   21 | 22 | 22 | 19 | $149
8004 Lely Resort Blvd.; 239-793-2600; 800-388-4653; www.lely-resort.com; 7217/5197; 75.2/70.5; 141/120

"If you love water, you'll love" this "lush and lovely" "challenge" laid out by Lee Trevino amid "rolling hills" and "lots of natural wetlands" at "a wonderful resort" on the Gulf Coast; "a few tough holes and an island green will make your stomach do flips", but a post-round meal in the "comfortable clubhouse" will "settle it right back down" again say "locals" who insist that "even a beginner can get some good experiences" playing the nine H_2O holes on this area "favorite."

Tiburón, Black 🏌 ⏰   25 | 26 | 26 | 18 | $250
2620 Tiburon Dr.; 239-594-2040; www.wcigolf.com; 7005/4909; 74.2/69.7; 147/119

"Prepare yourself for a date with the devil if you play from the tips" on this "long and tough" Greg Norman track where the "palmettos will eat your balls" and "coquina waste bunkers frame" "shaved fairways" that are "more challenging than they look"; "tight off the tee", it's "not for beginners", and it "can take forever during the high season" when you're advised to remember that the "homey and relaxing" Ritz-Carlton is only "a five-iron away."

Tiburón, Gold 🏌 ⏰   24 | 26 | 27 | 17 | $250
2620 Tiburon Dr.; 239-594-2040; www.wcigolf.com; 7288/5148; 74.7/69.2; 137/113

"It's always fun to play where the professionals play" gasp golfers going for the Gold at this "extra hard" home of the PGA Tour's Franklin Templeton Shootout; the Greg Norman layout dishes out "all you can handle" with "lots of pine needles" and shaved-down tall grasses that form fringes around "turtle-back greens that hold nothing"; this "top-of-the-line" track's facilities are "gorgeous", though duffers who would rather hold onto their dubloons dish that the "Ritz-Carlton seems to nickel and dime you for everything."

Ocala

El Diablo 🏌 | 23 | 11 | 17 | 24 | $55 |

10405 N. Sherman Dr., Citrus Springs; 352-465-0986; 888-886-1309;
www.eldiablogolf.com; 7045/5144; 75.3/69.8; 147/117

"If you can get past the trailer clubhouse", this "out-of-the-way" but "fabulous" course has a layout that's almost "second to none", with a strong opening hole, "lots of elevation changes and big trees" that require you to "hit it straight"; while some angelic aces describe it as "very picturesque" and an "amazing value", devil's advocates point their pitchforks at the "poor condition" that is forcing its "great reputation" to "go downhill fast."

Orlando

ARNOLD PALMER'S BAY HILL 🏌 ⛳ | 28 | 25 | 26 | 21 | $214 |

9000 Bay Hill Blvd.; 407-876-2429; www.bayhill.com;
7239/5235; 75.1/72.7; 139/130

"Arnie rocks!" rave knaves lucky enough to say "hello, Mr. Palmer" in the "clubhouse with the pros' names on the lockers" or "watch him" "cruising around" the course at this "golf fan's dream", a "first-class facility" where the King himself holds court; "even if it's just a flat Florida course" – albeit one with "incredible" conditioning, "bunkers, water", "tough rough", "difficult" greens and a finish you'd better "say your prayers on" – it's "worth waiting in line" to play the host of the PGA Tour's Bay Hill Invitational.

Baytree National 🏌 | 21 | 20 | 19 | 21 | $69 |

8207 National Dr., Melbourne; 321-259-9060; www.golfbaytree.com;
7043/4803; 74/68.4; 135/121

Golfing guys and gals both enjoy this "neat design" by Gary Player 45 minutes from Orlando; the large, flat greens and unusual red shale waste areas are kept in "great condition" on this "solid" "gem", but even if plenty of putters proclaim that a round here is "always fun", you may only need to "play it once", unless of course you live in one of the "many homes" along the fairways.

Black Bear 🏌 | 22 | 17 | 19 | 22 | $55 |

24505 Calusa Blvd., Eustis; 352-357-4732; 800-423-2718;
www.orlando-golf.com; 7002/5417; 74.7/70.4; 134/118

On a rare rolling lair for Florida, this daunting bear stalks golfers over some hilly holes; "don't let the wide-open fairways" of this "links-style course" lull you into hibernation because it's not "easy, by any means" – "outstanding undulations on the greens" "require an accurate short game to avoid collection areas" during a big game hunt that is "a challenge to any handicapper" and "a tremendous value" to all.

ChampionsGate, International 🏌 | 23 | 27 | 25 | 19 | $170 |

1400 Masters Blvd., Champions Gate; 407-787-4653; 888-558-9301;
www.championsgategolf.com; 7363/5618; 76.3/67.6; 143/117

A chip shot south of Disney World is where Greg Norman set this "British Isles–type links"; while mountain goats might kick it as "flat" and "kind of bland for the money", "target golfers" call it an "absolutely majestic" "test" where the Shark "lurks" in "dangerous water" hazards; it's also where top teacher David Leadbetter has his headquarters, which helps to make it "a wonderful experience from the time you park your car until you leave."

ChampionsGate, National 🏌️   20 | 24 | 24 | 17 |$160

1400 Masters Blvd., Champions Gate; 407-787-4653;
888-558-9301; www.championsgategolf.com;
7128/5150; 75.1/65.2; 133/111

"Very attentive service" and "great conditions" await would-be champions on this course that's "fun even for high-handicappers" who visit this "really great complex" where "you can play two outstanding spreads and get a lesson from one of the best" instructors in the business, fawn fans; opposing aces argue that, beyond the "best hole, the 600-yd. par-5 with traps and water on the left", the layout "seems engineered to fit the land", making this track "less inspiring than its sister."

DeBary 🏌️   ▽ 20 | 18 | 20 | 23 |$69

300 Plantation Club Dr., DeBary; 386-668-1705; www.debarycc.com;
6776/5060; 72.7/69.4; 137/119

"Shhhh, please don't let this secret get out" hush hackers hiding out on this "jewel" "set in a beautiful development" 20 miles north of Orlando amid Carolina-style woods; "each hole is private", including the 9th and 18th (the only two to dip into the drink), whose regular greens reopen in fall 2005 following renovations to fix "hurricane" damage.

Diamondback 🏌️   ▽ 23 | 16 | 20 | 21 |$65

6501 State Rd. 544 E., Haines City; 863-421-0437; 1-800-222-5629;
www.diamondbackgolfclub.net; 6903/5061; 73.3/70.3; 138/122

"Drive it straight" because, right from the opening hole, this "scenic layout" is "short but challenging" as it slithers through "lush" tropical foliage; a handful of hackers hiss that the place is "quite disorganized" with "some staff very accommodating, others not at all", and a few old-timers have shed this spread claiming what "used to be better" now has "no more bite."

Falcon's Fire 🏌️   22 | 21 | 22 | 20 |$139

3200 Seralago Blvd., Kissimmee; 407-239-5445; 877-878-3473;
www.falconsfire.com; 6901/5417; 73.8/71.6; 138/126

"While the kids are at Disney", take your inner child to this Rees Jones "must-play" where s/he can "bomb away" – the fairways are so "long and wide", s/he will "not be punished" (that is, if you avoid "mounds that only a plastic surgeon could love"); unlike that ball-blasting brat inside you, this "top-notch track" has "matured greatly" and, even "post-hurricanes", it's "immaculately kept" by a "great staff" that will "make you feel like royalty", albeit at "slightly expensive" rates.

Forest Lake 🏌️   ▽ 19 | 16 | 19 | 21 |$68

10521 Clarcona Ocoee Rd., Ocoee; 407-654-4653;
www.forestlakegolf.com; 7240/5773; 74.7/69.4; 128/117

A 15-minute drive west of Orlando, this "nice rolling course" (almost) "out in nature" amid lakes and trees is "well maintained", "fun to play" and spoiled by "no homes" whatsoever; nevertheless, it's still "next to an interstate", which "doesn't impress" visitors who have "many other courses to go for before they come back"; the "locals", however, "seem to like" that it's "cheap."

Grand Cypress 🏌 ⏱

25 | 27 | 25 | 18 | $175

1 N. Jacaranda St.; 407-239-4700; 800-835-7377; www.grandcypress.com
East/North: 6955/5056; 74.2/69.4; 135/117
North/South: 6993/5328; 74.4/71.2; 136/120
South/East: 6906/5126; 73.8/69.8; 135/117

There's "no mouse in sight", delight Disney-dodging duffers, so "pick your 18 and swing away" on this "almost surreal" 27-hole test designed by Jack Nicklaus with "elevated fairways", "severely penalizing rough" and "monster bunkers and traps"; "exceptional service" and a "fabulous clubhouse" with a "huge, chock-filled pro shop" and the "incredible Black Swan" restaurant, not to mention one of the "best golf school facilities ever", help make this "beautifully manicured" spread "so special" – as it should be "considering a round costs more than college tuition."

Grand Cypress, New 🏌 ⏱

24 | 26 | 25 | 19 | $175

1 N. Jacaranda St.; 407-239-4700; 800-835-7377; www.grandcypress.com;
6773/5314; 71.5/69.7; 122/113

The deep "pot bunkers and double greens" on this "tip-top" Nicklaus replica "whet the appetite" to play the "Old Course in St. Andrews"; given its cadre of "delightful staff and starters", it appears "more people maintain it than play on" this "stunning" "piece of Scotland in the middle Florida" where, "if the Epcot sphere weren't visible", you'd never know you were minutes from Disney World.

Hunter's Creek 🏌

18 | 16 | 16 | 19 | $70

14401 Sports Club Way; 407-240-6003; www.golfhunterscreek.com;
7432/5755; 76.1/72.5; 137/120

You can finish your round "in less than four hours" on this "long and challenging" but "forgiving" layout 15 minutes from the airport that's suitable "for all levels of play" with "fast greens", a "great range" and a rebuilt clubhouse following "significant hurricane and tornado damage in 2004"; hackers not hot on "mingling with seniors" on a "tight" track "situated in too many backyards" simply "skip it."

Legacy Club at Alaqua Lakes 🏌

23 | 21 | 21 | 18 | $109

1700 Alaqua Lakes Blvd., Longwood; 407-444-9995;
www.legacyclubgolf.com; 7160/5055; 74.5/69.1; 132/112

Environmentalists urge "do not miss playing" this "very pleasant surprise" "in a beautiful location" north of Orlando in Seminole County because the "great Tom Fazio design" was the first Audobon Certified semi-private in the world; it's "a pleasure to play", if only for its "really tough greens", but someone should tell the "helpful staff" to fix the "drainage problems" so that this Q-school host doesn't stay "wet, wet, wet" after the rainy season.

Marriott Grande Pines

20 | 20 | 22 | 18 | $130

6351 International Golf Club Rd.; 407-239-6108; www.grandepines.com;
7012/5418; 74.3/71.6; 140/126

"Bring a shovel and a bucket" and dig the "loads of fun" you can have on this "very nice" Joe Lee design recently redone by Steve Smyers and player/consultant Nick Faldo with tree-lined fairways that roll past lakes and tall pines to "well-trapped", "contoured", "very slick greens that fall off on all sides"; though "local rates are a steal", anti-development duffers dis "it's not worth" it when the "surrounding townhouses" make you "feel like you're playing downtown."

Mission Inn, El Campeon ⛳ 24 | 22 | 23 | 21 | $130
10400 County Rd. 48, Howey-in-the-Hills; 352-324-3101; 800-874-9053; www.missioninnresort.com; 6923/4811; 74.2/68.7; 135/119
"For South Floridians, it is lovely to go a bit up north and have some hills" say frazzled flatlanders who cherish this "charming place" "in the middle of nowhere" north of Orlando where "huge elevations" and a "design that's particularly fine" add up to "the way golf should be"; though postmodern putters proclaim this "older track" built in 1926 "not as interesting as anticipated", they admit that, "as always, the resort – and the food at the fancy restaurant – make up for" it.

Mission Inn, Las Colinas ⛳ 23 | 24 | 24 | 23 | $110
10400 County Rd. 48, Howey-in-the-Hills; 352-324-3101; 800-874-9053; www.missioninnresort.com; 6857/4720; 72.7/67.3; 130/110
If you're in search of a "great remote getaway vacation", make it your mission to check out this "nice change from Orlando courses", which rolls out "beautiful scenery", a "good pace of play" and an "unusual arrangement of golf holes" on an "interesting" but tight layout where accuracy is at a premium; particularly "if one is staying at the Mission Inn", it "should not be missed."

Orange County National, Crooked Cat ⛳ 25 | 24 | 22 | 24 | $140
16301 Phil Ritson Way, Winter Garden; 407-656-2626; 888-727-3672; www.ocngolf.com; 7277/5236; 75.4/70.3; 140/120
Crooked cats can relax – there are very few trees to stray into on this "fantastic" "links"; there are, however, numerous pot bunkers on rolling fairways kept in "A+++ perfect condition" to match the "wonderful facilities and super driving range"; "they're always running specials", so you might be able to "stay at the lodge" and play for a "tremendous value" at a course "where rarely seen other golfers" and "no mouse ears in sight" are a "visual treats" given its location "a short drive from Orlando."

Orange County National, Panther Lake ⛳ 26 | 25 | 22 | 24 | $125
16301 Phil Ritson Way, Winter Garden; 407-656-2626; 888-727-3672; www.ocngolf.com; 7295/5094; 75.7/71.5; 137/125
"The wild drive behind the Magic Kingdom" "dumps you in a golf paradise" proclaim would-be pros prowling for a "purrrrfect" round on this "jewel" that, while "unrecognized", is "even better than its great sister"; the "wonderful layout" is so "meticulously maintained" that your foursome will feel "like you're the first ones to ever play there", so "take a box lunch, enjoy the scenery" and pretend you're putting pioneers – the "nice folks in the pro shop" at this "top-notch facility" might just go along with the conceit.

Orange Lake, Legends ⛳ ▽ 20 | 20 | 18 | 17 | $105
8505 W. Irlo Bronson Memorial Hwy., Kissimmee; 407-239-1050; 800-887-6522; www.orangelake.com; 7072/5188; 74.3/69.6; 132/120
The legend himself, Arnold Palmer, crafted this "great course" in 1998 where the back nine, the Pines, is tighter and shorter than the Links front, but it boasts the layout's signature hole, the unique,

watery par-4 13th called Island Oak; nevertheless, despite pro-designer pedigree, a posse of players pooh-poohs "overpricing" for greens with "lousy conditioning" and the "worst bag boys ever at a high-end course."

Palisades
▽ 18 | 15 | 17 | 24 | $55

16510 Palisades Blvd., Clermont; 352-394-0085; www.golfpalisades.com; 6988/5524; 73.8/72.1; 127/122

With "severe elevation changes" that are "unique for central Florida", this "tough, long course" set among the rolling hills west of Orlando is "worth the trip out there", if for no other reasons than "the scenery is beautiful", and the enticing price makes it "a great value"; grooming-centric golfers gripe that this track suffers from "poor conditions."

Remington 🏨
18 | 18 | 19 | 22 | $69

2995 Remington Blvd., Kissimmee; 407-344-4004; www.remington-gc.com; 7111/5178; 73.9/69.8; 134/118

It may be "a typical Florida course", but its "all you can eat, play and practice" policy ain't; with a layout that's "even fun for the ladies", this "excellent value" 20 minutes from Disney is "pretty busy with tourists", and though the "staff tries hard" to provide a "very enjoyable day of golf", "heavy traffic affects course conditions slightly"; still, if "you're not a snob", it's a "real deal."

Ritz-Carlton Orlando, Grande Lakes
25 | 27 | 28 | 18 | $185

4048 Central Florida Pkwy.; 407-393-4900; www.grandelakes.com; 7122/5223; 73.9/69.8; 139/115

Roundsmen put on the Ritz to match the hotel's "fantastic" Greg Norman track, which "could not be in any better shape"; its "outstanding amenities" include an "excellent practice facility", "terrific food in the clubhouse" and greens that Tiger Woods described as the truest he ever putted; while you should "prepare to pay a steep price", the "amazing forecaddies", who contribute to the No. 1 Service Rating in Florida, ensure a "tranquil" experience that "exemplifies" a "best-of-both-worlds" stay-and-play.

Southern Dunes 🏨
25 | 19 | 20 | 23 | $104

2888 Southern Dunes Blvd., Haines City; 863-421-4653; 800-632-6400; www.southerndunes.com; 7227/4987; 74.7/72.4; 135/126

"The variety of holes keeps you on your toes" at this "awesome course" a "short drive from Tampa" and "even shorter from Orlando"; "in mint condition" with "tons of bunkers", "rolling hills" and "big, bold, well-contoured greens", it's "highly recommended" for a "strong" round at a "great value"; slicers and hookers simply "pity" the owners of "the houses so close to many fairways."

Stoneybrook West 🏨
▽ 19 | 19 | 18 | 20 | $75

15501 Towne Commons Blvd., Winter Garden; 407-877-8533; www.stoneybrookgolf.com; 7101/5173; 74.8/70.1; 135/117

"You have to think your way around" the "well-placed bunkers" on this "beautiful" but "very tough" Arthur Hills five-year-old, "one of the best newer courses in Central Florida"; its "well-run" facilities offer a "country-club atmosphere" at "public" prices just off the turnpike on the west side of Orlando, and its Tif Eagle greens are "tremendous" – that is, at times when they're not "a bit burnt."

Walkabout
▽ 22 | 13 | 17 | 23 | $55

3230 Folsom Rd., Mims; 321-385-2099; 866-465-3352;
www.walkaboutgolf.com; 7115/4873; 74.3/69.1; 143/127
Designed by former LPGA champ and Aussie ace Jan Stephenson
with Perry Dye, this "long", "fantastic layout" is set "in the middle
of nowhere" "amid the central Florida wildlife" at a club that
"has potential to be one of the best in the state once fully up and
running"; though the "facilities need a lot of work" and you can't, in
fact, have a walkabout on the carts-only track, the "staff is friendly",
and "the price is a steal", particularly given the extra par-3 with a
green shaped like Down Under.

Walt Disney World, Eagle Pines
24 | 25 | 25 | 20 | $154

1950 W. Magnolia-Palm Dr., Lake Buena Vista; 407-939-4653;
www.disneyworldgolf.com; 6772/4838; 72.5/68; 135/111
For a "great escape from Dumbo and the kids", you can watch
your ball fly like an eagle on "quite a variety" of "secluded holes" on
this "top-notch", "tough track" "carved into a nature preserve" by
Pete Dye; it offers "plenty of water and sand hazards to keep you
busy", "10-minute tee times that help with pace" and that "famous
Disney service" to ensure "your every need is taken care of", but
it's "worth playing for the beauty of the area alone."

Walt Disney World, Lake Buena Vista
21 | 22 | 24 | 18 | $119

2200 Club Lake Dr., Lake Buena Vista; 407-939-4653;
www.disneyworldgolf.com; 6819/5194; 73/69.4; 133/120
It may not be "the most popular" of the fab five, but "I'll stick to
this one" say loyal LBV linksters about "the easiest of the Disney
layouts", where even the "casual golfer" enjoys the Mouse's
"famous service"; "be sure to use your waterproof" waders as
"there's a lot of rain", and although "too many" "tree-house villas"
line its fairways, the otherwise "charming" "gem" is "still better
than Small World" after all.

Walt Disney World, Magnolia
23 | 24 | 24 | 19 | $144

1950 W. Magnolia-Palm Dr., Lake Buena Vista; 407-939-4653;
www.disneyworldgolf.com; 7200/5232; 74.9/70.5; 136/123
"Mickey does it again", as do his other "wildlife" friends, including
"lots of deer" who roam like Bambi around the 6th's Mouse-shaped
trap and elsewhere on the co-host of the PGA Tour's Funai Classic;
"nicely conditioned" and "long" with "so much sand you'd think
you were in a desert", the layout is "tougher than the pros make
it look", but the "wonderful staff and practice facility", "plus the
best hamburgers in town", help justify the stick and "sticker shock";
N.B. following 2005 renovations that added 300 yards, the track is
more challenging than ever.

Walt Disney World, Osprey Ridge
26 | 25 | 25 | 21 | $145

1950 W. Magnolia-Palm Dr., Lake Buena Vista; 407-939-4653;
www.disneyworldgolf.com; 7101/5402; 74.4/70.5; 131/122
Disney "does it again" cheer champs enchanted with Tom Fazio's
"terrific" "nature walk" on terrain dotted with scrub oaks and pines;
"heaven-on-earth" for brave ball blasters, it serves up "many
risk/reward" opportunities, "long carries over water", lots of
"fairway sand traps" and huge, undulating greens, but it's also

"lady-friendly" and nice to novices, with a "wonderful staff and practice facilities"; just don't get Goofy when you see how many "Mickey bucks" it costs.

Walt Disney World, Palm 🏌   23 | 24 | 23 | 19 | $139
1950 W. Magnolia-Palm Dr., Lake Buena Vista; 407-939-4653;
www.disneyworldgolf.com; 6957/5311; 73.9/70.4; 138/124
"Not too shabby for a Mickey Mouse course", this "good, solid resort" layout artfully designed by Joe Lee is "long and challenging" with "new greens that roll fast and true" and "typically Florida, flat" fairways "with lots of water" where gator-hunting golfers warn, "always use your longest club looking for a lost ball"; a PGA Tour stop for 35 years, it's "fun for all levels" "but enough of a test to keep you interested", even if you're an ace.

Palm Beach

Atlantis 🏌   18 | 17 | 19 | 18 | $79
190 Atlantis Blvd., Atlantis; 561-965-7700; www.atlantiscountryclub.com;
6610/5242; 72.2/71.1; 137/125
Hungry hitters can "pick a snack" at this "short, easy" course that "plays through the orange groves"; while the "flat", "mid-level track" may not be much of a draw for sweet swingers, average players find it "relaxing and pleasant"; lose yourself in the "soothing water views" at a spread that might need a "face-lift" but offers "reasonable rates" and readily available "tee times during season."

Boca Raton Resort,   21 | 25 | 24 | 15 | $182
Resort Course 🏌 ⛳
501 E. Camino Real, Boca Raton; 561-447-3000; 800-327-0101;
www.bocaresort.com; 6253/4577; 69.3/65.5; 128/112
This "lovely, old Florida course" dates back to the 1920s boom days and retains the characteristics of that era, "requiring good shotmaking" to relatively small greens with "wide-open fairways"; though longer lofters lament that this "recently redone" and meticulously landscaped layout is "too short, even from the blues", aesthetically minded aces anoint it "the most beautiful in the state", and while the greens fee is near the ceiling at this upscale resort, the "clubhouse is spectacular" and the staff is "superlative."

Breakers, The,   ▽ 18 | 17 | 18 | 16 | $175
Ocean Course 🏌 ⛳
2 S. County Rd.; 561-659-8407; www.thebreakers.com;
6167/5254; 68.1/69; 127/123
"If the winds are blowing, bring your A game" to this "fun resort course" that comes within three-wood distance of the Atlantic a couple of times; one of Florida's oldest layouts with portions dating back to 1898, it's "better since the redesign" by Brian Silva in 2000, which added bunkers and contoured greens, leading many fans to shrug, "it's pricey, but hey!"

Breakers, The,   – | – | – | – | $175
Rees Jones Course ⛳
1550 Flagler Pkwy., West Palm Beach; 561-653-6320;
www.thebreakers.com; 7404/5164; 74.9/70.8; 140/125
Expectations tend to soar when Rees 'The Open Doctor' Jones is summoned to restore a course; here, the good doc transformed a

handsome but tired 35-year-old track owned by the posh Breakers; 10 miles to the east of the main hotel, you'll find the resusitated patient looking healthy as ever and brimming with variety and excitement, sporting several new timber cart bridges and a quartet of eye-candy par-3s, three of which flirt with water.

Champions Club at Summerfield 🏌️ | 19 | 16 | 18 | 20 | $68

3400 SE Summerfield Way, Stuart; 772-283-1500;
6809/4941; 73/69.2; 131/117

"There are courses in the area for two and three times the price that can't hold a candle to this place – it blows the competition away" gasp supporters of this "excellent", "very scenic" spread with "lots of water and wildlife"; while critical club sluggers slam "hit-or-miss conditions" on a "rather dull design for Tom Fazio", its eight water holes "can be entertaining."

Links at Madison Green, The 🏌️ | 21 | 17 | 18 | 21 | $59

2001 Crestwood Blvd., Royal Palm Beach; 561-784-5225;
www.madisongreengolf.com; 7002/4800; 73.6/69; 143/117

If you want to "swim" in Florida, you'll have "no problem finding water" – and, given the "many blind shots", neither will your ball – on any of the 18 pond- and lake-laced holes on this "great" near-"newcomer"; beyond the drink, it's "one tough" links, with ample bunkering, "tight fairways" and "small greens" as "fast" as "glass"; "reasonable rates" put it "in the play-again category", even if "so much construction" going on means you "sometimes can't hear yourself think."

PGA National, Champ 🏌️👤 | 24 | 23 | 22 | 18 | $280

1000 Ave. of the Champions, West Palm Beach; 561-627-1800;
800-633-9150; www.pga-resorts.com; 7048/5145; 75.3/72.3; 147/136

"Now this is a golf course" that's "worth the drive from Miami" say fans who flock to the "classic home of the PGA of America" to play the "former host of the Ryder Cup and PGA Seniors Championship"; with "water on 17 of 18 holes, rock-hard greens and tight fairways", it's as "tough as advertised" and that's "just the way it should be", even if flubbing foes "don't see what the fuss is all about" for "a very flat and unimaginative" layout.

PGA National, Estate 🏌️👤 | 20 | 16 | 20 | 18 | $150

1000 Ave. of the Champions, West Palm Beach; 561-627-1800;
800-633-9150; www.pga-resorts.com; 6694/4943; 71.8/68.9; 137/123

A short drive from the main campus, you'll find this "nice course" with "great facilities" that "might not be the most memorable on one's trip but is certainly worth playing", say resort guests who want to sample all five PGA National tracks; it might appeal to "lots of convention golfers and tourists", but precision putters proclaim that their "least favorite" formation here has "no pizzazz."

PGA National, General 🏌️👤 | 21 | 22 | 20 | 19 | $150

1000 Ave. of the Champions, West Palm Beach; 561-627-1800;
800-633-9150; www.pga-resorts.com; 6768/5327; 73.1/71.3; 134/123

"Risk/reward holes" – including a strong set of par-5s that feature "water, water everywhere" – characterize this "early design by the King", which is nonetheless "enjoyable" "for the average golfer", who can "try to swing like Vijay Singh" at the PGA's home in Florida; putters expecting pampering pout "they treat you like you're on a municipal course" at this resort that might have "nice casitas" but "gets too much play", making it "not worth the price of admission."

PGA National, Haig 🏌️ ⛳️   19 | 22 | 20 | 16 | $150

1000 Ave. of the Champions, West Palm Beach; 561-627-1800; 800-633-9150; www.pga-resorts.com; 6806/5645; 73.5/73.1; 139/129

"All the PGA National courses are challenging, and the Haig is no exception", decree devoted duffers of this Tom Fazio homage to legend Walter Hagen, who likely would have been tested on this "sporty course" where "even the big hitters can end up in the water or the bunkers if their shots are not precise"; while less-impressed hackers harrumph that the layout is "boring", even they must concede that "the facilities cannot be beat."

PGA National, Squire 🏌️ ⛳️   16 | 23 | 20 | 14 | $150

1000 Ave. of the Champions, West Palm Beach; 561-627-1800; 800-633-9150; www.pga-resorts.com; 6465/4975; 72.5/70.2; 139/131

In 1981 in tribute to Hall-of-Famer Gene Sarazen, a kinder, gentler Tom Fazio designed this "nice, flat resort course", which some "summer boys on outings" nevertheless find "more challenging than The Champ, with more twists and turns and water hazards"; with "too many homes too close to the course" lending the round the aura of "playing in the middle of an apartment complex", some complain they "expect a lot more from PGA, especially for the steep price."

Polo Trace 🏌️ 🕐   24 | 19 | 19 | 18 | $139

13479 Polo Trace Dr., Delray Beach; 561-495-5300; 866-465-3765; www.polotracegolf.com; 7182/5445; 74.8/71.6; 139/125

"If you don't like to swim, stay away", but if you can deal with the drink, "you'll feel like you are at a private club" making your way across this "challenging" and "phenomenally" "interesting" layout with rolling dunes and (we warned you) "lots of water carries"; one of "the classiest and best groomed" courses "around Delray Beach" might also be "among the more expensive", but it's "well worth the price."

Panhandle

Camp Creek   ▽ 27 | 24 | 22 | 22 | $105

684 Fazio Dr., Panama City Beach; 850-231-7600; www.campcreekflorida.com; 7159/5150; 75.3/70.4; 145/121

"Not your boring, old Florida course" but "a beautiful glimpse of its rustic past" near the Gulf of Mexico, this "unique gem" mined by Tom Fazio boasts broad fairways on a desolate dunescape of native grasses with "very few trees" and "large, sandy waste areas" dotted with wetlands; "excellent in all respects", it gives "great golf", and afterwards, you can relax at the WaterColor Inn, where "the setting, service and ambiance is top flight."

Kelly Plantation 🏌️   25 | 22 | 24 | 18 | $123

307 Kelly Plantation Dr., Destin; 850-650-7600; 800-811-6757; www.kellyplantation.com; 7099/5170; 74.2/70.9; 144/114

Fans of Freddie Couples flock to this "first-class operation" in a gated Florida facility on Choctawhatchee Bay that's "close to all of the resorts and beach"; while pennywise players balk at the price, richer roundsmen rave that "great service" helps make this "terrific design" that meanders through woods and wetlands "one of the best courses on the Emerald Coast."

Regatta Bay 🏯 | 25 | 23 | 22 | 19 | $114

465 Regatta Bay Blvd., Destin; 850-337-8080; 800-648-0123; www.regattabay.com; 6864/5092; 73.8/70.6; 149/118

For a "great vacation", sail across one of the "favorites in the Panhandle area"; the "wonderful layout" will have you walking the plank between sprawling bunkers and the environmentally sensitive wetlands of the adjoining state parks, while the pro shop is a treasure trove of valuable booty; still, a mutinous crew of club wielders says this ship is "overpriced" because conditions are "not kept up."

Sandestin, Baytowne 🏯 | 21 | 22 | 22 | 18 | $109

9300 Emerald Coast Pkwy. W., Destin; 850-267-8155; www.sandestin.com; 6745/4690; 73.4/68.5; 127/114

Set between the Gulf of Mexico's emerald green waters and white mica sand dunes overlooking the expansive Choctawhatchee Bay, this "gorgeous bayside course" boasts scenic vistas with "water all around"; luckily for novice lofters, all that drink is "not intimidating", since it rarely comes into play on what lower handicaps call "the weakest of the Sandestin spreads."

Sandestin, Burnt Pine ⏱ | 25 | 24 | 23 | 19 | $159

9300 Emerald Coast Pkwy. W., Destin; 850-267-6500; www.sandestin.com; 7001/5153; 74.7/71.2; 144/122

"Bring a sand wedge" to this Rees Jones course that "Lawrence of Arabia would love" say trapped tracksters; despite its copious bunkers, this "tough but fair" test with huge greens framed by pines and wetlands delivers what a cadre of club carriers considers to be "one of Florida's best" rounds – "if you can get on it"; fortunately, the resort has plenty of other activities to keep you occupied while you're waiting for a tee time.

Sandestin, Links | 19 | 19 | 20 | 14 | $109

9300 Emerald Coast Pkwy. W., Destin; 850-267-8144; www.sandestin.com; 6710/4969; 72.8/69.2; 124/115

Sandestin's "old guard" – the first course built at the resort back in 1973 – is "a sentimental favorite" of local loopers dating from "the days before commercialization" of the area; with "a lot of water" in play, "accuracy is at a premium, not distance", so "leave the driver in the bag" and "use your seven-iron on every tee" on this links that big blasters call "rinky-dink."

SANDESTIN, RAVEN | 27 | 25 | 23 | 17 | $119

9300 Emerald Coast Pkwy. W., Destin; 850-267-8155; www.sandestin.com; 6931/5106; 73.8/70.6; 137/126

Like the bird in the poem, you too might quoth 'nevermore' when your "ball rolls off the fairway" into "water so clear, you can see it" on this "incredibly beautiful" track, "the best overall of the Sandestin group"; it's an "interesting layout" that "emphasizes distance on different holes", but you might "remember" it most for those "mango-scented face towels" the "great" staff brings you "in July's heat."

SouthWood 🏌 — | – | – | – | $70 |
3750 Grove Park Dr., Tallahassee; 850-942-4653;
www.southwoodflorida.com; 7172/4978; 74.5/63.7; 133/102
"I was surprised to find such a nice course" here claim shocked
swingers of this "Gene Bates/Fred Couples design that is full of
excitement, variety and playability" with "greens that are by-and-
large pretty quick" and "a stellar collection of par-3s"; with the
rolling terrain lined in hardwoods and live oaks, it doesn't always
feel like Florida, but indeed it is, as this "great experience for golfers
of all abilities" is "certainly the best course in Tallahassee", even
for the little ones who can play the 2,696-yard Wee tees.

Port St. Lucie

PGA Golf Club, North | 25 | 25 | 23 | 24 | $89 |
1916 Perfect Dr.; 772-467-1300; 800-800-4653; www.pgavillage.com;
7026/4993; 73.8/68.8; 133/114
There's "lots of water, alligators and fun" on this "prime" spread
at a "golfer's paradise" in Port St. Lucie; "not a typical, flat"
Sunshine State track, it serves up contoured fairways, "difficult,
undulating greens" and "zillions of deep bunkers" on long
par-5s and sporty par-3s designed by Tom Fazio and "beautifully
maintained" by a staff that's "all professionals"; some of "the
best all-around facilities you'll find", including the "excellent" 35-
acre Learning Center and six-hole par-3 short course, help make
this "a real deal."

PGA Golf Club, Pete Dye | 25 | 25 | 23 | 23 | $89 |
1916 Perfect Dr.; 772-467-1300; 800-800-4653; www.pgavillage.com;
7150/5015; 74.5/68.7; 141/119
"Everything is done right here – and at bargain-basement prices" –
on this "different kind of experience" provided by Pete Dye; "a
little more desert than Florida golf", it weaves over "beautiful
terrain" encompassing native wetlands as well as sandy coquina
"waste areas" and pine straw rough; it's "difficult for beginners",
but it's an integral part of "a great vacation" among "a threesome
to be savored."

PGA Golf Club, South | 25 | 26 | 24 | 25 | $89 |
1916 Perfect Dr.; 772-467-1300; 800-800-4653; www.pgavillage.com;
7076/4933; 74.5/68.7; 141/119
No questions asked – "just go" to this "wonderful", "forgiving" Tom
Fazio layout where "generous fairways" stretch between the
Atlantic Ocean and Lake Okeechobee amid native palmettos and
palms toward "plenty of challenge" on well-guarded greens; at
this "beautiful" "third leg of a golfer's trifecta", "great service
and pricing" plus "fantastic practice and training facilities" equal
an "excellent golf vacation spot."

Sarasota

Legacy at Lakewood Ranch 🏌 | 25 | 22 | 21 | 21 | $99 |
8255 Legacy Blvd., Bradenton; 941-907-7920; www.lakewoodranch.com;
7067/4886; 73.8/68.8; 140/115
Trumpeted as "the best public course in the Sarasota/Bradenton
area", this "rolling" Arnold Palmer layout features "lots of water
hazards" where afternoon gusts serve notice to happy hookers

and savvy slicers to carry "a large stock of balls"; yet with "five sets of tees", this "wonderfully diverse course" accommodates everyone from the most frustrated flubber to the sweetest swinger.

Riverwood ⌂
∇ 23 | 19 | 23 | 21 | $100

4100 Riverwood Dr., Port Charlotte; 941-764-6661;
www.riverwoodgc.com; 7004/4695; 74.2/68.3; 137/116
They should call it Woodriver because the front nine is set among pines, while the back is all wet on holes like No. 16, a par-3 framed in marshy preserve, on this "fantastic course" in a residential community in southwest Florida; it's "a little out of the way" but "really worth playing", particularly "in the warmer months when you can get a discount."

University Park Golf Course ⌂ ⊕
23 | 19 | 19 | 20 | $125

7671 Park Blvd., University Park; 941-359-9999; 800-394-6325;
www.universitypark-fl.com
Course 1/Course 10: 7001/4700; 73.6/68.4; 138/114
Course 10/Course 19: 7247/4960; 74.8/67.2; 136/111
Course 19/Course 1: 7152/4850; 75.2/67.8; 130/114
A development north of Sarasota is home to this "outstanding", "well-maintained" 27-holer, a "Florida-style" (read: "flat"), pine- and oak-lined "challenge for all levels" from "beginners to intermediates" to "shotmakers"; the "third nine is quite long", and so are the rounds "during football season" when it "gets crowded" "with duffer alumni and weekend warriors."

Venetian Golf & River Club
∇ 22 | 18 | 19 | 18 | $86

103 Pesaro Dr., North Venice; 941-483-4811; www.wcigolf.com;
6931/5038; 72.9/69.1; 127/115
"One of the favorites" of sentimental swingers, this "linksy course" designed by Chip Powell pays homage to Alister MacKenzie's fingered bunkers and Donald Ross' green complexes with nods to other Golden Age architects such as A.W. Tillinghast and C.B. Macdonald; this "interesting layout" with naturalistic mounding, slightly elevated, slick greens and ornamental grass edging many of the fairway traps "will be great" "once it grows in."

Tampa

Bloomingdale ⌂
∇ 22 | 17 | 18 | 23 | $79

4113 Great Golfers Pl., Valrico; 813-685-4105; www.bloomingdalegolf.com;
7165/5397; 74.4/72.1; 131/132
Golfers-in-the-know say this "really good, local, upscale course" "deserves a few rounds of play" – just "don't leave your lunch unattended" lest the "raccoons, foxes and other wildlife that abound" amid the oaks, pines and marsh areas steal it; its tough par-5s, featuring doglegs and island dance floors, might even make up for the fact that "the greens need to be greener."

Fox Hollow
21 | 18 | 19 | 22 | $85

10050 Robert Trent Jones Pkwy., New Port Richey; 727-376-6333;
800-943-1902; www.golfthefox.com; 7138/5203; 75.1/70.6; 137/127
Among the final formations by RTJ Sr., this "beautiful" but "not overly challenging" "links-style layout" northwest of Tampa is "not your typical Florida course"; winding amid abundant forests, marshland and creeks via "strong" routing that "will work for any

level golfer", its "spectacular shots" come at a "good value" –
except when "the course is in bad shape."

Lake Jovita, South 🏖️ ⏱️   22 | 21 | 19 | 16 | $119
12900 Lake Jovita Blvd., Dade City; 352-588-9200; 877-481-2652;
www.lakejovita.com; 7153/5145; 74.8/70.3; 136/121
Penny-pinching putters may pout about this hilly layout a half-hour
north of Tampa because it costs "a lotta money" – and may take
some "luck getting on", despite its "remote locale"; however, birdie
hunters and ball bangers willing to pay the fee will find a "very
good" course that "definitely plays long" with greens that are
"as challenging as they get" on "varied terrain" that's perhaps
"not quite North Carolina, but close"; N.B. its new sibling, North,
has opened here.

Saddlebrook,   19 | 20 | 20 | 18 | $180
Saddlebrook Course 🏖️
5700 Saddlebrook Way, Wesley Chapel; 813-907-4566; 800-729-8383;
www.saddlebrookresort.com; 6564/4941; 72/70.6; 127/126
A "Palmer course is always nice to play", and this "challenging"
30-year-old "a bit off the beaten path from Tampa" is no exception
as it winds through cypresses, pines and palms bringing water into
play on all 18 holes; renowned for its instruction programs, pro shop
and "excellent food and beverage", the resort is still considered
"overpriced" and "hardly breathtaking" because its "dated
architecture" is "a bit run-down"; N.B. Arnie's second course here
has reopened following renovations.

TPC of Tampa Bay   25 | 24 | 22 | 17 | $153
5300 W. Lutz Lake Fern Rd., Lutz; 813-949-0090; 866-752-9872;
www.tpc.com; 6898/4990; 73.6/69.7; 135/119
"We had a bloomin' good time" on the home of the Champions
Tour's Outback Steakhouse Pro-Am enthuse Aussie-style aces who
go "to play where the pros do" "45 minutes outside of Tampa"; with
"very well-maintained", "wide-open, forgiving" fairways and
"unmatched practice facilities", this "tough" "test lives up to what
you would expect from a TPC" – just "watch out for gators" cry croc
hunters who also feel bitten by the "pricey" fees.

Westin Innisbrook, Copperhead 🏖️ 27 | 24 | 23 | 20 | $220
36750 US Hwy. 19 N., Palm Harbor; 727-942-2000; 800-456-2000;
www.westin-innisbrook.com; 7340/5605; 75.6/71.8; 134/130
"Elevation changes", "thick rough" and "slick greens" guarantee
"you'll use every club" on this "long, tough, exciting" spread "just
north of Tampa"; though "the whole Innisbrook complex is great"
(including the "good golf school"), and "they go out of their way"
to make guests "comfortable", the resort is starting to "show its
age", and the layout often "needs sprucing up", so play "around
big events" like the Chrysler Championship when "the course is
at its best", and always "be prepared to pay a pretty penny."

Westin Innisbrook, Island 🏖️   24 | 24 | 25 | 21 | $200
36750 US Hwy. 19 N., Palm Harbor; 727-942-2000; 800-456-2000;
www.westin-innisbrook.com; 7063/5578; 74.1/73; 132/129
"Water comes into play on [almost] every hole", "hence the
name", so "bring plenty of balls" to this "top-drawer" "hidden
treasure", a "hilly", "perfectly manicured" and "ecologically

beautiful" "shotmaker's course" with "awesome facilities"; "these people know how to run" Copperhead's sib, so the spread "has it all", except perhaps distance and diversity – "it's pretty short" with "not much variety" disenchanted drivers say dryly, though they admit it's "a challenge nonetheless."

WORLD WOODS, PINE BARRENS   28 │ 22 │ 22 │ 26 │ $130

17590 Ponce de Leon Blvd., Brooksville; 352-796-5500; www.worldwoods.com; 6902/5301; 73.7/70.9; 136/124

"Pine Valley South" is how connoisseurs characterize this "truly picturesque" "monster" "in the midst of nature" with "many risk/reward" opportunites and "lots of sandy dunes in play"; its "excellent variety" of holes, "super-fast, smooth greens" and "dynamite practice facilities" "would be mobbed every day" if it weren't "in the middle of nowhere" an hour from Tampa, but no matter how "out of the way" it is, it's a "must-stop" for Fazio fans.

World Woods, Rolling Oaks   26 │ 21 │ 21 │ 26 │ $120

17590 Ponce de Leon Blvd., Brooksville; 352-796-5500; www.worldwoods.com; 6985/5245; 73.9/70.1; 133/123

Even the "skilled player" will find this an "outstanding value" "when the rough is high"; an "excellent track with all sorts of challenges" "carved out of a forest", it's a "one-two punch" with "big brother" Pine Barrens that's "worth a detour" an hour from the madding crowds of Tampa for those who are looking for "just golf" at one of the "better facilities" in Florida.

Georgia

★ **Top Courses in State**
27 Sea Island, Seaside, *Lowcountry*
    Cuscowilla, *Lake Oconee*
    Reynolds Plantation, Great Waters, *Lake Oconee*
26 Reynolds Plantation, Oconee, *Lake Oconee*
    Reynolds Plantation, National, *Lake Oconee*

Atlanta

Barnsley Gardens   24 │ 26 │ 26 │ 19 │ $115

597 Barnsley Gardens Rd., Adairsville; 770-773-7480; 877-773-2447; www.barnsleyresort.com; 7180/5450; 74.8/71.7; 142/129

Despite its location just "one hour" northwest of Atlanta, there's "not a house in sight" on this "diverse", "well-conditioned" course with "great par-3s" on lush resort grounds restored to their shipping-and-cotton baron namesake's mid-1800s aspect; fees are "on the pricey side", but this Jim Fazio design offers "private-club amenities" and "Southern hospitality at its best."

Bear's Best Atlanta 村⊡   24 │ 22 │ 25 │ 17 │ $105

5342 Aldeburgh Dr., Suwanee; 678-714-2582; 866-511-2378; www.bearsbest.com; 6857/5076; 72.5/70; 140/127

"Superlative service" stands out at this "special-event location", a collection of copycat holes culled by the Golden Bear from some of his finest tracks; the "required forecaddies" (until 3:30 PM) "make play more enjoyable" by taking the guesswork out of the tricky routing created by the "wide variety of layouts" on a "beautiful course that won't kill novices."

Brasstown Valley 🏨   26 | 20 | 23 | 24 | $75
6321 US Hwy. 76, Young Harris; 706-379-4613; www.brasstownvalley.com;
6957/5028; 73.2/69.2; 139/116

"Don't play here – leave this great track and its gorgeous views to the rest of us" say trailblazers who stumble upon this "great find" and "good value", an "unexpected beauty" in the Blue Ridge Mountains near the North Carolina border that is "hard to get to but worth the trip"; the "scenic" course's "excellent condition" and "changing elevation" are part of its appeal, as is sinking into a cushy chair by the 72-ft.-high stone fireplace in the rustic lodge.

Château Élan, Château   23 | 24 | 24 | 21 | $80
6060 Golf Club Dr., Braselton; 678-425-0900; 800-233-9463;
www.chateauelan.com; 7030/5092; 73.5/70.8; 136/124

With a winery, an equestrian center, eight restaurants, a spa and an art gallery, the resort that pharmaceutical patents built is "a real find if you don't mind a drive" 50 miles from Atlanta to a town once owned entirely by actress Kim Basinger; "crisscrossed by hidden creeks" and bumping along on "hills aplenty", the namesake course is "a solid challenge for any skill level"; the property's French country decor and "private-club atmosphere and facilities" could easily be indulged in for, say, nine-and-a-half weeks.

Château Élan, Woodlands   24 | 24 | 23 | 21 | $80
6060 Golf Club Dr., Braselton; 678-425-0900; 800-233-9463;
www.chateauelan.com; 6735/4850; 72.5/68.4; 131/121

"Make sure you're well-warmed up", or "you'll be playing within the woodlands most of the day" on Château Élan's younger sibling, a "must-play" that "requires a great deal of accuracy" ("try the up-slope side of the fairways for a good roll"); amid "beatific mountains and rolling hills" with "tremendous housing along the course", the "beautiful setting" alone makes it "worth the trip" northeast from Atlanta.

Cherokee Run   22 | 17 | 17 | 21 | $69
1595 Centennial Olympic Pkwy., NE, Conyers; 770-785-7904;
www.cherokeerun.com; 7016/4948; 75.1/70.6; 143/124

Leave the horsing around to the adjacent Olympic equestrian center because this "terrific place to play" is a "great-value" race around a "spectacular track"; yes, "it's a quagmire after a rain", but "when it is dry", this "challenging" Arnold Palmer Signature offers a "good variety of holes" dotted with "interesting items" from the "1996 steeple chase" and ending in "some of the fastest greens in the Atlanta area."

Cobblestone   22 | 17 | 17 | 23 | $63
4200 Nance Rd., NW, Acworth; 770-917-5151;
www.cobblestonegolf.com; 6759/5400; 71/71.5; 139/129

"Tight" holes, "rolling greens" and "lots of elevation changes" make this Ken Dye "challenge" "better than your average muni"; in fact, given its "beautiful Lake Acton views" and high-profile hosting of the PGA Tour's Bellsouth Classic qualifiers, snooty slammers say the "local good value" "would be a great private club"; hackers who huff it's "too difficult for a county-owned course" can at least eat up "great sandwiches at the turn" before "the last four holes eat them up" in turn.

Crooked Creek

21 | 20 | 20 | 19 | $89

3430 Hwy. 9 N., Alpharetta; 770-475-2300; www.crookedcreekgolf.com; 6917/4985; 73.4/70; 141/120

"Like to climb hills"? – then go cartless over "lots of elevation changes" at this "hidden gem" north of Atlanta where a layout with "no blind or tricked-up holes" means "you can easily see your next shot"; it's a "tough but fair" test that's probably even more "well conditioned" than you are, but you'd better play it now, as plans are for it to go private.

Georgia National

▽ 24 | 19 | 22 | 24 | $65

1715 Lake Dow Rd., McDonough; 770-914-9994; www.georgianational.com; 6907/5005; 74.1/70.5; 140/128

Maneuvering around water hazards on 13 holes on this "beautiful course" "worth the drive south of town", you'll understand why "they call it The Frog"; but this "scenic, peaceful, well-treed" track is actually a princely "pleasure to play" for a less-than-royal price; given "broad fairways" and "speedy greens" "designed for all skill levels", you'll find "challenges", but "you won't lose a lot of balls" on its "rolling terrain."

Nicklaus at Birch River 🏠

23 | 21 | 21 | 23 | $85

639 Birch River Dr., Dahlonega; 706-867-7900; www.nicklausgolfbirchriver.com; 6964/4999; 73.5/68.8; 140/124

If Jack Nicklaus were to direct a film, it would be *A River Runs Through It* on this "mountain valley" layout "in a beautiful part of Georgia" winemaking country, a scenic, "easy drive from Atlanta"; despite its name, it doesn't cross the Birch but the Chestatee – a full seven times, with the 4th green, 5th hole and 6th tee sharing an island in the stream; with turf "usually in excellent shape" and a staff that's "very interested in your business", it's "a lot of course for the money."

Renaissance Pine Isle 🏠

21 | 20 | 19 | 19 | $64

9000 Holiday Rd., Lake Lanier Islands; 770-945-8921; www.pineislegolf.com; 6514/5099; 71.4/70.2; 131/126

Don't forget to flash your gate receipt for a free sleeve of balls – you'll need them on this "short but tight" collaboration by Gary Player and Ron Kirby with "terrific water views" and "a lot of Lake Lanier coming into play" on eight holes including No. 15, a 250-yd. par-3 with a peninsula green, and No. 5, a left-curling par-5 that's reachable in two if the ball sails over the boats in intoxicating Cocktail Cove; even if you dunk every last one, there's still "lots of fun" to be had at the resort's beach, marina and tennis courts.

St. Marlo

19 | 18 | 18 | 18 | $89

7755 St. Marlo Country Club Pkwy., Duluth; 770-495-7725; www.stmarlo.com; 6923/5085; 73.5/70.3; 138/119

In a "secluded setting" 25 miles northeast of Atlanta, this "decent" Denis Griffiths design is "well landscaped" with cascading falls and rocky walls; despite some sentiment that the course was "tricked up to accommodate home sales", most of these "quality" holes – including massive par-4s measuring 474, 461 and 459 yards – are no joke; just "wait until summer to play" it, as it's in "great condition" then.

Windermere | 20 | 19 | 19 | 20 | $79 |

5000 Davis Love Dr., Cumming; 678-513-1000;
www.windermeregolfclub.com; 6902/4763; 73.3/68; 139/118
Davis Love III's "challenge" "winding through a high-end subdivision" "in the foothills of the Appalachians" is most "beautiful in spring, or in fall when the leaves are changing", but any time of year, the ferocious climbs up and down the "very hilly" Piedmont Plateau mean it "plays long"; thankfully, there's a special set of tees that, despite being a mix of the black and blue, won't bruise you nearly as bad as playing completely from the tips.

Columbus

Callaway Gardens, Lake View 🏨 | 21 | 20 | 21 | 19 | $85 |

US Hwy. 27 S., Pine Mountain; 706-663-2281; 800-225-5292;
www.callawaygardens.com; 6031/5347; 68.6/71.1; 123/121
Don't blast the Big Bertha on this "short", "fun" 1952 original at a 14,000-acre garden, nature preserve and resort founded by the clubmaker's cousin, Cason Callaway; prodigious flowering plantings make the "very scenic course" "pleasant to play" "particularly in the spring", and except for a few knee-knocking shots like No. 10's forced, over-the-creek carry from an island tee, a "leisurely round" here is as much a "picnic" as your outdoor meal with "the wife and kids" afterwards.

Callaway Gardens, Mountain View | 25 | 22 | 23 | 20 | $100 |

US Hwy. 27 S., Pine Mountain; 706-663-2281;
www.callawaygardens.com; 7057/6630; 73.7/71.9; 139/134
Dick Wilson and Joe Lee's "difficult" PGA Tour–caliber course, host to The Buick Challenge for 12 years, "will test any golfer, especially from the back tees"; the par-5 15th, which flirts with water on all three shots, is typical of the "tough-to-play" layout, but even "hacking good ol' boys" say "I'd go back anytime", especially "when the magnolias and azaleas are in bloom."

Lake Oconee

Cuscowilla 🏌 ⏲ | 27 | 24 | 24 | 21 | $150 |

640 Old Phoenix Rd., Eatonton; 706-484-0050; 800-458-5351;
www.cuscowilla.com; 6847/5348; 72.3/69.6; 130/123
"Walking is a must for the full effect", so lose the cart and make your required caddie work for his tips on this "winner", a "natural", rugged-bunker design "well-worth the journey" southeast from Atlanta; Coore and Crenshaw "outdid themselves" laying out "brilliant" "shotmaking values" and "one of the toughest putting tests you'll experience" on a spread that duffers dub "Georgia's Pinehurst"; "stay in one of the cottages" along the fairway or on Lake Oconee and enjoy the resort's "good community of people."

Harbor Club | ▽ 24 | 19 | 25 | 21 | $79 |

1 Club Dr., Greensboro; 706-453-4414; 800-505-4653;
www.harborclub.com; 6930/5084; 73.7/70.2; 135/123
Perhaps reflecting the disposition of its cantankerous co-architect Tom Weiskopf, this "well-maintained" and "challenging" woodland collaboration with Jay Morrish is a "very hard test of golf"; just ask participants in the 1996 PGA Tour Qualifying Tournament and the Georgia State Open who grappled with tee shots over Lake Oconee

on the 8th, a long par-3, and the 16th, a short par-4; N.B. the course
will be closed until November 2005 during a greens renovation.

Reynolds Plantation,   27 | 25 | 25 | 19 | $195
Great Waters 🏌 ⌐

100 Linger Longer Rd., Greensboro; 706-467-0600; 800-800-5250;
www.reynoldsplantation.com; 7048/5082; 73.8/69.2; 135/114
"There are few things in life better than the last eight" "scenic"
holes "bordering the water" at this "Reynolds favorite"; run by a
"super golf director", Jack Nicklaus' "player-friendly" "challenge"
is "beautiful, quiet and secluded"; "the Ritz is nice" indeed, and
you can "impress your friends" with "the ability to boat to the
course from your [rented] condo"; N.B. look for Jim Engh's slated
2007 spread to compete with it for popularity here.

Reynolds Plantation, National 🏌 ⌐   26 | 24 | 24 | 18 | $165
100 Linger Longer Rd., Greensboro; 706-467-0600; 800-800-5250;
www.reynoldsplantation.com
Bluff/Cove: 7034/5296; 73.8/71.5; 137/127
Ridge/Bluff: 6955/5318; 73.4/71.4; 137/124
Ridge/Cove: 7025/5386; 73.6/71.6; 136/126
In familiar Tom Fazio fashion, this "fantastic" forest foray is
designed for you to "see from tee to green on all" 27 holes, so it will
be clear to you that "every club and shot you have" is required to
nail par; "always in top condition" and graced with hardwoods,
pines and dogwoods, this beauty leads fans "staying in the golf
cabins at the Ritz" to rave that it "might be the closest thing to
Augusta" – even if they "still have not built a clubhouse on it."

Reynolds Plantation, Oconee 🏌 ⌐   26 | 28 | 28 | 18 | $260
100 Linger Longer Rd., Greensboro; 706-467-0600; 800-800-5250;
www.reynoldsplantation.com; 7393/5198; 75.5/70; 143/126
"Those who don't mind dropping money" should drop everything
and play this Rees Jones "treat", a "beautifully manicured"
"challenge" "by the lake" with "no houses in sight"; offering the
"service you would expect" from a spread located "right next to the
Ritz-Carlton", the "staff does a good job spacing out tee times, so
when you're out there, you feel like you have the place to yourself" –
along with your "required caddie" and lots of "wildlife."

Reynolds Plantation,   22 | 24 | 26 | 16 | $165
Plantation 🏌 ⌐

100 Linger Longer Rd., Greensboro; 706-467-0600; 800-800-5250;
www.reynoldsplantation.com; 6698/5121; 71.7/68.9; 128/115
Since emerging from a back-nine greens renovation, this Bob
Cupp/Fuzzy Zoeller/Hubert Green collaboration is now "awesome
in every category, including the price"; its calling-card fairways
roll and ripple past pretty pines and ponds – "this is where I am
planning to die" sigh sports swinging toward that great beyond.

Lowcountry

Hampton Club, The 🏞   21 | 22 | 22 | 23 | $85
100 Tabbystone, Saint Simons Island; 912-634-0255; 800-342-0212;
www.hamptonclub.com; 6465/5233; 71.7/71.3; 137/121
Though the Sea Island Club's courses get the most attention on
St. Simons, The King and Prince resort's "hidden gem at the north

end" of the isle on a former cotton, indigo and rice plantation is "one of the best"; with "wide fairways" and "beautiful greens", the "strong" but "forgiving" layout features a fabulous four-hole fling (Nos. 12–15) that finds you island-hopping through salt marshes and tidal creeks over a network of wooden bridges.

Sea Island, Plantation 🏌 ⛳   25 | 29 | 28 | 21 | $190

100 Retreat Ave., Saint Simons Island; 912-638-5118; 800-732-4752; www.seaisland.com; 7058/5048; 73.9/70.4; 135/122

"When the wind is howling and the Seaside is too tough", take a crack at architect Rees Jones' "inviting" fusion of the original Plantation and Retreat nines, a "beautiful" amalgam accented with towering oaks, vibrant flowerbeds and "ocean views"; for more serenity, repair to the on-site Lodge, which, though "frightfully expensive", combines "Southern hospitality with European elegance", making this "five-star facility" a "must" for an offshore Georgia golf vacation.

Sea Island, Retreat 🏌 ⛳   23 | 28 | 27 | 22 | $190

100 Retreat Ave., Saint Simons Island; 912-638-5118; 800-732-4752; www.seaisland.com; 7000/5100; 73.9/70; 135/119

In 2001, island resident and PGA Tour pro Davis Love III and his brother, Mark, "did a terrific job" transforming the former St. Simons Island Club course into a "wonderful" routing with "mostly wooded fairways"; sure, compared to its dazzling sibling, this one can appear "plain", but with a "very customer service–oriented" staff, it's "a good value" for an "easy" round; the only real drawback is that "it's not at the Lodge."

SEA ISLAND, SEASIDE 🏌 ⛳   27 | 29 | 29 | 23 | $240

100 Retreat Ave., Saint Simons Island; 912-638-5118; 800-732-4752; www.seaisland.com; 7005/5048; 72.3/68.8; 137/120

Tom Fazio's "superb" reincarnation of a Golden Age gallop along the St. Simons Sound is "everything you want in high-end golf, and then some", ranking as Top in Georgia for Course, Facilities and Service; on "strikingly beautiful" grounds with "breathtaking" views of the ocean, marshlands and enormous cedars and oaks, the windswept, linksy layout offers a "hard" but "rewarding" round that, along with the "impeccable" staff and the "first-rate" clubhouse and pro shop, is at the "pinnacle of the Sea Island" experience.

Savannah

Club at Savannah Harbor, The   ▽ 23 | 25 | 22 | 18 | $115

2 Resort Dr.; 912-201-2007; www.theclubatsavannahharbor.net; 7288/5261; 75.1/70.8; 137/124

Credit goes to Bobb Cupp and the late, great Sam Snead for this "tremendous" Champions Tour host on an islet between the Savannah and Back rivers with holes, such as Washington's Guns and Moonshiner's Haven, named to commemorate Southern history and culture; "watch out for gators if you get off the beaten path" or even in the fairway on No. 14, aka Alligator Alley, but a "bug infestation" is a more likely nuisance on this "pricey" but "above-average" Lowcountry layout at a resort that includes a Westin and The Greenbrier Spa.

| C | F | S | V | $ |

Hawaii

★ **Top Courses in State**
28 Kapalua, Plantation, *Maui*
   Princeville, Prince, *Kauai*
   Challenge at Manele, *Lanai*
27 Kauai Lagoons, Kiele, *Kauai*
   Mauna Kea, Mauna Kea Course, *Big Island*

Big Island

HUALALAI ⟳ | 26 | 28 | 29 | 21 | $190 |
100 Kaupulehu Dr., Kaupulehu-Kona; 808-325-8480;
www.hualalairesort.com; 7117/5374; 73.7/65.8; 139/119
If "lava formations on fairways, ponds with fish jumping out of
them" and "spectacular ocean views" ("especially on the 17th
where the waves almost crash at your feet") are "distracting" on
this "gorgeous course", just wait till you get a load of fees made
"even more expensive" because "you have to pay the Four Seasons
hotel rates to be able to play it"; "who cares about losing balls
with this scenery?" ask "Senior Tour" pros of this "neat" Nicklaus
"paradise" with "top-drawer" Facilities and Service that rank
Hawaii's No. 1.

Kona Country Club, Ocean ⛳ | ∇ 22 | 19 | 18 | 21 | $155 |
78-7000 Alii Dr., Kailua-Kona; 808-322-2595; www.konagolf.com;
6700/5400; 72.8/71.7; 129/119
"A great deal" after 1 PM, this "well-maintained" country-club
course sporting "nice views" hosted the Takefuji Classic in 2000
and 2001; LPGA Tour stars who couldn't negotiate the windblown
carries over the jagged lava pits and the ocean – including one
aggravated by a geyserlike blow hole – had a short, 20-minute ride
back to the Keahole International Airport.

Mauna Kea, Mauna Kea Course ⛳ | 27 | 21 | 23 | 19 | $195 |
62-100 Mauna Kea Beach Dr., Kamuela; 808-882-5400;
www.maunakearesort.com; 7124/5277; 75.3/70.2; 142/124
"One of the first of the great island courses", this "classic" RTJ Sr.
design remains "the standard by which others are measured"
because it offers "everything you expect to find in paradise":
"postcard beauty", "lots of variation" and shots "across ocean and
lava", including a "gut check" on the 3rd hole, "one of the scariest
par-3s in the world"; granted, it's "very expensive", but "hey, it's
Hawaii" – and "worth it if you include watching whales offshore"
and taking in the 1,600 Asian and Pacific artworks in the hotel.

Mauna Lani, North | 26 | 25 | 26 | 20 | $195 |
68-1310 Mauna Lani Dr., Kohala; 808-885-6655; www.maunalani.com;
6913/5383; 74/67.2; 135/115
Though "the contrast between the green fairways, black lava and
white sand traps can't be beat", "if you don't hit a straight ball,
bring lots of them" to these "velvet ribbons of emerald winding
through" dormant volcano fields; you'll share the spread with
grazing "wild turkeys" and goats, while non-feral foodies forage
at the CanoeHouse restaurant at a resort where guests get "a
good value" on a round and anyone "paying the afternoon rate"
scores "a steal."

Mauna Lani, South　　　27 | 26 | 26 | 20 |$195

68-1310 Mauna Lani Dr., Kohala; 808-885-6655; www.maunalani.com;
6938/5128; 72.8/69.6; 133/117

Though the "unbelievable ocean views" and fairways that "wind through a licorice-colored" landscape make this former site of the Senior Skins Game "like playing golf on a postcard", beware: "the lava eats balls", so "bring your Fred Flintstone wedge", or hope they bounce off a dormant volcanic rock and "come right back at you"; taken with a staff that "learns your name immediately and remembers it forever", the entire experience is "a feast for the eyes and soul."

Waikoloa Beach Resort, Beach 🏌　21 | 20 | 21 | 18 |$175

1020 Keana Pl., Waikoloa; 808-886-6060; www.waikoloabeachresort.com;
6566/5094; 71.6/64.8; 134/115

"Lava, lava and more lava makes for an exciting challenge" at this Robert Trent Jones Jr. layout that is "always in great shape" for those "Kodak" moments "along the shoreline", including at the signature par-5 12th that practically dives off the edge of a cliff high above the pounding surf; afterward, "relax with a beverage" in the "clubhouse restaurant filled with colorful locals", and you've got "a great way to spend the day."

Waikoloa Beach Resort, Kings 🏌　23 | 21 | 21 | 18 |$175

1020 Keana Pl., Waikoloa; 808-886-7888; 877-924-5656;
www.waikoloabeachresort.com; 7074/5459; 73.4/66.3; 135/116

In addition to the "mountain views" and "well-maintained" grass, one of the best features of this "resort track" "carved out of the lava" is that it "doesn't feel resorty"; this is thanks to architects Tom Weiskopf and Jay Morrish whose design "looks easy but challenges your course management", especially when the "Waiko-blow-a" winds steer your balls into the volcanic "rough" – which is "really rough" rough – "making St. Andrews look like mini golf."

Kauai

Kauai Lagoons, Kiele 🏌　27 | 25 | 24 | 21 |$170

3351 Hoolaulea Way, Lihue; 808-241-6000; 800-634-6400;
www.kauailagoonsgolf.com; 7070/5417; 75.2/67.7; 140/121

"The more challenging of the two at Lagoons" is a "phenomenal" Jack Nicklaus "experience" for its "fantastic back nine above the ocean" and "breathtaking views of Nawiliwili Harbor"; a properly timed tee shot on the "stunning par-3s", including the 17th, which must carry the ocean, will take on the "roar of the jets from nearby Lihue Airport", then ride the "tropical breezes" down to the "well-bunkered" greens.

Kauai Lagoons, Mokihana　　19 | 24 | 24 | 22 |$120

3351 Hoolaulea Way, Lihue; 808-241-6000; 800-634-6400;
www.kauailagoonsgolf.com; 6960/5607; 73/66.8; 126/110

It's "less expensive and attractive than Kiele", but this "Hawaiian links" layout by Jack Nicklaus is "almost as good as its brother" and still manages to deliver some "wonderful island views"; take advantage of the benign tee shots, because approaches to the rippling greens fortified with unique mounding and bunkers are "challenging" indeed.

Poipu Bay

| 26 | 25 | 24 | 21 | $185 |

2250 Ainako St., Koloa; 808-742-8711; 800-858-6300;
www.poipubaygolf.com; 7081/5372; 73.9/70.4; 134/122

The host of the Grand Slam of Golf, this RTJ Jr. design hits "a home run" with "goosebump"-inducing "coastline views" and "huge winds that make an awesome course even more challenging"; the "great attitude of the staff" and on-course remains of ancient *heiau* (places of worship) – not to mention "deeply discounted locals" – solidify its reputation as "the epitome of Hawaiian golf."

Princeville, Makai

| 21 | 21 | 22 | 19 | $125 |

5520 Ka Haku Rd., Princeville; 808-826-9644; 800-826-4400;
www.princeville.com
Ocean/Lakes: 6306/5516; 70.5/69.9; 127/116
Ocean/Woods: 6365/5631; 70.4/70.4; 126/116
Woods/Lakes: 6357/5543; 70.1/69.6; 125/115

Though it "doesn't compare to the Prince", this formation is no frog, as island hoppers jump at the chance to play its "27 holes of sheer pleasure" for the same "unbelievable vistas" as on its brother but at a more "affordable" price; there are "lots of contrasts between each nine", but they're all "easy", so "even if you're a beginner, you can relax here" – unless you're a neat freak and can't abide by its "suffering maintenance."

PRINCEVILLE, PRINCE

| 28 | 26 | 25 | 20 | $175 |

5520 Ka Haku Rd., Princeville; 808-826-9644; 800-826-4400;
www.princeville.com; 7309/5338; 75.3/72; 145/127

"Playing through a tropical rain forest" amid the "ocean, mountains and waterfalls", this RTJ Jr. design is simultaneously "one of the prettiest courses known to man" and "one of the toughest", a "ball-eating monster" armed with "blind shots", "forced carries" and "no recovery" options from "the jungle"; given "a serious whooping if the wind is up and a moderate beating if not", by the time you putt out on the 18th, "you've earned that martini."

Puakea

| 23 | 15 | 22 | 23 | $125 |

4150 Nuhou St., Lihue; 808-245-8756; 866-773-5554; www.puakeagolf.com;
6954/5225; 73.5/69.3; 135/113

Not even 1992's Hurricane Iniki, which originally halted work on eight holes, could keep this "unknown gem in Lihue" from its appointed rounds; it's "a real sleeper, now that it is a full 18" fairways of "inspired, bold yet not overbearing" golf punctuated by "spectacular views" of Mount Haupu; the "dramatic" routing, utilizing the "ever-present wind" from "all four directions", is "genius", as was new owner (and former AOL chairman) Steve Case's re-hiring of architect Robin Nelson to finish the job.

Wailua

| 22 | 14 | 17 | 25 | $44 |

3-5351 Kuhio Hwy., Kapaa; 808-246-2793; www.gvhawaii.com;
6981/5974; 73.3/73.4; 129/119

If you're not made of moolah, and "you want to play every day you're in Hawaii", join "all the locals" "who recognize the best value in the islands" on this "great muni" "warm-up" to the "big-bucks" spreads; sure, the facilities are bare-bones, but "it's well groomed", you can "keep a nice, leisurely pace" and there are "spectacular ocean views on several holes" – all that and plenty of "sandtraps" too, for under $50 a round.

Lanai

CHALLENGE AT MANELE ⌂   28 | 27 | 27 | 21 | $225
1 Manele Bay Rd., Lanai City; 808-565-2222; www.lanai-resorts.com;
7039/5024; 73.7/68.8; 135/119
"Those who know golf understand" it's "worth going to Lanai just
for this" "exciting" Nicklaus "gem" with "postcard views on every
hole", "greens so manicured they could melt a heart" and "no
crowds"; even if the "friendly, helpful staff" does let you "play all
day for one fee", it's "expensive", partly because the "challenging
carries over the Pacific Ocean" (where "whales and dolphins play"
"150 feet below") make it a "golf ball disposal machine."

EXPERIENCE AT KOELE ⌂ ⊕   27 | 25 | 26 | 20 | $225
1 Keamoku Dr., Lanai City; 808-565-4653; www.lanai-resorts.com;
7014/5425; 75.3/72.6; 143/130
With "deer, pheasant" and "wild turkeys trotting across fairways"
lined with trees, not only does this "dramatic" Greg Norman design
"on top of Lanai" look "like you're in New England", but the
"weather at the higher altitude is not typical of Hawaii", either; "no
matter the conditions at the beach, bring a jacket", "your wind
game" and "vertigo" pills for holes like No. 17, "one of the world's
most spectacular" – launching a shot "through a belt of fog" to the
green 250 feet below will have you "feeling like Superman."

Maui

Dunes at Maui Lani   22 | 18 | 19 | 22 | $110
1333 Maui Lani Pkwy., Kahului; 808-873-7911; www.dunesatmauilani.com;
6841/4768; 73.5/67.9; 136/114
"You feel like you might be in Europe on some holes" on "underrated
architect Robin Nelson's" "links", a "different Hawaiian course"
winding through natural sand dunes (rather than lava rock) "in a
valley" where "the wind howls in the afternoon"; since it's "not
affiliated with a resort", this "nice alternative" tends to attract "lots
of locals" who praise it as the "best value on Maui."

KAPALUA, BAY 廿 ⌂   24 | 24 | 24 | 20 | $200
300 Kapalua Dr., Kapalua; 808-669-8044; 877-527-2582;
www.kapaluamaui.com; 6600/5124; 69.2/69.6; 133/121
If you're susceptible to sticker shock, "sign the credit card slip
with your eyes closed" before taking in the hilltop "views of the
ocean" from Kapalua's original course; the scenery is so "majestic"
that you might "take more pictures than golf shots", particularly
since this is "the most forgiving of the three layouts" here; but
even if "the trades start blowing" your balls astray, it's the "vistas
that will be remembered long after your score is forgotten."

KAPALUA, PLANTATION 廿 ⌂   28 | 27 | 25 | 21 | $250
2000 Plantation Club Dr., Kapalua; 808-669-8044; 877-527-2582;
www.kapaluamaui.com; 7263/5627; 74.9/73.2; 138/129
"You'll never watch the Mercedes Championship the same way
again" after tussling with this refurbished Crenshaw/Coore design,
where "idyllic views of the Pacific and neighboring mansions"
combine with "monstrous fairways", "majestic swales" and
"elevation changes galore" to form "paradise with teeth"; it can be
"tough to get a tee time" at Hawaii's Top Course, so "try the sunset

special" when the "expensive" fees and "crowds" go down, but the "treacherous winds" and pace of play pick up.

Kapalua, Village 🏌🛺　　　21 | 24 | 23 | 18 |$185

2000 Village Rd., Kapalua; 808-669-8044; 877-527-2582;
www.kapaluamaui.com; 6378/4896; 71.9/68; 135/116

For those who don't want to "pony up for the Plantation", this "least crowded" Kapalua course can be "just as much fun" for an "unpretentious romp through the Maui countryside, with gorgeous views of Molokai", including the one from No. 7, which is 800 feet above sea level; nature lovers especially like that "it displays the flora and fauna of the island extremely well", while bird dogs dig that it begins and ends with par-3s.

Makena, North　　　25 | 19 | 21 | 20 |$175

5415 Makena Alanui, Makena; 808-879-3344; 800-321-6284;
www.makenagolf.com; 6567/5303; 72.1/70.9; 139/128

Flag down the beverage cart and fuel up with "the best breakfast burritos on the island" before taking on the newer of the pair of "lush" "gems" at Makena because you'll "climb the back of Mt. Haleakala" for "fantastic ocean views" before "winding back to the shore"; along the way, most of the "diverse" holes emphasize "shotmaking value", which, taken with its "remote location", likely "cuts down on crowds" that just want to let their big dog eat.

Makena, South　　　24 | 19 | 22 | 21 |$180

5415 Makena Alanui, Makena; 808-879-3344; 800-321-6284;
www.makenagolf.com; 7014/5489; 72.6/71.1; 138/130

Time your round so you're "on 15 or 16 around sunset" as these "two holes along the ocean" provide "beautiful" "Molokini views" in a "less crowded", more "quiet setting" than other island courses, epitomizing what "makes this track worth playing"; even during the rare times when "they need to take better care of fairways and tee boxes", the friendly, PGA-trained staff "makes it more palatable."

Wailea, Blue 🛺　　　23 | 21 | 24 | 19 |$145

100 Wailea Golf Club Dr., Wailea; 808-875-7450; 888-328-6284;
www.waileagolf.com; 6765/5208; 72.2/69.3; 129/117

Never mind that its wide fairways and large greens make this the "easiest of the three courses" at Wailea: you can always "play from the tips" to increase the "fun" and the depth of the "magnificent views" of the ocean, Mt. Haleakala and the flowering "plumeria trees that line the fairways"; though parts of the clubhouse "could use an upgrade", Mulligan's is as good as it gets, a delightfully out-of-place Irish pub where shepherd's pie is served side-by-side with sashimi.

Wailea, Emerald 🛺　　　26 | 25 | 25 | 20 |$155

100 Wailea Golf Club Dr., Wailea; 808-875-7450; 888-328-6284;
www.waileagolf.com; 6825/5256; 71.7/69.5; 130/114

The "dazzling views" of the "ocean and other islands from almost every hole" make the "prettiest of the three" courses "the real jewel at Wailea"; it's also a "confidence builder", "especially for women", because Robert Trent Jones Jr. "creatively shortened the course" while "leaving trouble in play"; save your money, skip the "video of your tee shot they try to sell you" and spend it instead in the SeaWatch Restaurant, where "you will enjoy no better sunset."

Wailea, Gold 🏌　　　　　25 | 22 | 23 | 19 | $155
100 Wailea Golf Club Dr., Wailea; 808-875-7450; 888-328-6284;
www.waileagolf.com; 7078/5317; 73.4/70.1; 137/119
"Hey, the big boys from the Senior Tour play here" in the Champions
Skins Game, so follow suit and take the "short drive from the hotel"
to wrestle with the "toughest of the Wailea courses", another "gold
standard" from RTJ Jr. that bobs and weaves through lava rock and
kiawe trees; bring along the whole family and let 'em watch you get
skinned, since the "fantastic" scenery, "unbelievable pro shop" and
"great restaurant" make it "worth the trip for non-golfers", too.

Oahu

Kapolei 🏌　　　　　▽ 20 | 19 | 19 | 17 | $140
91-701 Farrington Hwy., Kapolei; 808-674-2227;
7001/5490; 72.7/71.9; 134/124
Across Pearl Harbor from Honolulu in Oahu's second city, this
Ted Robinson design hosted the LPGA Tour's Hawaiian Ladies
Open until 2001; a "windy" and water-laden "resort" course "easily
managed" and enjoyed, it features No. 10's island tee and a
finishing hole that caps off the round with the sight and sound of
a cascading waterfall.

Ko'olau　　　　　　　25 | 20 | 21 | 23 | $130
45-550 Kionaole Rd., Kaneohe; 808-247-7088; www.koolaugolfclub.com;
7310/5102; 76.4/72.9; 152/134
"If your game doesn't defy gravity", then plan a post-round soul-
soothing at Don Ho's mom Honey's restaurant because "the
toughest course on U.S. soil" forces "long, difficult" "carries over
dense vegetation", and if you miss the fairway, "you're in the
rain forest" amid "mountains that shoot straight up 2,000 feet";
granted, tough "isn't always fun, but this is", so either "bring lots of
balls – both kinds", or "bring a machete", plus "your oldest shoes"
to slosh across the "soggy", "junglelike terrain."

Ko Olina　　　　　　　23 | 23 | 24 | 18 | $160
92-1220 Aliinui Dr., Kapolei; 808-676-5309; www.koolinagolf.com;
6867/5361; 72.3/71.8; 135/126
"Riding your cart under a waterfall" amid "ocean views" is fun, but
it's "the right mix" of holes that makes this "lush" Ted Robinson
design "near the beautiful JW Marriott Ihilani and Ko Olina Resort"
"a pleasure to play", meaning "it's challenging, but not such that
you want to toss your clubs"; despite the "top-notch staff" and
opportunity to "dine at Roy's (as in Yamaguchi) afterward",
"the course is never crowded", perhaps because it's "a bit of a
drive" from Honolulu.

Luana Hills　　　　　　▽ 21 | 20 | 21 | 21 | $120
770 Auloa Rd., Kailua; 808-262-2139; www.luanahills.com;
6595/4654; 70.9/61.7; 136/117
The verdant Maunawili Valley is perfect for the "wild boars" that
roam here, but the "*Jurassic Park*"–like landscape "is hard for
tourists to play" across, particularly given the "blind shots" to
bountifully buttressed fairways and green on this "hard", "target
golf" design by Pete Dye; it's like a "lighter" and "less expensive
version of Ko'olau" with an actual 19th hole, a peninsula-green
par-3 that sometimes substitutes for No. 12.

Makaha　　　　　　21　15　17　19　$140
84-626 Makaha Valley Rd., Waianae; 808-695-9544;
www.makaharesort.com; 7077/5856; 74.3/73.9; 137/129
"If you're willing to drive" an hour or so from the airport, you will come across this "beautiful resort course" "hidden in a valley in west Oahu"; despite your typical Hawaii-style "breathtaking views of the Pacific", it's "usually not crowded", perhaps because the "hard-to-read greens" and sometimes severe "wind" can make it "one tough baby" – and the potentially "rude" staff ain't easy, either.

Pearl Country Club 🖾　　　20　15　14　20　$110
98-535 Kaonohi St., Aiea; 808-487-3802; www.pearlcc.com;
6787/5536; 72.7/67.1; 136/120
Located at the base of the Ko'olau mountain range, this "solid" course owned by the founder of Honda Motor Company is "very hilly with big changes in elevation" to "fast greens" offering "great views of Pearl Harbor"; though the high-profile same-named "Open is played here every year", it remains mainly the province of "locals", sometimes even making it "difficult for a single visitor to get a tee time."

Royal Kunia 🖾　　　▽ 26　11　16　22　$135
94-1509 Anonui St., Waipahu; 808-688-9222; www.royalkuniacc.com;
7007/4945; 73.8/68.1; 135/110
"What a blessing the money issues were sorted out" because this "Robin Nelson masterpiece" – the course with the longest grow-in time in history (completed in 1993, opened in 2003) – finally has a "chance to be great"; its "wonderful variety" of "interesting" holes afford "great views of Pearl Harbor", but don't get too distracted, as you have to "think your way around the course, taking the wind into consideration on many shots", including on the back-to-back, 600-plus-yd. par-5s at the turn.

Turtle Bay, Arnold Palmer　　　25　22　22　19　$165
57-049 Kuilima Dr., Kahuku; 808-293-8574; www.turtlebayresort.com;
7199/4851; 74.4/64.3; 143/121
No wonder Arnold Palmer chose to marry on this namesake in 2004 just before the Champions Tour's annual stop – the "views are amazing" from the "oceanfront setting" of this "absolutely gorgeous course"; but if you're going to take shots instead of vows, you'll "have to be able to shape them" around "a lot of dogleg holes", negotiate a "number of carries over water" and manage "loads of surprises" courtesy of its "remote location" surrounding the Punaho'olapa Marsh, a wetlands preserve and bird sanctuary.

Turtle Bay, George Fazio　　　▽ 19　23　23　20　$155
57-049 Kuilima Dr., Kahuku; 808-293-8574; www.turtlebayresort.com;
6535/5355; 71.2/70.2; 130/116
Though it's "not as interesting as the Palmer", George Fazio's only design on the island "is getting better with age"; the "friendly" staff at the "fun" thirtysomething layout, former host of the LPGA Hawaiian Open and site of the first Senior Skins Game, helps make it "worth the trip to the North Shore if you have an extra day", and since most of the Turtle Bay action is on its sister spread, you can "feel like you have this course to yourself."

Idaho

Coeur d'Alene

Circling Raven
– | – | – | – | $79

US Hwy. 95, Worley; 800-523-2464; www.cdacasino.com;
7189/4708; 74.5/66.6; 140/122
"I defy anyone to find fault with this golf club" declare duffers
defending "one of the most beautiful tracks you'll ever play on",
a track that twists through ponderosa pines and hopscotches
wetlands on its wildlife-laced journey; outside the forest primeval
is the jumping, on-property Coeur d'Alene Casino, but out on the
course, the main action is on the par-3s, where most whackers
warn "you better make sure you hit straight."

Coeur d'Alene Resort 🏌 ⏲
27 | 27 | 29 | 21 | $225

900 Floating Green Dr.; 208-667-4653; 800-688-5253; www.cdaresort.com;
6735/4448; 71.1/64.4; 119/105
From the "generous fairways and mandatory, ball-finding caddies"
to the "beautifully groomed" grounds considered "among the best
in the country", this "epitome of a resort course" with "gorgeous
lake views" offers "the most pampered golf" – "although you
definitely pay for it"; technically, it's not "cart-path-only all the time"
because to reach the moveable, "floating green" on the 14th hole,
you have to leave the pavement for the water via a small boat.

Sun Valley

Sun Valley Resort 🏌
▽ 19 | 17 | 20 | 18 | $145

1 Sun Valley Rd.; 208-622-2251; 800-786-8259; www.sunvalley.com;
6938/5380; 72.5/68.6; 141/125
Go ahead and play the four holes from the special, beyond-blue
tees at this Robert Trent Jones Jr. redo of a 1936 original because
"the ball flies at this elevation" and, from way back there, the
"fantastic vistas" of Bald Mountain produce their full effect; just be
sure to take a cart or the "elevation could kill you", if the "narrow
fairways" that constantly jump Trail Creek don't get you first;
granted, it's "expensive" for a track that "needs a new clubhouse",
but you may get to "play with a star" because this spread "still
charms" plebs and celebs alike.

Illinois

★ **Top Courses in State**
28 Cog Hill, No. 4 (Dubsdread), *Chicago*
27 Eagle Ridge, The General, *Galena*
   Thunderhawk, *Chicago*
   Annbriar, *Peoria*
26 Cantigny, *Chicago*

Chicago

Big Run
22 | 13 | 14 | 20 | $67

17211 W. 135th St., Lockport; 815-838-1057; www.bigrungolf.com;
7050/5420; 74.6/72; 142/130
"Bring your long game" because "they don't call it Big Run for
nothing", though the "killer hills", "uneven lies" and "many trees

that punish stray balls" also help make this "wonderful old course" really "difficult"; it "could use a driving range" and "the clubhouse is a relic" – "don't expect tablecloth service" – but the "fun" "challenge" of the "great topography" keeps it "crowded, even during the week."

Cantigny 🕴

26 | 24 | 24 | 20 | $85

27 W. 270 Mack Rd., Wheaton; 630-668-3323; www.cantignygolf.com
Hillside/Lakeside: 6831/5183; 72.6/70.1; 131/119
Lakeside/Woodside: 7004/5425; 73.9/71.9; 138/127
Woodside/Hillside: 6961/5236; 73.5/70.3; 132/120

This "high-end" 27-holer on the estate of former *Chicago Tribune* publisher Robert McCormick "reminds you of the way golf used to be": "a little short but a great challenge" with "nice diversity" in a "country club–like atmosphere" complete with a thriving caddie program; with its "Dick Tracy bunker" on No. 9, the "Lakeside course seems to be a crowd favorite", but "always friendly and accommodating service" and "gorgeous landscaping" throughout make the "entire experience top-notch."

Chalet Hills 🏑

23 | 19 | 20 | 21 | $79

943 Rawson Bridge Rd., Cary; 847-639-0666; www.chaletgolf.com;
6877/4934; 73.6/69.1; 137/121

Architect Ken Killian says this "awesome" redesign "in the far northern suburbs" is his greatest work, thanks to natural "elevation changes", 200-year-old trees that pinch the "narrow fairways" and lakes, creeks and wetlands on 13 of the 18 "tough" holes, including the island-green 17th; "if the course were closer to the city, it would get a lot more play" because it's "usually in great condition."

Cog Hill, No. 2 (The Ravines) 🕴

21 | 21 | 21 | 21 | $52

12294 Archer Ave., Lemont; 630-257-5872; www.coghillgolf.com;
6576/5639; 71.3/72.8; 126/121

"If you can't afford or get a tee time on Dubs", the "best of the rest at Cog" is a "very affordable alternative"; "shorter with fewer bunkers" but still an option for "challenge and interest", Bert Coghill's 1929 "classic parkland course" is not only well priced, it's "well treed" and "well maintained" by people "who know how to extend a good golfing experience."

COG HILL, NO. 4 (DUBSDREAD) 🕴

28 | 21 | 21 | 20 | $132

12294 Archer Ave., Lemont; 630-257-5872; www.coghillgolf.com;
6940/5590; 75.4/70.6; 142/133

"You thought you could play golf, but let this course show you otherwise" say bunker blasters bitter that the home of the PGA Tour's Western Open has "more sand than the Sahara", making it "much tougher than it looks on TV"; still, it's "impossible not to fall in love" with this "American classic", a "refreshing, old-style" spread with "bigger-than-life trees and greens" and "no throwaway holes"; some swingers say service "could improve" on Illinois' No. 1 Course, since the "ornery rangers" might be dubbed Duffers' Dread.

Glen Club, The 🕴

26 | 26 | 23 | 14 | $155

2901 W. Lake Ave., Glenview; 847-724-7272; 7149/5324; 74.5/71.5; 138/127

"It's hard to believe" the Nationwide Tour's La Salle Bank Open venue "was once completely flat" Naval "aircraft runways", but thanks to Tom Fazio's "amazing earth moving", it now falls 40 feet and features fairways so full of fescue that "when it's windy and rainy, you'll swear you can hear bagpipes"; the fees are "terribly expensive", though, so it "caters to corporate clients" clamoring for "facilities that are second to none", including lodging "with balconies overlooking the course."

Harborside International, Port   25 | 23 | 22 | 21 | $92

11001 S. Doty Ave.; 312-782-7837; www.harborsideinternational.com; 7123/5164; 75.1/69.4; 132/120

"Who cares that you glow after you play this great links" atop "a former landfill" "surrounded by some of the most beautiful paint factories in America?" – it's still "a lot of course for a muni", given its "great driving range" and "true Scottish" feel complete with "flawlessly conditioned" "high mounds", "tall grass" and "constant wind"; "you don't need a weather vane to know which way it blows" because "some days it can smell", and as for "the black goo bubbling up from below", just "watch where you toss your stogie."

Harborside International, Starboard   25 | 23 | 22 | 21 | $92

11001 S. Doty Ave.; 312-782-7837; www.harborsideinternational.com; 7104/5110; 75/68.8; 132/118

Known for its "excellent practice facilities" and "pretty cool views of the Sears Tower", the second 18 of these "36 holes close to the city" is a "mirror of the Port course" in that the linksy landfill is "devilish when the wind is blowing" (which tends to be "all the time"), while "the long grass eats golf balls for lunch"; also, "like its twin, it's a long haul to the finish", so start early or you'll have to "watch out for the gnats and coyotes" that show up at dusk.

Heritage Bluffs   24 | 15 | 17 | 24 | $46

24355 W. Bluff Rd., Channahon; 815-467-7888; www.heritagebluffs.com; 7106/4967; 73.9/68.6; 138/114

Just remember, "it's all about the golf" at this "unpretentious" muni with "some prairie-style holes and others carved out of the woods"; the "layout and challenge are exceptional", but "the conditions vary" from "well kept" to "terrible", and "the clubhouse is less than memorable"; it is, however, "an outstanding value" "for the budget-minded", and the grill's one-pound, three-cheese Bluff Burger will fill your tank for the "long drive" back to Chicago.

Naperbrook   18 | 18 | 17 | 22 | $58

22204 W. 111th St., Plainfield; 630-378-4215; www.naperbrookgolfcourse.org; 6755/5381; 72.2/70.1; 125/118

Built in 1991, this "links-style" muni is considered "above-average", partly because it's so "well maintained" and partly because the "open" layout "is a good test for all players", especially when there's "lots of wind" knocking shots about; you might even consider moving to this "upscale community" to play it often, as it's "a great value if you are a Naperville resident."

Oak Brook   18 | 16 | 18 | 22 | $50

2606 York Rd., Oak Brook; 630-990-3032; www.oak-brook.org; 6541/5341; 71.1/70.7; 126/120

"Play from as far back as you can" because this muni "next to Butler National" is "a little short"; despite expansions and renovations in 2000 that created "some of the best greens for a public" course and helped make it "crowded and slow on the weekends", it's "nothing fancy, just a solid spread" with "lots of doglegs and lakes" and "service and facilities that fall short like a missed putt."

Orchard Valley

26 | 22 | 21 | 24 | $57

2411 W. Illinois Ave., Aurora; 630-907-0500; www.orchardvalleygolf.com; 6745/5162; 72.8/70.9; 134/128

"Bring your ball retriever" because "almost every hole has water" on this "thinking-man's course" presenting "numerous risk/reward opportunities" over wetlands and lakes to bulkheaded fairways and greens; a "wonderful, upscale" "value" with "consistently good conditions", it's so "well managed in every regard" that it "doesn't feel like a Park District course", but it's "a long drive from Chicago", so "only its location prevents it from shining."

Pine Meadow

24 | 17 | 18 | 20 | $77

1 Pine Meadow Ln., Mundelein; 847-566-4653; www.pinemeadowgc.com; 7141/5203; 74.6/70.1; 138/126

Cog Hill's "Jemseks run a good golf program" at their "Dubsdread of the north side" where the "diversity of challenges" on a "variety" of "holes surrounded by forest preserves and lakes" gets "even better when you walk it"; now, if only the "rangers would lighten up a little bit", the course, "built on the grounds of a seminary", would really feel like "another world" where, "if you can't read the undulating greens, you won't have a prayer."

Plum Tree National

20 | 17 | 18 | 20 | $65

19511 Lembcke Rd., Harvard; 815-943-7474; www.plumtreegolf.com; 6648/5760; 71.8/73.1; 130/129

Located between Woodstock and Harvard in McHenry County, this "once great tournament course" "still has some bite", as well as some "very nice employees" who make it "easy to get a tee time" on "challenging holes" including the signature par-4 8th wedged between a lake and a bunker-strewn sidehill lie; however, this 35-year-old track "has not aged well" and "course conditions tend to be somewhat variable", so the experience here is "sometimes very good, sometimes very average."

Prairie Landing

24 | 22 | 20 | 20 | $96

2325 Longest Dr., West Chicago; 630-208-7600; www.prairielanding.com; 6950/4859; 73.2/68.3; 136/116

Do yourself a favor and "play the [three] practice holes" at this "upscale, links-style" layout by Robert Trent Jones Jr. because "wind is always a factor" and, if you let it steer your shots into the "knee-high rough just off the fairway", "the course can really eat you up"; as it's located "next to DuPage Airport", its name makes some sense, but rather than flat, homogeneous runways, these "diverse" holes offer "plenty of playing options", so "be prepared to think about every shot."

Ruffled Feathers

23 | 22 | 20 | 16 | $99

1 Pete Dye Dr., Lemont; 630-257-1000; www.ruffledfeathersgc.com; 6898/5273; 74.1/71.7; 140/129

"The only Pete Dye course in the area" is "gorgeous" and "surrounded by homes of equal beauty", but some say it's "guaranteed to ruffle your feathers", either through the "mean-spirited design", the fees that are "too expensive" or the staff's "country-club attitude"; "bring your best game" to this "South Side" scoundrel only if you're looking for a course that "really tests your skills", or the "tough forced carries" and tons of "pot bunkers" can turn its 18 holes into "18 headaches."

Schaumburg ▽ 20 | 17 | 17 | 22 | $60
401 N. Roselle Rd., Schaumburg; 847-885-9000; www.parkfun.com
Baer/Players: 6525/4871; 70.4/67.4; 118/113
Players/Tournament: 6412/4892; 69.8/67.4; 119/112
Tournament/Baer: 6559/4900; 70.5/67.2; 121/114
Way back when, the Schaumburg Park District "renovated a deteriorating property" from the 1920s and created this 27-hole "surprising find" with bent-grass fairways and strategically placed bunkers where now "you get your money's worth"; it's an especially "great value for the locals" and, thus, it "can be very crowded and slow", but pop inside the prairie-style clubhouse for the daily specials at Chandler's Chop House, and all is right with the world.

Seven Bridges 🏌 20 | 19 | 19 | 15 | $99
1 Mulligan Dr., Woodridge; 630-964-7777; www.sevenbridges.com;
7103/5262; 74.6/65.6; 135/114
It "would be nice to warm up" before embarking on "the suicide mission" that comprises this "pricey" place's opening "wet nine", a collection of holes "with water on either side" and "domed fairways" that slope toward it, but, alas, there's no driving range; regardless, this outing and event specialist "still seems to pack them in" mainly because it is "generally well run and waits are minimal", a real surprise since it "eats up low-handicappers" and hackers with equal aplomb.

Shepherd's Crook ▽ 22 | 18 | 21 | 25 | $42
43125 Greenbay Rd., Zion; 847-872-2080; www.shepherdscrook.org;
6769/4901; 72.1/67.7; 128/115
Even though "it's a pain to drive to", "serious golfers should flock to this course", a 1999 Keith Foster muni known to be a "very good value" considering you're grazing across a links-style layout woven with bent grass from tee to green, where some of the "tricked-up" putting surfaces will truly test your prowess; truth be told, "the last 12 holes are the reason to play here" so, if you can initially get past "the stench" from the "garbage dump" nearby, it's not b-a-a-d.

Steeple Chase 22 | 18 | 18 | 21 | $71
200 N. La Vista Dr., Mundelein; 847-949-8900; 6827/4831; 73.1/68.2; 136/118
"For the golfer that loves variety", this 1993 Mundelein Parks muni, which is "usually in impeccable shape", "challenges all aspects of the game" with "some great holes", lots of water and "not many flat lies"; however, the golfer that likes a proper warm-up might be put off because there's "no driving range", only two hitting nets that, like the course, "can get crowded at peak times."

Stonewall Orchard 26 | 20 | 21 | 21 | $74
25675 W. Hwy. 60, Grayslake; 847-740-4890; www.stonewallorchard.com;
7074/5375; 74.1/71.2; 140/126
This "sleeper" might be "immature", but suburban swingers say golf "can't get any better, especially at this price", as the 1999 track is "extremely well conditioned", and Arthur Hills' "imaginative layout" provides "lots of different looks" across "diverse terrain";

just make sure you play from the proper box, because the "regular tees require a long ball" to negotiate the many "forced carries" over water that could stonewall your progress toward a decent score.

Thunderhawk

27 23 22 22 $98

39700 N. Lewis Ave., Beach Park; 847-872-4295; www.lcfpd.org;
7031/5046; 73.8/69.2; 136/122

"You could slip this in on the tour and nobody would complain" because "one of the best courses owned by a government" is "a beauty" designed by RTJ Jr., who crafted "challenging yet fair holes" that are "generous at times" but "really test your accuracy" at others when, "if you stray, you pay"; surprisingly, it "does not seem to get much play", perhaps because it's "a hike from Chicago" and the "price is too high for non-residents" of Lake County.

Water's Edge

20 18 18 21 $65

7205 W. 115th St., Worth; 708-671-1032; www.watersedgegolf.com;
6904/5332; 72.9/70.4; 131/122

"Don't let its less-than-scenic location dampen your enthusiasm" because this Rick Robbins and Gary Koch collaboration with the Saganashkee Slough bordering its south side "has water, trees, marsh, elevation and everything else that makes golf fun", plus a "great practice area" that's lit for sundown sand shots; taken with the "friendly starters" and cart rates that are "a steal", this truly is "a diamond in the rough, or at least a cubic zirconium."

Galena

Eagle Ridge, North

24 23 25 21 $165

444 Eagle Ridge Dr.; 815-777-2444; www.eagleridge.com;
6875/5578; 73.2/72.1; 132/125

"Set on rolling hills" in Illinois' "lovely" northwest corner, this "outstanding" layout affords "beautiful water views", such as the one from the tee box on No. 8, a 165-yd. par-3 that drops 80 feet and forces a shot across the corner of Lake Galena; it's "part of a great resort" with the No. 1 Service in the state, so it's "usually in good shape", but penny-pinching putters call it "overpriced" for "rounds that can be long if it's crowded."

Eagle Ridge, South

24 23 24 20 $165

444 Eagle Ridge Dr.; 815-777-2444; www.eagleridge.com;
6762/5609; 72.7/72.3; 134/129

A "good breather after The General", this wooded, streamside spread still manages to be "fun" while offering "scenic views" of the "beautiful land" at Eagle Ridge resort; granted, "it needs a range on-site", since "having one five minutes down the road doesn't account for this kind of money", but with "great conditions" and pace of play that "rarely backs up", "it's hard not to like."

Eagle Ridge, The General

27 24 24 21 $165

444 Eagle Ridge Dr.; 815-777-2444; www.eagleridge.com;
6820/5337; 73.7/71.8; 141/128

"You've got to be a straight shooter" when you're waging war with this "scenic" but "severe" spread sporting "some of the narrowest fairways" around; "lots of bold contouring and risk/reward" options mean "nearly every hole could be a signature", but you'll have to advance your cart battalion "on the path all the time", which ensures "impeccable conditions" but also a "long day" with "lots of additional walking" to win this uphill "hell" of a battle.

Moline

TPC at Deere Run
▽ 29 | 26 | 23 | 22 | $70

3100 Heather Knoll, Silvis; 309-796-6000; 877-872-3677; www.tpcatdeererun.com; 7183/5179; 75.1/70.1; 134/119

It's easy to "see why the PGA Tour moved" "the home of the John Deere Classic" to this former horse farm in 2000 – for a "newer course", it "looks as if it has been here for a long time" as it "fits the land very well and does not look contrived"; plus, sitting between the Rock and Mississippi rivers, it offers "true tournament playing conditions" including "plenty of water to test your mettle and tricky holes to test your skill" at executing a variety of shots.

Peoria

Annbriar
27 | 22 | 24 | 24 | $69

1524 Birdie Ln., Waterloo; 618-939-4653; 888-939-5191; www.annbriar.com; 6863/4792; 72.8/66.4; 136/110

The "links holes to start" on this "gem" are a "windy" "change from the usual Midwest course", and "then you go to Augusta National for the final" stretch, with "awesome Nos. 11 and 14" highlighting the "best nine in all of St. Louis"; it's "quite a drive from Downtown", but it's "worth it" for "lots of good memories" from the tee-off onto a layout with "no houses around" to a post-round pig-out on pulled pork at the Smokehouse.

WeaverRidge
▽ 26 | 24 | 22 | 22 | $73

5100 Weaverridge Blvd.; 309-691-3344; www.weaverridge.com; 7030/5046; 73.1/68.9; 136/115

This "local favorite" that bobs between "bluffs and lowlands" is a "real surprise" to first-timers who can't believe the "old-looking", "scenic" Hurdzan/Fry layout has only been around for "less than 10 years"; it's "challenging" for better players but "not too difficult for the average golfer", as per this design duo's devoted directive.

Rockford

Aldeen
– | – | – | – | $45

1900 Reid Farm Rd.; 815-282-4653; 888-425-3336; www.aldeengolfclub.com; 7131/5075; 74.2/69.1; 134/117

Rockford has been long recognized as a hotbed for quality, affordable golf, and regulars rave about this walkable, 1992 park-district prizefighter that provides private club–style conditioning, amenities and service; the imposing layout is laced with deep-faced bunkers, rough that's lose-your-ball thick and heroic holes like No. 8, a 203-yd. 17th-at-Sawgrass simulation.

St. Louis Area

Gateway National
▽ 24 | 18 | 21 | 22 | $67

18 Golf Dr., Madison; 314-421-4653; www.gatewaynational.com; 7092/5187; 74.6/64.5; 138/109

Though it is "styled as a links" with mounding, deep bunkers, stone bridges and "rough that can be deadly when they let it grow", Keith

Foster's 1998 Midwestern mecca features "bent-grass fairways", providing a lushness lacking in most Scotts-style spreads; it sports "views of the Arch on a couple holes" and "distracting noise from the Speedway if a race is in town", though swingers still cry "gentlemen, start your engines", because this "golfer's golf course" is definitely worth a lap.

Piper Glen

– | – | – | – | $33

7112 Piper Glen Dr., Springfield; 217-483-6537; 877-635-7326; www.piperglen.com; 6985/5138; 73.6/70.3; 132/123

Ninety miles might seem like a long drive to play golf, but St. Louis sluggers sick of static settings steer north to experience 60-ft. elevation changes, old oak trees and wildly undulating greens that held all but two 2003 state amateur participants to par or higher; grass depressions, pot bunkers and an omnipresent creek lurk around every turn on this Sangamon County course, but you can find some relief in The Stewart Grill, an homage to the late pro Payne, when you make the one from the 9th to the 10th.

Spencer T. Olin 🏌

▽ 24 | 18 | 16 | 25 | $50

4701 College Ave., Alton; 618-465-3111; www.spencertolingolf.com; 6941/5049; 73.5/65.6; 135/110

Named for the son of the Olin metals and munitions maker, who once partnered with the King in a pro-am, this "challenging Arnold Palmer design" with "many different types of holes" and boldly sloped greens is "a great value" and "worth the trip over from St. Louis" even if additional services are sparse; after playing the 1999 men's and 1996 women's U.S. Amateur Public Links Championship venue, you can stop and smell the roses in this community park's garden, or take a loop around its additional par-3 executive track.

Stonewolf 🏌

▽ 23 | 22 | 19 | 17 | $65

1195 Stonewolf Trail, Fairview Heights; 618-624-4653; www.stonewolfgolf.com; 6943/4849; 73.4/68.2; 136/114

Nobody can deny that the dramatic elevation changes, forest-flanked fairways and "first few holes that may be the toughest opening in the state" don't provide "big fun" for floggers "on the east side of St. Louis"; still, "the Nicklaus name can only go so far" – the "gimmicky setup on the front nine" has some ball-whacking wolves howling "just because the Golden Bear designed it doesn't make it great."

Indiana

Carmel

Prairie View

▽ 25 | 22 | 21 | 18 | $90

7000 Longest Dr.; 317-816-3100; www.prairieviewgc.com; 7073/5203; 74.5/70.5; 138/122

"Either they had too much sand delivered and had to use it or else" Robert Trent Jones Jr. "was a sadist", considering that some of the 90 bunkers on this "great public track" are monstrous enough to engulf a city bus; the design also features abundant streams, wetlands and lakes, making for a "top-notch" round, though someone should tell the "snobbish" staff that their "service could be better."

Cincinnati Area

Belterra
∇ 23 | 25 | 24 | 21 | $100

777 Belterra Dr., Florence; 812-417-7783; 800-594-5833;
www.belterracasino.com; 6910/5102; 73.3/69.2; 136/117
Unlimited practice balls (which help make the facilities here
"unmatched in the area") are appreciated at any Tom Fazio
layout, but they're particularly useful at this "nicely conditioned"
"casino course" near the Ohio River and Log Lick Creek that is
"open off the tee" but then weaves dangerously close to several
lakes; if you're a better gambler than golfer you can "win back your
losses to your buddies with some craps inside" – "come on, 7!"

Indianapolis

Brickyard Crossing
25 | 20 | 21 | 17 | $90

4400 W. 16th St.; 317-484-6572; www.brickyardcrossing.com;
6994/5038; 74/68.3; 143/116
Even though it comes with a "big price tag" for Indiana, this
former pit stop on the Champions Tour designed by Pete Dye is a
"great experience" because "four holes are inside the historic
Indianapolis Motor Speedway" and they, along with the rest of
the "challenge", are "always in outstanding condition"; if that's
not enough reason to put the pedal to the metal, there's a stay-
and-play deal (based on double occupancy) that costs just $9
more than the daily fee.

Fort, The
25 | 22 | 21 | 22 | $55

6002 N. Post Rd.; 317-543-9592; www.golfus.com/thefort;
7148/5045; 74.5/69.2; 139/123
"Who would have thought there were hills in Indiana?"; certainly
not locals, who marvel at the "unbelievable" elevation changes
that Pete Dye incorporated into this "visually interesting" "find"
"close to Indianapolis" in Fort Harrison State Park; though it's "not
championship" caliber, the course is "challenging enough for
any double-digit player" and, given the charming Harrison House
accommodations and "Callaway rentals", perhaps a better
question is: who would have thought this was a state-run facility?

Links At Heartland Crossing
∇ 26 | 24 | 22 | 24 | $50

6701 S. Heartland Blvd., Camby; 317-630-1785;
www.heartlandcrossinggolf.com; 7267/5536; 75.4/69; 134/121
"If you like sand, you will love this place", an "interesting and
challenging layout" noted for its huge, free-formed bunkers and
use of fescue, prairie grass and wildflowers that create linkslike
playing conditions and shot options; it's "a bit of a drive from
downtown" Indy and it "needs to mature a little to be an excellent
course" but it's already considered "a great value" so "don't miss
it if you're in town."

Otter Creek
∇ 24 | 22 | 21 | 25 | $75

11522 E. 50 N., Columbus; 812-579-5227; www.ottercreekgolf.com
East/North: 7224/5581; 75.6/73; 137/125
North/West: 7258/5690; 75.6/73.5; 138/128
West/East: 7126/5403; 75/71.9; 137/123
Thirty-one years after RTJ Sr. designed the original 18 holes of
this "old-style course" his son, Rees, added another linksy nine,

completing in 1995 a 27-hole "top-of-the-line" experience that's "scenic", "memorable" and a "true test of golf"; you'd "better be driving it well or pay", though if you factor in the "great value" of the "play-all-day feature" for $100, that's something most would gladly do.

Purgatory
▽ 26 | 20 | 22 | 21 | $70

12160 E. 216th St., Noblesville; 317-776-4653; www.purgatorygolf.com; 7754/5683; 78.1/73.4; 142/126
"Play the correct tees" or this "outstanding layout", a 45-minute drive north of Indianapolis, is "tougher than it needs to be"; with "lots of sand" (125 bunkers to be exact) and 7,754 total yards, including a 741-yd. monster par-5, the longest course in Indiana is a hell of a challenge from all but the shortest of the six sets; thankfully, there's salvation to be found in the "new clubhouse" where the "friendly staff's" "Hoosier hospitality" helps soothe the burn.

Rock Hollow
▽ 24 | 16 | 20 | 25 | $49

County Rd. 250 W., Peru; 765-473-6100; www.rockhollowgolf.com; 6944/4967; 74/69.1; 136/118
Pete Dye protégé Tim Liddy designed this "fabulous" formation to bound "through a quarry" formerly mined by the father of PGA Tour player Chris Smith (whose 63 is the course record), which has helped it gain notoriety as one of the "best values in the state"; despite being nicknamed The Rock, it isn't that hard "if you choose the correct tees", though the old-growth forests, wetlands and boulders can pulverize weak shots.

Trophy Club, The
▽ 24 | 21 | 20 | 24 | $60

3887 N. US Hwy. 52, Lebanon; 765-482-7272; www.thetrophyclubgolf.com; 7280/5050; 75.3/64.9; 138/113
This "central Indiana sleeper" might win the trophy for "one of the best bargains around" because its fescue-framed layout "moves from links-style into the trees" and features "fun and challenging" "short par-4s and long par-3s", yet it's "far enough from Indianapolis to drive down the greens fee"; several lakes and Prairie Creek provide the punch on certain holes, but the 60-yd.-wide fairways mean it's a "not-too-difficult" "joy to play" at any skill level.

Iowa

Cedar Rapids

Amana Colonies ⛳
25 | 20 | 20 | 22 | $52

451 27th Ave., Amana; 319-622-6222; 800-383-3636; www.amanagolfcourse.com; 6824/5228; 73.3/70; 136/119
It's "worth the drive" to this "great value" with such drastic elevation changes that "you won't believe you're in Iowa", except that it's surrounded by the landmarked villages of a utopian religious community not uncommon in this part of the country in the 18th-century; some say the "layout is a little redundant at times", but when the holes are "playable for all levels", that's not necessarily a bad thing; just be sure to visit when the "cart-path-only rules" aren't in effect or your legs will be praying for mercy.

Des Moines

Harvester, The

∇ 27 | 22 | 21 | 20 | $80

1102 330th St., Rhodes; 641-227-4653; www.harvestergolf.com;
7300/4950; 75.6/68.9; 137/120

The only thing this former farm has harvested since 2000 is national acclaim for its uniquely hilly Keith Foster design with "lots of risk/reward holes" laid out around its 60-acre lake and "firm-and-fast" conditions that "allow for a variety" of playing styles; though "it seems like a steal" for those on a heartland holiday, locals lament that "the fees should better offset the gas money it takes to get there" — once you do arrive, you might want to stay, as buying an on-site condo reaps a lifetime of free golf.

Kansas

Garden City

Buffalo Dunes

– | – | – | – | $20

5685 S. Hwy. 83; 620-276-1210; www.garden-city.org/golfcourse;
6774/5150; 72.1/69.5; 127/118

Thirty years young, this country course keeps 'em coming back for humps, bumps, ripples and rolls that make you feel like you're not in Kansas anymore; the narrow fairways, constant wind and tall, native grass that locals call 'the gunch' may have you tapping your heels for home; the only thing more undulating than the fairways are the pristine greens, which will undoubtedly produce powerful putts when the State Amateur Championship is held here in 2006.

Kansas City

Alvamar Public

24 | 19 | 20 | 23 | $40

1800 Crossgate Dr., Lawrence; 785-842-1907; www.alvamar.com;
7092/4892; 75.5/68.1; 141/112

"Great greens and fairways" on the public 18 at the home of the University of Kansas golf team and regular Kansas Open site make it "one of the better offerings" in Lawrence; but the "long holes" can also make it a "tough course from the back tees, especially on the par-3s", so first avail yourself of the on-site Jayhawk Golf Training Center, and then give it the ol' college try.

Deer Creek

23 | 19 | 20 | 19 | $69

7000 W. 133rd St., Overland Park; 913-681-3100; www.deercreekgc.com;
6811/5126; 74.5/68.5; 137/113

It may be "a little overpriced" for these parts, but this RTJ Jr. course offers a "country-club feel" and a layout that's "still fantastic after 15 years+", despite the fair amount of play it gets from the locals in this residential development; its "variety of terrain" includes some "very tight holes" hemmed in by mature trees and plentiful water hazards on the front side, and it gets even "tougher on the back."

Falcon Ridge

25 | 22 | 20 | 18 | $75

20200 Prairie Star Pkwy., Lenexa; 913-393-4653;
www.falconridgegolf.com; 6820/5160; 72.8/69.6; 130/119

You normally don't find "hills in Kansas" but this course "has them", and while the elevation on No. 4 provides "great views" of the city, golfers still feel secluded because you generally "can't see another hole at any point while playing" on one; all 18 "have their own identities", which forces you to "think your way around", while "tons of distance from green to tee" demands the big stick.

Ironhorse   20 | 25 | 21 | 16 | $70
15400 Mission Rd., Leawood; 913-685-4653; www.ironhorsegolf.com; 6889/4745; 73.7/67.5; 138/118
The "great staff and practice facilities" help make this 1995 Dr. Michael Hurdzan design "a good choice", but with "fairways and bunkers that need a little touch up" and "some muggy holes" with "disease on the greens", this creek-teased muni is "a little expensive" for the conditions; if you really want your money's worth, enter a tournament here, then break for the Player's Grill, which bestows a bountiful burger and 'brat buffet on its ball beaters.

Prairie Highlands   25 | 22 | 21 | 22 | $50
14695 S. Inverness Dr., Olathe; 913-856-7235; www.prairiehighlands.com; 7066/5122; 74.5/69.6; 129/114
Architect Craig Schreiner picked a winner for his first ownership stake in a course, as this "gorgeous", "links" layout that is "almost always in good shape" offers "a little bit of everything", including lakeside holes, "rolling hills" that either advance or buffer drives, "rough that will eat your ball" and, overall, "lots of playing options"; the designer also created the clubhouse, which has a round window and stone chimney that are fashioned after a club hitting a ball, as well as a roof pitched to the trajectory of a five-iron.

Sycamore Ridge   ▽ 27 | 19 | 19 | 21 | $49
21731 Clubhouse Dr., Spring Hill; 913-592-5292; www.sycamoreridgegolf.com; 7055/4877; 76.2/65.4; 150/118
Its designers "did a fine job" combining links and parkland nines into one of the "hardest courses in Kansas City", a 150-slope savage that is "always in great shape" and, even better, "always running a special" because it's "located in the boonies"; for some, visiting the nearby "strip clubs" that can "double as the 19th and 20th holes is the draw" after seeing the course's back side.

Topeka

Colbert Hills 衣 🖾   ▽ 27 | 19 | 21 | 19 | $79
5200 Colbert Hills Dr., Manhattan; 785-776-6475; www.colberthills.com; 7525/4947; 77.5/65.1; 152/119
The paw-print bunker doesn't appear until the 5th hole, but the severe "elevation changes", "native grass" and "deep rough" on the "very long", "links-style" home of the Kansas State Wildcats are instant signs that alum Jim Colbert's design is "a real beast"; especially on a typical "windy" day "in the middle of Kansas" where, despite the breeze, it's "not hard to crank up the heat."

Kentucky

Cincinnati Area

Lassing Pointe   – | – | – | – | $37
2266 Double Eagle Dr., Union; 859-384-2266; 6724/5153; 72.2/69.5; 132/122
This former maple syrup farm made a smooth transition to top-notch muni in 1994, promptly hosting two state championships on its

generous fairways and massive greens, the last of which is 101 yards long and surrounded by water on three sides; despite being located at the highest point in Boone County, the grade is benign, but the tall native grasses and 63 bunkers are more than enough to justify the 10-minute tee-time interval.

Lexington

Marriott's Griffin Gate 🏨   ▽ 19 | 21 | 20 | 17 | $62

1720 Newtown Pike; 859-288-6193; www.marriott.com; 6784/5053; 72.2/68.6; 133/122

"Seeing the cars whiz by on I-75 makes you know how lucky you are to be playing" this 1981 Rees Jones design 10 minutes from Downtown, but with "a lot of houses within hitting distance" and water in play on 12 holes, there can be "slow play typical of hotel courses"; there's nothing ordinary about the resort's restaurants, however: the Mansion at Griffin Gate in a restored, antebellum manor house and JW Steakhouse, serving up fire-grilled beef.

Old Silo   – | – | – | – | $59

350 Silver Lake Dr., Mount Sterling; 859-498-4697; www.oldsilo.com; 6977/5509; 74.5/67.8; 139/125

Australian Champions Tour player Graham Marsh designed his first course in the U.S. amid the rolling hills of thoroughbred country where Somerset Creek meanders and, boy, did he make the most of it on holes like No. 6: called 'First Glimpse' for its opening view of the namesake silo, it drops 95 feet off the tee; don't horse around on the 13th, or you'll get kicked into one of the sandy troughs that split the fairway or guard the green.

Louisiana

Baton Rouge

Bluffs on Thompson Creek   ▽ 26 | 22 | 19 | 22 | $77

Hwy. 965 at Freeland Rd., Saint Francisville; 225-634-5551; www.thebluffs.com; 7151/4781; 75.3/68.6; 150/117

"Months after you've played it, you'll remember" this "picturesque" Palmer "gem" for its "great par-3s, multiple-fairway par-4s" and surprising elevation changes; stay a few days at its quaint, B&B-like lodge and intersperse rounds with tours of nearby "historic homes, antique shopping" and, in April or October, "the Angola Prison Rodeo at the Louisiana State Penitentiary just down the road."

Carter Plantation   ▽ 26 | 26 | 27 | 22 | $85

23475 Carter Trace, Springfield; 225-294-7555; www.carterplantation.com; 7049/5057; 74.4/69.8; 140/122

PGA Tour star David Toms' first signature course is a "wonderful" "women-friendly" woodlander with facilities that are "second to none"; still an "infant", it's "going to be great" once it grows into three distinct sections of oak flats, cypress wetlands and pine forests, which should justify "prices a bit out of the average guy's range"; you'll want to stay for dinner, not only because it's "in the middle of nowhere" but because its Plantation Dining Room proffers "great gumbo", pecan wood–broiled steaks and "the epitome of Southern hospitality."

Lake Charles

Gray Plantation   – | – | – | – | $36

6150 Graywood Pkwy.; 337-562-1663; www.graywoodllc.com;
7238/5392; 73.6/71.9; 138/128

"Watch out for gators in the water hazards" warn herpetologically
minded hackers who "really enjoy playing" this "nice", flat,
Audubon-certified spread in Cajun country that's "challenging for
all golfers", mostly due to liquid-laced trouble on 12 holes; with
continuing refinements that include a clubhouse expansion
scheduled for completion in November 2005, it's no wonder that
folks say this "good course has gotten better"; N.B. following
work on the back tees, the track is awaiting a new USGA rating
and slope at press time, both expected to be higher.

New Orleans

Belle Terre   ▽ 17 | 17 | 16 | 22 | $56

111 Fairway Dr., La Place; 985-652-5000; www.belleterregolf.com;
6849/5409; 72.2/71.8; 130/122

Some swamp swingers "like the bayou atmosphere" of this "basic"
"old Pete Dye course", while others swear that 10 soupy holes
amount to "too much water"; "affordable rates" and a location 15
minutes from the airport make it "convenient during visits" to the
Big Easy, but until a layout that's "showing its age" gets a "needed
upgrade", there's "no reason to drive very far to play here."

Oak Harbor 🏫   19 | 17 | 19 | 22 | $79

201 Oak Harbor Blvd., Slidell; 985-646-0110; www.oakharborgolf.com;
6897/5226; 72.7/68.8; 132/115

"Water comes into play" on 12 holes at this bayou links sporting
Pete Dye–esque railroad ties and bulkheads, making it "a bear
when the wind blows, which is most of the time"; "the course has
been up and down in shape and service", but with "new greens
and a recent face-lift", "it's on the upswing"; play it during "the
twilight special when the value is" at its sweetest.

TPC of Louisiana 🏫   24 | 26 | 26 | 17 | $155

11001 Lapalco Blvd., Avondale; 504-436-8721; 866-665-2872;
www.tpc.com; 7520/5121; 76.6/69.7; 138/119

"Still in its infant stages", the new home of the PGA Tour's Zurich
Classic by Pete Dye, Steve Elkington and N'Awlins native Kelly
Gibson was born to be "devilish from the tips", and its "long" "holes
with cypress trees and lots of traps on either side" are only going to
get "tougher when the rough grows in"; unlike the distances from
its tees to its greens, the "well-groomed" "Tiger-proofed" "loop in
the middle of a swamp" is just a "quick drive from The Quarter."

Maine

Central Maine

BELGRADE LAKES 🏌️   27 | 16 | 24 | 21 | $100

West Rd. at Clubhouse Dr., Belgrade Lakes; 207-495-4653;
www.belgradelakesgolf.com; 6572/4803; 71.6/67.6; 142/117

Walking the "difficult" course with a caddie is actually encouraged
at this "pure golf" experience "hidden in the lakes region" with "no

development", "no memberships" and "no waiting" thanks to "well-spaced tee times"; all this plus "stunning views of the water" "almost makes nine months of winter worthwhile", but the place "needs a better clubhouse" and an on-site range "to be perfect."

Kebo Valley

– | – | – | – | $76

Eagle Lake Rd., Bar Harbor; 207-288-3000; www.kebovalleyclub.com; 6131/5473; 69.5/72.6; 124/128

America's eighth-oldest course dates to 1888 and its facilities don't appear to have been modernized much since then, but if a rolling, semi-forested throwback with an abundance of natural, quirky holes sounds appetizing, this is your spot; take the unforgettable, recently restored par-4 17th where President Taft once took 27 shots – most of them from the Sahara-size trap fronting the green – and combine it with the handsome scenery of Acadia National Park, and it adds up to a golf experience that oozes character.

SUGARLOAF

28 | 17 | 20 | 22 | $110

Rte. 27, Carrabassett Valley; 207-237-2000; 800-843-5623; www.sugarloaf.com; 6910/5289; 74.4/72.5; 151/131

"Don't loaf" at "one of the toughest tracks east of the Mississippi" or you'll be "lucky if you break 100", though scores are unimportant when you "cannot imagine a more picturesque mountain layout"; "fall is the best time" to play because the "greens tend to be in rough shape early in the season" but you can see "moose tracks" any time of year, or if you're lucky, spy the big, antlered guys from the new, million-dollar clubhouse.

Southern Maine

Dunegrass 🏌

26 | 21 | 20 | 22 | $79

200 Wild Dunes Way, Old Orchard Beach; 207-934-4513; 800-521-1029; www.dunegrass.com; 6602/4728; 72.1/68; 137/113

Subtly rolling fairways peppered with pines make this "well-maintained", 18-hole portion of a "well-run" 27-hole facility a bit "surprising" because it's "like playing golf in North Carolina"; though it "can be seen from the turnpike", it offers "impressive" wooded seclusion between holes, which are "seriously tough from the back tees" – if the long par-4s don't get you, the "fantastic", "challenging greens" will.

Ledges, The

24 | 18 | 19 | 24 | $65

1 Ledges Dr., York; 207-351-3000; www.ledgesgolf.com; 6981/4997; 74/70.9; 137/126

This "rugged", "beautiful" "challenge" "lives up to its reputation" as "one of the best in the region", say seasonal swingers who "play it every summer" in attempts at taming the "tricky greens" and thought-provoking finishing hole, a 618-yd. par-5 where a second-shot lay-up leaves a 175-yd. carry to the green; even weekenders can take a few cracks at it as there are dozens of B&Bs and inns around York, Kennebunkport and Oganquit.

Samoset

24 | 23 | 22 | 19 | $130

220 Warrenton St., Rockport; 207-594-2511; 800-341-1650; www.samoset.com; 6548/5083; 70.8/70.2; 133/120

With seven seaside holes and "gorgeous ocean views" from 14 in total, this nifty 1902 number located "in an area where the pickin's

are slim" is "justifiably called the Pebble Beach of the East" – though it's "very playable for all levels", so you might have to "intentionally hit a ball into the Atlantic" to imitate the real thing; it's almost as "expensive" as the West Coast wonder, but with restored resort rooms and Marcel's fine dining with "vistas of Penobscot Bay", "what more could you ask for?"

Maryland

★ **Top Courses in State**
29 Bulle Rock, *Baltimore*
28 Links at Lighthouse Sound, *Ocean City*
26 Whiskey Creek, *Frederick*
     Beechtree, *Aberdeen*
     Atlantic Golf At Queenstown, River, *Easton*

Aberdeen

Beechtree   26 | 25 | 25 | 24 | $95
811 S. Stepney Rd.; 410-297-9700; 877-233-2487; www.beechtreegolf.com; 7023/5363; 74.9/70.4; 142/121
"You better think out there" and visit the "excellent practice facility" because "Tom Doak is simply a genius", and his I-95 IQ test includes "lots of interesting holes", "long grasses" and "lightning-fast greens" on "two distinct nines", a links-style front and parkland back; "the amazing thing is the lack of crowds", perhaps because it "suffers in comparison to nearby Bulle Rock", but the devoted declare it's "every bit as challenging as its much more expensive neighbor."

Annapolis

Atlantic Golf at South River   23 | 19 | 19 | 18 | $85
3451 Solomons Island Rd., Edgewater; 410-798-5865; 800-767-4837; www.mdgolf.com; 6723/4935; 71.8/66.9; 133/115
The "ocean provides inspiration if not difficulty" to this "well-managed course" "through a residential setting" in Anne Arundel County where "just enough water", "old-growth trees" and traps add "challenge" to "narrow fairways" that "straighten out your game . . . or increase your expenses in balls"; the "practice area needs an upgrade", but the "new greenskeeper is doing a much better job" of maintaining the course "in great shape."

Baltimore

BULLE ROCK 朼   29 | 27 | 26 | 20 | $145
320 Blenheim Ln., Havre de Grace; 410-939-8465; 888-285-5375; www.bullerock.com; 7375/5426; 76.4/71.1; 147/127
"One of the few places you can play a best-in-state course without knowing a member", this "Pete Dye masterpiece" and host to the 2005 LPGA Championship is "as good as you've heard", but "take a caddie" because it's "a killer: long and steep" where "any shot that finds the rough is unlikely to be advanced", if you can locate it at all; hackers can still have a "great" day, though, by "lowering their expectations", seeing if they can "find just one weed anywhere" or simply enjoying being treated "like an Augusta member" for a day.

Greystone   24 | 19 | 19 | 25 | $69
2115 White Hall Rd., White Hall; 410-887-1945;
www.baltimoregolfing.com; 6925/4800; 73.5/67.5; 139/112
A course "run by Baltimore County", this "woman-friendly" Joe
Lee design with 140 feet of elevation changes "in the heart of
horse country" is "an opportunity for the masses" to enjoy a
"country-club-for-a-day" experience at a "fair price"; like some
of its "hidden greens", the course itself is "not very easy to find",
though "repeat plays will reduce your score" and the number of
wrong turns you make getting to its location "close to York, PA."

Timbers at Troy, The   18 | 16 | 18 | 21 | $59
6100 Marshalee Dr., Elkridge; 410-313-4653; www.timbersgolf.com;
6652/4899; 72.1/68.5; 134/115
"Well-designed holes" and "reasonable" rates make this muni
"appealing" (and "crowded"), though sodden swingers say go
"only in dry weather" because "poor drainage" means you get "no
roll whatsoever"; on fairways "bordered by woods and creeks",
offline shots can get "kicked into severe positions" – maybe that's
why it "tends to be slow", with weary whackers left to wonder if
the "disinterested" staff's "ever heard of a marshall."

Waverly Woods   22 | 19 | 19 | 20 | $71
2100 Warwick Way, Marriottsville; 410-313-9182;
www.waverlywoods.com; 7024/4808; 73.1/68.1; 132/166
This Arthur Hills track west of Baltimore befits the designer's name
with a "good mix of tight holes and wide fairways" routed across
"dramatically rolling countryside" for "tough shotmaking" and a
"brutal walk" – in other words, there are "only about 18 flat lies,
all of them on the tee boxes"; equally "steep greens fees" are
offset by "remarkable vistas" that may become a little less so as
the "houses grow like weeds around the course."

Cumberland

Rocky Gap Lodge 🏨   ▽ 23 | 22 | 19 | 20 | $85
16701 Lakeview Rd., NE, Flintstone; 301-784-8500;
www.rockygapresort.com; 7002/5198; 74.3/69.4; 141/123
Jack Nicklaus routed this "lovely", "state-owned" facility in
Flintstone's Rocky Gap State Park past Lake Habeeb and Evitt
Mountain, adding "punishing rough" to the "scenic", wooded,
mountainous front nine and rippling the back; it's "challenging",
but playing the proper tees makes it "suitable for all", and even if
it "feels like it's run by bureaucrats", the lodge is a welcome
place for Fred, Wilma and the whole family because it offers
Dino-friendly rooms and Pebbles stays for free.

DC Metro Area

Swan Point   25 | 20 | 21 | 21 | $80
11550 Swan Point Blvd, Issue; 301-259-0047; www.swanpointgolf.com;
6761/5009; 73.2/69.3; 130/116
On the banks of the Potomac with "great views of the shore", this
Lowcountry-look-alike "gem" is "unknown to many" due to its
"remote location"; "if you can get there", you'll see why some say
it's "the best public course in the area", with a "picturesque" layout
that includes an island-green par-5 and back-to-back par-3s; dock

your dinghy for free at the Cuckold Creek marina near the 16th and let a member of the "great staff" pick you up in a cart.

University of Maryland Golf Course   17 | 15 | 13 | 21 | $57

University of Maryland, College Park; 301-314-4653; www.golf.umd.edu; 6734/5563; 71.6/71.7; 125/120

Maybe it's "not going to win any awards", but "nowhere else near DC can you get this kind of value" than on this 1958 design where, for half the price of a textbook, you can load up on "tall, old trees", a "fair amount" of blind shots and holes ranging "from simple par-4s to ones that would challenge any low-handicapper"; the Terrapin terrain "can be patchy", but with a "good practice area" supporting it, it's still an "excellent golf course for a college campus."

Easton

Atlantic Golf at   23 | 20 | 23 | 20 | $69
Queenstown Harbor, Lakes

310 Links Ln., Queenstown; 410-827-6611; 800-827-5257; www.mdgolf.com; 6569/4606; 71/66.8; 126/108

"The little sister of the two courses here" may be known as the "pretty" one, but even though it's "not as challenging as the River", its water on 15 holes and toughness "when the wind blows" mean "it's still not for the faint of heart" – particularly if you're coming from the western shore on beach weekends when "the traffic will eat you alive"; granted, the "greens fee is a little high", but "the wildlife makes you feel like you're playing in an enchanted forest."

Atlantic Golf at   26 | 20 | 21 | 20 | $99
Queenstown Harbor, River

310 Links Ln., Queenstown; 410-827-6611; 800-827-5257; www.mdgolf.com; 7110/5026; 74.2/69.4; 137/123

"Leave your slice at home" but "bring your knockdown shot" to "the tougher, stronger sibling" of this 36-hole facility because "the best course in Maryland for risk/reward golf" "will test your shotmaking abilities" "especially on windy days" – thank goodness there are "good practice facilities" and the "beautifully kept" layout provides great lies; just "be careful of the Bay Bridge traffic."

Hog Neck   22 | 18 | 20 | 24 | $65

10142 Old Cordova Rd.; 410-822-6079; 800-280-1790; www.hogneck.com; 7049/5434; 73.7/71.3; 131/125

Despite being a muni, native son Lindsay Ervin's first solo design "has everything: practice greens and sand traps, driving range, locker rooms" and, most importantly, an "excellent variety of holes" between the "wide-open front" with "Chesapeake inlet views", and the harder, "tree-lined back"; oddly, this "low-priced gem on the way to the beach" is usually "not too crowded", perhaps because the "much improved snack bar and staff attitude" are still "tacky."

Frederick

Little Bennett   20 | 16 | 17 | 22 | $53

25900 Prescott Rd., Clarksburg; 301-253-1515; 800-366-2012; 6706/4921; 73.2/68.2; 137/115

If Little Benny's "thoughtful layout", with "lots of hills", "blind shots" and "tricky, sloping greens", is tough enough to hold "qualifiers for the [PGA Tour's] Booz-Allen Classic", imagine what his big brother would be like; perhaps he'd have facilities that didn't exude a "muni feel", though the "gigantic" practice area here is "one of the best grass driving ranges around", and even if your smooth swings don't carry over to the course, the "long and wide-open" fairways won't beat you up too badly.

Maryland National ⛳　　　23 | 21 | 20 | 19 | $89

8836 Hollow Rd., Middletown; 301-371-0000; www.marylandnational.com; 6811/4844; 73.1/68.3; 137/120

With a relatively "new clubhouse", this Arthur Hills design literally "gives Bulle Rock a run for the money": in addition to "memorable holes" "loaded with risk/reward" and Catoctin Mountains views, it's in "excellent condition", but it's also "very pricey" given a "location remote from Baltimore and Washington"; though parts of the course convey "a links feel", "proximity to I-70 is not the same as proximity to the ocean", but if you're looking for a truly seaworthy experience, sink into a softshell crab sandwich in Schroyer's Tavern after your round.

P.B. Dye　　　23 | 22 | 20 | 16 | $89

9526 Doctor Perry Rd., Ijamsville; 301-607-4653; www.pbdyegolf.com; 7036/4900; 74.2/68.3; 140/123

This "challenge" north of Washington, DC, "will raise your handicap" – and possibly your ire – with its "dastardly" P.B. Dye design replete with railroad ties and "blind approach shots" to "ridiculously fast" greens; though its firm, forgiving fairways allow even raw rippers to roll it closer to the pin, "a few unfair, gimmicky" setups make this one "difficult for average players"; "first-class service" (including free WiFi access), "terrific food" and "wonderful views" of Sugarloaf Mountain take away the sting – just "be like Tiger and practice putting on a gym floor" beforehand.

WHISKEY CREEK　　　26 | 23 | 22 | 20 | $95

4804 Whiskey Ct., Ijamsville; 301-694-2900; 888-883-1174; www.whiskeycreekgolf.com; 7001/5296; 74.5/70.5; 137/121

Although co-designed by Ernie 'The Big Easy' Els, this is a "tough" but "fair" course that "rewards good play and penalizes poor play" on "rolling farmland" "nestled in the hills of northern Maryland" where plentiful "elevation changes" "put shotmaking at a premium"; it's "expensive", but "well worth the price – heck, the [alternate-route] 18th alone is worth the fee", as are the lodgelike clubhouse and "picturesque" panoramas of the surrounding Catoctin Mountains.

Worthington Manor　　　22 | 16 | 19 | 21 | $79

8329 Fingerboard Rd.; 301-874-5400; 888-987-2582; www.worthingtonmanor.com; 7034/5206; 74.4/70.1; 144/116

Set in Maryland's foothills, this "poorer cousin" of nearby Whiskey Creek makes up for "sparse practice facilities" with an "excellent mix of holes" and "enough undulation" to "make anyone happy", even the USGA, which holds U.S. Open and U.S. Amateur qualifiers here; you'll "need to play twice to appreciate" the "fast greens" and sometimes "unfair pin locations", but players will be glad to go it again given "pretty" environs, an "attentive staff" and a "price-to-quality ratio that's tough to beat."

Ocean City

Bay Club, East   17 | 17 | 18 | 18 | $75
9122 Libertytown Rd., Berlin; 410-641-4081; 800-229-2582;
www.thebayclub.com; 7004/5231; 74.6/67.4; 134/115
Credit the "great staff attitude" for making this "average resort
course" outside Ocean City "worth playing" because, while it
makes "good use of water in the design" and turf techies "love
the zoysia fairways", other say the layout "doesn't stand out"; the
"fairways are in better condition off-season than in-season", but
check the Web site for regularly posted discounts and specials
throughout the year.

Eagle's Landing   24 | 18 | 19 | 22 | $65
12367 Eagles Nest Rd., Berlin; 410-213-7277; 800-283-3846;
www.eagleslandinggolf.com; 7003/4896; 73.6/67.9; 126/112
"Heck, even the bunkers are well manicured" at this "immaculate"
muni with nest boxes installed throughout, literally making the
"very, very scenic" and "walk-able" layout with "beautiful views"
of the Sinepuxent Bay and Assateague Island National Seashore "a
sanctuary for both birds" and birdie-seekers; the only problem is
that "one of the better values in the Ocean City area" has "no
driving range" to help prepare for the "many tough shots" over and
around the "marshy" areas.

LINKS AT LIGHTHOUSE SOUND 🏳   28 | 24 | 23 | 19 | $169
12723 Saint Martins Neck Rd., Bishopville; 410-352-5767;
www.lighthousesound.com; 7031/4553; 73.3/67.1; 144/107
If you're in the mood to "treat yourself", this "expensive but oh-
so-nice" "Arthur Hills treasure" is the place because the only thing
better than the "memorable and diverse" combination of a "windy
links front" (with "spectacular views" of the Ocean City skyline
and Assawoman Bay) and marsh- and "tree-lined back" is the
"immaculate condition" in which it is kept; you'll feel like you're
motoring forever on "the longest cart bridge" in the country, but
it's actually the staff that "goes out of its way – to serve you."

Ocean City Golf Club, Newport Bay   22 | 19 | 19 | 21 | $98
11401 Country Club Dr., Berlin; 410-641-1779; 800-442-3570;
www.ocgolfclub.com; 6657/5205; 71/71.5; 126/119
Granted, there are "many better Eastern Shore tracks to choose
from", but not if you want to play an entire back nine on the
Sinepuxent Bay, as at this 1998 "remake" with "some challenging
holes" that carry "links-style rough from the tee"; now if only the
"service could be worked on": the "slow pace of play" might
have you eaten alive by critters while you wait warn wallopers
who whine "they did not give us any complimentary bug spray
until we asked."

River Run   21 | 17 | 18 | 18 | $92
11605 Masters Ln., Berlin; 410-641-7200; 800-733-7786;
www.riverrungolf.com; 6705/4818; 70.4/73.1; 128/117
Like the man himself, this 1991 Gary Player design on the St. Martin's
River is "short but sweet", a "well-maintained" and "well-marked"
"shotmaker's course" with "lots of water" in play on both a "links-
style" front and amid marshes and "trees on the back"; despite
such hazards, it's "great for mid- to high-handicappers", though

there's always the risk of "hitting a house or two" given "condos and beach homes" that "seem to be right on top of you."

Rum Pointe   25 | 22 | 22 | 21 | $129

7000 Rum Pointe Ln., Berlin; 410-629-1414; 888-809-4653;
www.rumpointe.com; 7001/5276; 72.6/70.3; 122/120

You might want a shot of rum after playing "one of the best courses at the beach" because "wind is a factor . . . a huge factor" at this "wide-open", "visually impressive" Pete and P.B. Dye links that "plays along the [Sinepuxent] Bay" with 17 waterview holes; if you tire of trying to keep the ball down amid "howling" gales, wait for calmer climes in the posh, eight-person apartment you can let above the clubhouse.

Massachusetts

★ **Top Courses in State**
27 Ranch, *Berkshires*
    Taconic, *Berkshires*
    Crumpin-Fox, *Berkshires*
    Farm Neck, *Martha's Vineyard*
26 Pinehills, Jones, *Boston*

Berkshires

Cranwell   18 | 21 | 19 | 15 | $99

55 Lee Rd., Lenox; 413-637-1364; 800-272-6935; www.cranwell.com;
6204/5104; 70/70.2; 123/121

First it was Reverend Henry Ward Beecher's estate, then a hunt club, a private school for boys and now this luxe vacation destination, which includes a course that is "not long" and "great for high-handicappers" – if they "take a caddie or buy a yardage book" because, unlike the resort's ambiance, there's "nothing elegant" about "blind shots" and "a few holes that are impossible to understand"; however, "thoughtful amenities" abound, such as a "great golf school", a "spa for non-players" and four tantalizing restaurants for non-dieters.

Crumpin-Fox   27 | 20 | 23 | 24 | $69

Parmenter Rd., Bernardston; 413-648-9101; 800-943-1901;
www.crumpin-fox.com; 7007/5432; 73.8/71.5; 141/131

Thank goodness this "special place" is deep "in the hinterlands" because "if it were near anything, you could never get on" to experience "one of the most challenging [tracks] in New England", a "tree-lined", "target-golf" test with "demanding elevation changes", "sidehill lies" and "rock outcroppings" that "leave great golfers shaking their heads" – and "immediately planning their return trip"; in addition to being a "fall foliage stunner", it's a "must-play" for the "compelling combo package with dinner."

Ranch, The   27 | 24 | 23 | 21 | $110

65 Sunnyside Rd., Southwick; 413-569-9315; 866-790-9333;
www.theranchgolfclub.com; 7171/4983; 74.1/69.7; 140/122

Good thing "roller-coaster golf" is just a figure of speech because it would be a shame to lose one of the "great sandwiches for lunch" on this "absolutely awesome" "links-style" track "north of Hartford" that peers over the Pioneer Valley before descending in a whoosh through woodlands and wetlands; at Massachusetts' Top Course, the price of admission includes a GPS-equipped cart, bottled water, use of the "fine facilities" and a "welcoming, friendly staff", making this "uphill and downhill" ride over "natural terrain" "one of the finest in New England, period."

Taconic ⏱   27 | 18 | 20 | 23 | $145

19 Meacham St., Williamstown; 413-458-3997;
www.williams.edu/go/taconic; 6640/5202; 72.5/70.2; 129/121
What began in 1896 as three tomato cans buried in Williams College's Weston Athletic Field is now "a fine example of an old, rustic, charming New England layout" known for its "unique" holes and "incredibly fast greens"; the practice facility is about a mile away, there's only a "small pro shop" and "everyone walks" the course, but somehow this makes it "especially endearing in this small college town" located in a "scenic corner of western Massachusetts" that is "a real treat in the autumn months."

Boston

Atlantic Country Club   22 | 18 | 19 | 21 | $58

450 Little Sandy Pond Rd., Plymouth; 508-759-6644;
www.atlanticcountryclub.com; 6728/4918; 73/68.3; 131/116
Players make a pilgrimage to Plymouth for this "beautiful" course, which is "great for the price" because it's religiously "well kept" and its "tight fairways" "test all levels"; "it's hilly, so you may want a cart", though the "nice staff" lets purists walk and will later get you a table on the deck overlooking the 9th and 18th greens.

George Wright 🕴   15 | 9 | 10 | 22 | $36

420 West St., Hyde Park; 617-364-2300; 6440/5131; 69.5/70.3; 126/115
"For a quickie when you can't go far from the city", head to Hyde Park "in the heart of Boston" for this "classic Donald Ross design", a "longer-than-average city course" with "shorter-than-average waits" because weekday tee times are first-come, first-served and local kids caddie for you in summer; "it takes a beating", so the "conditions can be questionable", "but for under 40 bucks, it is a steal" – lest someone "watching you" gets a similar idea, "be careful of leaving things in your car" in this neighborhood.

Granite Links at Quarry Hills   22 | 14 | 18 | 19 | $100

100 Quarry Hills Dr., Quincy; 617-296-7600; www.granitelinksgolfclub.com;
6818/5001; 73.4/70.6; 141/124
Spread between Quincy and Milton "close to Boston's Downtown", this "windy", "links-style" layout built amid boulders "on an old quarry" in 2003 is "still growing up" but could be "spectacular", particularly when "the new clubhouse" is completed by fall 2005 and another nine holes are added; it already boasts "astounding views" of the skyline, a lighted, grass-and-mats range and the distinction of having hosted a Women's Senior Golf Tour event, though, surprisingly, it's still "not too congested on weekends."

Olde Scotland Links   18 | 11 | 14 | 18 | $47

695 Pine St., Bridgewater; 508-279-3344; www.oldescotlandlinks.com;
6790/4949; 72.6/68.4; 126/111
With its wide-open fairways, "limited elevation" and "short par-5s", referencing this "user-friendly" course and "Scotland in the same

breath" is "a big stretch"; but if you "go on a windy, overcast day" and pretend the marshland is heather and gorse, the Town of Bridgewater's "blue-collar" "bang for your buck" can be "fun" for playing both golf and make-believe.

Pinehills, Jones　　　　26 ￤ 26 ￤ 26 ￤ 21 ￤ $100 ￤
54 Clubhouse Dr., Plymouth; 508-209-3000; 866-855-4653;
www.pinehillsgolf.com; 7175/5380; 73.8/71.2; 135/125
A big "bravo" to Rees Jones whose "beautifully sculpted fairways" set amid "abundant pine scrub and sandhills" with "fantastic views of the ocean popping up across" them "make you think you are way out on the Cape"; smack dab in Plymouth, the state's Most Popular is a "lush, green" "country-club experience" – complete with an "inviting clubhouse", "great practice facilities" and a "friendly staff" that rank Top for Facilities and Service in the state – all for a "reasonable price."

Pinehills, Nicklaus　　　　26 ￤ 26 ￤ 24 ￤ 19 ￤ $100 ￤
54 Clubhouse Dr., Plymouth; 508-209-3000; 866-855-4653;
www.pinehillsgolf.com; 7285/5185; 74.3/69.4; 135/123
Though it was "designed by Jack Jr., not Jack", this "great walk" through an "unspoiled" "Carolinas"-like landscape is a "classic Nicklaus design" with "open tee shots, challenging second shots (to say the least)" and "huge greens"; though it's "a little pricey", "great facilities" at this regional U.S. Open qualifying site still have pros and schmoes alike wondering "why can't all courses be like this?"

Poquoy Brook　　　　20 ￤ 15 ￤ 18 ￤ 22 ￤ $46 ￤
20 Leonard St., Lakeville; 508-947-5261; www.poquoybrook.com;
6762/5415; 72.4/71; 128/114
Even if you "play here in winter" when it's "so cold", you can "hit a ball into a pond, walk out on the frozen water and hit it again", this 1962 Geoffrey Cornish design is "always in great shape", and its "huge greens" are "lightning-fast and tricky" any time of year; "bring your bug spray" in summer because flies in sizes both "large" and "tiny" make it "truly hell", even though the "wider-than-they-look" fairways and "great finishing hole" are heavenly.

Shaker Hills　　　　24 ￤ 21 ￤ 20 ￤ 19 ￤ $85 ￤
146 Shaker Rd., Harvard; 978-772-2227; www.shakerhills.com;
6850/4999; 74/69.8; 137/122
Better study a yardage book, because the "amazing terrain" at this Harvard hit "45 minutes outside metro Boston" not only "provides incredible views" but also "plenty of challenges" on "unique", "tight" holes with a few "blind" shots thrown in for good measure; the facilities exude a "private-club feel", but the sometimes "rather pompous" staff and the "cart-path-only rule" make the "rising prices" that much tougher to justify.

Widow's Walk　　　　16 ￤ 11 ￤ 15 ￤ 18 ￤ $42 ￤
250 The Driftway, Scituate; 781-544-0032; www.widowswalkgolf.com;
6062/4562; 74.9/66.2; 131/113
"Man, the wind blows hard" across Boston Sand & Gravel's former worksite, now an "extremely challenging", "total target-golf" test through wetlands and sand dunes where you're "forced to use all of your clubs" except for the driver; make sure you "play the tees

that match your handicap or this course will own you", though some think the town of Scituate, which owns this early example of environmentalist course design, "should have left it a quarry" as it only had 100 acres to work with.

Cape Cod

Ballymeade ⌂ ⏱
20 | 22 | 21 | 17 | $82

125 Falmouth Woods Rd., North Falmouth; 508-540-4005;
www.ballymeade.com; 6928/4871; 74.7/69.6; 140/123
This "friendly" facility "in Falmouth" with "beautiful vistas of Buzzards Bay" is "much improved since a redesign" by Jim Fazio and Chi Chi Rodriguez, who widened the ultra-"tight", tree-lined holes into "playable, not impossible" challenges; however, it still "makes up for [what it lacks in] length" with "some funky holes" that "demand accuracy" and are "unforgiving on slight mishits"; play "only off-season" if you "want to spend less than $100" on golf, grub and Guinness.

Bayberry Hills
21 | 16 | 16 | 24 | $57

635 W. Yarmouth Rd., West Yarmouth; 508-394-5597;
www.golfyarmouthcapecod.com; 7172/5323; 74.3/69.7; 127/119
"Wide fairways and tough greens highlight this track on the Cape", which has "drastically improved in the last three years" to become "forgiving" and "enjoyable for the high-handicapper" while remaining long enough to "challenge the par shooter"; though the "people are nice", "carts are sadly mandatory in the summer" (on weekends and before 2 PM) on this Yarmouth-owned muni.

Brookside
∇ 21 | 15 | 19 | 22 | $65

11 Brigadoone Rd., Bourne; 508-743-4653; www.thebrooksideclub.com;
6400/5130; 71.1/69.6; 126/118
Besides its "convenient location" and "good value", the first golf course you hit on Cape Cod via the Bourne Bridge is a "memorable experience" sporting a "new clubhouse with views of Cape Cod Canal"; though it stretches to only 6,400 yards, it's "very difficult if you get off the fairways" because the "rough is thick, and there are no flat lies" – not to mention the "gale-force winds" that can sometimes swoop in without notice.

Cape Cod Country Club
19 | 14 | 16 | 21 | $56

Theater Dr., North Falmouth; 508-563-9842;
www.capecodcountryclub.com; 6429/5348; 71.7/71; 129/120
"The Cape is more than boats" and this "very old" course, rumored to have been tweaked by Donald Ross, is "fun for an outing" away from the docks or "an ad hoc round" after tying up because it's as "dependable as an old raincoat"; though the "basic" facility "lacks a driving range", the "classic layout with plenty of challenge yet plenty of scoring opportunities" "always seems to be in great shape" and exudes the "old Cape Cod charm", so take a "sail around this course" – "you'll enjoy the trip."

Captains, Port
21 | 17 | 18 | 22 | $60

1000 Freemans Way, Brewster; 508-896-1716; 877-843-9081;
www.captainsgolfcourse.com; 6724/5799; 72.1/73.5; 131/126
"Tee times are tough" to get aboard this vessel, but the "portrait of a New England course", owned and operated by the town of

Brewster, is "worth the wait" as long as you "don't expect seaside holes" or mind a "surly" crew; even though the blending in of new holes is "not what the old course used to be" and the "conditions have hurt" what had been a shipshape track, the "creative design has kept the layout challenging" and "a solid value on the Cape."

Captains, Starboard   22 | 20 | 20 | 24 | $60
1000 Freemans Way, Brewster; 508-896-1716; 877-843-9081; www.captainsgolfcourse.com; 6776/5833; 71.5/73.3; 122/127

Though it "lost a little with the redesign a few years back", "you will not be disappointed" in this muni that Brewster ballers say is "just a fathom better" and "a nice change" from its "overplayed" "mate"; too bad the "staff needs an education in service" because "the only decent courses accessible to the Upper Cape" would be even better without the "unwarranted smugness."

Cranberry Valley   22 | 14 | 15 | 20 | $60
183 Oak St., Harwich; 508-430-5234; www.cranberrygolfcourse.com; 6482/5568; 71.6/72.2; 127/124

You won't feel the ocean spray at this "inland" track owned by the town of Harwich, but it's still "a great course for the money" because the fine "mix of long and short holes" is "manicured" to "country-club conditions", despite a "huge amount of play"; it's this overload that can lead to "pro shop arrogance" and "grumpy starters", but they "allow walking", which helps to mitigate the "slowness" and prickly vibes.

Dennis Pines   19 | 14 | 17 | 22 | $55
50 Golf Course Rd., East Dennis; 508-385-8347; www.dennisgolf.com; 7000/5567; 74.4/73; 134/131

"Book tee times way ahead in summer" if you want to play this "good alternative to some of the higher-priced courses in the area" because the "fine, old" spread gets "a bit backed up with vacationers" trying to navigate the "rolling Cape Cod landscape" fraught with "sand and lots of pine trees"; granted, the "facilities are a bit spartan" because it's "owned by the town of Dennis", but this "done-right muni" is "a nice test for the money."

New England Country Club   20 | 14 | 17 | 17 | $75
180 Paine St., Bellingham; 508-883-2300; www.newenglandcountryclub.com; 6483/4927; 70.9/68.9; 135/122

Don't expect the cart's GPS to locate your ball if it "disappears in the rough" at this "long and challenging" 1991 Hale Irwin course near the Rhode Island border; just keep the vehicles "off" the "well-maintained" grass and "keep up your speed" or the "strict rangers" might send you back to the clubhouse "about 400 miles from the first tee", which makes "riding an unfortunate must" in the first place; it might not be all bad, though, especially if it's a Friday when Egan's Pub offers all-you-can-eat prime rib.

Ocean Edge   19 | 19 | 19 | 17 | $64
832 Villages Dr., Brewster; 508-896-9000; www.oceanedge.com; 6602/5179; 72.6/69.6; 130/118

"Be accurate, not long", or this "magnificent" combo of "links and wooded holes" on the historic Nickerson estate, an English country–style manor in a "beautiful area of Cape Cod", "can kill your handicap"; as it is, playing it "for the first time, you'll be clueless on where to aim" on a few "wacky" holes that "need some updating"; "staying there" for repeat rounds "makes things better", in part because the condos, restaurants, tennis courts and beach add to a "superb vacation."

Olde Barnstable Fairgrounds   20 14 16 22 $60

1460 Rte. 149, Marstons Mills; 508-420-1141; www.obfgolf.com; 6479/5122; 71.4/69.1; 128/119

If you're willing to write a check, you can make a reservation anytime after January 1st for this "Cape favorite", a "well-run", "well-maintained" "municipal course" opened in 1992 with "interesting holes" and "lots of challenges" to which past participants in U.S. Mid-Amateur, Amateur and Open qualifying tournaments can attest; but, because it's "not too difficult" for mere mortals, it's "the type of course you could play three times a week and never get bored with", even if there's "little in the way of service" and amenities.

Martha's Vineyard

Farm Neck   27 22 23 22 $135

1 Farm Neck Way, Oak Bluffs; 508-693-3057; 6815/4987; 72.8/68.4; 135/121

This "beautiful, beautiful, beautiful" course "starts in the pines, moves to the shoreline" and features several holes "hard by the ocean" and "top-notch facilities that seem almost like a private club's" – thus it earns the nickname "Pebble Beach of the East"; it's "not easy to get to" and "not easy getting on" (only two-day advance tee times in season) but even mainlanders will "take the ferry over" to this neck of the woods for a round on the "expensive" "course Bill Clinton plays" when he's not chowin' down on chowda.

Nantucket

Miacomet   ▽ 17 13 14 15 $95

12 W. Miacomet Rd.; 508-325-0333; www.miacometgolf.com; 6831/5159; 73/69.6; 123/118

The 2003 addition of nine holes with wide fairways and large, undulating greens completed the only 18-hole, public golf course on Nantucket Island, "the perfect setting to enjoy the links" that offer ocean views on four occasions; now it just "needs a professional staff with personality" – and perhaps another nine holes because it's "hard to get a tee time"; what's easy is finding a good prix fixe deal in the clubhouse restaurant.

Worcester

Blackstone National   24 18 19 18 $79

227 Putnam Hill Rd., Sutton; 508-865-2111; www.bngc.net; 6909/5203; 73.5/70; 132/122

Ball whackers who wind up in Worcester will see why the smiley face was invented here when visiting this "hidden gem" nearby, a "challenging" Rees Jones layout "maintained like a private course"; but "put your bag on a cart" because "you have to be a goat to walk" the 300 acres of steep, "rolling hills" in the Blackstone Valley; some say it's "rather expensive for central Massachusetts", but it's "a real treat" amid fall foliage.

Cyprian Keyes
24 | 23 | 23 | 20 | $59

284 E. Temple St., Boylston; 508-869-9900; www.cypriankeyes.com;
6844/5079; 72.7/69.2; 132/119

Here are the keys to enjoying this course: put away the big stick and "use your most accurate iron" because the "very tight fairways", "blind shots" and 22 acres of wetlands – restricted to all but the endangered marbled salamander – provide "few opportunities to hit driver or even cut loose with a wood"; "don't attempt to walk it" as it is "extremely hilly" and "some holes are 800 to 1,000 yards apart", but do avail yourself of the "excellent facilities", including the bistro where you can dine on a burger made from the exotic, but less imperiled, ostrich.

Red Tail
26 | 14 | 19 | 19 | $88

15 Bulge Rd., Devens; 978-772-3273; www.redtailgolf.net;
7006/5049; 73.9/69.4; 138/120

Although this "wonderful, new course" is named for a family of hawks that reside on the former military training base, the "tight", "target-golf" layout fortified with "rolling terrain", mature oak trees, "lots of big sand traps" and "fast greens" is also aptly labeled for the butt kicking it doles out; there are "no real facilities yet" but the "clubhouse overlooking the 18th green" (scheduled for 2006) will help make it "a blast to play", especially if the ammunition storage bunker off the 17th isn't entirely empty.

Stow Acres, North
21 | 17 | 17 | 19 | $56

58 Randall Rd., Stow; 978-568-8690; www.stowacres.com;
7046/5936; 74.2/74.4; 131/132

The 1995 host of the U.S. Amateur Public Links Championship is a "nice, long track that winds through some tall groves" offering "all the challenge you could want": a "very tight and tricky" front nine, "many doglegs" and plenty of ponds and streams to negotiate; be warned, however, it "gets worked to death in the summer" causing "ragged" conditions and "slow play", while snow play is more the norm in January and February when the course is generally closed for golf.

Stow Acres, South
19 | 18 | 18 | 19 | $56

58 Randall Rd., Stow; 978-568-8690; www.stowacres.com;
6520/5412; 71.7/71.6; 128/123

"Ugly sister of the two Stow courses", this spread 25 miles west of Boston "doesn't hold a candle to the North", but it's "still a challenge with significant elevation changes" and "narrow" holes where "woods come into play a lot"; plus, "during crowded times on the North, you can sneak on the South and play in peace" as long as you don't mind a sluggish pace and "so-so facilities."

Wachusett
∇ 20 | 16 | 15 | 20 | $35

187 Prospect St., West Boylston; 508-835-2264; www.wachusettcc.com;
6567/5573; 71.7/74.6; 124/121

This 1927 Donald Ross layout 45 minutes west of Boston has been family owned and operated since 1939 and has likely been "a local's favorite" for exactly as long because the "beautiful and scenic" course is "consistently well maintained" and offers "great value, great views . . . and cold beer"; from the Ross Tavern's deck, you can follow the action on the first three holes or simply gaze at the waters of the Wachusett Reservoir with a frosty pint in hand.

Michigan

★ **Top Courses in State**
29 Arcadia Bluffs, *Traverse City*
28 Lakewood Shores, Gailes, *Bay City*
27 Boyne Highlands, Arthur Hills, *Petoskey*
   Shanty Creek, The Legend, *Traverse City**
   Treetops, Robert Trent Jones Masterpiece, *Gaylord*

Bay City

Lakewood Shores, Blackshire   ▽ 23 | 12 | 17 | 20 | $63
7751 Cedar Lake Rd., Oscoda; 989-739-2075; 800-882-2493;
www.lakewoodshores.com; 6898/4936; 71.9/66.8; 125/105
"Pine Valley north", the newest of this resort's courses, mimics
the trees, rugged terrain and sandy waste areas of New Jersey's
illustrious private club; anyone who has never played the real
thing will probably "love it", especially if they first perfect their
precision on the complimentary pitch-and-putt course and after
go for a cholesterol count way higher than their golf score with a
baked cheese casserole and prime rib in the main dining room.

LAKEWOOD SHORES, GAILES   28 | 18 | 21 | 24 | $63
7751 Cedar Lake Rd., Oscoda; 989-739-2075; 800-882-2493;
www.lakewoodshores.com; 6954/5246; 75/72.2; 138/122
"It's worth going off the beaten path to play" what is "perhaps the
best mirror image of a Scottish links course in the USA", a "pure"
experience "without gimmicks" but full of deep bunkers, wispy
fescue and wind whipping off Lake Huron; "bring lots of balls and
then pack some more" because "the finishing holes are brilliant"
at this "extremely fun course", and it would be a shame to run out
of ammo before the final battle is won — or lost.

Red Hawk   ▽ 25 | 22 | 23 | 23 | $79
350 W. Davison Rd., East Tawas; 989-362-0800; www.redhawkgolf.net;
6589/4883; 71.6/69; 139/120
Beware the course bearing small yardage and high slope, because
it usually means a succession of short but nasty holes; this Arthur
Hills design on the state's northeastern shore is no exception to
the rule, with its superb string of serene, challenging, attractive
numbers that skirt wetlands and tumble down from ridgetops into
valleys; this is one tough bird, but "hands down, it's a keeper for
the price"; just don't let it leave you seeing red — cool down in the
handsome glass-and-cedar clubhouse after your round.

Detroit

Majestic at Lake Walden ⛳   ▽ 24 | 17 | 19 | 19 | $69
9600 Crouse Rd., Hartland; 810-632-5235; 800-762-3280;
www.majesticgolf.com
10/27: 6904/4896; 72/67.6; 136/109
1/18: 7009/5081; 73.8/68.7; 132/111
19/9: 6749/5033; 71.6/67.9; 134/113
Probably the most unique aspect of this "interesting", "enjoyable"
27-hole course encircling 150-acre Lake Walden is that "you must
take a boat across the water" between the third and first nines;
"kids love it", but it adds time to what is "usually a very long round"

to begin with, what with "lots of balls" lost to the dense forests that insulate the holes from one another; newcomers might not notice, but the clubhouse and bunkers have been recently renovated, possibly outdating the Facilities score.

Orchards, The ▽ 24 | 19 | 19 | 18 | $80

62900 Campground Rd., Washington; 586-786-7200; www.theorchards.com; 7036/5158; 74.5/70.3; 136/123

"You'll enjoy every hole" hail tree-hugging hackers of this "nice job" by Robert Trent Jones Jr. on a "great piece of property" that rolls out "a solid, picturesque layout" with a forested front and a "links-style" back nine where "stray shots are punished in the unplayable heather"; though it's considered "fairly pricey", the views of the Motown skyline are worth it on this "outstanding course" where 93 daunting bunkers made for an "excellent test" at the 2002 U.S. Amateur Public Links.

Shepherd's Hollow 26 | 24 | 23 | 19 | $85

9085 Big Lake Rd., Clarkston; 248-922-0300; www.shepherdshollow.com
10/19: 7235/4982; 76.1/70.4; 144/120
1/10: 7236/4906; 76/69.7; 147/120
19/1: 7169/4960; 75.5/69.7; 143/120

Perhaps it was divine intervention, but architect Arthur Hills was able to craft 27 "amazing, absolutely amazing" holes into "varied" and "wooded" terrain that was leased from a Roman Catholic order of priests; with 160 feet of elevation changes, this "very challenging" millennial spread is "just like being up north" in the mountains, though the "high-end", "country-club atmosphere", complete with rocking chairs for post-round relaxation on the veranda, is more refined than rustic.

Gaylord

Elk Ridge 26 | 23 | 20 | 25 | $75

9400 Rouse Rd., Atlanta; 989-785-2275; 800-626-4355; www.elkridgegolf.com; 7072/5261; 75.7/74.2; 145/133

Wolfish wallopers howl "too bad Atlanta is in the middle of nowhere" because it's the site of "the only course in America featuring a pig-shaped bunker"; you can't blow the house down on this "beautiful, wooded course" by "the creators of HoneyBaked Ham" unless you "learn to play left-to-right doglegs", though; it's "never crowded" – or it seems that way because there's "nice spacing for tee times so you don't feel constantly pushed", except perhaps to pig out on the owner's product afterwards.

Treetops, Rick Smith Signature 27 | 26 | 25 | 23 | $115

3962 Wilkinson Rd.; 989-732-6711; 888-873-3867; www.treetops.com; 6653/4604; 72.8/67; 140/123

If there is a signature style to golf-teacher-to-the-stars Rick Smith's namesake layout at his five-course, four-season resort, it's the "elevated greens" and "scenic, challenging and playable" holes coaxed from the "wonderful topography" of the Pigeon River Valley; regulars say it's "a pleasure to come back to every year" because there are "very reasonable golf package prices" and Legends is an "excellent, high-end (but casual) restaurant with a good wine list."

Treetops, Robert Trent Jones Masterpiece
27 | 26 | 25 | 22 | $115

3962 Wilkinson Rd.; 989-732-6711; 888-873-3867; www.treetops.com;
7060/4972; 75.5/70; 144/123

Spend a "great day" with "the granddaddy of northern Michigan golf", this Robert Trent Jones Sr. "masterpiece" that climbs and dips through the mountains for miles of "middle-of-nowhere" vistas; an "interesting" layout, it's "tough" from the tips but "enjoyable and playable" if you choose the proper set of tees for your skills; otherwise, the "excellent resort's" aptly named Broken Club Pub, with more than 60 types of beer, might be your sole salvation.

Treetops, Tom Fazio Premier
27 | 26 | 25 | 22 | $115

3962 Wilkinson Rd.; 989-732-6711; 888-873-3867; 800-444-6711;
www.treetops.com; 6832/5039; 73.6/70; 136/125

"Bring the hiking boots" because you'll be "playing right in the tree tops" at this "very hilly course" where the "large elevation changes" help you "hit some of the longest drives in your life" on Michigan's only Fazio course; the bunkering is "outstanding", the greens are "tricky" and the fairways are "tight", but they "funnel to the middle" for a "user-friendly" foray on a layout kept in "good condition" ("grass grows well in northern Michigan!"); afterward, "checking out the spa is a must."

Grand Rapids

Pilgrim's Run
▽ 27 | 23 | 24 | 27 | $65

11401 Newcosta Ave., Pierson; 888-533-7742; www.pilgrimsrun.com;
7093/4863; 74.1/67.7; 138/114

It's "a little remote" out "in the middle of nowhere", but somehow, two-time U.S. Open champion Lee Janzen found this "hidden gem" and shot 65, the course record; perhaps he went so low because he had "no distractions like houses, a pretentious staff or pestering rangers" to bother him on a "classic" where "wide, forgiving fairways" and "true greens" are "literally cut from a forest."

St. Ives Resort, St. Ives
▽ 26 | 24 | 25 | 20 | $99

9900 St. Ives Dr., Stanwood; 231-972-4837; 800-972-4837;
www.stivesgolf.com; 6702/4821; 73.3/68.7; 140/120

"When the Director of Golf is loading your bag, you know you're getting the best service anywhere" comment coddled club clingers about this 1995 Lake Mecosta "mixture of resort golf and a private club" in a "great setting" of highlands and wetlands with "stunning views" and "impeccable maintenance"; unlike its sister, Tullymore, this namesake track is located right next to its inn, yet both offer a free summer shuttle to nearby Soaring Eagle Casino.

St. Ives Resort, Tullymore
▽ 27 | 19 | 21 | 21 | $99

11969 Tullymore Dr., Stanwood; 231-972-4837; 800-972-4837;
www.stivesgolf.com; 7148/4668; 74.9/66.8; 148/115

Even though the affiliated 36-hole Canadian Lakes Resort is for members only, it's this "excellent" 2001 Jim Engh endeavor that "feels like a private golf sanctuary" because there are "no back-to-back holes", you "never see another group" and it has the "best beverage carts in the business"; it's "challenging" and "fair for all abilities because of the multiple tees", so those looking for "a true test" should head for the tips – just "don't expect a great score."

Lansing

Forest Akers MSU, East
| 19 | 20 | 18 | 24 | $27 |

Harrison Rd., East Lansing; 517-355-1635; www.golf.msu.edu;
6559/5111; 70.3/67.8; 114/110

"The play is slow, but the price is right; go green, go white!" chant cheerleaders of this "good college layout" that's "pretty flat" and therefore playable "no matter what your level"; don't be fooled by the mild terrain, though – West's sibling is "harder than it looks", so take advantage of the "great driving range" on this "value", particularly for MSU students.

Forest Akers MSU, West
| 25 | 24 | 22 | 27 | $42 |

Forest Rd., East Lansing; 517-355-1635; www.golf.msu.edu;
7013/5278; 74/70.3; 136/123

Students involved in the MSU Turfgrass Environmental Stewardship Program ensure this "great layout" is "well taken care of", keeping it in "better-than-country-club condition", despite coeds clamoring for the "tremendous value" here; redesigned in 1992 by alum Arthur Hills, the "tough" track is "one of the best college courses anywhere", "a long ball hitter's" baby that's still "fun for the rest of us", particularly if we stop in first at the "top practice area."

Hawk Hollow 🏨
| ▽ 27 | 24 | 21 | 22 | $65 |

15101 Chandler Rd., Bath; 517-641-4295; 888-411-4295;
www.hawkhollow.com
10/19: 6693/4962; 72.8/70; 134/120
1/10: 6974/5078; 73.7/69.7; 136/120
19/1: 6487/4934; 71.7/69.1; 129/117

Warm up on the "wonderful ranges, short-game area and putting course", and you'll be in as "fine shape" as these three "diverse nines" at this "superb complex"; only "getting better as it matures", this track's "risk/reward style" "gives lots of options", especially on the "great holes around a large pond" called Hawk Lake; the "beautiful clubhouse" and new Eagle Eye sister course round out the options at this "bang for the buck in central Michigan."

Pohlcat
| 21 | 17 | 20 | 19 | $75 |

6595 E. Airport Rd., Mt. Pleasant; 989-773-4221; 800-292-8891;
www.pohlcat.net; 6889/5140; 73.3/69.5; 133/126

"A great place for intermediate golfers looking for the next step" is this design by Champions Tour player and Mt. Pleasant native Dan Pohl; while the "wide-open fairways and well-trimmed rough" on the front "leave more to be desired", "the back tightens up your skills" with "lots of different holes to keep it interesting", including ones with forced carries over the Chippewa River; unfortunately, with those "bread-and-butter outings" in the "last half of the season", the track "takes a pounding" – just like you will afterward at "the nearby casino."

Timber Ridge
| 21 | 18 | 19 | 21 | $69 |

16339 Park Lake Rd., East Lansing; 517-339-8000;
www.golftimberridge.com; 6585/5175; 73/71.4; 144/132

The holes are named to reflect the character of each as per the Scottish tradition, but far from the British Isles–style, this "fun" spread with "trees, trees, trees" (60 types in all) is "a northern Michigan golf experience at lower Michigan prices" making it a "good value" "without having to travel" there; not only that, but the conditions are some of the "best" around for a public course.

Muskegon

Double JJ Ranch, Thoroughbred 🏌

▽ 23 | 22 | 21 | 20 | $79

6886 Water Rd., Rothbury; 231-894-4444; www.doublejj.com; 6900/4851; 73.6/68.3; 146/121
Its name refers to the "attached dude ranch" that anchors this "nice resort", but this "scenic" 1993 Arthur Hills design has plenty of kick of its own; "how about a 475-yd., uphill par-4 to start the round", followed by a bevy of "blind shots" and "a couple of tricked-up holes"?; if it weren't for the three other sets of tees, "one of the highest sloped courses" in the country would be "almost too hard."

Petoskey

Bay Harbor 🏌

27 | 27 | 27 | 17 | $199

3600 Village Harbor Dr., Bay Harbor; 231-439-4028; 800-462-6963; www.bayharborgolf.com
Links/Quarry: 6810/4151; 73.1/71.2; 146/136
Preserve/Links: 6810/4087; 72.9/69.1; 143/123
Quarry/Preserve: 6726/3906; 73/69.7; 147/128
These "awesome 27 holes" designed by Arthur Hills are "played by the few, the proud" and those with "deep pockets" but "one of Michigan's most high-priced courses" is "deservedly so"; "all three nines are special in their own way", linked only by equally "narrow fairways", "breathtaking views of the countryside and Grand Traverse Harbor", Michigan's Top Facilities and the "friendly and helpful guys in the pro shop"; just play this "head turner" "before it becomes private!"

BOYNE HIGHLANDS, ARTHUR HILLS 🏌

27 | 26 | 27 | 23 | $134

600 Highland Dr., Harbor Springs; 231-526-3028; 800-462-6963; www.boynehighlands.com; 7312/4811; 76.4/68.5; 144/117
Of Boyne Highlands' "four challenging courses", "the best of the bunch" is this Arthur Hills design that tempts you to "grip it and rip it" while simultaneously cooling your confidence with "steep slopes", "huge bunkers", unnerving water holes and "nary a flat putting surface"; after the round, there are "many restaurants" and the entertaining Young Americans Dinner Theatre to choose from, proving the resort "knows how to keep a golfer busy" – and pampered with its "great attention to customers" making for Michigan's Top Service.

Boyne Highlands, Donald Ross Memorial 🏌

26 | 23 | 24 | 21 | $109

600 Highland Dr., Harbor Springs; 231-526-3029; 800-462-6963; www.boynehighlands.com; 6814/4929; 74.5/68.5; 136/119
A "novel idea", this "great tribute" to Donald Ross replicates his "finest holes", cribbing from courses such as Aronimink, Inverness, Oakland Hills, Pinehurst No. 2 and Seminole; the "interesting layout" is "like playing in a museum", albeit one with "a high degree of difficulty", but that's still easier than "traveling to every location" where the architect did his handiwork.

Boyne Highlands, Heather | 25 | 25 | 25 | 24 | $129 |

600 Highland Dr., Harbor Springs; 231-526-3029; 800-462-6963;
www.boynehighlands.com; 6890/4794; 74/67.8; 136/111

"Another great course at Boyne" that is "not to be missed", this "absolutely classic" RTJ Sr. design dipping into woods and a blueberry bog "started the resort boom" in these parts in 1967; it gets "a lot of play", but it offers such a "great round" that "everyone who plays the track loves it", especially "in September" when it's "a great deal", so even if you think that Boyne Highlands' "lodging facilities need a blood transfusion", you'll probably agree that this layout is still beating strong.

Boyne Highlands, Moor | ▽ 20 | 25 | 24 | 21 | $79 |

600 Highland Dr., Harbor Springs; 231-526-3029; 800-462-6963;
www.boynehighlands.com; 6809/5061; 74.6/72; 135/122

Though it's "dwarfed by the other three" courses, this "good", "traditional layout" is "a nice complement" to its more heralded cousins because it's less crowded and "lots of fun to play", "providing a challenge" to newer roundsmen (like the swingers of the National Junior Golf Academy) as it doglegs and gallops "through the woods" and then splashes through water on 13 holes.

Traverse City

ARCADIA BLUFFS 🏌 | 29 | 27 | 27 | 22 | $175 |

14710 Northwood Hwy., Arcadia; 231-889-3001; 800-494-8666;
www.arcadiabluffs.com; 7300/5107; 75.4/70.1; 147/121

"You need a good windbreaker and a great knockdown shot" to play "around the many huge dunes" and "cavernous bunkers" on this "roller-coaster" links peering "over Lake Michigan", though the "wide fairways help compensate" for knock-hockey swings; just like its 225-ft. grade, its cost is "steep", but "it's a bargain" if you consider the "Kodak moments on every hole" of Michigan's No. 1 Course; caddies are only available in the summer, but the "excellent clubhouse dinner" is yours to devour all season.

Black Lake | ▽ 27 | 25 | 23 | 27 | $85 |

2800 Maxon Rd., Onaway; 989-733-4653; www.blacklakegolf.com;
7046/5058; 74.3/69.9; 140/125

Even anti-unionists who "hate supporting the UAW" admit that this Rees Jones design "in the beautiful setting" of the auto workers' family education center "about 240 miles north of Detroit" is "one of America's greatest unsung gems"; "if you're sponsored by a member, the rates drop" on a "fun and challenging" round featuring the par-3 14th with nine tees to choose from to avoid a tangle with the tentacled bunker; director of golf Pam Phipps, the first female PGA Master Professional, helps make this one women-friendly.

Dunmaglas 🏌 | ▽ 25 | 13 | 15 | 18 | $89 |

9031 Boyne City Rd., Charlevoix; 231-547-1022; www.dunmaglas.com;
6901/5175; 73.5/69.8; 139/123

On a treasure hunt for this "hidden gem", you might "question if you're lost", but it's "worth the search" to find "one of the toughest tests of golf you'll ever play"; the "difficult" and varied terrain dictated a "parkland-style front nine" and "links back", but all over the course there are "wildlife" and "wonderful views" of Lakes Michigan and Charlevoix, especially "in the fall" when the foliage is "stunning" – just tee off before mid-October when it closes until the following May.

Grand Traverse, The Bear ⛳ | 24 | 22 | 21 | 17 | $140 |
100 Grand Traverse Blvd., Acme; 231-938-1620; 800-748-0303;
www.grandtraverseresort.com; 7065/5281; 76.8/73.1; 146/137
"This course that started it all in northern Michigan" might be "getting a little long in the tooth", but the "Nicklaus classic" still puts up a "struggle"; indeed, "every challenge in golf is here" on "target"-style holes with "some hard carries", deep rough, lakes, mounds and "strategically placed" pot bunkers – and this is after "Jack toned it down"; "the facilities are starting to show their age" too, however, and some Michigan mashie masters say there are "more interesting" experiences "for a fraction of the price."

High Pointe | ▽ 21 | 15 | 17 | 24 | $51 |
5555 Arnold Rd., Williamsburg; 231-267-9900; 800-753-7888;
www.highpointegolf.com; 6890/4974; 73.3/68.7; 136/120
"Rumor has it" that the owner of this Traverse-area track "mucked up Tom Doak's original plans", though that might just be an easy explanation for the "completely different front and back nines", the first looking like "Scotland" and the second like "northern Michigan"; even if he did diddle with the design, he wound up with a "fun layout" in "great shape" that's "like playing two courses" for the price of one "cheaper than most nearby."

Shanty Creek, Cedar River | ▽ 25 | 22 | 21 | 21 | $120 |
1 Shanty Creek Rd., Bellaire; 231-533-6076; 800-678-4111;
www.shantycreek.com; 6989/5315; 73.6/70.5; 144/128
The newest course at this four-season family resort was made by Tom Weiskopf to be "fun" for the entire clan with a "variety of holes" ranging from parkland- to links-style and "great views" across rolling terrain that's kept in "fabulous condition"; the "fog can be brutal", as can the fees, but all around, it's "a nice golf experience."

SHANTY CREEK, THE LEGEND | 27 | 24 | 25 | 20 | $120 |
1 Shanty Creek Rd., Bellaire; 231-533-6076; 800-678-4111;
www.shantycreek.com; 6764/4953; 73.6/69.6; 137/124
You "don't want to miss" the "best course at Shanty Creek" golf and ski resort, a "beautiful and challenging" Arnold Palmer layout in a "great setting" amid thousands of trees along Lake Bellaire; "enjoy the first hole because No. 2 is a really tough" "debacle" designed for "those who hit sky drives."

Minnesota

Brainerd

GRAND VIEW LODGE, | 28 | 24 | 24 | 22 | $105 |
DEACON'S LODGE
Breezy Point, 9348 Arnold Palmer Dr., Pequot Lakes; 218-963-0001;
888-437-4637; www.deaconslodge.com; 6964/4766; 73.1/68.4; 134/120
Its name may refer to a deacon, but this "manicured" "challenge" "cut out of the northern woods" belongs to the King; Arnold Palmer crafted the Gull Lake resort's "crown jewel" with "large fairways", "great views" and "nasty rough", so "bring an extra ball" or spring for a sleeve in the excellent pro shop.

Grand View Lodge, Pines   ▽ 22 | 24 | 24 | 23 | $95

23521 Nokomis Ave., Nisswa; 218-963-0001; 888-437-4637;
www.grandviewlodge.com
Lakes/Woods: 6874/5134; 74.1/71; 144/131
Marsh/Lakes: 6837/5112; 74.1/70.7; 151/131
Woods/Marsh: 6883/5210; 74/70.6; 147/131

At a grand old resort on Gull Lake, this "classic northwoods" 27-holer sports three nines aptly named for their terrain; though word is that "the Lakes/Woods is the best combination", they're all "exceptionally scenic", and their multiple tees are "great for beginners" as well as "experts" looking for "quick play"; if the layout's "conditions have been dropping over the last several years", the weekend, all-you-can-eat prime rib special at Freddy's Tavern is as satisfying as ever.

Grand View Lodge, Preserve   24 | 22 | 23 | 22 | $95

23521 Nokomis Ave., Nisswa; 218-568-4944; 888-437-4637;
www.grandviewlodge.com; 6601/4816; 72.8/69.4; 140/126

Though six years younger, this "absolutely beautiful course" is "better than the Pines now"; it "plays like a dream" "through the woods" with "lots of elevation" changes and "breathtaking views from the first hole to the last", some of which take in the clubhouse where you can gobble a deep-fried walleye sandwich and sip a glass of Greg Norman Shiraz after your round.

MADDEN'S ON GULL LAKE, CLASSIC   29 | 26 | 26 | 22 | $104

11266 Pine Beach Peninsula; 218-829-2811; 800-642-5363;
www.maddens.com; 7102/4859; 75/69.4; 143/124

"You would think it was designed by a famous architect", but Minnesota's Top Course is the dreamchild of this Brainerd-area resort's golf superintendent, Scott Hoffman; an "amazingly beautiful northwoods course" on which "wildlife abounds", it "wraps around" Bass Lake and rides 60 feet of elevation changes amid enormous red oaks; even the "overpriced" fees can't ruin what is "a good day, no matter how you hit the ball."

Duluth

Giants Ridge, Legend 🏡   ▽ 29 | 25 | 27 | 28 | $80

County Rd. 138, Biwabik; 218-865-3001; 800-688-7669;
www.giantsridge.com; 6930/5084; 74.3/70.3; 138/124

"Awesome, awesome, awesome" sums up this "wonderful layout", which leverages proximity to the Superior National Forest and water holes to the max for a "very entertaining" round; the "service and conditions always exceed expectations" yet come at a "bargain compared to other Minnesota resorts" that probably don't offer game burgers (venison, elk and buffalo) in their grills; "you can't improve on perfection", rave fans, but you can avoid nature's little quirks by playing before "5 PM when the bugs come out."

Giants Ridge, Quarry   ▽ 29 | 22 | 25 | 27 | $80

County Rd. 138, Biwabik; 218-865-3088; 800-688-7669;
www.giantsridge.com; 7201/5119; 75.6/70.8; 146/125

Designer Jeff Brauer made "beautiful use of the land" at this resort, routing holes around gaping pits, massive boulders and scraggly waste areas of the former mineland and sand quarry and in and out of wetlands and woods, finding "incredible views" from the tees perched high above the fairways; swingers sweet on a pure experience say "together with the Legend", this is "the best golf destination in the state and maybe the region", "with value to boot."

Minneapolis

Baker National
19 | 18 | 19 | 24 | $36

2935 Parkview Dr., Medina; 763-694-7670; www.bakernational.com; 6762/5313; 73.9/72.7; 135/128

"The back in particular is high-caliber" on this muni "favorite" where a regulation nine-hole course was fleshed out into a full spread by Michael Hurdzan in 1991; with their woods and wetlands, Nos. 10–18 contrast the more wide-open front, which begins with a view of a red barn and, later, spies Lake Spurzem; along with a 60-station grass range, it's a "pretty" place with "reasonable costs."

Chaska Town
26 | 20 | 19 | 24 | $55

3000 Town Course Dr., Chaska; 952-443-3748; www.chaskatowncourse.com; 6817/4853; 73.8/69.4; 140/119

Given an "even better value for Chaska residents" on a course that already has one of the "best quality-to-cost" ratios near Minneapolis, you "may consider moving" to the town that runs this Arthur Hills layout; "you can't ride carts in the fairways" of the "forgiving front nine" or "tougher back" that bounds through oak groves, open prairie and marshes, but that's what helps keep it in such "excellent shape", especially for a "busy muni."

Edinburgh U.S.A.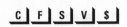
20 | 22 | 19 | 20 | $48

8700 Edinbrook Crossing, Brooklyn Park; 763-315-8550; www.edinburghusa.com; 6888/5319; 74.2/71.5; 149/133

This Robert Trent Jones Jr. design that hosted the LPGA Tour in the '90s is "convenient to downtown Minneapolis", but locals would even travel for its mind-over-muscle setup, "great" conditions and "resort/private-class" facilities at muni prices; the "houses are kind of tight" on the course, so do your best to "hit really straight", and even if you fail this "good test", at least you can say you played on the largest green in the U.S., a 43,000-square-footer that multitasks for the 9th, 18th and practice area.

Legends Club
▽ 27 | 25 | 21 | 21 | $75

8670 Credit River Blvd., Prior Lake; 952-226-4777; www.legendsgc.com; 7046/5297; 74.1/71.1; 144/126

"One of the best courses in the metro area" "gets better every year" as its "interesting holes" mature into "testing all aspects of your game" – especially your course management skills as there are lakes, ponds and creeks, 20 acres of wetlands and copious white sand bunkers to circumvent; at the turn, parkland changes to links, but both halves offer "sweeping vistas" and a cart path that leads back to the "great bar and restaurant after your round."

Les Bolstad
▽ 17 | 11 | 14 | 24 | $30
University of Minnesota Golf Course

2275 Larpenteur Ave. W., St. Paul; 612-627-4000; www.uofmgolf.com; 6278/5478; 70.2/72.3; 123/123

These Gophers truly are Golden because they can play this "old and venerable" course for "a very good price" whenever they

want; it's on the "shorter" side, but it's also "deceptively tough because the strategically mounded fairways" are bordered by "mature trees" and the "small, elevated greens" demand precision; just ask the 2002 men's team that won the NCAA Championship.

Rush Creek
25 | 25 | 22 | 18 | $99

7801 County Rd. 101, Maple Grove; 763-494-8844; www.rushcreek.com; 7125/5422; 74.8/72; 144/131

Almost "no homes on the course makes the experience more pure", while "lots of interesting holes" put a premium on "shotmaking" at this "exceptionally maintained" female-friendly formation, host to the 2004 U.S. Amateur Public Links Championship and several LPGA events; the "A+++ staff" "helps you feel like a member", and one of the "best practice setups" "in the metro area" is partially covered so you can brush up your drive in the "pouring rain"; still, cut-rate roundswomen aren't rushing here as it's "expensive."

StoneRidge
24 | 21 | 21 | 23 | $79

13600 Hudson Blvd. N., Stillwater; 651-436-4653; www.stoneridgegc.com; 6992/5247; 74.2/71.3; 140/131

"You won't be disappointed" in this links because there are "no homes on-course", the fine conditioning is matched by "great service" and the "pace is fantastic", thanks to "courteous groups" letting faster folks through; it is "a little expensive", "but rarely do you have to pay full price" because there are "lots of specials", making this Bobby Weed work "a good value" more often than not.

Wilds, The
24 | 22 | 21 | 17 | $99

3151 Wilds Ridge Ct., NW, Prior Lake; 952-445-3500; www.golfthewilds.com; 7025/5095; 74.9/70.5; 147/125

Though foozlers fuss about "long tee shots over lakes", "greens that are a bit fast" and "too much O.B." near "surrounding homes", this Weiskopf/Morrish "champion" has a personality that's not as wild as its name; it's a "fair, forgiving" loop around ponderosa pines and wetlands past plenty of wildlife; though the "service doesn't live up to the upscale price", if you "play on one of the specials", such as the pay-the-temperature deal in the fall, you can narrow the gap.

Willinger's
26 | 19 | 21 | 26 | $42

6900 Canby Trail, Northfield; 952-652-2500; www.willingersgc.com; 6775/5166; 74.4/71.8; 150/135

Sure, they're "straight, traditional holes", but they're "way hard", too, on this "jewel" that's "tremendous for the money" and the mere "45-minute drive from Downtown"; "when the wind blows", it's "easy to get your lunch eaten straying" into "hazards on the front" or "trees on the back", so a day here "never gets boring", especially "during deer season when you hear gunshots" ("wear orange").

Mississippi

Gulfport

Bridges at Casino Magic
▽ 23 | 24 | 23 | 23 | $105

711 Casino Magic Dr., Bay Saint Louis; 228-467-9257; www.casinomagic-baystlouis.com; 6841/5108; 73.5/70.1; 138/126

"Bring plenty of extra balls" to the only Arnold Palmer course in Mississippi because, if the "thick rough" doesn't "swallow them", the "excess of water" will; 17 of 18 holes have the drink in play, so "accuracy is key", or "it will be a long day" at this "fine layout" "adjacent to the casino" offering "bargain" "package deals" that combine rounds with overnight stays at the elegant Bay Tower or more basic Casino Magic Inn.

Grand Casino Gulfport, Grand Bear ⚲
∇ 27 | 25 | 24 | 17 | $109

12040 Grand Way Blvd., Saucier; 228-604-7100; www.grandcasinos.com; 7204/4802; 75.5/68.4; 143/120

Jack Nicklaus left one of Mississippi's "most beautiful" courses "meandering down through the trees" in DeSoto National Forest, replete with pines and cypress wetlands; 25 minutes from the casino "out in the boonies" with "no houses, no development" encroaching on an "inspiring" round, the host of the 2002 and 2003 Hooters Tour has a "private-club feel" that is augmented by free bottled water and range balls.

Oaks, The
∇ 23 | 19 | 21 | 23 | $95

24384 Club House Dr., Pass Christian; 228-452-0909; www.theoaksgolfclub.com; 6885/4691; 72.5/66.4; 131/107

Just south of I-10 in the historic town of Pass Christian, you'll find this "golfer's course" in a gated community on the Gulf Coast to be a "tough" but "beautiful" test with "tight fairways and strategic wetlands" that "require a couple of sleeves of balls"; just ask the PGA Tour hopefuls who play the first round of Q-school on it and they'll likely confirm that it's a "good track" with a few "surprises here and there", including "greens that can be a little shady."

Shell Landing 🏌
∇ 27 | 23 | 21 | 20 | $109

3499 Shell Landing Blvd., Gautier; 228-497-5683; 866-851-0541; www.shelllanding.com; 7024/5047; 73.2/68.6; 128/112

"Davis Love III has done a great job creating a golf mecca in the middle of nowhere" (actually, between Biloxi and Pascagoula), a "beautifully designed" and "well-maintained" "secret on the Mississippi Gulf Coast" with tees named for turtles on a "good variety" of "fair but challenging" holes; though the course "needs to mature", the 25-acre practice facility with complimentary range balls is a "nice place to knock it around."

Jackson

Dancing Rabbit, Azaleas
26 | 23 | 19 | 22 | $78

1 Choctaw Trail, Choctaw; 601-663-0011; 888-372-2248; www.dancingrabbitgolf.com; 7128/4909; 74.4/68.6; 135/115

"It doesn't get much better than this" "well-conditioned" Tom Fazio/Jerry Pate "Mississippi gem" near Philadelphia, sigh Yankees staying in a guestroom in the antebellum clubhouse in the spring "when the azaleas are in bloom" and the course is "breathtaking"; unfortunately, they'll have to get on sultry Southern time to stomach the "slow play" on a layout that "should be called Dancing Turtle."

Dancing Rabbit, Oaks
∇ 23 | 24 | 21 | 23 | $78

1 Choctaw Trail, Choctaw; 601-663-0011; 888-372-2248; www.dancingrabbitgolf.com; 7076/5097; 74.6/69; 139/123

The Azaleas course's "fantastic" younger sister is "great fun" but not overly marked with yardage guides or signage, since its owner, the Mississippi Band of the Choctaw Indians, minimized the amount of artificial structures imposed on their sacred land; it's just as well, because, like the site's Big and Little Dancing Rabbit Creeks, the course flows naturally around the rolling terrain's rock formations.

Missouri

Kansas City

Tiffany Greens
▽ 24 | 25 | 21 | 19 | $65

6100 NW Tiffany Springs Pkwy.; 816-880-9600;
www.tiffanygreensgolf.com; 6977/5391; 74.4/71.3; 136/121
Even if this RTJ Jr. design is "still trading on the fact that it used to host the Senior Tour's" TD Waterhouse Championship, there's no denying that it's a "championship course", a "difficult but not impossible" links whose "large greens offer a wide variety of options"; aesthetes argue that, after "a wonderful opener", "about six holes look the same: 400 yards, fairway bunkers on right, woods left", but even they have to admit that it's kept in "nice condition."

Lake of the Ozarks

Club at Old Kinderhook, The
▽ 29 | 24 | 25 | 23 | $75

54-80 Lake Rd., Camdenton; 573-346-4444; 888-346-4949;
www.oldkinderhook.com; 6855/4962; 72.8/69.5; 137/123
"The top course these days down at Lake of the Ozarks" is this "very impressive" Tom Weiskopf design with an "interesting variety of holes" that dramatically dipsy-doodle into valleys, "through trees" and over "lots of water"; at tees like No. 8 that plays 100 feet downhill to a narrow landing en route to a hardwood- and wetlands-guarded green, it's a "breathtaking golf experience", but it's "more costly than most", so look for "coupons in the tourist brochures" for a discount.

Lodge of Four Seasons, Witch's Cove 🎧 🕐
▽ 23 | 24 | 21 | 18 | $85

Horseshoe Bend Pkwy., Lake Ozark; 573-365-8544; 800-843-5253;
www.4seasonsresort.com; 6557/5238; 71/70.8; 133/124
It's not just superstition that the "lake's level plays a big part in the challenge" on holes like the two par-3s carrying the water at this "beautiful" but scary "difficult" RTJ Sr. spread, so prepare to "use every club in your bag" and possibly "every ball"; still, chased by a filet at the sumptuous H.K.'s Steak House (now relocated to the main resort), it's a "nice golf experience", even if the grounds are "not maintained very well."

Osage National 🎧
23 | 20 | 19 | 21 | $65

400 Osage Hills Rd., Lake Ozark; 573-365-1950; 866-365-1950;
www.osagenational.com
Links/River: 7103/5026; 74.6/69.1; 141/120
Mountain/Links: 7165/5076; 74.7/69.9; 139/121
River/Mountain: 7150/5016; 75.6/69.2; 145/119
Though most people think all "27 excellent holes" were "designed by Arnold Palmer", he only created the original Mountain/River combo; still, "each nine" in this "beautiful setting" along the Osage River is "a joy to play" and "provides a different experience, from links to target to traditional, tree-lined golf"; lately, the course

"doesn't seem to be as crowded as others in the lake area", however, perhaps because it "has seen better times."

Tan-Tar-A, The Oaks
▽ 18 | 18 | 18 | 12 | $75

State Rd. KK, Osage Beach; 573-348-8521; 800-826-8272; www.tan-tar-a.com; 6432/3931; 72.1/61.3; 143/92

With water affecting play on 11 of its 18 holes, this "great layout" by Bruce Devlin and Robert Von Hagge places a premium on approach shots; unfortunately, no one seems to have placed a premium on its conditioning – the spread "requires a greater deal of care and attention" to merit its "expensive" fees; on the plus side, the "staff is great" and so is the variety of accommodations to choose from at a resort with nearly 1,000 rooms and suites.

Springfield

Branson Creek 🏌
▽ 26 | 14 | 20 | 23 | $94

144 Maple St., Hollister; 417-339-4653; www.bransoncreekgolf.com; 7036/5032; 73/68.6; 133/113

It's still "relatively new", but already "the premier course in the area" is this Tom Fazio design with "challenging holes" "laid out beautifully" for "great views", especially on the back, which is carved out of the Ozarks and drops dramatically from elevated tees; the experience "will be great when the clubhouse, etc., are built" and the layout "ages" to "maximum" effect.

St. Louis

Innsbrook Resort
19 | 20 | 18 | 20 | $52

1 Aspen Circle, Innsbrook; 636-928-6886; www.innsbrook-resort.com; 6465/5035; 70/67.7; 130/120

Though a "couple holes are a little contrived", this Lake Aspen resort sports "a fun course for all types of players"; it rolls through tree-lined corridors, skirts glistening ponds and culminates with four "great finishing holes"; "bring a fishing pole" and a wildlife field guide because birds, deer, snakes and turtles are pampered visitors to this "peaceful" Audubon Cooperative Sanctuary, even if management "has forgotten how to take care of the course."

Missouri Bluffs
24 | 21 | 19 | 17 | $95

18 Research Park Circle, St. Charles; 636-939-6494; www.mobluffs.com; 7047/5191; 73.2/69.2; 131/115

Tom Fazio cut the wide fairways for this "beautiful challenge" from an old oak and hickory forest, and its "great variety" of "reachable par-5s and challenging par-4s and -3s", as well as its "spectacular topography", separates it from other local courses"; play it while you can, because the club is soon "going private, and it shows" in the "excellent practice facilities", "well-kept" turf and "great marshals" who "keep the pace flowing even on weekends."

Pevely Farms 🏌
21 | 20 | 20 | 16 | $69

400 Lewis Rd., Eureka; 636-938-7000; www.pevelyfarms.com; 7115/5249; 74.6/70.7; 138/117

Once a farm for cows and goats, this 1998 Arthur Hills design is now home to the Rams, St. Louis' football-playing foozlers who touch down "in the middle of nowhere" for the "great views" across the Meramec River Valley from dramatic fairways that bob and weave through lush terrain to "fast greens that read true"; though money is no object to professional athletes, local linksters lament that "the price is too high" for a layout that has a couple of "hokey, tricked-out holes."

Quail Creek | 18 | 16 | 17 | 19 | $58 |

6022 Wells Rd.; 314-487-1988; www.quailcreekgolfclub.com; 6980/4374; 73.6/69.2; 141/109

Three-time U.S. Open winner Hale Irwin is no pushover, and neither is his "well-maintained" 1986 design, the toughest in town thanks to rolling hills, narrow fairways and forced carries over creeks and ponds; a "great value", the "above-average" club is a "very popular tournament site", so "call ahead" because it can get "busy", and the "friendly" but harried staff can turn "unapproachable."

Montana

Butte

Old Works | - | - | - | - | $41 |

1205 Pizzini Way, Anaconda; 406-563-5989; 888-229-4833; www.oldworks.org; 7705/5348; 76/69.1; 133/119

The remnants of a copper smelting plant at a cleaned-up Superfund site form the unlikely backdrop for a "terrific place and incredible course" that benefits from "some of Jack Nicklaus' best design work"; though the "black slag is tough to hit out of", "you won't be bored" attempting it on this "great way to spend $50 and play a Golden Bear" beauty.

Kalispell

Big Mountain | - | - | - | - | $49 |

3230 Hwy. 93 N.; 406-751-1950; 800-255-5641; www.golfmt.com; 7015/5421; 72.5/69.5; 121/117

Formerly known as Northern Pines, this formidable Flathead Valley find, designed by two-time U.S. Open Champion and investor Andy North, changed its name to get in the groove with the resort community down the road; its rolling, open meadow front is eclipsed by parkland on the back, where several holes play along and over the rushing river against a backdrop encompassing snow-capped Glacier National peaks, Big Mountain ski runs and the occasional bear or mountain lion.

Nebraska

North Platte

Wild Horse | ▽ 29 | 23 | 24 | 29 | $38 |

40950 Rd. 768, Gothenburg; 308-537-7700; www.playwildhorse.com; 6805/4688; 73/67.7; 125/108

"It's worth driving two days" to "the middle of nowhere" because this jaw-droppingly "fantastic" re-creation of "Scotland in the heartland" is "one of the best courses you will ever play" at just about the "best value in the U.S."; it's "surprising the golf carts are not John Deere" at this links "smack dab in the corn belt", but you don't need a tractor to get across the well-groomed spread say "avid golfers" who wouldn't let wild horses drag them away from "playing it multiple times."

Omaha

Quarry Oaks ▽ 27 | 27 | 25 | 24 | $72

16600 Quarry Oaks Dr., Ashland; 402-944-6000; 888-944-6001;
www.quarryoaks.com; 7010/5068; 75.1/72.3; 143/124

Eyes shut, swingers swallow "lots of eye candy" as well as "blind tee shots" on this "hidden gem along the Platte River close to metropolitan Omaha and the football hotbed of Lincoln"; with the water "running along several holes", it's a tough track to tackle, though gridironists aren't being sarcastic when they rave "I can't wait to go back" – particularly so they can visit afterward with the "wild turkeys, buffalo and elk roaming in the nearby reserve."

Nevada

★ **Top Courses in State**
28 Shadow Creek, *Las Vegas*
Reflection Bay, *Las Vegas*
Wolf Creek, *Las Vegas*
27 Bear's Best Las Vegas, *Las Vegas*
26 Primm Valley, Lakes, *Las Vegas*

Las Vegas

Angel Park, Mountain 🏞 17 | 19 | 18 | 19 | $155

100 S. Rampart Blvd.; 702-254-4653; 888-629-3929; www.angelpark.com;
6722/5150; 71.1/69.1; 130/114

"Take the whole family" and "warm up with a wonderful putting course or fun par-3" track before tackling the "longer and more challenging" of the two Arnold Palmer/Ed Seay designs at Angel Park; besides "a few tough holes that require you to carry multiple hazards", it's "forgiving and playable" with "wide-open, reachable par-5s" and "beautiful mountain views"; just note, at prices that "won't break the bank" "by Vegas standards", "it's so crowded that nobody goes there anymore."

Angel Park, Palm 🏞 17 | 18 | 15 | 19 | $155

100 S. Rampart Blvd.; 702-254-4653; 888-629-3929; www.angelpark.com;
6525/4570; 70.9/66.2; 129/111

Since it sits next to robust practice facilities just 15 minutes from the Strip, it's no surprise that this "flat", "short" yet "tricky" track designed by Arnold Palmer and Ed Seay (then redesigned by Bob Cupp and John Fought) sees "lots of play" from Vegas vacationers looking for "a great deal of fun"; unfortunately, there are so "many bad golfers" among them, "a six-hour round is not uncommon."

Bali Hai 🏌 21 | 23 | 23 | 12 | $295

5160 Las Vegas Blvd. S.; 702-450-8000; 888-397-2499;
www.waltersgolf.com; 7002/5535; 73/71; 130/122

They spared no expense (and neither will you) at this "artificially perfect" "tropical paradise in the middle of the desert" with "elevation changes, water features", palm trees and volcanic rocks; those required forecaddies "don't come cheap", and the "somewhat cramped" layout with "constant airplane" "noise overhead" "would be considered marginal but for the superb location" right on the Strip where you can almost "feel the presence of Dean Martin."

Bear's Best Las Vegas 27 | 24 | 26 | 19 | $245

11111 W. Flamingo Rd.; 702-804-8500; 866-385-8500; www.bearsbest.com; 7194/5043; 74/68.7; 147/116

"It costs a small fortune to play" this "excellent anthology", "but it's not every day" you get a crack at "signature" holes from Jack Nicklaus courses all over the West and in Mexico; "you need to be on your game", so it's a good thing the "friendly, helpful" forecaddies are "mandatory", since they'll probably "save you at least six strokes"; "if you don't like this" after ogling the Golden Bear's photos in the clubhouse restaurant overlooking the Red Rock Mountains and the Vegas skyline, "you must be a bowler."

Cascata ▽ 29 | 29 | 29 | 18 | $500

1 Cascata Dr., Boulder City; 702-294-2000; www.golfcascata.com; 7137/5591; 74.6/67.2; 143/117

Only Caesars guests have the privilege of forking over the über-"expensive" fee or losing "money on the blackjack tables to get comped" at this Rees Jones oasis; it's "worth it" because there "isn't a blade of grass out of place" on this "long, tight track with lots of elevation changes", "awesome vistas" and a "spectacular" 418-ft. waterfall that spills into "a river running through the clubhouse" where "your own name is on your locker"; "the course, the staff, the food and beverage – all of it rates a huge wow!!"

DragonRidge 25 | 20 | 22 | 17 | $225

552 S. Stephanie St., Henderson; 702-614-4444; www.dragonridgegolf.com; 7039/5040; 72.9/68.3; 143/118

"Bring your hiking boots" since "one of the best golf experiences in the immediate Vegas vicinity" sports some "steep climbs to and from the tee boxes and greens" on the McCullough Mountains where there are "terrific views" of the city; whether at "high-priced" peak times or "in the off-season when it's a great value" for the area, it offers a "well-designed", "well-conditioned" "mix of target golf and traditional holes" – just "hurry" up and play it "before the houses are all constructed."

Falls at Lake Las Vegas Resort 25 | 23 | 25 | 17 | $270

101 Via Vin Santo, Henderson; 702-740-5258; 877-698-4653; www.lakelasvegas.com; 7243/5300; 74.7/68.3; 136/118

Golfers "gotta love the man-made lake" that punctuates this "wind-blown" Weiskopf wonderland, a "dramatic challenge" that requires "lots of different shots", especially on the back nine that rolls "uphill and downhill" past "views of the Strip, the mountains and even some long-horned sheep"; granted, it's "a little expensive" and the property is "being overbuilt with real estate", but hey, "it's Vegas after all."

Las Vegas Paiute Resort, Snow Mountain 26 | 24 | 24 | 22 | $175

10325 Nu Wav Kaiv Blvd.; 702-658-1400; 866-284-2833; www.lvpaiutegolf.com; 7146/5341; 73.9/70.4; 125/117

"You don't have to rob a bank to pay the greens fee" at this Paiute Resort getaway full of "fine Pete Dye features" like holes that accentuate the "magnificent" "desert and mountain views" and a "remarkable finish"; "the wind takes the bite out of the heat", but when it "howls", "the course will win every time" – it's a happy concession, though, since it's "always in the best possible shape" and the "attentive" staff makes it "one of the better Vegas values."

Las Vegas Paiute Resort, Sun Mountain 🏌

`25 | 24 | 25 | 22 | $155`

10325 Nu Wav Kaiv Blvd.; 702-658-1400; 866-284-2833; www.lvpaiutegolf.com; 7112/5465; 73.3/71; 130/123

With its "wide fairways" and other "forgiving" features, this Pete Dye design offers high-handicaps "the most fun of the three courses" on the Paiute reservation where all the spreads sport "mountain and desert" "scenery that is over the top"; from the "terrific" staff that "makes you feel welcome" to the "excellent conditions, even in January", this "classy operation" that is "not surrounded by housing tracts" is "worth the trip from Downtown" especially at twilight rates that are "a deal."

Las Vegas Paiute Resort, Wolf 🏌

`26 | 25 | 24 | 21 | $215`

10325 Nu Wav Kaiv Blvd.; 702-658-1400; 866-284-2833; www.lvpaiutegolf.com; 7604/5130; 76.3/68.8; 149/116

This "Pete Dye monster" lurking in the "Las Vegas hinterlands" is "Jekyll when calm and Hyde when the wind gets going", so "practice your knockdown shot" on the "large grass driving range" before confronting its "undulating" fairways and greens "built through arroyos"; "the most difficult of the three" Paiute courses, this Wolf will sink its teeth into your game on holes like No. 15, a "longer, harder version" of "the island green from Sawgrass", but the bite will be "absolutely unforgettable."

Legacy, The 🏌

`22 | 21 | 20 | 20 | $155`

130 Par Excellence Dr., Henderson; 702-897-2187; 888-446-5358; www.thelegacygc.com; 7233/5340; 74.5/71; 137/120

Though the mansions lining the fairways "make you want to hit big in the casinos", this "open and beautiful" layout just a "short trip from The Strip" is a "primo alternative to gambling" – when it's not "backed up"; "wider than most desert courses", it's so "easy", that it might be "a bit of a bore" for scratch players, but it gives high-handicaps "a sense of confidence" that even the "nets in front of the big homes" can't rattle.

Oasis Golf Club, Oasis 🏌

`24 | 20 | 21 | 24 | $140`

100 Palmer Ln., Mesquite; 702-346-7820; www.theoasisgolfclub.com; 6633/4508; 71.7/64.9; 133/109

Shhh, this "great Arnold Palmer course" and host to the Nevada Open only "about an hour" northeast of Las Vegas is a "local secret"; once you've experienced the "breathtaking views" from the 125-ft. "elevated tees" and "must-play" holes "cut out of the mountains", it's your tough job to keep it quiet – at least until its sister, Canyons, opens in the fall of 2005.

Primm Valley, Desert 🏌

`25 | 23 | 24 | 24 | $175`

31900 S. Las Vegas Blvd., Primm; 702-679-5510; 800-386-7837; www.primmvalleyresorts.com; 7131/5397; 74.6/71.6; 138/129

"If you aren't enough of a high roller to get to Shadow Creek", this "super" spread is "your best alternative" because, as at the aforementioned luxe layout, MGM Mirage guests receive priority access and discounts, and the "almost butlerlike staff" treats you like a bigwig from the moment you step onto the "incredible driving range" until you finish this Fazio formation festooned with flowers, "palm trees, big waste bunkers and beautiful views"; best of all, it's only "a short drive from Vegas . . . at 80 m.p.h."

Primm Valley, Lakes 🔊
26 | 24 | 23 | 24 | $175

31900 S. Las Vegas Blvd., Primm; 702-679-5510; 800-386-7837; 6945/4842; 74/68.5; 134/121
"As its name implies", there's "lots of water", plus "a forest of evergreens" on this "beautiful" Fazio track with "wider fairways and landing areas" than its sister; it's still a "desert layout" though, so you might need "your own water boy" to douse you during the "intense summer heat"; luckily, a staff that "treats you like a king" leaves you "little to complain about" besides "lots of sun", so play it along with the other course for a "first-class" "one-two punch."

REFLECTION BAY AT
LAKE LAS VEGAS RESORT
28 | 26 | 25 | 18 | $270

75 Montelago Blvd., Henderson; 702-740-4653; 877-698-4653; www.lakelasvegas.com; 7261/5166; 74.8/70; 138/127
This "dramatic but playable" Nicklaus design "has something for everybody": "a little bit of mountain golf, desert golf and lake golf", all in "mint condition"; from the "breathtaking waterfalls" to the "interesting par-3 to a peninsular green", the course "exudes class", as do the "very kind" staff and "top-notch facilities"; "look for the room-and-round package deals" to manage the "ridiculous cost", and expect "the overall experience to improve when the surrounding construction is done."

Revere, Concord
23 | 22 | 21 | 20 | $195

2600 Hampton Rd., Henderson; 702-259-4653; 877-273-8373; www.reveregolf.com; 7034/5306; 72.8/70; 126/119
Though it's set on "long, steep" "mountainous terrain", the newer of the Revere courses is "more forgiving", with "greener-than-life" "fairways and rough geared to get the ball to roll back into play" so you don't have to "take relief from the desert"; there's nothing forgiving about heat that's "over 100 in the shade", but the "friendly staff" will steer you toward the "nice facilities" where you can take liquid relief at Buckman's Grille with its sweeping skyline views.

Revere, Lexington 🔊
23 | 22 | 21 | 20 | $235

2600 Hampton Rd., Henderson; 702-259-4653; 877-273-8373; www.reveregolf.com; 7143/5305; 73.6/69.6; 139/116
Good thing there's a "great range and putting/chipping greens" because this desert duel "designed by sadists" PGA veteran Billy Casper and architect Greg Nash involves plenty of target-golf and risk/reward shots from elevated tees through rocky canyons to small, "tough greens"; it's so "immaculately groomed", it "looks painted" on, but so do the lawns of the "many homes around it."

Rio Secco
25 | 24 | 22 | 17 | $275

2851 Grand Hills Dr., Henderson; 702-889-2400; 888-867-3226; www.riosecco.net; 7332/5778; 75.7/70; 142/127
"Yikes" — "narrow valleys and long carries over canyons and water" make this Rees Jones "thrill" "extremely difficult", and

the "tough-to-putt" greens "will leave you wondering which way is up"; don't worry – "once you've been humbled by the terrain", you can "take some lessons from Tiger's former teacher", Butch Harmon, whose school is headquartered here; it's "pricey", but "gamblers staying at Harrah's properties can golf cheaply."

Royal Links 村   17 | 19 | 20 | 13 | $250

5995 Vegas Valley Dr.; 702-450-8123; 888-427-6682; www.waltersgolf.com; 7029/5142; 73.7/69.8; 135/115

"Except for the cactus" and a climate that's "sans wind and rain", these "18 copies of British Open holes", complete with "unforgiving rough and truly terrifying pot bunkers", are "quite like their counterparts across the pond"; however, "fescue just will not grow in the desert", so, though the required forecaddies' "royal service", the castle-style clubhouse and Stymie's Pub feel authentic, Anglophiles argue "the attempt to imitate holes doesn't work that well", and the location "near a waste treatment plant" doesn't help.

SHADOW CREEK 村 ⌐   28 | 28 | 28 | 16 | $500

3 Shadow Creek Dr., North Las Vegas; 702-791-7161; 866-260-0069; www.shadowcreek.com; 7239/6701

"Bring your camera, your A game and a high-limit credit card" because the MGM Mirage's Fazio "fantasy come true" – where stars like "Michael Jordan" play around waterfalls and creeks on "meticulously maintained" grounds – is "the second coming of Shangri-La", but at a "ridiculous price"; still, considering that the layout (which remains unrated by the USGA) is "phenomenal", "the condition of the driving range is better than most courses' greens" and "they pick you up in a limo" to play here, Nevada's No. 1 Course, Facilities and Service are a better value "than gambling."

Siena 🏠   19 | 20 | 21 | 21 | $175

10575 Siena Monte Ave.; 702-341-9200; 888-689-6469; www.sienagolfclub.com; 6843/4978; 71.5/68; 129/112

There's "plenty of room off the tee", but "get ready for three-putts on the ultra-undulating greens", and try not to sink into "all the sand in Italy" in the 97 bunkers on this "nice course" in a Tuscan-themed development; just give yourself ample time to get to the finish: "too many houses around" it means there are "too many" locals on it, so a round can "take about six hours during the week."

TPC at The Canyons 🏠   24 | 24 | 22 | 18 | $250

9851 Canyon Run Dr.; 702-256-2000; www.tpc.com; 7063/5039; 73/67; 131/109

You might "need to sell your home to afford" to play the PGA Tour's Michelin Championship venue in the winter, but it's "a bargain out of season", "if you're willing to play in 106-degree" "dry heat"; use the leftover cash on bottled water and "an extra sleeve of balls", as "it's not called The Canyons for nothing" – the "tight" corridors, arroyo "carries" and blind shots over *Flintstones*-style landscape can cause "slow rounds", but it's still "target golf at its finest."

WOLF CREEK 🏠   28 | 20 | 22 | 22 | $180

401 Paradise Pkwy., Mesquite; 702-346-9026; 866-252-4653; www.golfwolfcreek.com; 6994/4169; 75.4/61; 154/106

Though "the fairways are wider than you think", heat-seeking hackers take a "blissful beating" at the third-toughest track in the country, "a desert course where water will get you"; these "surreal" holes "flanked by sand, arroyos, red rock cliffs, a stream" and waterfalls with "jaw-dropping vistas" are "spectacular" – "and completely punishing if you're off target"; since the smallish driving range "isn't good for woods", just "lose the pride and drop down a tee box for a more enjoyable round."

Wynn Las Vegas 🏌 ⚬₸ | – | – | – | – | $500
3131 Las Vegas Blvd. S.; 702-770-3575; 888-320-9966;
www.wynnlasvegas.com; 7042/6464
Crank the switch and blast the neon, because Vegas showman Steve Wynn (of Bellagio, Mirage and Shadow Creek fame) has unveiled his eponymous Strip hotel and must-stay-to-play golf course; with co-designer Tom Fazio, the developer imploded the old, flat Desert Inn formation and built this predictably jaw-dropping, tight, rolling track blanketed with pines, flowers and water features, including a 37-ft. drive-through waterfall that backdrops the closing green; N.B. the luxe layout has not been rated by the USGA.

Reno

Edgewood Tahoe 🏌 | 26 | 24 | 23 | 18 | $200
180 Lake Pkwy., Lake Tahoe; 775-588-3566; 888-881-8659;
www.edgewood-tahoe.com; 7445/5567; 75.5/71.3; 144/136
"Feel like a star teeing off" on the host of the Celebrity Golf Championship, George Fazio's "spectacular course along the shores of Lake Tahoe"; this "good test of golf" combines "some challenging holes and some breathers" with a "great finishing stretch" starting with "the 16th, one of the most beautiful" par-5s in Nevada; if you find the "cart-path-only policy" "unforgiveable", the bar and restaurant might inspire you to leniency – overlooking the water, they "deserve a visit even if you don't play golf."

Lake Ridge | ▽ | 19 | 17 | 17 | 22 | $95
1200 Razorback Rd.; 775-825-2200; 800-815-6966; www.lakeridgegolf.com;
6715/5156; 71.8/68.5; 130/121
After a few "relatively weak opening holes" on this 1969 RTJ Sr. design, "the rest of the course is quite stunning", especially the "stronger back nine" with its "spectacular elevation changes" on holes like "incredible" No. 15, a 239-yd., island-green par-3 perched 140 feet above Lake Stanley; perhaps it's best that it starts off easy because this "Reno standard" can get "crowded on weekends", and there are "no practice facilities" to help grease the gears.

New Hampshire

Colebrook

Balsams Panorama ⊙ | 24 | 21 | 22 | 20 | $60
Rte. 26, Dixville Notch; 603-255-4961; 800-255-0600;
www.thebalsams.com; 6804/4978; 72.8/67.8; 130/115
"You can see Canada" from this "beautiful mountaintop course", a "Donald Ross classic" "at the northern tip of New Hampshire" that began as six holes in 1897, but you'd better "bring your greens-reading glasses" because many of the "tough" dance floors appear to "break uphill"; it "can be played on a day trip, but treat yourself to the full Balsams experience" in which "the food is as stupendous

as the golf", the accommodations "transport you back to the grand hotel era" and your rounds are on the house.

Keene

Bretwood, North   ▽ 21 | 15 | 16 | 21 | $38
E. Surry Rd.; 603-352-7626; www.bretwoodgolf.com; 6976/5140; 73.7/69.8; 136/120
Don't bother with weekday reservations for this "very casual" course in the southwest corner of the state, as it's first-come, first-served; the Ashuelot River bisecting it provides "plenty of scenery as well as challenge", making it "tough for beginners", not to mention past participants in the New Hampshire Open and State Amateur; like all the holes, the island-green par-3 is tricky in the ever-present wind, but "when the weather is ideal", this track with its quaint covered bridges is "a real pleasure to visit."

Shattuck   20 | 11 | 16 | 18 | $55
53 Dublin Rd., Jaffrey; 603-532-4300; www.shattuckgolf.com; 6764/4632; 73.5/73.1; 153/139
"At the base of Mt. Monadnock" is "as tough a course as was ever designed", a "scenic" but "punitive" promenade through oak, birch and pine forests and wetlands with "multiple bogs to hit over" onto "narrow fairways" and "tiny greens", if you can avoid "the rough that swallows balls whole"; "be prepared to lose a dozen, even when you're playing well" on a layout that "would be packed if it were more accessible" with a clubhouse that wasn't so "poor."

Portsmouth

Portsmouth Country Club ⊕   ▽ 23 | 21 | 19 | 19 | $90
80 Country Club Ln., Greenland; 603-436-9719; www.portsmouthcc.net; 7072/5134; 73.6/64.8; 123/108
An hour north of Boston, the "only Trent Jones Sr. course in New Hampshire" is in "excellent condition" with "typically fast greens"; it's "forgiving if the wind isn't blowing", though the holes along Great Bay – including a "par-5 into the prevailing breeze with the green sitting in the harbor" – "can get hairy" when it gusts; it's "loaded with locals" who clean their plates of fried haddock in the Clipper Lounge, even if some claim "the hot dog stand is far better."

New Jersey

★ **Top Courses in State**
27 Crystal Springs, Ballyowen, *NYC Metro*
     Pine Hill, *Cherry Hill*
26 Hominy Hill, *Freehold*
     Twisted Dune, *Atlantic City*
25 Architects, *Trenton*

Atlantic City

Blue Heron Pines, West ⊕   24 | 22 | 22 | 19 | $126
550 W. Country Club Dr., Cologne; 609-965-4653; 888-478-2746; www.blueheronpines.com; 6777/5053; 72.9/69.2; 132/119
"You can't go wrong" at this early proponent of the "upscale public course" trend in the Atlantic City area because it's "always in

great shape" and the "elevated tees on many holes" allow an "easy view" of the "sand" to avoid and the "slick greens" to hold; hopefully, its new owner will revise the rates because, even with a "professional staff" that provides "private-club treatment", it's "a bit pricey for what you get"; N.B. its former sister, East, is to be ploughed under for development.

HARBOR PINES | 24 | 22 | 21 | 20 | $130 |

500 Saint Andrews Dr., Egg Harbor Township; 609-927-0006; www.harborpines.com; 6827/5099; 72.3/68.8; 129/118

"Well designed for all levels of golfer", this "nice place to play when down the shore" offers "a decent mix of risk and reward with some short holes" on "beautiful grounds"; just "be prepared to three-putt" on the "huge greens" and to pony up a huge wad of green for the "expensive" fee; "the pro shop is well stocked", and the "staff is very friendly" to the "large AC" "bachelor party" crowds, even if some best men find the layout "uninteresting."

McCullough's Emerald Golf Links | 19 | 13 | 17 | 20 | $80 |

3016 Ocean Heights Ave., Egg Harbor Township; 609-926-3900; www.mcculloughsgolf.com; 6535/4856; 71.7/67.2; 130/118

"If you don't want take out a second mortgage to play golf down the Jersey shore", skip the other "pirates" and set sail on this "neat little" muni collection inspired by fabled British Isles holes; its "challenges" will "keep your attention", but so will the "tinge of funny odor" and "oozing coming up" from the "old garbage dump" it's built on; if you don't mind that, the lack of a driving range and "slow pace in summer" surely won't bother you either.

Sea Oaks ☺ | 24 | 24 | 23 | 21 | $105 |

99 Golf View Dr., Little Egg Harbor Township; 609-296-2656; www.seaoaksgolf.com; 6950/5150; 72.4/68.9; 129/119

If you're looking for "a pleasant drive to a pleasant place", hop "off the Garden State Parkway" "near Long Beach Island", and get "mentally massaged" by a "fun challenge" sporting a "good variety of holes" including "reachable par-5s"; just remember to "bring bug spray" because "the mosquitos are deadly" and it would be a shame to flee the flying foes before experiencing the "nice practice area" and the "good food" in the "beautiful clubhouse."

Seaview Marriott, Bay | 21 | 24 | 23 | 18 | $129 |

401 S. New York Rd., Absecon; 609-748-7680; 800-932-8000; www.seaviewgolf.com; 6247/5017; 70.7/68.4; 122/114

Swingers with a soft spot for "the way courses used to be" melt over this 1921 Hugh Wilson/Donald Ross design where Sam Snead won the 1942 PGA Championship and the LPGA holds its Shoprite Classic; while it is "dated" and "short by today's standards", the "classic" design elements, "wicked wind" and "tricky greens" provide plenty of plot twists; just "bring bug repellent" – "or a flamethrower" – because the "nasty greenhead flies" can be "a huge problem."

Seaview Marriott, Pines | 23 | 24 | 23 | 19 | $129 |

401 S. New York Rd., Absecon; 609-748-7680; 800-932-8000; www.seaviewgolf.com; 6731/5276; 71.7/69.8; 128/119

Though it "doesn't have the cachet of the Ross-designed Bay", this "inlander" is the "better of the two at Seaview"; "longer and tighter" with "beautiful, tall pines" lining the "narrow" fairways, it certainly doles out more of a "butt whipping"; the "traditional" layout and old-world yet "top-flight" facilities lend a "turn-of-the-century ambiance" to a round that, if priced for the postmodern pocket, is still "cheaper than the tables" in nearby Atlantic City.

Shore Gate
25 | 17 | 19 | 19 | $99

35 School House Ln., Ocean View; 609-624-8337; www.shoregategolfclub.com; 7227/5284; 75.3/71.2; 136/126
Despite being "a little far", this "dramatic" four-year-old is "a great place to spend an afternoon away from the casinos"; the layout, with a "good mix of water hazards", "massive waste bunkers and traps" (some cut into the outer faces of fairway mounds), "will not get boring", no matter how many times you play it, though once might be enough given "shore"-style "overpricing" for a spread that has the potential to be "one of the best" but "still needs some seasoning."

Twisted Dune
26 | 18 | 20 | 20 | $99

2101 Ocean Heights Ave., Egg Harbor Township; 609-653-8019; www.twisteddune.com; 7384/5831; 74.8/71.5; 132/124
"If you like links but don't want to fly to the other side of the pond", this "surreal design" with "moonscape" dunes mimics the auld sod; there are "no houses" and "no trees on the entire course", just "fescue, fescue, fescue" and "amphitheatre bunkering" that mitigate the "wide, wide fairways and big, big greens", which you'd better not miss unless you're looking for "big, big trouble" and a "long, long round"; the "clubhouse needs improvement" but not the BYOB policy: if you "bring a cooler full of beer, they'll supply the ice."

Vineyard Golf at Renault
– | – | – | – | $89

72 N. Bremen Ave., Egg Harbor; 609-965-2111; www.renaultwinery.com; 7213/5176; 75.3/68.8; 132/117
After months of delays, the owners of one of the oldest continuously operated wineries in the nation finally popped the cork on this gem; its fairways are wide enough for vine-oriented vacationers to skirt the ripening grape clusters, ponds and bunkers that connoisseurs of club swinging will be coerced to carry; everyone will enjoy a seven-course feast at the vineyard's gourmet restaurant or a Mediterranean-inspired meal at Joseph's located in its adjacent Tuscany House hotel.

Bridgewater

Neshanic Valley
– | – | – | – | $65

2301 S. Branch Rd., Neshanic Station; 908-369-8200; www.somersetcountyparks.org
Lake/Meadow: 7069/5096; 73.8/69.4; 130/119
Meadow/Ridge: 7079/5050; 73.8/69.4; 130/119
Ridge/Lake: 7108/5098; 74/70.2; 132/123
When does a muni cost $20 million? – when it's a 27-hole, Michael Hurdzan/Dana Fry design with an additional executive spread, state-of-the-art practice center and only the second on-course Callaway club-fitting center in the country; the final Ridge third opens in fall 2005 on this long, treeless test with tons of bunkers, wind, native grass and massive greens that are lumpy, bumpy and often leave players grumpy.

Royce Brook, East   – | – | – | – | $105
201 Hamilton Rd., Hillsborough; 908-904-4786; 888-434-3673;
www.roycebrook.com; 6950/5062; 73.9/69.6; 135/121
Though slightly less linksy than his work on the private West, this
Steve Smyers spread still sports mounds, slopes and chutes carved
from firm-and-fast fairways, as well as behemoth bunkers that
could hide a herd of hippos; there's always a stampede to use the
24-acre, tour-quality practice area that's so good, they used to sell
memberships to it.

Cape May

Cape May National   19 | 16 | 16 | 19 | $85
Florence Ave. & Rte. 9; 609-898-1005; www.cmngc.com;
6905/4711; 73.4/66.7; 136/116
At the southernmost tip of the state, you'll find a "great layout" on
"beautiful" terrain that includes a 50-acre bird sanctuary; this linksy,
"beach town experience" with "some great carry challenges" over
water, sand and wetlands is nicknamed "The Natural", a point
sometimes lost on the summer "vacationers" who mistake it for
being "poorly cared for"; though there are "not too many facilities",
Skee Riegel, the 1947 U.S. Amateur champion and runner up to Ben
Hogan in the 1951 Masters, makes daily appearances.

Sand Barrens   25 | 20 | 21 | 20 | $115
1765 Rte. 9 N., Swainton; 609-465-3555; 800-465-3122;
www.sandbarrensgolf.com
North/South: 6969/4946; 72.7/68; 133/120
South/West: 6895/4971; 71.7/68.3; 130/119
West/North: 7092/4951; 73.2/67.9; 135/119
"They don't call it Sand Barrens for nothing" say swingers sinking
in the "traps as big as Egg Harbor" splayed out "all around" these
"three great nines"; the "huge greens and fairways" "look tougher
than they are", and they're all "in excellent shape", as is the pace
of play since "27 holes ease the crowding"; the only "setback" in
the "great clubhouse" overlooking a peninsula-green par-3 is its
lack of a public liquor license.

Cherry Hill

PINE HILL ⏱   27 | 26 | 24 | 19 | $99
500 W. Branch Ave., Pine Hill; 856-435-3100; 877-450-8866;
www.golfpinehill.com; 6969/4922; 74.2/68.3; 144/121
"The closest most golfers will ever get" to the exclusive Pine Valley
is this Tom Fazio "roller coaster" on a "former public ski area" "only
1.5 miles away"; the "fast greens, steep slopes" and "blind shots"
on this "visually daunting" and "punishing" "test" will "take your
breath away" along with your cash, but it's "worth the splurge once
in a while" for the "masochistic enjoyment" and "beautiful" "views
of the Philly skyline" from the "immaculate" course and "first-
class" clubhouse; just "play it quick because it's going private" too.

Scotland Run   23 | 23 | 22 | 19 | $105
2626 Fries Mill Rd., Williamstown; 856-863-3737; www.scotlandrun.com;
6810/5010; 73.3/69.5; 134/120
Architect Stephen Kay devised "the best use ever for a converted
sand pit": a "links" that "looks like it met the moon"; its "difficult

holes" include No. 16, with "a tee-off over a ravine so big there's an airplane in it", a dubious endorsement for the "Dive and Drive packages with the skydiving place next door"; regain your footing in the "beautiful" clubhouse with "great food and drinks" amid extreme execs from nearby Philly on one of their "frequent outings", during which the "rangers earn their money keeping pace of play."

Freehold

Charleston Springs, North ⏱ | _ | _ | _ | _ | $66 |
101 Woodville Rd., Millstone; 732-409-7227;
www.monmouthcountyparks.com; 7011/5071; 73.4/69.7; 126/117
As if having Hominy and Howell weren't enough, Monmouth County residents recently got another 36 holes of heaven; this linksy layout came first in 1999, bringing with it just enough fairway bumps to make flat lies elusive and plenty of bunkering to make them important; however, missing a green doesn't automatically result in sandblasting because large, closely mown chipping areas are positioned where misses tend to stray.

Charleston Springs, South ⏱ | _ | _ | _ | _ | $66 |
101 Woodville Rd., Millstone; 732-409-7227;
www.monmouthcountyparks.com; 6953/5153; 73.2/69.7; 125/118
The only thing this 2002 addition shares with its predecessor is designer Mark Mungeam and a classy clubhouse with comfy leather chairs, a picture-window view and a patio overlooking the course; this spread is pure parkland with hilly holes framed by trees, long grasses and well-bunkered greens; polish your putter in the practice area as there's more than a half-acre of Poa to ponder.

Eagle Ridge | 20 | 21 | 20 | 20 | $95 |
2 Augusta Blvd., Lakewood; 732-901-4900; www.eagleridgegolf.com;
6607/4792; 72.4/68.3; 132/125
"Golf's version of a splasher rather than a lap swimmer", this Ault/Clark design is "hilly", "challenging" and "perfectly manicured", but despite some "great scenery", there's "not enough land" here and too many "houses blocking the wind" to merit "greatness"; the same can't be said for its "nice facilities", including an expanded clubhouse with wood-paneled lockers, the View Restaurant and the area's only MODELGOLF computerized teaching program.

HOMINY HILL | 26 | 17 | 17 | 25 | $68 |
92 Mercer Rd., Colts Neck; 732-462-9223;
www.monmouthcountyparks.com; 7049/5793; 74.2/73.6; 131/129
"Designed by RTJ Sr.", this "jewel" "may not be on par with Bethpage Black" but it's close and actually "seems harder to get on", "even for county residents"; the extra effort is "worth it", because the "conditions" and "horse-farm setting" "make it feel like a private club" (minus the clubhouse), while the "narrow fairways, tough rough and elevated greens" "make you play your best"; it's a "treat", "if you can tolerate abrasive employees."

Howell Park | 23 | 14 | 16 | 24 | $56 |
Preventorium Rd., Farmingdale; 732-938-4771;
www.monmouthcountyparks.com; 6964/5698; 73/72.5; 126/125
The question of whether this "Monmouth County gem" ranks "behind Hominy Hill" or is "even better than the more well-known"

relative may never be answered, but it sure would be fun doing the research; this one may be a shade more "forgiving" but it's still a "fun, challenging track" with some of the "most interesting" holes around – and "flower beds" by some tee boxes for good measure; if only the local "politicians" would "take better care of it", the competition would be even tighter.

NYC Metro

Berkshire Valley ☉
— | — | — | — | $75

28 Cozy Lake Rd., Oak Ridge; 973-208-0018; www.morrisparks.net; 6810/4647; 72.2/66.9; 128/113

Constrained by the nature of this former brownfield, designer Roger Rulewich had to route the first few holes of Morris County's latest and greatest course on the side of a huge hill that drops off sharply to the right, with high grass to snare errant shots, making the opening a real knee-knocker for right-handers; if you make it past this purgatory with your sanity and ball supply intact, the open valley offers sweet relief in bailout areas on either side of the greens.

Bowling Green
19 | 14 | 16 | 19 | $84

53 School House Rd., Milton; 973-697-8688; www.bowlinggreengolf.com; 6812/5051; 72.5/69.4; 132/123

A course within an hour of NYC where "weekend walking is permitted" is rare, so grab your cushiest cleats and cruise to this "well-maintained", renovated 1967 Geoffrey Cornish design; also "bring your tree wood" because while the "greens are the size of a parking lot", the fairways are extremely "tight" and the holes can get "tricky" when your ball is "ricocheting" off branches and trunks; the "grill could use updating and better service", but the "laid-back and friendly atmosphere" makes it easy to mete out a mulligan.

CRYSTAL SPRINGS, BALLYOWEN 🎏
27 | 25 | 24 | 19 | $125

105-137 Wheatsworth Rd., Hamburg; 973-827-5996; www.crystalgolfresort.com; 7094/4903; 73.6/66.9; 131/106

Not only is this take on "Scotland in the rolling farmland of New Jersey" the "best of Crystal Springs", it ranks as the state's Top and Most Popular Course; the "links-style" layout "with lots of natural fescue" is a "visual treat" and "a challenge all the way through", complemented by a "magical atmosphere" that includes "sheep" on No. 12 and a "bagpiper who plays at the end of the day"; the only low points on this faux highlander are the "cart-path-only rule" and "patronizing starters" – it's "hard to take a lecture from a guy in a kilt."

Crystal Springs, Black Bear 🏕
19 | 19 | 19 | 19 | $79

138 State Rte. 23 N., Franklin; 973-827-5996; www.crystalgolfresort.com; 6673/4785; 72.2/67.7; 130/116

Unlike some courses named for wildlife, "you might actually see black bears" or other "animals run across" this Crystal Springs track that's nevertheless just "a little closer to civilization than its sisters"; despite its "huge elevation changes", it's also said to be "not as difficult", though that might have more to do with its proximity to the "great practice area" housing the David Glenz

Academy; the "least expensive" of the resort's 18-holers is "reasonably priced" – "for New Yorkers", that is.

Crystal Springs, Crystal Springs Course 🏌

20 | 21 | 20 | 18 | $90

1 Wild Turkey Way, Hamburg; 973-827-5996; www.crystalgolfresort.com; 6808/5111; 74.1/70.5; 137/123

Swingers who spring for this "hilly adventure" with "swales and ridges", fairway "moguls" and "uneven lies" call it an "exciting", "shotmaker's paradise" that offers "spectacular views" from the "elevated tees", such as the 11th's 80-ft. perch above a rock-walled, lake-fronted green; detractors denounce the "gimmicky", "tricked-up" holes for penalizing good shots, which makes for a round that's about as satisfying as "staying home and hitting yourself with a hammer."

Crystal Springs, Wild Turkey 🏌

24 | 24 | 22 | 19 | $90

1 Wild Turkey Way, Hamburg; 973-827-5996; www.crystalgolfresort.com; 7202/5024; 74.8/69; 131/118

Like any turkey, this one "needs to mature to be great", but despite being hatched only in 2001, the newest member of the resort's rafter has already been gobbling up accolades for "rolling fairways" in "pristine condition" with "elevation changes" affording "stunning" views of the Kittatinny Mountains; the panoramas are slightly marred by the "outer areas constantly under construction" for condos, but you barely notice from inside the "great clubhouse", a lodge-style pleasure palace housing Restaurant Latour and its celebrated wine list.

Crystal Springs, Great Gorge 🏌

21 | 17 | 18 | 19 | $89

State Rte. 517, McAfee; 973-827-7603; www.play27.com
Lakeside/Quarryside: 6710/5354; 72.7/66.6; 133/119
Quarryside/Railside: 6758/5502; 72.9/66.8; 129/115
Railside/Lakeside: 6852/5518; 73.3/67.2; 132/117

It's "too bad the old Playboy Club is such an eyesore" because the adjacent "granddaddy of courses" in "New Jersey's high country" "still delivers the goods" with "lots of challenges" on three "interesting" nines that are "distinctly different" except, unfortunately, for their shared "poor drainage"; the "facilities need a serious face-lift", but now that Crystal Springs has assumed management of this track, hopefully it will get every bit of attention that it deserves.

Farmstead ☉

17 | 14 | 17 | 21 | $61

88 Lawrence Rd., Lafayette; 973-383-1666;
www.farmsteadgolf.com
Clubview/Lakeview: 6680/5094; 71.9/74; 129/126
Lakeview/Valleyview: 6161/4713; 69.7/66.9; 121/112
Valleyview/Clubview: 6221/4929; 70.1/73.1; 124/125

"Lots of water" and "rolling hills" make this "value for a non-muni course in northern NJ" a "true test" "no matter what nine you play"; still, you might want to "keep off the Valleyview when possible" because it appears "squeezed in" compared to the "wide fairways" of the Clubview and Lakeview holes; you'll also do well to steer clear of the "cranky starter" who contrasts the otherwise "friendly staff" and "relaxing atmosphere" "out in the country."

Flanders Valley, Red/Gold   21 | 13 | 14 | 24 | $50
81 Pleasant Hill Rd., Flanders; 973-584-5382; www.morrisparks.org; 6770/5540; 72.3/72.8; 130/127
The "flat front" on this "surprisingly well-maintained" muni is "pretty easy", but "the back will ruin your score", beginning at the "long hike up steep No. 10" to a "tough" "Alps-like" landscape with "tall, towering pines" providing cover for "deer, falcons" and lost balls; if you can tolerate the "basic facilities" and "soup kitchen–style service" provided by "grumpy", "old guys", it's an "excellent value even if you're not a Morris County resident", but "good luck getting a tee time."

Flanders Valley, White/Blue   21 | 12 | 14 | 24 | $49
81 Pleasant Hill Rd., Flanders; 973-584-5382; www.morrisparks.org; 6765/5534; 72.7/71.6; 126/122
If you have ever lived "in the middle of northern NJ" in Morris County, you might be "tempted to move back" for this "very good municipal course" that's "flatter" than its sister but "more balanced overall", with a fine "finishing hole, a long par-4 with water in play"; just "don't come expecting service of any kind" or facilities more elaborate than a "little shack of a snack bar" because it's simply "great golf without anything else."

High Bridge Hills   21 | 13 | 16 | 21 | $75
203 Cregar Rd., High Bridge; 908-638-5055; www.highbridgehills.com; 6640/4928; 72/68.9; 130/116
Legend has it that the "fescue is so deep that golfers have gotten lost" at this "poor man's Ballyowen", a mounded muni with "no trees" but "narrow fairways", "dramatic" "elevation changes" and a "variety of fun holes"; perhaps that's the reason "it can take up to six hours" to play on summer weekends; one thing's for sure: players aren't losing track of time in the clubhouse, because this linksy layout "lacks a good-looking 19th hole."

Sunset Valley   21 | 11 | 13 | 22 | $49
47 W. Sunset Rd., Pompton Plains; 973-835-1515; www.morrisparks.net; 6483/5274; 71.4/71; 129/122
"C'mon now", these "greens will give you an ulcer!" rage red-faced residents on this "very pretty", "hilly" hike where there's "never a flat lie", even near the pins; still, "three of the best and toughest finishing holes in the state" help make the "excellent" layout yet another "gem in the Morris County consortium"; that's why it's usually "tough to get a tee time" and "rounds can be long on weekends" – certainly, nobody's coming for the "bare-bones clubhouse" or "rather rude staff."

Trenton

ARCHITECTS   25 | 15 | 20 | 19 | $100
700 Strykers Rd., Phillipsburg; 908-213-3080; www.thearchitectsgolfclub.com; 6863/5233; 73.3/71.1; 130/123
Rather than designing replicas, Stephen Kay and *Golf Digest*'s Ron Whitten paid "homage to the great architects" of golf from 1885 to 1955 by incorporating their "strategic ideas" into the "rolling hills" of "western New Jersey" where "each hole is distinct", yet they "blend seamlessly" into the landscape; the "friendly staff" and "magnificent scenery" mean the "only negatives" are that the

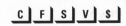
"clubhouse is still a glorified double-wide" and it's "way too pricey for being 70 miles west of NYC."

New Mexico

Albuquerque

PAA-KO RIDGE
28 | 23 | 23 | 26 | $71

1 Clubhouse Dr., Sandia Park; 505-281-6000; 866-898-5987;
www.paakoridge.com
Back Nine/New Nine: 7667/5846; 75.8/71.9; 139/134
Front Nine/Back Nine: 7562/5702; 75.2/71.7; 137/134
New Nine/Front Nine: 7579/5896; 75.6/72.2; 137/134

If you "miss the fairways, you're dead", but this "inspiring" 27-holer "winding through the mountains" with "extreme elevation changes" "makes you forget the high score you'll get" because "even bad shots look good in this scenery", a contrast of green turf, dark arroyos and rock outcroppings against the Sandia Mountains; it "may get overrun by homes" but, even then, this "great value" is "well worth the trip" 30 minutes from Albuquerque, particularly now that its final nine has opened.

Piñon Hills
▽ 26 | 16 | 19 | 27 | $50

2101 Sunrise Pkwy., Farmington; 505-326-6066; www.farmington.nm.us;
7249/5522; 73.9/71.1; 139/126

One of "the best golf deals in the USA", this 1989 Farmington muni "needs better conditioning to shine again", but its "tough greens" and "pretty", challenging forced shots over sandstone canyons and arroyos keep it on must-play lists; out-of-towners who trek to the northwest corner of the state to play here might consider relocating, as residents within a 100-mile radius pay less than $21, on weekends no less.

Twin Warriors
24 | 25 | 23 | 18 | $145

1301 Tuyuna Trail, Santa Ana Pueblo; 505-771-6155;
www.twinwarriorsgolf.com; 7736/5843; 75/69.6; 130/125

The "many memorable holes" routed through a "great setting" composed of ancient Santa Ana Pueblo cultural sites along arroyos and the sacred Snakehead butte will make you "want to play it over and over", but this "tough course" is the longest in the state, so rethink moving to the back tees that stretch it out to a full 7,736 yards of high-desert hijinks; afterward, stretch yourself out by the swimming pool or in the spa at the "wonderful" Hyatt Regency Tamaya.

University of New Mexico Championship Golf Course
25 | 18 | 18 | 25 | $54

3601 University Blvd., SE; 505-277-4546;
7272/5451; 74.6/69.1; 133/128

It's no wonder UNM has produced so many top golfers: its course is "an excellent layout" that "challenges all parts of one's game" with a "nice variety of long and short holes" and "moderate elevation changes"; it's even "walkable for those in shape", like the youngsters making "frequent stops on the NCAA tournament rotation" here; besides being "a must for any aspiring amateur", it's also a "value" for a "pre-flight round" "right next to the airport."

Santa Fe

Black Mesa ▽ 26 | 18 | 20 | 25 | $50 |
115 State Rd. 399, La Mesilla; 505-747-8946;
www.blackmesagolfclub.com; 7307/5162; 73.9/71.2; 141/125
The Santa Clara Pueblo tribe's ridge-riding, arroyo-leaping layout
"carved right out of the mountains" 20 miles north of Santa Fe is
"not for beginners", and even seasoned swingers find its "many
blind shots difficult at first"; "play it multiple times to really see it
all", including the "classic rattlesnake signs", which might lead
urban roundsmen to find this "out-of-body golf experience" "a
little too natural."

New York

★ **Top Courses in State**
29 Bethpage, Black, *Long Island*
28 Grossinger, Big G, *Catskills*
27 Seven Oaks, *Finger Lakes*
25 Turning Stone, Shenendoah, *Finger Lakes*
    Links at Hiawatha Landing, *Finger Lakes*
    Bethpage, Red, *Long Island*
    Leatherstocking, *Albany*
    Saratoga National, *Albany**
    Montauk Downs State Park, *Long Island*
    Sagamore, *Adirondacks*

Adirondacks

Lake Placid Resort, Links 21 | 20 | 21 | 22 | $69 |
1 Morningside Dr., Lake Placid; 518-523-2556; 800-874-1980;
www.lpresort.com; 6936/5021; 73.6/71; 138/125
Located in the Adirondacks, this "great links" may be "where you
least expect it", but golfers who've "played it on a stormy day" say
you "would swear you were on a rain-swept spread in England";
accordingly, the transporting track is "a nice experience for a
vacation", but "it's not an easy round, so you can feel pretty good
about a low score", particularly on a "windy afternoon when it's
even more of a challenge"; it's "a good value too", even though
"its condition can be hit-or-miss."

Lake Placid Resort, Mountain 20 | 20 | 20 | 22 | $30 |
1 Morningside Dr., Lake Placid; 518-523-2556; 800-874-1980;
www.lpresort.com; 6294/4985; 71.6/72; 127/120
"With the Sentinel Range as your backdrop, breathtaking views
are your only real distraction" on these "18 different holes" – some
of them "quirky" – "carved on the mountainside" at Lake Placid
Resort; "a magnificent play from start to finish", it's "tighter" and a
slightly "better value" than the Links, with "a few daunting water
shots and off-camber approaches" and enough elevation changes
to "humble" vacationing "Floridians used to nice, flat courses."

Sagamore, The 25 | 23 | 22 | 20 | $135 |
Frank Cameron Rd., Bolton Landing; 518-644-9400;
www.thesagamore.com; 6821/5176; 73.8/73; 137/122
It's "wonderful to play in the fall with the leaves turning colors"
on this "Donald Ross gem in the heart of the Adirondacks"; on

"reachable par-5s" and "challenging par-3s", the "tee boxes play tricks with your aim" onto "very tight" fairways where "immense trees" "require accuracy" and clearings offer glimpses of Lake George; the "courteous" staff helps the resort feel "first-class", but they haven't done anything yet about the "shoddy" practice range and the course's "poor drainage."

Whiteface

| ▽ 21 | 19 | 20 | 22 | $50 |

Whiteface Inn Rd., Lake Placid; 518-523-2551; 800-422-6757;
www.whitefaceclub.com; 6500/5635; 70.5/71.6; 122/125
"A true woodlander in every sense of the word", this "picturesque course" boasts the "stunning" "Adirondacks looming in the background"; with "tight tee-off alleys", "plenty of doglegs, uphill shots" and "carries over treetops", its "challenging" holes will leave your face as white as a ghost's – and it gets "noticeably harder on the back nine" where there are "no flat spots on any of the fairways" and two new ponds on the 18th; "get there quick as development is encroaching on this once hidden gem" built in 1898.

Albany

Leatherstocking

| 25 | 21 | 23 | 19 | $90 |

60 Lake St., Cooperstown; 607-547-9931; 800-348-6222;
www.otesaga.com; 6401/5180; 70.8/70.2; 135/122
An "ideal" "summer's day" in "historic" Cooperstown includes "the Baseball Hall of Fame in the morning and a late 18" topped off by "supper in the Hawkeye Grill" or the elegant main dining room at this "charming throwback" resort; "you can card a good round" on the "classic lakeside layout", "but the closing holes can alter that if you're not careful", particularly on the finisher's "unique island tee"; it's a "tough little test", but supplicants still sigh "I hope heaven has a course like this."

Saratoga National 🏌

| 25 | 23 | 23 | 19 | $155 |

458 Union Ave., Saratoga Springs; 518-583-4653; www.golfsaratoga.com;
7265/4954; 74.5/70; 143/125
The "friendly" "staff makes you feel like a member for the day" at the "*Cheers* of golf courses" "near the race track", and the "wonderful clubhouse and 19th-hole patio" clinch the comparison; as for the layout, it's "beautiful, testing", even "frustrating at times", "but many holes have a fabulous risk/reward quotient", so get with your most "rock-solid game", and "avoid it during the wet season" when the course itself is far from rock solid.

Catskills

Concord Resort, Monster

| 24 | 16 | 17 | 19 | $95 |

209 Chalet Rd., Kiamesha Lake; 845-794-4000; 888-448-9686;
www.concordresort.com; 7650/5442; 76.8/70.6; 137/125
"Bring the Daly stick" to this "looong" layout, then "get humbled" anyway; yard for yard, this "endless" stretch on the old matzoh-ball circuit is "hard to conquer", but at least it's "fair and in front of you"; "bored" ballers say it "needs new blood" to transform "ordinary" routing, "dated facilities" and "falling apart paths" that make it "feel like an old friend you have had so many good times with, you don't have the heart to say get the face-lift"; perhaps it "will thrive when the hotel reopens" and "gambling takes off in the area."

GROSSINGER, BIG G
| 28 | 16 | 19 | 24 | $85 |

127 Grossinger Rd., Liberty; 845-292-9000; www.grossingergolf.net;
7004/5730; 73.5/72.3; 133/127

You "must be able to hit long drives" and "keep the ball below the hole" to tackle the "evil pin placements" on this "secret of the Catskills" with "good conditioning" and "great panoramas"; players who know the "wooded, rolling" "classic" are "glad it survived the hotel closing", though they'd like the "minimal pro shop and bar" back in shape "before they're focused on trying to get casinos" here – either way, this "good value" isn't a gamble for a "magnificent" round.

Nevele Grande
| 17 | 15 | 16 | 17 | $75 |

1 Nevele Rd., Ellenville; 845-647-6000; 800-647-6000; www.nevele.com
Blue/Red: 6823/5145; 73.5/69.8; 126/118
Red/White: 6532/4570; 71.8/66.6; 126/113
White/Blue: 6573/4881; 71.7/68; 124/116

This "cute, little" Catskills track is a "pleasant resort course with a nice variety of holes but hardly memorable" – except for the "many bugs"; "bring insect repellent" to "enjoy the views of the Valley and the Gunks" without being devoured, and "don't miss the fairway because balls are easily lost even in the first cut of rough"; though a "drink by the pool" might be a "highlight", kvetchers find that the "facilities need a major overhaul."

Windham
| 20 | 17 | 19 | 20 | $55 |

36 South St., Windham; 518-734-9910; www.windhamcountryclub.com;
6024/4673; 70.4/69.2; 120/112

Even long hitters will "enjoy" a round "much more than anticipated" on this "well-maintained", "tough, short course with small greens to match"; "set in the hills" of the Catskills, it's "filled with doglegs and ups and downs", so the golf is "not easy", but the living sure is courtesy of a "friendly staff" that makes you "feel like a club member without the dues."

Finger Lakes

Bristol Harbour 🏌
| 21 | 20 | 19 | 19 | $69 |

5410 Seneca Point Rd., Canandaigua; 585-396-2460; 800-288-8248;
www.bristolharbour.com; 6662/5482; 73.4/72.5; 136/132

"Sensational all around" the calendar, this Canandaigua layout is "a must in the fall" when "the scenery is spectacular"; with "a wide-open, flat front and a tree-lined, hilly back", the Robert Trent Jones Sr. design is "like playing two great courses at one time", each "surprisingly good for the middle of nowhere"; just try to ignore the "staff that needs to get over itself" and enjoy the "killer lake views from the Adirondack chairs at the 19th hole."

Chenango Valley State Park
| ▽ 22 | 17 | 18 | 26 | $24 |

153 State Park Rd., Chenango Forks; 607-648-9804;
6271/5200; 70.4/69.4; 125/127

"Over the river and through the woods" to this "great little track" you go – just "watch your balls in the trees" on the tight fairways and don't run afoul of No. 4, just about "the hardest par-5 in New York"; the "amazing" Binghamton-area course is so "tough", it's a "surprise it's run by the state", but it's "fun" nevertheless as, "at this price, you can afford to slice."

Conklin Players Club
25 | 20 | 22 | 26 | $49

1520 Conklin Rd., Conklin; 607-775-3042; www.conklinplayers.com;
6772/4699; 72.5/67.8; 127/116

Panhandling players have struck "great gold in Binghamton" on this "scenic" suburban layout with "excellent conditioning"; "a bargain and a bear", this "good challenge from the back tees" boasts No. 10's "island-green par-3", "beautiful course vistas" from its many hills and pricing that's downright "cheap compared to the city."

En-Joie
22 | 17 | 18 | 23 | $40

722 W. Main St., Endicott; 607-785-1661; 888-436-5643;
www.enjoiegolf.com; 7034/5477; 74.4/71.7; 130/123

It's "fun to play but more fun to watch the big boys in July" on this "PGA Tour course that's open to the public at very reasonable rates" in the Finger Lakes; just "keep it straight or your score will balloon" on the "tight, tree-lined" layout of the "home of the B.C. Open", and don't expect much from the staff or the "laughable" digs: "the facilities are likened to a bingo parlor", and you can get "more courteous service from the IRS."

Greystone
22 | 21 | 20 | 20 | $43

1400 Atlantic Ave., Walworth; 315-524-0022; 800-810-2325;
www.234golf.com; 7215/5277; 74.3/70.4; 128/118

"If the tall grass doesn't get you, the water will" on this "fantastic, links-style course" "nestled in the woods outside of Rochester"; with its pond-guarded green, "the signature 18th is a favorite finishing hole" of duffers who don't mind a dunk in the drink; even if you end up all wet, the "friendly" staffers are lifesavers: they "treat everyone the same – excellent", and at the very least, the "starters will get you off the first tee with a good laugh."

Links at Hiawatha Landing
25 | 21 | 21 | 23 | $65

2350 Marshland Rd., Apalachin; 607-687-6952; 800-304-6533;
www.hiawathalinks.com; 7150/5101; 74.4/69.8; 133/118

"Bring lots of balls, as the tall grass is everywhere" waiting to ambush your shots on this "beautiful links course in upstate New York"; landing parties "wish the pro shop and lounge were as big as some of the sand traps", but it does have the "best practice area around", so brush up on your wedge shots and have "fun, fun, fun", at least "until the bugs get ya."

Ravenwood
22 | 18 | 20 | 17 | $55

929 Lynaugh Rd., Victor; 585-924-5100; www.ravenwoodgolf.com;
7026/4906; 73.7/68.7; 138/118

"Quirky holes" like the par-4 Nos. 2 and 7 with their pedestal greens might "take some getting used to", but this "upscale public course" from 2002 "is coming into its own as it matures"; even foozlers are "fond of the challenging par-4 5th and par-5 6th", an uphill-downhill pair, while yardage-happy yipsters "love the GPS in the carts and digital readout display of distance for the next shot."

Seven Oaks ⏰
27 | 16 | 18 | 25 | $60

13 Oak Dr., Hamilton; 315-824-1432; www.sevenoaksgolf.com;
6915/5352; 74.4/72.1; 144/125

"Send your kid to Colgate just to visit often" on this "hidden gem" "right next to campus", the "first course Robert Trent Jones ever designed"; even green, the architect "did a great job" fashioning an "awesome" formation with "small creeks and tight fairways that challenge any golfer"; it's got a "nice pro shop", too, though you'll want to "go somewhere else to eat."

Turning Stone, Atunyote – | – | – | – | $200

5218 Patrick Rd., Verona; 315-829-3867; 800-771-7711; www.turning-stone.com; 7315/5120; 75.6/69.8; 140/120

One of the "best bets you can make at Turning Stone" Resort and Casino is this 2004 Tom Fazio design whose name means 'eagle', say soaring swingers; in an open, rolling parkland setting a couple of miles from the main complex, it features a 13-acre lake along its finishing fairways, culminating in a closing hole with a tough dogleg left skirting the water to a bunker-beleaguered green; budget birdies' only beef is that it's "a little too expensive."

Turning Stone, Kaluhyat 赴 ▽ 24 | 25 | 26 | 21 | $125

5218 Patrick Rd., Verona; 315-361-8518; 800-771-7711; www.turning-stone.com; 7105/5293; 75.1/71.5; 146/134

"If you like to golf and gamble", the Oneida Nation's casino-based club "is the best place east of Vegas", thanks in part to this "superb layout" designed by Robert Trent Jones Jr. in 2003; "built for the next generation of equipment", it might be "too tough and long" for high-handicappers, but high rollers rave that "three nice courses", a "great restaurant and awesome range" are helping to make the entire facility "one of the Northeast's finest golf resorts."

Turning Stone, Shenendoah 25 | 26 | 25 | 19 | $125

5218 Patrick Rd., Verona; 315-361-8518; 800-771-7711; www.turning-stone.com; 7129/5185; 74.1/71.6; 142/120

"The casino is second-rate, but their golf courses are excellent"; a round might be pricey, but "you get what you pay for", which are "facilities that are A+" and a "challenging", "fantastic" "links that plays long" and "more interestingly than Kaluhyat"; if you're an "average golfer" without "local knowledge", "could shoot a big number here, but you won't care" – "you'll love the place."

Hudson Valley

Branton Woods ⏱ 23 | 21 | 21 | 17 | $100

178 Stormville Rd., Hopewell Junction; 845-223-1600; www.brantonwoodsgolf.com; 7100/4956; 73.7/67.8; 131/117

"Carved out of the woods" of Dutchess County, this "pricey" but "well-manicured" "beauty" is a "good public in the land of the privates" – but not for long: it's slated to go members-only in 2006; "until then, they treat you great", the facilities are "swanky" and the "mix of pars" makes for an "excellent layout", if a bit too "level" not to "bore" mountaineers; sit on the "nice patio" and enjoy the "great scenery" with an "adult beverage after the round."

Garrison Golf Club 20 | 15 | 17 | 18 | $85

2015 Rte. 9, Garrison; 845-424-4747; www.garrisongolfclub.com; 6497/4902; 71.3/69.3; 130/122

High above the Hudson, this "mountain golf" "challenge" "offers some of the most gorgeous downhill tee shots in the state"; just "keep your balance when you get close to the edge", and try to "hit it straight", "especially in fall when any ball that misses" the "narrow" fairways is lost to "the thick layers of leaves"; in other words, "danger lurks everywhere", even among a staff that "makes you feel like you're doing it a favor by being there."

Links at Union Vale ☺   24 | 21 | 20 | 22 | $65
153 N. Parliman Rd., LaGrangeville; 845-223-1000;
www.thelinksatunionvale.com; 6954/5198; 73.3/72; 132/126
There are three options for dealing with the fescue on this "lovely", "long links" "looking out over the Hudson Valley hills": "bring a weed whacker", land "on the fairway or kiss your balls goodbye"; it "can torture you right off the first tee", the final holes are natural-born "killers" and the whole round is a "bear in the wind and rain" – still, it "takes you back to Ireland" where it's "warm inside the clubhouse" and, "of course, there's a good bar."

Tennanah Lake Golf & Tennis Club   20 | 17 | 19 | 23 | $47
100 Fairway View Dr., Roscoe; 607-498-5000; 888-561-3935;
www.tennanah.com; 6546/5164; 72.1/70.1; 128/120
"Value" outweighs all else at this "nice Catskills design" where you "basically get an all-you-can-golf deal for a great bargain with a stay right on the premises" of this historic resort; you'll want to check in, too, because the setting is "gorgeous", particularly "in the fall"; historical hackers cite this Sam Snead layout as evidence of "why he was not a golf course designer", noting "greens that are small and flat and a course that is just straight", making it perhaps "too far to drive from NYC for blandness."

Town of Wallkill Golf Club   20 | 16 | 17 | 23 | $48
40 Sands Rd., Middletown; 845-361-1022; www.townofwallkill.com;
6470/5125; 72.5/70.7; 125/118
"Home of the dogleg", this "hilly", wooded "treasure" northwest of NYC also hosts "many blind shots that make it a challenge"; "yardage books are a bonus", though they don't tell you where the "snakes in the rough" are; the staff keeps it "well maintained", but "they need to improve their attitude toward customers", since "they don't make it easy for non-residents to get a tee time."

Long Island

BETHPAGE, BLACK   29 | 20 | 18 | 28 | $98
99 Quaker Meeting House Rd., Farmingdale; 516-249-0700;
www.nysparks.state.ny.us/golf; 7297/6684; 76.6/73.1; 148/140
Sink your teeth into "a filet mignon course for McDonald's prices", the 2002 U.S. Open host and this *Survey*'s No. 1 Value, though truth be told, Bethpage's "beautiful beast" will probably "eat you up" in turn; "bring your A game or your hanky" because the "king-daddy of munis" shows his "walk-only" subjects "no forgiveness", with "narrow fairways", "killer rough, forced carries", "roller-coaster" elevation changes and "more doglegs than *101 Dalmations*"; not only is it still "worth sleeping in your car for", it's "a reason to move to New York."

BETHPAGE, BLUE   22 | 19 | 17 | 26 | $34
99 Quaker Meeting House Rd., Farmingdale; 516-249-0700;
www.nysparks.state.ny.us/golf; 7297/6158; 71.5/69.4; 128/123
"A tale of two completely different nines will deliver your fate" on "the Dr. Jekyll and Mr. Hyde of the state park system"; "bring a

helmet" to deal with the "many hackers" on the "difficult front" ("as good as any at Bethpage"), and "expect six-hour rounds" on a "solid but overcrowded" course that offers "challenge enough" when you "can't wait forever to play big brother Black."

BETHPAGE, GREEN   21 | 18 | 17 | 27 | $39

99 Quaker Meeting House Rd., Farmingdale; 516-249-0700; www.nysparks.state.ny.us/golf; 6124/5866; 73.0/69.8; 128/121
"For the strong beginner", Bethpage's "original" is "excellent for the dough"; it "runs adjacent to the Black", so it gets "backed up" with gawking golfers, but its "generous fairways" sport "some of the technical doglegs and sand traps" typical of its pro-level sib, while its "elevated tee boxes make you feel like you could drive the ball to Mars"; best of all, "you can say you played the site of the U.S. Open – just don't tell anyone it wasn't the exact course."

BETHPAGE, RED   25 | 19 | 17 | 28 | $39

99 Quaker Meeting House Rd., Farmingdale; 516-249-0700; www.nysparks.state.ny.us/golf; 7297/6206; 76.6/75; 148/126
"After you stagger off the Black", playing here "is like leaving the ring with Ali and going a few rounds with Frazier"; this "phenomenal second fiddle" is "in better shape than ever" and "just what you would expect from a New York muni: tough as nails but still a heck of a lot of fun" with "lots of doglegs and length" that "will gobble ya up if you don't watch out"; its only drawbacks are the "dismal practice facilities" and "slow rate of play, especially on weekends."

HARBOR LINKS   21 | 16 | 17 | 17 | $101

1 Fairway Dr., Port Washington; 516-767-4807; www.harborlinks.com; 6927/5465; 73.4/69.1; 129/121
"Mother Scotland would be proud" rave fans of this "true links" on the North Shore that reclaimed "pretty environmental areas" once ravaged by sand mining; "some split fairways give you options", but "it's harder than it looks", with "knee-high fescue that slows play"; critics crab "beware high non-resident fees" for staff relations, pacing and conditions that "degrade as the season gets going" – at least "they're finally building a much-needed clubhouse."

Island's End   20 | 16 | 18 | 21 | $54

Rte. 25, Greenport; 631-477-0777; www.islandsendgolf.com; 6655/5017; 71.5/69.6; 123/117
When you're "high on a bluff overlooking Long Island Sound" at the "religious" signature 16th, "the East Coast's most picturesque par-3," you'll probably find this North Fork course aptly named; given "the nearness of the sea" and the "wineries", a round here could be New York's version of a "*Sideways* experience", but "what about the other 17 flat, uneventful, obstacle-free holes?" snipe sober swingers who add that the track is "not usually in good shape either."

LONG ISLAND NATIONAL   24 | 20 | 21 | 16 | $129

1793 Northville Tpke., Riverhead; 631-727-4653; www.americangolf.com; 6838/5006; 73.6/65.3; 132/114
"Use your mashie and niblick" on this "beautiful links" in a "former potato field" "amid the vineyards" on the "eastern end of Long Island"; "if the wind is blowing, this sucker has some teeth" – milk teeth, that is, as it "separates the heavy cream from the skim" in

"tough fescue grass" and "craterlike bunkers" and on "large, usually fast" greens; with "no trees for shade" and "slow play", "it can be a killer" on those "unbearable hot" summer days.

MONTAUK DOWNS
| 25 | 17 | 17 | 25 | $78 |

50 S. Fairview Ave., Montauk; 631-668-1100; 6874/5787; 74.7/75.5; 141/137

"You don't have to pay an arm and a leg", but the "breeze will bring you to your knees" on this "Shinnecock for everyone"; "there must be something in the sea air" that makes for "18 holes of bliss" capped off by "a beer and some clams at a roadside bar" – just "don't tell the Hamptonites that it's better than some of their clubs"; "with a bit" of "conditioning and revamping of service" ("retired fishermen aren't great marshals"), this "gem would shine" even on "crowded summer weekends."

Oyster Bay Town Golf Course
| 20 | 16 | 15 | 19 | $67 |

Southwoods Rd., Woodbury; 516-677-5980; 6376/5101; 71.5/70.4; 131/126

Though it's "popular with pro ball" blasters from other sports, this "shorty but goodie" is "extremely narrow and not for the long and wrong"; in other words, "don't get greedy the first time around" – "manage this course with your irons, not your driver", and "let it come to you", especially on the three "great" finishing holes; "now if only the staff could get a sense of humor . . ."

Rock Hill
| 20 | 17 | 18 | 20 | $69 |

105 Clancy Rd., Manorville; 631-878-2250; www.rockhillgolf.com; 7050/5390; 73.4/71.4; 131/121

It's as if "you were in the mountains" on a front that "emphasizes the 'hill' in Rock Hill", but once you get to a "wide-open" back that's "flat as a pancake", you know you're in Long Island at this "good course for the intermediate" golfer; "the greens could be faster", and the "condition varies", but what really stops it from becoming "a premier spread for the Westhampton area" is its "need of a locker room and grill"; maybe that's why "afternoon tee times" are "1000% more accessible than on other East Enders."

Smithtown Landing ☉
| 19 | 15 | 18 | 21 | $33 |

495 Landing Ave., Smithtown; 631-979-6534; www.mikehebron.com; 6114/5263; 69.3/69.8; 127/121

"Mike Hebron rules!" – "one of the best teaching pros in the country" and his "excellent staff" run a "good golf school" at this "cute, short, little" muni, so take a few classes in "creative shotmaking" before venturing onto its "sidehill lies" and "small greens"; "don't plan on walking it unless you're a mountain goat", in which case you'll probably want to snack on grounds that are "a little rough around the edges from a conditioning standpoint."

Swan Lake
| 20 | 15 | 17 | 20 | $64 |

388 River Rd., Manorville; 631-369-1818; 7011/5245; 73.2/69; 125/112

One might expect to see "monster-sized" swans floating in the "swimming-pool greens" on this "plain ol' nice" track where you can "easily have a 70-ft. putt"; the rest of the spread is "hilly and interesting with lots of good and bad rolls" to "test your course management", but there's "no driving range" here, it's "not really scenic" and the layout is "short" enough that bombers find it "nothing to write home about"; at least the "recently upgraded clubhouse" now matches grounds that are "always in good shape."

NYC Metro

Blue Hill
19 | 15 | 17 | 22 | $49

285 Blue Hill Rd., Pearl River; 845-735-2094; www.orangetown.com
Lakeside/Pines: 6500/5464; 70.8/69.8; 128/119
Pines/Woodland: 6400/5200; 70.8/69.8; 128/119
Woodland/Lakeside: 6400/5100; 70.8/69.8; 128/119

"It's easier to get Springsteen tickets than a tee time" on this "super well-maintained" 27-hole "town course" in Rockland County, "but once on, it's gorgeous and challenging" "for the average golfer" – and "inexpensive" for the average wallet; "lots of doglegs and short par-4s" make it "not bad in a pinch" for "practice" "close to Manhattan", but "bring a helmet" to protect yourself from wayward shots as well as a staff made "cranky" by the "crowds."

CENTENNIAL
22 | 22 | 20 | 16 | $125

185 Simpson Rd., Carmel; 845-225-5700; 877-783-5700;
www.centennialgolf.com
Fairways/Meadows: 7050/5208; 74.2/70.7; 137/122
Lakes/Fairways: 7133/5208; 75.3/70.5; 145/126
Lakes/Meadows: 7115/5208; 74.7/70.3; 136/126

"What used to be a horse farm" is now "27 holes of pure joy" in Carmel, "especially during the fall" when views are "spectacular"; though all three combos are "interesting", "Lakes/Meadows is best" – warm up on the "top-notch practice facilities", but be warned: as "one of the few publics accessible to Manhattanites", it "gets a lot of play, so it's in rough shape", and an "expensive" "round can reach 5+ hours."

Hudson Hills
22 | 17 | 19 | 18 | $105

400 Croton Dam Rd., Ossining; 914-864-3000; www.hudsonhillsgolf.com;
6935/5102; 73.3/64.3; 129/110

Westchester's "excellent new" muni offers "plenty of challenges and beautiful vistas" on holes including "interesting par-5s" that "will develop as time goes on"; still, "if you're not a resident", "it's a little overpriced" for a potentially "dangerous round" where "too many blind shots" and "parallel fairways" "mean you'll duck for cover" against "balls flying everywhere"; in these circumstances, its lack of a practice range is "a major drawback."

Mansion Ridge 🏠
23 | 20 | 19 | 16 | $139

1292 Orange Tpke., Monroe; 845-782-7888; www.mansionridge.com;
6889/4785; 73.5/67.9; 138/121

"The first four holes are links, and then the real fun begins" on this Nicklaus design that "starts off easier and gets more difficult", climaxing at the 9th, a "gimmicky" par-5 "requiring plenty of carry"; "old stone walls run through" the landscape where "the views from the tees are fantastic" – "thank God" since "the snail's pace gives you plenty of time" to ogle them; "the rangers must be enjoying the cozy outdoor setting at the bar" because lord knows they're not having a party at the "annoying" "irons-only driving range."

Spook Rock
22 | 15 | 16 | 21 | $57

233 Spook Rock Rd., Suffern; 845-357-6466; www.ramapo.org;
6806/5521; 72.9/68.3; 136/121

"If you're not a resident, you have to book well ahead of time" and "pay a little more", but don't let that spook you from "one of the better munis in the NYC area"; it's a "good, solid layout" where the "nice variety of holes and terrain" "offer a challenge to all skill levels" except, perhaps, "quasi-pros"; despite one or two "doglegs and blind shots", there are no tricks on this "nicely maintained" "local treat" – just "pack your bug spray" lest the insects haunt you.

North Carolina

★ **Top Courses in State**
28 Pinehurst Resort, No. 2, *Pinehurst*
27 Pinehurst Resort, No. 8, *Pinehurst*
   Pine Needles Lodge, Pine Needles, *Pinehurst*
26 Pinehurst Resort, No. 4, *Pinehurst*
   Duke University Golf Club, *Raleigh-Durham*
25 Carolina Club, *Pinehurst*
   Pinehurst Resort, No. 7, *Pinehurst*
   Currituck, *Outer Banks*
   Tobacco Road, *Pinehurst*
24 Oyster Bay, *Myrtle Beach Area*

Asheville

Linville 🏬 ⌐   ▽ 28 | 24 | 25 | 28 | $90
83 Roseboro Rd., Linville; 828-733-4363; www.eseeola.com; 6959/4948; 72.7/69.1; 139/122
"Hidden in the mountains" of western North Carolina is this "Donald Ross gem", a scenic woodlander from 1924 that remains "magnificent" for a relatively "cheap" round; the layout is classic, but so is the grub, say hungry hackers: "the chicken salad at the halfway house will make you question whether to play the back nine or stay for a while" and order seconds; check into the historic and recently renovated, antique-filled Eseeola Lodge for playing privileges.

Mt. Mitchell   ▽ 26 | 15 | 19 | 24 | $79
11484 Hwy. 80 S., Burnsville; 828-675-5454; www.mountmitchellgolfresort.com; 6495/5455; 70/69.5; 121/117
Take a break from furniture shopping with a round on this "hard" but "fun" "must-play" near Asheville in the Blue Ridge Mountains; amid a "nice mix of hills, moving water and forests", the wide-open layout offers no blind shots, but the "breathtaking views" are so distracting that you might find yourself swimming for stray balls with the rainbow trout in the South Toe River.

Charlotte

Highland Creek 🏬   20 | 16 | 18 | 18 | $65
7001 Highland Creek Pkwy.; 704-875-9000; www.highlandcreekgolfclub.com; 7043/5080; 74.2/70.1; 138/127
"Premiums are put on tee shots" say eggheads pondering this "thinking man's" parklander in Charlotte; offering "lightning-fast greens" and water in play on 12 holes including the "great finish", the "relatively new" "challenge" will only "become more memorable with age"; for now, what you might remember are the "severe penalties for slight mishits" that land in the namesake "meandering creek", as well as plenty of bites from "mosquitoes buzzing everywhere."

Greensboro

Tot Hill Farm   ▽ 25 | 14 | 19 | 25 | $49

3185 Tot Hill Farm Rd., Asheboro; 336-857-4455; 800-868-4455;
www.tothillfarm.com; 6614/4853; 72.2/69.1; 135/122

With a "design that's pure magic" at prices "more often associated
with third-rate munis", this Mike Strantz "gem within easy driving
distance of Durham, Charlotte and Winston-Salem" is "not to be
missed" for some "not-so-simple pleasure" in the "pines"; plenty
of players pass it by, though, as it's "not well publicized"; all the
better for you, since you'll have all to yourself its "wonderful
vistas" and "memorable holes" like "stunning beauty" No. 12, a
par-3 with a boulder- and pond-guarded green.

Myrtle Beach Area

Angels Trace, North 🏌   ▽ 19 | 18 | 19 | 20 | $91

1215 Angels Club Dr., SW, Sunset Beach; 910-579-2277; 800-718-5733;
www.golfangelstrace.com; 6640/4524; 72.7/66.7; 137/111

Don't let the name of this "little piece of heaven" just north of
Myrtle Beach fool you: the devil lurks in "hidden water, which is
not marked very well" but which you'll have to fly over on five
holes to get to the green; too bad your balls don't have the wings
of the visiting egrets on this links that offers "more challenge" than
its sister course.

Bald Head Island   23 | 19 | 18 | 15 | $102

301 S. Baldhead Wind, Bald Head Island; 910-457-7310; 866-657-7311;
www.bhigolf.com; 6844/4861; 74.3/70.1; 137/117

Though it's "not long", this "island oasis" an hour from Myrtle
"has some very tough holes" with "water in play in many places",
including on No. 9, a lagoon-surrounded par-4, and No. 11, a par-5
that puddle jumps off the tee and to the green; "you have to take a
ferry" from Southport to get there, so count on an "all-day affair",
"bring bug spray" and don't expect as much of the salty soup as
the fresh – given "all the condos, forget seeing the ocean unless
you're on a crane."

Carolina National 🏌   ▽ 25 | 22 | 23 | 22 | $97

1643 Goley Hewett Rd., SE, Bolivia; 910-755-5200; 888-200-6455
Egret/Heron: 7017/4738; 74.4/67.3; 138/104
Heron/Ibis: 6961/4675; 72.5/66.8; 140/109
Ibis/Egret: 6944/4737; 72.3/67.3; 136/100

It's "challenging but not overpowering" say birdie hunters stalking
this "visually appealing", waterfowl-themed 27-holer that "takes
advantage of its oceanfront location" "a little out of the way"
between Wilmington and North Myrtle Beach; "Freddie [Couples]
created a masterpiece" with "many nice touches" "for the average
player", including "great greens", which are kept in "excellent
shape" by a "pleasant, helpful staff."

Ocean Ridge Plantation,   20 | 22 | 20 | 20 | $77
Lion's Paw 🏌

351 Ocean Ridge Pkwy., Ocean Isle Beach; 910-287-1703;
www.lionspaw.com; 7003/5363; 75/70.3; 137/129

Slinking through the marshlands on Ocean Isle Beach a mere 15
minutes from Myrtle, Williard Byrd's leonine layout is "ok" for play

on a mix of feral and domesticated holes, though roundsmen roar "if you have a choice, play Tiger's Eye instead"; with this cat dipping its paw in the drink on a dozen holes, some duffers dryly remark that it's "too wet to really enjoy", though the practice putting green and amply stocked pro shop have plenty of players purring.

Ocean Ridge Plantation, Panther's Run
22 | 22 | 20 | 20 | $87

351 Ocean Ridge Pkwy., Ocean Isle Beach; 910-287-1703; www.panthersrun.com; 7089/5023; 75.2/70; 148/123
"Bring your game", particularly your short one, or this Ocean Ridge Plantation feline might draw its claws and "snag" you in "the grass surrounding the greens"; rouse your putter from its cat nap on the practice holes before you tee off, and pack "lots of balls", because there's plenty of drink to dunk in around the "outstanding", marshy track's wide fairways, with views of the neighboring nature preserve to distract you.

Ocean Ridge Plantation, Tiger's Eye
23 | 25 | 23 | 21 | $112

360 Ocean's Edge Pkwy., Ocean Isle Beach; 910-287-7228; www.tigerseye.com; 7014/4502; 73.5/66.6; 144/108
The leader of the pack of "wild animals" at Ocean Ridge has the "best pro shop on The Strand", so buy plenty of balls to tangle with "well-placed sand and water" on its "very pretty", "terrifically conditioned", "challenging layout" where "serious" holes like the par-3 island-green No. 11 "deserve the accolades"; "if it were softened a little, it would be great for high-handicappers as well as low" say lobbers, but as it is, this "tough" top cat is "awesome!"

Oyster Bay
24 | 20 | 19 | 21 | $112

614 Lakeshore Dr., Sunset Beach; 910-579-3528; 800-552-2660; www.legendsgolf.com; 6685/4665; 71.6/68; 134/118
"Herons and alligators" watch you swing from their perches in the "great marsh surrounding" this off-site "hidden jewel" run by the Legends Resort; swamp-waders say No. 5's "par-5 is classic – when the water level is high, you'll know what I mean", while "holes 13 through 17 are as good a stretch as you can find"; unfortunately, the "driving range is too small, the cart area is way too crowded" and "the conditions are terrible on this wonderful design" say hackers "heartbroken over how they've let the course slide."

Porters Neck Plantation
▽ 21 | 22 | 19 | 20 | $75

8403 Vintage Club Circle, Wilmington; 910-686-1177; 800-947-8177; www.porters-neck.com; 7112/5145; 75.3/70.5; 136/121
You'd better "hope the wind isn't in your face" but rather on the back of your neck "on the back nine" of this "fabulous" Tom Fazio–fashioned design, a rolling, "classic country-club layout" in a gated community in Wilmington; it's "fun every time", particularly if you start off with a few lessons with a "great teacher" and a spin around the "excellent" all-grass practice area.

Rivers Edge
23 | 18 | 20 | 21 | $129

2000 Arnold Palmer Dr., Shallotte; 910-755-3434; 877-748-3718; www.river18.com; 6909/4692; 74.7/68.2; 149/119
"Unusual for a Palmer course", this "tough" track touts "tons of blind shots" and a layout "where you're punished if you don't stay in

the fairway"; situated between Myrtle and Wilmington, the course itself is as "hard to get to" as the greens are from the tees, so it's "not for amateurs", but "the friendliest staff around" and a "great value" have aces "playing it again and again" – in fact, you might "like it so much", you'll "buy property and build a house" here.

Sea Trail, Dan Maples ⛳   ▽ 21 | 21 | 20 | 21 | $85

210 Clubhouse Rd., Sunset Beach; 910-287-1150; 800-546-5748; www.seatrail.com; 6751/5090; 71.5/69.2; 135/111
"Summertime value" abounds on the eponymous designer's "comfortable playing course" with "more wooded holes" than the other two tracks in the "enjoyable collection" at Sea Trail; this "relatively flat" teenager plays "nice and easy" – if you "can hit them straight" to avoid the huge waste bunkers, old oaks, soaring Carolina pines and alligators of Calabash Creek.

Sea Trail, Rees Jones ⛳   ▽ 23 | 21 | 19 | 21 | $100

75 Clubhouse Rd., SW, Sunset Beach; 910-287-1150; 800-546-5748; www.seatrail.com; 6761/4912; 72.4/68.5; 132/115
"I could play this course every day for the rest of my life" gushes one Jonesing swinger; "if you want a break but also a challenge", this links offers "great golf with interesting features", including mounding, numerous bunkers, water hazards on 11 holes and – "watch out"! – "the occasional alligator"; along with the resort's children's activities and "excellent food", it's "great" for a family vacation in Sunset Beach.

Sea Trail, Willard Byrd ⛳   ▽ 21 | 19 | 19 | 21 | $85

75 Clubhouse Rd., SW, Sunset Beach; 910-287-1150; 800-546-5748; www.seatrail.com; 6750/4717; 72.1/69.1; 128/121
Sea Trail's youngest and shortest, this "well laid-out" Byrd is full of "picturesque Carolina scenery", which translates into a test composed of "lots of sand and water"; asocial swingers say the "only problem is many of the fairways are lined with houses and condos", which "does not give you a feeling of being alone in some isolated location like other courses do."

St. James Plantation, Players Club ⛳   ▽ 24 | 18 | 21 | 20 | $75

3640 Players Club Dr., SE, Southport; 910-457-0049; 800-281-6626; www.stjamesplantation.com; 6940/4463; 74.6/66.6; 150/113
At St. James Plantation, this "lovable" course is "fair and pretty" with "very good holes" in fine shape; you can't walk it unless you're a member, but if you don't mind a cart, "there's no drawback to taking the trip" to Southport to play it, especially now that its Georgian-style clubhouse is complete; N.B. look for Mike Nicklaus to steal some of its thunder when his Reserve Club course opens here in the spring of 2006.

Outer Banks

Currituck   25 | 22 | 22 | 16 | $160

620 Currituck Clubhouse Dr., Corolla; 252-453-9400; 888-453-9400; www.thecurrituckgolfclub.com; 6885/4766; 74/68.5; 136/120
"The without-question best course on the Outer Banks" is "worth" its "expensive" price tag; with "ocean on one side, the Sound on the other" and a "nice mix of holes" in between designed by Rees

Jones, it's a "tight" links layout with an "old-world feel that brings back the true meaning of the sport"; you might get "crushed" by the "wind" out there, but "the nature and quality of the location" make the tussle a whole lot of blustery "fun."

Nags Head

20 | 17 | 19 | 17 | $110

5615 S. Seachase Dr., Nags Head; 252-441-8073; 800-851-9404; www.nagsheadgolflinks.com; 6126/4415; 71.2/68.5; 138/117

Leash the big dog because this "short" links requires "pinpoint accuracy" for "placement shots" on holes "framed by dunes"; if the sand doesn't "add to your misery", then "lots of water to hit over" will, but the degree of difficulty "depends" on the "havoc-wreaking" "wind", ranging from a "medium" test on a quiet day to "one of the toughest seaside courses ever designed" when it's "blowing too hard"; either way, long shots nag "it could've been something if there were 50 more acres."

Pinehurst

Carolina Club, The 🏨

25 | 18 | 21 | 24 | $84

277 Ave. of the Carolina; 910-949-2811; 888-725-6372; www.thecarolina.com; 6928/4828; 73.2/68.6; 142/117

With "no condos along the fairways" and traffic that's "not as busy as some of the other tracks" nearby, The King's "meticulously maintained", "high-quality" "challenge" offers a "great deal" on a "very nice" round; warm up in the practice putting area first, or the "gimmicky pin positions" on the "tricky greens" might foil your efforts; until they build their clubhouse, "you'll feel right at home if you live in a trailer, albeit one with a great golf course next to it."

Legacy 🏨

23 | 18 | 19 | 23 | $99

12615 Hwy. 15-501 S., Aberdeen; 910-944-8825; 800-344-8825; www.legacypinehurst.com; 7018/4948; 73.2/68.3; 132/120

"If you cannot get into Pinehurst", this "very pleasant" 2000 U.S. Women's Amateur Public Links host is "worthwhile" for a "great" round; designed by Jack Nicklaus II, it's set in "beautiful" seclusion in the Sandhill woods where the ample practice facilities include a putting green, a chipping/bunker area and a grass driving range.

Little River Farm

18 | 12 | 15 | 20 | $95

500 Little River Farm Blvd., Carthage; 910-949-4600; 888-766-6538; www.littleriver.com; 6909/5710; 73.5/70.5; 134/124

This "tough" Dan Maples links "has potential", but all is not well down on the farm: the fees are so reasonable that the course suffers "overcrowding" and "marginal" conditions – add to that a "cart-path-only" rule, and you're looking at a "prolonged" round; still, with a brand-new clubhouse, pool and condos built just in time for the 2005 U.S. Open at Pinehurst five minutes away, they're "making improvements" here for a decent stay-and-play.

Mid Pines Inn 🏌 ⌐

23 | 22 | 23 | 22 | $160

1010 Midland Rd., Southern Pines; 910-692-2114; www.pineneedles-midpines.com; 6528/4921; 71.3/68.2; 127/120

"Exactly what you'd expect from Donald Ross", this 1921 "classic" is "not very long, but it's sneaky tough" with a layout that "makes you use every club" and "quick", "small greens" that are "sloped from back to front"; miss the fairways, and you can "practice hitting off of the pine needles", then "land above the pin and you're guaranteed the embarrassment of putting it off the green"; owner and teaching legend Peggy Kirk Bell is "visible and welcoming", offering "well-priced packages" that include fine dining at the inn.

Pinehurst Resort, No. 1 🏌 ⚲   20 | 28 | 26 | 21 | $160

1 Carolina Vista Dr.; 910-295-6811; 800-795-4653; www.pinehurst.com; 6128/5297; 69.4/70.5; 116/117

Step back in time on this majestic resort's "short", "old-style" "Donald Ross gem"; it might be "much more forgiving than famed No. 2", but it still offers a "nice warm-up for the other Pinehurst courses", with "impeccable greens" and a "pretty" layout; snide modernists snipe "it's a great track – if you play with 100-year-old clubs and balls", but "otherwise skip it", as it's "at a distinct disadvantage with today's equipment."

PINEHURST RESORT, NO. 2 🏌 ⚲   28 | 28 | 27 | 19 | $375

1 Carolina Vista Dr.; 910-295-6811; 800-795-4653; www.pinehurst.com; 7274/5045; 75.6/68.9; 137/123

Experience "what the pros go through" at this "home of many famous tourneys", including the 2005 U.S. Open; "suckers for the great Donald Ross design" say "you'd never think that such a straightforward course could be so tough", until you "pull out the short stick" and go for a "spiritual orgasm" on those "brutal" "turtleback greens"; the Carolina Inn's "remarkable Ryder Cup Lounge", the "Payne Stewart statue at the 18th" and "history" lessons from the "best caddies in the world" add to the "unbridled nostalgia" of this "expensive" but "top-notch" test.

Pinehurst Resort, No. 3 🏌 ⚲   21 | 28 | 27 | 21 | $160

1 Carolina Vista Dr.; 910-295-6811; 800-795-4653; www.pinehurst.com; 5682/5232; 67.2/69.9; 115/117

"All of the Pinehurst courses are worth the time and costs", including this "very playable", short Ross layout with recently renovated greens that are usually in "fantastic condition"; some swingers like it as "an afternoon, best-ball, fun course" while big game hunters say it's a solid "prelude to No. 2"; either way, top off the day with a deluxe treatment at the resort's spa after your round.

Pinehurst Resort, No. 4 🏌 ⚲   26 | 28 | 27 | 22 | $250

1 Carolina Vista Dr.; 910-295-6811; 800-795-4653; www.pinehurst.com; 7117/5217; 74.5/70.6; 136/123

"Tom Fazio did a masterful job of updating this Donald Ross classic", and now some "modernists" claim "it can rival No. 2 any day"; it's certainly "a much better value", and its pair of water holes on No. 13 and 14 help make it "more scenic" – just "bring your sand game, as you'll need it" to grapple with the more than 140 pot bunkers; golf "doesn't get any better" than when you "play this back-to-back" with its more famous sister.

Pinehurst Resort, No. 5 🏌 ⚲   21 | 29 | 26 | 21 | $160

1 Carolina Vista Dr.; 910-295-6811; 800-795-4653; www.pinehurst.com; 6848/5248; 73.4/70.1; 137/119

"If you're tired of the other courses beating you senseless" at Pinehurst, this tame track is "fairly mellow", though with elevation changes, fade and draw opportunities and a mix of long and short par-4s, it's "still not a walk in the park"; it's in the same "great condition" as its "monstrous" cousins with the same "fantastic service", but it offers dragonslayers a "playable" "second round" when they won't get burned – "hit it from the back tees" for a more heated "challenge."

Pinehurst Resort, No. 6 🏌 ⟶

24 | 23 | 23 | 20 | $250

1 Carolina Vista Dr.; 910-295-6811; 800-795-4653; www.pinehurst.com; 7008/5001; 74.4/70; 139/121

"The most underrated course at Pinehurst" has just undergone a redesign by Tom Fazio, its original co-architect, who refurbished bunkers, renovated and relocated greens for better shot values and created a new par-4, so if you didn't have the muscle before, "you'd better be a long hitter to play this track" now; it's "a little bit away from the main facility", so it's a good thing they've also expanded the practice area, added a new events pavilion and spruced up the clubhouse with its "smaller, more intimate pro shop."

Pinehurst Resort, No. 7 🏌 ⟶

25 | 25 | 26 | 20 | $250

1 Carolina Vista Dr.; 910-295-6811; 800-795-4653; www.pinehurst.com; 7216/5183; 75.5/71.7; 149/127

Pinehurst's "prettiest" isn't all looks – this "strategic challenge" on hilly terrain riddled with wetlands requires "tough" thinking as well; "bring lots of balls, pray for no wind" and plot your approach to Rees Jones' undulating greens, or you'll find yourself "checking for ticks after heading into the woods again and again to retrieve wayward shots"; afterward, let the "good staff" pamper you in the "nice clubhouse" at "the golf resort all others should look to model."

Pinehurst Resort, No. 8 🏌 ⟶

27 | 26 | 26 | 20 | $250

1 Carolina Vista Dr.; 910-295-6811; 800-795-4653; www.pinehurst.com; 7092/5177; 74.2/69.8; 135/122

"Everything about Pinehurst is top-notch", including this "fun Fazio" spread, "the epitome of North Carolina gentrified golf" "with amazing waste areas and devilish par-3s" in "gorgeous" "wilderness" with "cart paths out of sight" and "no homes" to spoil the views; the resort's "newest" course "doesn't resemble any of the others" (in the shadows of which it gets "overlooked"), but it offers a "phenomenal" round nonetheless on an "immaculate" 18.

Pine Needles Lodge, Pine Needles 🏌

27 | 22 | 25 | 23 | $175

1005 Midland Rd., Southern Pines; 910-692-7111; 800-747-7272; www.pineneedles-midpines.com; 7015/5536; 73.5/68.6; 135/119

Dating from 1921, this "classic parklander" has had a "great upgrade" that "keeps true" to the "theme and approach originally architected by Donald Ross" "at his best", "offering the challenging shots that only he could design"; "who said the ladies weren't the smart ones?" – "they picked" the "female-friendly" track "for their Open" twice already and again for 2007; with a "great women's golf school" and "deals in late August and winter", you'll want to pick Mid Pines' sister resort yourself for a "lovely weekend."

Pinewild, Holly

22 | 20 | 18 | 20 | $135

801 Linden Rd.; 910-295-5145; 800-523-1499; www.pinewildcc.com; 7021/5968; 73.3/68.7; 138/123

Though "it's still being broken in", this "whimsical" Gary Player design offers a "good variety of holes"; compared to its sister,

Magnolia, half of which will be closed during renovations until 2007, it sports smaller greens, more water and fewer bunkers – except on the sand-menaced 12th, "one of the most challenging par-3s in the area"; improve your game at the "excellent practice facilities", which include a three-hole short-game warm-up and the "best driving range in the area."

Pit Golf Links, The 22 | 16 | 17 | 22 | $109
110 Pit Links Ln., Aberdeen; 910-944-1600; 800-574-4653; www.pitgolf.com; 7018/6138; 74/69.9; 139/123
"Aptly named" for its "numerous" pits and downscale "facilities that pale compared to Pinehurst", Dan Maples' "diabolical" design on an old sand and gravel mine is a "real fun" "test", but "only for the brave"; "frustrated" foozlers fuss that the traps are "annoying", but the spread is "scenic enough to compensate"; you "might need a helicopter to find your ball in the dunes", "water" or "pine forest", but be careful at that chopper's controls because this mind-bending layout makes you feel like you're "playing golf after taking [magic] mushrooms."

Talamore 24 | 21 | 21 | 22 | $125
48 Talamore Dr., Southern Pines; 910-692-5884; 800-552-6292; www.talamore.com; 6840/4993; 73.2/68.7; 140/120
"Look for the llamas" who "carry clubs", and (figuratively speaking) beware the "bears", including "the toughest opening hole ever" on this "solid Rees Jones design" in the Sandhills; a "well-maintained track that winds through an appealing and appropriately set-back housing community", it features "greens as good as you'll get on a public-access course"; if the "gimmicky moguls" and "swaths of rough cut through the fairways" "annoy" you, the "friendly staff", "great stay-and-play packages" and some of "the best BBQ around" are "not to be missed."

Tobacco Road 25 | 20 | 23 | 23 | $115
442 Tobacco Rd., Sanford; 919-775-1940; www.tobaccoroadgolf.com; 6554/5094; 73.2/66.1; 150/124
"If you like wacky, putt-putt, larger-than-life architecture, this is your mecca" marvel Mike Strantz fans of this "fast and funky" Sandhills spread; "don't let the yardage fool you" – it's "not long", but "with many doglegs, lots of blind spots and an acre of sand, you'll need accuracy and every club in your bag", and "you'll either love it or hate it"; those in the latter camp lament "golf on steroids with shots that give you hemorrhoids and swales that look as if hit by steroids", sighing "somewhere Donald Ross is weeping."

Raleigh-Durham

Duke University Golf Club 26 | 21 | 22 | 23 | $85
3001 Cameron Blvd., Durham; 919-681-2288; www.dukegolfclub.org; 7111/5505; 74.5/71.5; 139/124
"And I thought the academics at Duke were hard" gripe grads – "they were nothing compared" to this "championship-level" "challenge" "winding" "narrowly" through a "gorgeous pine setting"; Rees Jones did such a "masterful job of reengineering" his father's "devilish" Durham design that it's no wonder "the university's golf teams are always so competitive"; "when the greens are fast, watch out", especially on the "long par-4s" –

warm up first at the new practice center, and celebrate success at nearby Washington Duke Inn where "a post-round bite or drink is a must."

North Dakota

Bismarck

Hawktree
    – | – | – | – | $60

3400 Burnt Creek Loop; 701-355-0995; 888-465-4295; www.hawktree.com; 7085/4868; 75.2/69.7; 137/116

There's nothing little about this links on the prairie just north of Bismarck by Colorado-based designer Jim Engh; since its 2000 debut, happy hackers have enjoyed the big views, black sand traps and water hazards on this par-72 highlighted by the narrow, slight dogleg on the par-5 5th hole; fix your game at the two-sided, 17-acre range or drown your sorrows at the Hawk's Nest after the round.

Williston

Links of North Dakota
    – | – | – | – | $50

Hwy. 1804 E.; 701-568-2600; 866-733-6453; www.linksnd.com; 7092/5249; 75.1/71.6; 128/121

The wind's always sweeping down the plains 28 miles southeast of Williston, where Stephen Kay's design draws duffers to the northwest corner of the state; known as Red Mike, the layout sits atop bluffs overlooking Lake Sakakawea, but there are no water hazards in play, just 82 bunkers providing defense, especially on the 6th, an uphill par-4 where straying left toward the green tumbles you into those pesky traps.

Ohio

Akron

Windmill Lakes
    23 | 21 | 22 | 24 | $53

6544 State Rte. 14, Ravenna; 330-297-0440; www.windmill-lakes-golf.com; 6936/5368; 73.8/70.4; 128/115

Though "each hole looks straightforward", the "tough" "home course for Kent State golf" "often leaves you shaking your head wondering how it beat you up when you least expected it"; blame it on the barometrics, which make the layout play "difficult and long when the wind kicks up"; on the other hand, there's no catch to the "friendly staff" that keeps the spread in "excellent shape" and the "amazing pro shop" stocked for "an enjoyable outing every time."

Cincinnati

Shaker Run
    27 | 22 | 22 | 22 | $76

4361 Greentree Rd., Lebanon; 513-727-0007; www.shakerrungolfclub.com
Lakeside/Meadows: 6991/5046; 73.7/68.4; 136/118
Meadows/Woodlands: 7092/5161; 74.1/69.6; 134/119
Woodlands/Lakeside: 6953/5075; 74/68.8; 138/121

"If you can find it, play it" navigators nag about the "absolutely best" Cincinnati-area non-private offering; the 2005 U.S. Amateur

Public Links venue is "a blast and beautiful" with "no homes, just trees and trees and trees" (which you'll "bang it into" "all day" if you "hit a big draw"), plus "five or six holes you'll remember forever" on Arthur Hills' original 18 and Hurzdan/Fry's newer Meadows nine; "you inevitably get slow novices on occasion" "who need a push from the rangers to maintain a better pace."

Vineyard, The   24 | 17 | 19 | 25 | $44 |
600 Nordyke Rd.; 513-474-3007; www.greatparks.org;
6789/4747; 72.8/67.9; 132/114
"Bring lots of Titleists – or, on second thought, bring lots of shag balls and save your Titleists for a wider course" than this "narrow, hilly" 1986-vintage muni with three ponds and "thick woods to lose shots" in; south of the city in Hamilton County on the Ohio-Kentucky border, it offers "reasonable value for a Cincinnati public facility."

Cleveland

Avalon Lakes   ▽ 25 | 21 | 21 | 17 | $135 |
1 American Way, NE, Warren; 330-856-8800; www.avalonlakes.com;
7523/4904; 76.9/68.4; 142/117
This multimillion-dollar Pete Dye redo of a 1967 original may be "out of the way" northwest of Youngstown, but the "pretty" "challenge" is worth the drive; it now incorporates loads of undulations, 150 bunkers, countless maples and oaks and water on 12 holes; the range and teaching facilities were also recently redone, while the steaks and seafood at the upscale restaurant are as good as ever.

Fowler's Mill   25 | 19 | 17 | 21 | $68 |
13095 Rockhaven Rd., Chesterland; 440-729-7569;
www.fowlersmillgc.com
Lake/Maple: 6595/5828; 72.1/72.3; 128/120
Maple/River: 6385/5712; 70.7/71.1; 125/119
River/Lake: 7002/5950; 74.7/71.8; 136/118
"Can you say 'forward tees'?" – this "long" 27-hole Pete Dye "classic" "exceeds many of his resort courses" for a "tough, straightforward" challenge "with no gimmicks"; "score well here and you know you've played great golf because little slip-ups cost big" on holes like the Lake nine's signature No. 4 with a peninsula tee; duffers "biting off more than they can chew" lead to "slow" rounds, despite the "storm trooper–like rangers."

Little Mountain 🏌️ ⏱   25 | 20 | 24 | 21 | $75 |
7667 Heritage Rd., Concord; 440-358-7888; www.lmccgolf.com;
6628/4982; 72.7/68.3; 131/115
Sandmen dig the "unbelievable bunkers" on this "beauty" where "a great mixture of both tight and open holes" gives golfers some relief from sifting and shovelling; "conditions are pristine" on this young layout, but if you find the greens "too bouncy", rest assured it "will come along nicely in a few years", while the new driving range and those memorable Lake Erie views are ready for you now.

Reserve at Thunder Hill, The   21 | 17 | 19 | 21 | $64 |
7050 Griswold Rd., Madison; 440-298-3474; www.thunderhillgolf.com;
7504/4769; 78.5/68.5; 152/121
"They went overboard (pun intended) with the water hazards" on this "long course" that doubles as a "fishery"; it's "in extremely

good shape", but "bring at least two dozen balls to replace the ones you hit into the hundreds of lakes, ponds and creeks" suggest landlubbers who blubber "I've never seen so much blue in my life!"; aquatic aces who "can't get enough of the place" say "accuracy is key", as is a course map – "if you don't know the layout, you'll find yourself in trouble all day."

Sawmill Creek   20 | 21 | 21 | 20 | $63

2401 Cleveland Rd. W., Huron; 419-433-3789; 800-729-6455; www.sawmillcreek.com; 6702/5074; 72.3/69.4; 128/115

Get your putter ready for "the most undulating greens in northwest Ohio" at this Tom Fazio design; part of a resort overlooking Lake Erie with a 240-room lodge, six restaurants, a marina and shops not far from Cedar Point amusement park, it's a joyride itself with coastal breezes, water in play on 14 holes and those "great" dance floors.

StoneWater ⛳   24 | 24 | 23 | 19 | $106

1 Club Dr., Highland Heights; 440-461-4653; www.stonewatergolf.com; 7020/4952; 74.8/69.2; 138/123

You'll "need to play here more than once to figure out some holes" on this "immaculate" wooded wetlands layout that "changes dramatically depending on the tees you select"; stone throwers say "management has an attitude that trickles down to the staff", none of whom seem to know if they want it "to be a championship course or a housing development"; still, you'd better "hurry" and get in a round (followed by a fine French-Asian meal in the StoneWater Grill), since it's "looking to go private."

Columbus

Cooks Creek   24 | 19 | 19 | 22 | $60

16405 US Hwy. 23, Ashville; 740-983-3636; www.cookscreek.com; 7071/5095; 73.7/68.2; 131/120

PGA Tour pro John Cook worked with Michael Hurdzan and Dana Fry in his home state and built a "great combo of long and short holes, all challenging and scenic"; south of Columbus on Scioto River wetlands, it's a "great course for the money, especially after 2:30 PM"; its "only problem is it doesn't drain well – when there's rain, it floods and takes weeks to get back to ideal conditions" for golfers, though the herons in the rookery don't mind a little water.

Eaglesticks   25 | 19 | 22 | 26 | $50

2655 Maysville Pike, Zanesville; 740-454-4900; 800-782-4493; www.eaglesticks.com; 6508/4233; 70.1/63.7; 120/96

"Bring your A putt" to sink it on the "hard-to-hold greens" at this "hilly course that looks inviting to play on every hole" – until you reach those "too fast" putting surfaces (and excluding No. 7 altogether where the adjacent "trailer park" is "not pretty"); still, "excellent conditions", "bargain" prices and a "staff that always aims to please" make it "worth the trip" "a little out of the way" to the pottery capital of the nation.

Granville   25 | 17 | 18 | 23 | $39

555 Newark Rd., Granville; 740-587-0843; www.granvillegolf.com; 6559/5197; 71.3/69.6; 128/123

You'll "use every club" on the rolling, wooded terrain and "tricky greens" of this "incredible beauty" east of Columbus that builds to the finish, where the tee shot with a 122-ft. drop to the green "is astounding, like you're hitting off the side of a mountain"; for a "perfect day", get a post-round "beer and hamburger at Brew's Cafe down the street" where you'll meet Granvillers who might gripe "they messed up a great Donald Ross course when they put houses on it", though they'll eventually concede "it's a pleasure"

LONGABERGER 29 | 27 | 28 | 20 | $125

1 Long Dr., Nashport; 740-763-1100; www.longaberger.com; 7243/4985; 75.2/68.9; 138/122

"The Longaberger company can obviously make more than baskets" – they've also fashioned "by far the best public course in the state" bellow ball whackers gone buckeye over "immaculate conditioning and a nice overall design" "spread out over acres and acres" on which "every hole is dedicated to itself"; "if you're within 500 miles" of "middle-of-nowhere Ohio", it's a "must" for "the feeling of playing on a PGA tournament track without the pesky crowds"; after April 1st, practice "repeat dialing" to score an elusive, "expensive" tee time.

Dayton

Heatherwoode 19 | 20 | 18 | 20 | $51

88 Heatherwoode Blvd., Springboro; 937-748-3222; 800-231-4049; 6730/5069; 72.2/70.1; 134/123

On a "weekday summer evening", you "can't beat" the "discount rate combined with late sunsets" for "18 holes for next to nothing" at this "solid", soupy parklander with lots of water in play; it's "not as good as nearby Yankee Trace", but then again, it's "less crowded", perhaps because Dayton divas dis it as "golf's answer to *Sunset Boulevard* – aging and past its glory."

Yankee Trace 24 | 22 | 21 | 22 | $47

10000 Yankee St., Centerville; 937-438-4653; www.yankeetrace.org; 7139/5204; 74.1/70.6; 136/121

Eager eagle-seekers "endure I-75 north from Cincinnati to get to" this "very nice daily fee" "with a country-club feel" "just south of the Dayton Beltway"; most of the layout might "not be real exciting", but it's "fun, playable and a challenge" enough – until you get to the "best four finishing holes in the area", a creek-guarded par-4 followed by a long, tight par-3, a par-4 with a bunker-bumpered green and a water-laced par-5 No. 18; play it on a Sunday morning and follow up with a "great" brunch buffet at the clubhouse.

Toledo

Maumee Bay ▽ 20 | 16 | 15 | 22 | $28

1750 Park Rd., Oregon; 419-836-9009; www.maumeebayresort.com; 6941/5221; 73.5/70.4; 131/120

"When the wind is up, so are the scores" at this "tough links" "challenge" with an "open feel" that cuts through wetlands at a resort located in a state park; get yourself a "pin sheet" and "better yardage" since it "requires accurate shots" executed only "if you can hit the ball straight" despite "Lake Erie breezes", and avoid the ubiquitous "goose droppings."

Oklahoma

Durant

Chickasaw Pointe – | – | – | – | $45
Hwy. 70 E., Kingston; 580-564-2581; www.oklahomagolf.com;
7085/5285; 74.5/72.2; 125/126

Club-wielding kinfolk claim this "course is fabulous – we played it twice when we went to visit grandma last September"; grab your golf gear and your fishing rod because this "great, all-around experience" from the Oklahoma State Parks Department hooks you with "beautiful views" from 15 holes abutting Lake Texoma; though the wind blows more often than not on Randy Heckenkemper's hilly, wooded layout, down-home drivers still say "wow" to "one of the best public courses in the three-state area."

Oklahoma City

Jimmie Austin ▽ 24 | 19 | 20 | 23 | $40
University of Oklahoma Golf Course
1 Par Dr., Norman; 405-325-6716; www.ou.edu/admin/jaougc;
7197/5310; 74.9/71.6; 134/119

"Boomer Sooners" stake their claim to the University of Oklahoma's "great traditional" track, tweaked in 1996 by Bob Cupp; penny-pinching prairie putters can play it for pocket change, planting their pooped persons on the patio afterwards for a peek at others teeing off on Nos. 1 and 3 or approaching the final two holes; despite the view, "underwhelmed" college competitors complain the "unimaginative" spread "can't keep up with the course at OSU."

Stillwater

KARSTEN CREEK ⛳ 28 | 23 | 22 | 18 | $250
1800 S. Memorial Dr.; 405-743-1658; www.karstencreek.net;
7285/4906; 74.8/70.1; 142/127

Saddle up in "Cowboy country" among Oklahoma State students and alums and "see why one under par won the 2003 NCAA championship" on this "humbling" layout where you "must be an accurate ball striker"; if you find it "eating your lunch", you can do the same at the "outstanding clubhouse" before heading over to the "amazing practice facility" for a much-needed brush-up; sure, a round's "expensive", "but treat yourself and play it once" – "you won't be disappointed."

Tulsa

Forest Ridge ▽ 24 | 21 | 21 | 21 | $90
7501 E. Kenosha St., Broken Arrow; 918-357-2443; www.forestridge.com;
7012/5341; 74.8/73.3; 137/132

"When visiting Tulsa kin", bring your sticks to this "wonderfully hard" layout just east of Downtown; set inside a 1,000-acre residential community, it's "long from the tips" with "very fast greens"; the "value goes up if you buy a yearly membership", but that doesn't guarantee country club–level facilities – snobby swingers complain that "they call it semi-private but the clubhouse, range and restaurant say 'public.'"

Oregon

★ **Top Courses in State**
29 Bandon Dunes, Bandon Dunes, *Coos Bay*
    Bandon Dunes, Pacific Dunes, *Coos Bay*
    Sunriver, Crosswater, *Bend*
27 Pumpkin Ridge, Ghost Creek, *Portland*
24 Sunriver, Woodlands, *Bend*

Bend

Black Butte Ranch, Big Meadow   24 | 21 | 25 | 22 | $65
13457 Hawksbeard Rd., Black Butte; 541-595-1500;
800-399-2322; www.blackbutteranch.com;
6850/5673; 71.3/70.5; 125/125
"With improved play and bunker placement" following 2005 renovations, Robert Muir Graves' 1972 parklander has become more "aesthetically" "interesting"; a "beautiful course" in the "fantastic setting" of the evergreen- and lake-laced eastern Cascades, it's a "nice place to play in the Bend area" close to the arty little town of Sisters; just shoot straight because it's "narrow with large trees on every hole."

Black Butte Ranch, Glaze Meadow   22 | 19 | 22 | 21 | $65
13457 Hawksbeard Rd., Black Butte; 541-595-1500;
800-399-2322; www.blackbutteranch.com;
6574/5545; 70.8/70.9; 122/125
"Winding through the ponderosa pines in the Cascade Mountains" northwest of Bend is an "outstanding venue with some of the best views anywhere" around its many doglegs, declare Black Butte beaus; eyes glazed over by its many "gimmicks", disgruntled golfers grump "they should stop wasting the gas it takes to mow the course and give it back to the elk"; N.B. perhaps its few new additional tee boxes, bunkers and elevation changes will convince them otherwise.

SUNRIVER, CROSSWATER ⚬   29 | 26 | 25 | 22 | $160
17600 Canoe Camp Dr., Sunriver; 541-593-1221; 800-547-3922;
www.sunriver-resort.com; 7683/5359; 76.5/71.1; 153/133
"Unless you can take Tiger and Vijay straight up, don't play from the tips" on this "scary", "long and fast" 7,683-yd. monster "in the high desert"; "the club ensures the pace is maintained" on the "interesting design", "which must be hard" given its "difficulty" and distractingly "beautiful views" of Broken Top, Mt. Bachelor and the Three Sisters; this is Sunriver's "premier" 18, but "the entire resort and all the courses are worth a long weekend."

Sunriver, Meadows   20 | 24 | 25 | 20 | $125
1 Center Dr., Sunriver; 541-593-1221; 800-547-3922;
www.sunriver-resort.com; 7012/5287; 72.9/70.4; 131/131
"Old but ok" with seven holes along the river, this twentysomething spread is "great for players with a range of skills", though scratch swingers shelling out "a lot of money for a fairly boring experience" say "there are better ways in the area to spend your golf day", like tackling "Crosswater instead" or practicing your short game on the resort's putting course; at least animal lovers admire this track, since they "almost always see deer" on it.

Sunriver, Woodlands
24 22 23 20 $125

1 Center Dr., Sunriver; 541-593-1221; 800-547-3922;
www.sunriver-resort.com; 6946/5446; 72.7/71.2; 134/132

Hackers hail this "high-desert gem" as "fun to play", since it's
"not very technical" – "just stay straight for low scores" on the
"expensive but beautiful" tree-lined and meadow-laced layout;
though this "worthwhile" woodland/parklander is a "good change
of pace" for double-digiters discouraged by its difficult sister,
aces argue "you should play Crosswater" instead.

Central Coast

Salishan
19 19 21 15 $115

7760 Hwy. 101 N., Gleneden Beach; 541-764-2371; www.salishan.com;
6470/5237; 72.2/71.3; 134/128

"Bring your rain gear" to the central coast for this course that's
been "remodeled" by PGA Tour pro and Oregon native Peter
Jacobsen; roundsmen who "like what he has done" here rave over
the "awesome views" from the 15th and 16th, while sea-seeking
swingers say there's "not much use for the nearby ocean" on the
inland front nine at a spread that would be "fun to play – but at half
the price"; N.B. they might change their minds if they bring a kid,
since it's free for accompanied juniors.

Coos Bay

BANDON DUNES, BANDON DUNES COURSE ⏃
29 27 28 26 $225

Round Lake Dr., Bandon; 541-347-4380; 888-345-6008;
www.bandondunesgolf.com; 6732/5072; 73.9/71.0; 142/120

"Don't waste time going to Scotland" when links "perfection" is
"right here" at this "windswept wonder"; "heaven for the pure
golfer" with "nothing to see but ocean, mountains, trees and
sky", Oregon's Top Course is "a less commercial, more low-key
alternative to Pebble Beach" with equally "superb facilities and
accommodations", "great food" and an "above-and-beyond" staff;
your "first-rate caddie" will tell you to "bring long pants and a
jacket", "play early" to avoid "offshore winds" and "make tee
times nearly a year in advance" for this "sublime experience."

Bandon Dunes, Bandon Trails ⏃
– – – – $225

Round Lake Dr., Bandon; 541-347-4380;
www.bandondunesgolf.com; 6765/5064; 73.4/70.6; 130/120

Encores aren't easy when you've already got two of the top public
courses in the nation, but leave it to the masters of minimalism,
Bill Coore and Ben Crenshaw, to crash the party in June 2005 with
this walking-only layout that commences in densely covered
inland dunes, then disappears into the forest before emerging onto
a lick of linksland; though it doesn't touch the ocean like its elder
siblings do, the elevated terrain provides for stunning vistas.

BANDON DUNES, PACIFIC DUNES ⏃
29 27 28 27 $225

Round Lake Dr., Bandon; 541-347-4380; 888-345-6008;
www.bandondunesgolf.com; 6633/5088; 72.6/69.3; 138/128

"Breezy, foggy, sunny and salty" all at once, this "rugged" sister
"hits all your senses" and "humbles your game" with "more waste

areas" and "unforeseen hazards" than Bandon Dunes – but "arguing over which course is better" is "splitting hairs", even if you "don't like the back-to-back par 3s" on this one; the "weather can be chancey, but if there's nae wind there's nae golf, as they say in Scotland", so "abandon hope of a good score but have fun" with the "caddies worth their weight in gold" at this "fabulous destination" for linksters.

Eugene

Sandpines   21 | 14 | 18 | 23 | $89
1201 35th St., Florence; 541-997-1940; www.sandpines.com; 7252/5345; 76.3/72.7; 131/129

The "poor man's Bandon", designed by Rees Jones, is an "excellent value" "on the way" to the Dunes; "lots of wind and sand" make for a "challenging", "majestic-looking course, especially on the finishing holes", even if putting picture-hounds pout that it "should have better views considering its proximity to the Pacific"; the spread "needs sprucing up", but "better facilities" are in the works, beginning with construction of a new clubhouse late in 2005 – in the meantime, the "smallish pro shop" has "plenty of warm, dry gear."

Tokatee   ∇ 24 | 13 | 16 | 24 | $40
54947 McKenzie Hwy., Blue River; 541-822-3220; 800-452-6376; www.tokatee.com; 6806/5018; 72.4/67.8; 127/109

"Nestled in the middle of the Cascades with views of snow-capped mountains" is a "beautiful" "dream course", with "no houses or traffic" to ruin the "serenity" of "some spectacular holes"; however, the "dated", "spartan" facilities and "snooty pro shop staff" might have you waking up to the fact that the whole package is "not worth the drive" or the "money."

Klamath Falls

Running Y Ranch   ∇ 26 | 22 | 19 | 20 | $70
5790 Coopers Hawk Rd.; 541-850-5580; 888-850-0261; www.runningy.com; 7133/4842; 73.2/66.4; 131/120

Cutting through pine forests and wetlands two hours south of Bend, "one of Oregon's best layouts" is "very difficult from the black tees" but still a "terrific" "backcountry resort-style course"; overlooking the 10th fairway is a "great place to stay", an 83-room "lodge that's simple yet comfortable" for an overall "quality experience" – if you can stand the "mosquitoes eating you alive."

Portland

Heron Lakes, Great Blue   20 | 15 | 15 | 23 | $40
3500 N. Victory Blvd.; 503-289-1818; www.heronlakesgolf.com; 6902/5258; 73.2/70.7; 140/127

"Buy extra balls before teeing off" and "watch out for No. 2" where the "water seems to have some magnetic pull" on this "very good muni" in Portland; the rest of the "flat" front is "pedestrian", but the "back nine gets brutal" on its sloping greens; though it's "obviously" city-owned with "mucky" grounds that "don't have the care a private course gets", it's at least playable "for a great price", and "maybe someday they'll have a real clubhouse instead of a double-wide mobile home."

Heron Lakes, Greenback
▽ 20 | 15 | 16 | 25 | $30

3500 N. Victory Blvd.; 503-289-1818; www.heronlakesgolf.com; 6615/5240; 71.4/69.1; 124/122

"More traditional" and "easier" than Great Blue, this "wonderful" muni features "quick greens", a "super" RTJ Jr. layout and all the "fun" of higher-priced golf "without all the pretentiousness"; it can get "very busy and very soft", but "local weather is its worst problem" – in dry conditions, "it'll do" for a "superb value."

Langdon Farms
21 | 24 | 23 | 22 | $100

24377 NE Airport Rd., Aurora; 503-678-4653; www.langdonfarms.com; 6931/5246; 73.3/70.7; 125/124

"The natural grass putting area, red barn clubhouse and new meeting hall make the facilities top-notch" at this "underutilized gem"; the "generous" fairways are "meticulously maintained" on its "challenging yet fair" layout where mounding, fir trees, a creek and a large pond come into play, though loopers lament that the "greens get lumpy in the late afternoon."

Oregon Golf Association
Members Course at Tukwila
▽ 20 | 19 | 16 | 25 | $48

2850 Hazlenut Dr., Woodburn; 503-981-6105; 6650/5498; 71.7/71.8; 131/128

Association membership has its privileges with reduced rates at this William Robinson–designed layout 45 minutes from Portland; "golfers of all abilities" say the drive to "the middle of nowhere" is "well worth it" for views of Mt. Hood on a somewhat "flat" but "nice, little" "playable" course; though step-to-it rangers help "guarantee a typically four-hour round or less", some ageist aces argue that, overall, "service could be better" if the staff wasn't composed of "crusty old retirees."

Persimmon ◷
▽ 23 | 24 | 24 | 21 | $65

500 SE Butler Rd., Gresham; 503-667-7500; 6445/4705; 71.9/68; 136/120

"My advice: get a cart!" gasp golfers groaning over the "very interesting elevation changes" on this mountainous woodlander east of Portland; at least the hills make for "beautiful views" of the "lightning-fast greens", the "water features" on four holes and, in the distance, Mt. Adams, Mt. Hood and Mt. St. Helen's; topped off by a "clubhouse and facilities that are very nice", it's a "great" place for a round, so play it now before it goes private.

Pumpkin Ridge, Ghost Creek
27 | 26 | 25 | 18 | $135

12930 Old Pumpkin Ridge Rd., North Plains; 503-647-9977; 888-594-4653; www.pumpkinridge.com; 6839/5111; 74/70.7; 145/128

"If you don't have the time to drive to Bandon", pull up near Portland at this "incredibly well-tended" track, a "world-class" Robert Cupp "classic" that has hosted the Nike Tour; a "fantastic" staff oversees a "terrific golf environment" where "fairways to die for" and "very fast greens" make for such a "stunning course" that "the chosen ones across the range" at "the private Witch Hollow" might be haunted by a "dirty secret": its "great public" sister is "better."

Reserve Vineyards, North
24 | 24 | 24 | 19 | $85

4805 SW 229th Ave., Aloha; 503-649-8191; www.reservegolf.com; 6845/5278; 73.5/70.9; 135/132

The coast comes inland to the Willamette Valley where Bob Cupp has carved out a "fantastic" links-style spread; it's a good track with "great service" and a "nice practice range", but don't try to play it in the first half of the month when it's reserved for members; "ho-hum" yawn yipsters over "slow play" and "fairways that need to be cut" on this frequent tournament host; perhaps they'll be more interested in the fine local fare and wines at the club's restaurant.

Reserve Vineyards, South ▽ 25 | 23 | 21 | 20 | $85
4805 SW 229th Ave., Aloha; 503-649-8191; www.reservegolf.com; 7172/5189; 74.5/69.9; 133/126
As pros playing in the JELD-WEN Tradition can attest, this "wide-open course with young trees is deceptive at first", but in the end, Portland native John Fought's design epitomizes the Willamette Valley with tree-lined fairways that contrast its open sister North; it's "very nice only if you don't have to drive far or during peak times", but at least the "snooty staff" is "proud of their 114 bunkers, each ready to eat your shots" harrumph hackers, who have to be members to play it in the second half of the month.

Pennsylvania

★ **Top Courses in State**
27 Nemacolin Woodlands, Mystic Rock, *Pittsburgh*
26 Hartefeld National, *Philadelphia*
  Golf Course at Glen Mills, *Philadelphia*
25 Olde Stonewall, *Pittsburgh*
  Hershey, East, *Harrisburg*

Allentown

Center Valley Club 22 | 17 | 20 | 18 | $75
3300 Center Valley Pkwy., Center Valley; 610-791-5580; www.centervalleyclubgolf.com; 6916/4925; 73.7/68.6; 138/116
"Starters who dress the part" in "Payne Stewart–style" knickers are "a scream", but they're just the beginning of the "fun" at this "very nice public course" offering "the best of both worlds": a "front nine patterned after the great links courses, and a back done in the American tradition with woods and water"; it's "nothing fancy" like nearby "world-class" Saucon Valley, but it's "entertaining", "forgiving and enjoyable for all ages and skill levels."

Olde Homestead 20 | 16 | 15 | 20 | $60
6598 Rte. 309, New Tripoli; 610-298-4653; www.oldehomesteadgolfclub.com; 6800/4953; 73.2/68.2; 137/116
"No matter which tees you play from, you have beautiful vistas" at this "well-manicured" track in "the rolling hills of Pennsylvania"; with undulating greens and water in play on 10 holes, it's a "fun as well as challenging course", even if the facilities have "little character" and the "pushy and demanding" staff has too much.

Whitetail 18 | 16 | 18 | 22 | $53
2679 Klein Rd., Bath; 610-837-9626; www.whitetailgolfclub.com; 6432/5152; 70.6/65.3; 128/113
"From the ups and downs" of the "hilly" layout, to the "water in play, the tricky par-3s" and "the covered bridge that you motor through to the tee box" on No. 3, this "tough little" track is a "good experience", particularly given "extremely reasonable twilight rates and replays"; however, because it's squeezed onto "enough

land for 14 holes" only, with "several short par-4s that tend to hold up the round", locals say "it's not the first choice in an area with many outstanding courses."

Gettysburg

Bridges, The
| 20 | 19 | 19 | 23 | $57 |

6729 York Rd., Abbottstown; 717-624-9551; 800-942-2444;
6713/5134; 71.7/69.6; 132/113
"Country yet sophisticated", this "attractive" "Pennsylvania Dutch course" built over wildlife-filled wetlands and woods in the south-central part of state offers "a nice test" at a "great value"; "women love this track", while events planners "come back again and again" for a "staff that works with you to create a pleasant outing", even if bridge burners call a round here "contrived target golf."

Carroll Valley, Carroll Valley Course
| ▽ 17 | 16 | 18 | 24 | $56 |

121 Sanders Rd., Fairfield; 717-642-8211; 800-548-8504;
www.carrollvalley.com; 6688/5022; 72.3/68.8; 128/116
"Many babbling brooks and two large lakes make this a challenging course" gush valley golfers of this layout southwest of Gettysburg near the Maryland border; combine an "efficient, courteous and friendly staff" with "comfortable accommodations and excellent meals", and you'll see why package deals are "a fantastic value" for a "very pleasant" vacation.

Links at Gettysburg
| 22 | 23 | 22 | 23 | $80 |

601 Mason-Dixon Rd.; 717-359-8000; 888-793-9498;
www.thelinksatgettysburg.com; 7031/4861; 73.9/68.8; 140/120
Combine "history and golf in one trip" with a stop at the Civil War battlefield followed by a skirmish on one of the "best secrets in southeast Pennsylvania", a "solid design" with "exceptional fairways" set amid red rock cliffs, lakes and waterfalls; the "links-style" layout features "some tricked-out holes that offer great challenge", especially the "awesome closer", a 539-yard water-and sand-guarded par-5 that doglegs right — watch the war-weary drag themselves home from the clubhouse overlooking its near-fortressed green.

Penn National, Founders
| ▽ 24 | 21 | 22 | 24 | $52 |

3720 Club House Dr., Fayetteville; 717-352-3000; 800-221-7366;
www.penngolf.com; 6972/5378; 73.9/71.4; 139/123
If the staff has a "slightly overblown opinion of itself" at this traditional course in a Gettysburg-area retirement community, perhaps it's because it keeps Edmund Ault's original 1968 tree-lined fairways, generous greens, sculpted bunkers and playing areas around the lake looking "extremely well"; from the par-5 14th through to the end, the finish provides a "real challenge" here.

Penn National, Iron Forge
| ▽ 25 | 19 | 22 | 26 | $52 |

3720 Club House Dr., Fayetteville; 717-352-3000; 800-221-7366;
www.penngolf.com; 7009/5246; 73.8/70.3; 133/120
A "good place for a double" round near Gettysburg is this club on land where, as the name of this "great course" tells it, iron was once forged; though some swingers say sister spread Founders "has so much more character", this wide-open links-style track

with Michaux State Forest views is a fine follow-up, if only to learn about the history of the area when you reach the lime kiln at the 18th hole.

Harrisburg

Hershey, East 🏨 ⛳   25 | 24 | 25 | 21 | $99
1000 E. Derry Rd., Hershey; 717-533-2464; www.hersheypa.com; 7061/5645; 74.5/73.6; 136/128
"One of the best courses in PA that no one talks about" is a "tough par-71 that will take every club in your bag"; "the most undulating of Hershey's" sweet spreads, the former Nationwide Tour venue takes strokes away with "difficult, elevated greens", but it's "both panoramic and serene", if you "watch out for the black flies"; despite the critters, this "true gem" from 1970 is only "improving with age", particularly given the new clubhouse slated for 2006.

Hershey, Parkview   22 | 20 | 20 | 23 | $50
600 W. Derry Rd., Hershey; 717-534-3450; www.hersheypa.com; 6332/4979; 71/68.6; 129/119
"Smell the chocolate and avoid the water" at this "older layout with lovely routing" around a meandering stream and "huge, old trees" on hilly terrain; built in the 1920s, this "historical classic" features "narrow fairways" and "crowned greens" for a "fun, fairly priced" round that offers "the best value of all the Hershey courses."

Hershey, West 🏨 ⛳   22 | 22 | 22 | 18 | $99
1000 E. Derry Rd., Hershey; 717-533-2464; www.hersheypa.com; 6860/5598; 72.6/72.6; 130/129
The local treat's "smell pervades" this "beautiful classic course" with some of "the best greens" seen by the LPGA and PGA pros who've played across the lawn of Milton Hershey's estate high atop the town; the resort is only "better now that they've upgraded the hotel and spa", and the upcoming clubhouse will clinch the deal for an addictive "place to spend a weekend."

Lancaster

Pilgrim's Oak   22 | 13 | 18 | 24 | $59
1107 Pilgrim's Pathway, Peach Bottom; 717-548-3011; www.pilgrimsoak.com; 6766/5063; 73.4/70.9; 146/123
A "great bargain anywhere", this "interesting" "Hurdzan design" "offers a lot of different shot options" on "some outstanding holes" at cut-rate prices; "if you're not down the middle", however, you might encounter "strange lies" in "some funky" places, and the "rough is so high" that "hackers spend most of their time looking for balls, resulting in rounds often exceeding five hours when it's busy" – regulars "suggest making the drive" out to Lancaster County only "during the week."

Philadelphia

Downingtown Country Club   20 | 18 | 17 | 18 | $69
85 Country Club Dr., Downingtown; 610-269-2000; www.golfdowningtown.com; 6642/5092; 72.3/69.6; 129/122
It "feels like Ben Hogan will walk around the corner any moment" at this "gem" "from a forgotten era", now "hidden" behind an all-too-

contemporary "strip mall"; George Fazio's 1965 layout is "flat" and "old-fashioned" but "as tough as they come" thanks to "tight", tree-lined holes, some of which are "played backward with irons off the tee and fairway woods to" "slow, bumpy greens"; its "country-club feel" could be enhanced if they added a driving range.

Golf Course at Glen Mills
26 | 20 | 21 | 23 | $90

221 Glen Mills Rd., Glen Mills; 610-558-2142; www.glenmillsgolf.com; 6636/4703; 72.3/67.3; 138/116

"Carved out of the countryside with no sign of civilization through most of the loop, this course is worth a trip" if only to support the "local boys' school", whose pupils in "course management" keep the "wonderful greens" and fairways looking as if they've "been here for a hundred years instead of just five"; with "some blind shots" and a "character that changes with every hole", it's "tough to play first time out", so "bring extra balls" and perhaps a flask, since "the restaurant doesn't have a liquor license."

Hartefeld National ⊙
26 | 24 | 23 | 17 | $110

1 Hartefeld Dr., Avondale; 610-268-8800; 800-240-7373; www.hartefeld.com; 6969/5065; 74.4/64.6; 143/107

You'll "relish the roll" on the "large greens" at this "upscale country club" (where non-members can play up to six rounds a year), but "pay attention to pin placement", or "you'll be looking at a three-putt"; you'll "work off enough calories to drop a waist size" climbing its "challenging elevations", so you can splurge at the "fabulous 19th hole" run by a staff that "treats you like you belong"; just visit the "excellent practice facility" first, as it's "impossible to score if you spray drives" around fairways "overcrowded with new homes."

Hickory Valley, Presidential
▽ 20 | 14 | 14 | 22 | $56

1921 Ludwig Rd., Gilbertsville; 610-754-9862; www.hickoryvalley.com; 6676/5271; 72.8/71.2; 133/128

Its wide "front nine is great" for slicers and hookers alike, but the "back is too narrow, forcing irons off tees" at what some straight shooters vote "one of the best courses for the money in Pennsylvania"; despite the many environmental areas and an interesting tee box inside the foundations of an old stone barn, opponents who call it "nice but not that nice" impeach it for being "not as plush" as other local candidates.

Turtle Creek
21 | 12 | 17 | 24 | $58

303 W. Ridge Pike, Limerick; 610-489-5133; www.turtlecreekgolf.com; 6702/5131; 72.1/68.6; 127/115

"The most fun you can have with a nuclear reactor as a backdrop", rave irradiated roundsmen, is this "local favorite" where everything, "especially the greens, is impeccably maintained, despite heavy play"; the "finish will decide most contests" on the "links-style" spread, culminating in the "great fun" of the 18th near a 1740 stone farmhouse; "walking is encouraged", but relaxing post-round is not – that is, until they're done "constructing the new clubhouse."

Wyncote
24 | 20 | 20 | 19 | $78

50 Wyncote Dr., Oxford; 610-932-8900; www.wyncote.com; 7148/5454; 74/71.6; 130/126

A "mighty wind" strokes this "good, treeless" "dairy farm links", making it "four shots harder" when it "blows", which seems to be almost "always"; adding to the "deceptively" difficult round are "fast, undulating greens" and a lack of "directional markers in the center of fairways", making it nearly impossible to "know where to hit the ball"; there are "few amenities" this "far out" from Philly, but the facilities, featuring the new Ball & Thistle Pub, "are coming online and should improve over time."

Pittsburgh

Deer Run   ▽ 22 │ 19 │ 21 │ 22 │ $50

287 Monier Rd., Gibsonia; 724-265-4800; 7066/5255; 74.2/70.9; 135/127
You "get more for your money" than at other spreads in the Pittsburgh area at this "challenging but not impossible" woodland layout in "very pretty surroundings" featuring a covered bridge over a portion of a lake in play on one hole, just a 25-minute drive from Downtown; still, your dollar could stretch even further if they "kept the course well" and hired a "more knowledgeable staff."

Hidden Valley 🖩   21 │ 18 │ 20 │ 24 │ $45

1 Craighead Dr., Hidden Valley; 814-443-8444; 800-458-0175;
www.hiddenvalleyresort.com; 6589/5027; 73.1/70.3; 142/127
"If you can find" this "fantastic course" "meandering through the Laurel Highlands almost cookie-cut from the woods", you'll discover it's "worth the trip" for "fun", "value" and solitude; "each hole is enclosed by trees", so "you feel like the only foursome" on a "nice family resort" track where the one distraction is the "beautiful scenery"; hungry hackers "appreciate the call-ahead ordering from No. 9" so that your "yummy" "snack is ready at the turn."

Nemacolin Woodlands,   27 │ 27 │ 26 │ 20 │ $175
Mystic Rock 🎌

1001 Lafayette Dr., Farmington; 724-329-8555; 800-422-2736;
www.nemacolin.com; 7516/4803; 78.1/68.8; 151/126
It's "obvious that not a dollar was spared" redoing Pennsylvania's No. 1 Course; this "fantastic" formation on "rolling hills" with "beautiful" "mountain views" has "become a top-notch track", "deserving of hosting the annual 84 Lumber Classic" in September; in "typical Pete Dye" fashion, it's "lovely, interesting" and "kind of gimmicky", making it "tough for high-handicaps"; with an "opulent hotel", spa and fine dining, the resort is a "great facility overall", but the golf gets "very busy", so "get there early to get a fast round in."

Nemacolin Woodlands,   20 │ 24 │ 23 │ 20 │ $84
Woodlands Links

1001 Lafayette Dr., Farmington; 724-329-8555; 800-422-2736;
www.nemacolin.com; 6661/4709; 73/67.3; 131/115
"From the perspective of a high-handicapper", this "lovely layout" is "much more enjoyable than Mystic Rock", even if aces "don't waste their time" on the easier sister (except in winter when its fabled sib is closed); its links-style layout is "beautiful" and kept in "great condition", "but your wallet will be much lighter afterwards."

Olde Stonewall   25 │ 23 │ 23 │ 15 │ $160

1495 Mercer Rd., Ellwood City; 724-752-4653; www.oldestonewall.com;
6944/5051; 73.2/69.7; 140/123
"Pack an overnight bag, a compass and a GPS system, and don't forget to leave a bread crumb trail" when finding your way to the

fairy-tale "Sir Lancelot clubhouse" at this "immaculate" "hidden gem" "carved out of rocky hills" 40 minutes from Pittsburgh where "extensive elevation changes" make for "spectacular panoramas" from "mountainside tee boxes"; stone-cold swingers who find the "castle motif sort of silly" say it's "not worth the fee when equal, more affordable courses abound in western Pennsylvania."

Quicksilver   ▽ 21 | 21 | 20 | 19 | $65
2000 Quicksilver Rd., Midway; 724-796-1594; www.quicksilvergolf.com; 7083/5069; 75.7/68.6; 145/115

"Tour players, amateurs and groups all feel at home" on this "top-notch" Arnold Palmer design, a former Senior PGA and Nationwide Tour stop a short drive from Pittsburgh; some duffers beg to differ, calling it a "long, tough course" on which, true to its name, the "greens are quick" while "conditioning is good but not great."

Seven Springs Mountain   ▽ 22 | 21 | 21 | 17 | $72
777 Waterwheel Dr., Champion; 814-352-7777; 800-452-2223; www.7springs.com; 6454/4934; 71.7/68.9; 131/119

"Wow!" – you can see all the way to Maryland and West Virginia from this "nice mountain layout" with "fantastic greens" in the Laurel Highlands; from the family rec center to the chalets, all of the "facilities are very nice" at this "beautiful" "getaway", though someone might tell the "customer-oriented" staff that conditions are "a bit rough" due to carts "driving anywhere they want."

Tom's Run at Chestnut Ridge   ▽ 27 | 23 | 24 | 24 | $69
1762 Old William Penn Hwy., Blairsville; 724-459-7188; www.chestnutridgeinn.com; 6812/5363; 73/71; 135/126

You'd think "all skill levels" would want to run from the "tricky" holes on this resort course that's both "scenic and challenging", with "wide fairways" but with a ball-swallowing namesake creek on the front and "lots of statues" around the property to knock with stray shots; still, what "may be the best value in the region" is "busy", making for "slow play" on a track that might only get more tough in the near future if they increase their yardage as planned.

Poconos

Hideaway Hills   24 | 18 | 20 | 24 | $59
Carney Rd., Kresgeville; 610-681-6000; www.hideawaygolf.com; 6933/5047; 72.7/68.4; 127/116

"Thank goodness they make you take a cart because walking would be impossible" on this "Poconos layout", but the "extreme elevation changes" on a "good variety of holes" across "rolling hills" not only "make it challenging", they also afford "excellent views" "in the mountains"; "weekend play is slow", but the "friendly staff" helps ensure "you won't be disappointed" by this "hidden gem."

Shawnee Inn   20 | 16 | 17 | 21 | $70
1 River Rd., Shawnee-On-Delaware; 570-424-4000; 800-742-9633; www.shawneeinn.com
Blue/Red: 6800/6290; 72.8/70.4; 129/126
Blue/White: 6665/6250; 72.4/70.2; 131/128
Red/White: 6425/6250; 72.2/69.4; 132/130

A "great old-time feel" still exists 75 miles west of Manhattan on this layout that "may seem short but is very challenging"; almost

100 years young, the course features 24 holes built on an island with "beautiful views" in the Delaware at a resort haunted by the ghosts of celebs past, but despite "immaculate conditioning", claustrophic club wielders claim that original designer "A.W. Tillinghast would cry if he saw" that they "squeezed 27 holes into the original 18's space", with "all of it suffering as a result."

State College

Toftrees   20 | 20 | 20 | 20 | $95

1 Country Club Ln.; 814-234-8000; 800-458-3602; www.toftrees.com; 7056/5384; 74.3/72.2; 138/125

Alumni agree it's "great to come back" to State College, "watch a football game on Saturday and play a round on Sunday" on this "enjoyable" woodlander with "tree-lined fairways", "nice, bentgrass greens" and "large elevation changes" at a resort set amid "beautiful" "mountain" scenery; the fine clubhouse and "friendly staff" make tackling this "challenging but reasonable track" a "pleasant" "way to forget another PSU loss."

Puerto Rico

Dorado

Dorado Del Mar ⛳   21 | 18 | 20 | 18 | $102

200 Dorado Del Mar; 787-796-3070; www.embassysuitesdorado.com; 6940/5245; 75.2/71.9; 138/125

The girl golfers of the NCAA enjoy "spectacular views", especially on the 10th hole, during the Lady Puerto Rico Classic on this Chi Chi Rodriguez "classic", "which goes along the ocean, up into the hills" and around the Embassy Suites; "get the twilight rate, and it's a steal" for the island, though what you get away with might be "nothing much" – critics claim the "not-terribly-challenging" track "gets beaten hands-down by the Hyatt courses down the road."

Hyatt Dorado Beach, East ⛳   24 | 23 | 23 | 18 | $195

Hwy. 693; 787-796-8961; www.doradobeach.hyatt.com; 7005/5735; 75.7/75.4; 140/135

You'll "feel as if you're in a fairy tale" – complete with a villainous "wind to watch out for" – when you "go to the beach while golfing" in the "beautiful", "tropical" setting of the "world-class" Hyatt resort an hour west of San Juan; this former "Champions tour stop" designed by RTJ Sr. has been a mainstay of island golf since 1958, "worth the trip" for its "excellent conditioning", "incredible views" and No. 4's "famous double dogleg."

Hyatt Dorado Beach, West ⛳   23 | 23 | 24 | 19 | $195

Hwy. 693; 787-796-8961; www.doradobeach.hyatt.com; 6975/5730; 74.5/75.2; 132/132

Though it "doesn't have the ocean views that the East course has", this Robert Trent Jones Sr. spread is still "good for resort" golf, particularly since its 2002 redo by Raymond Floyd; it's "slightly easier" than its sister with "player-friendly hazards" and a "pace that's not as slow as expected" so that "everyone can enjoy it" "again and again", particularly discounted resort guests; follow it up with lunch at the Hyatt's Ocean Terrace Cafe – "even if your game is off, the sea will comfort you."

Las Croabas

Wyndham El Conquistador　　22　23　21　19　$190

1000 El Conquistador Ave.; 787-863-6784; 800-468-8365;
www.wyndham.com; 6662/5131; 72.5/70.1; 131/120

If "you enjoy hilly courses" (and Hills courses) "with beautiful views of the sea and mountains", then you'll love the "elevated tee boxes" high above the "palm trees everywhere" on what goatlike golfers gush is "not the Caribbean's toughest but its prettiest" track; the "design requires evaluation of club selection" at "several par-4s", including the finishing hole, which shares a "unique double green with No. 9"; the *muy expensivo* tabs are as "severe" as "all of the sloping", but a "great lunch" on the resort's "gorgeous patio" is a fine follow-up to a nonetheless "wonderful" morning round.

Rio Grande

Westin Rio Mar, Ocean 🏌　　23　24　24　20　$165

6000 Rio Mar Blvd.; 787-888-6000; 888-627-8556; www.westinriomar.com;
6782/5450; 73.8/72.6; 132/126

"Iguanas at the tee boxes add a surreal quality" to this "good warm-up for the tougher River", as does its misleading name – in fact, "only one green is by the ocean", but it's "a real devil of a par-3 in the wind"; "in resort fashion", this World Amateur Team Championship co-host "offers challenge yet not too much frustration", except for non-guests who can only book a tee time on the day of play.

Westin Rio Mar, River 🏌　　24　24　23　19　$165

6000 Rio Mar Blvd.; 787-888-6000; 888-627-8556;
www.westinriomar.com; 6931/5088; 74.5/69.8; 135/120

Greg Norman's handiwork at the Westin Rio Mar resort is "perfecto" – "if you can hit it long"; the lengthy stretch is also "tight" and "tough" "with various holes with a high degree of difficulty", due in part to "tricky" shots over the tropical wetlands "adjacent to the rain forest" of El Yunque; it's "well maintained" and "worth a repeat" round, so if "no one else seems to be here" "to play with", you can blame it on either the "challenging" layout or the "expensive" fees.

Rhode Island

Providence

Triggs Memorial　　▽ 20　11　16　24　$51

1533 Chalkstone Ave.; 401-521-8460; www.triggs.us;
6522/5392; 71.5/70.5; 129/126

An "excellent Donald Ross design" and a location just two miles off I-95 in the Mount Pleasant neighborhood make this muni "a decent place to have tournaments or for those learning to love the game" in Providence; a short, 1932 layout with "good tees, greens and fairways", it's well bunkered and "tough at times", but it "gets a lot of play, so the conditions can be a challenge", and the "old clubhouse" offers "no frills" beyond "loads of local character and charm."

South Carolina

★ **Top Courses in State**
29 Kiawah Island, Ocean, *Charleston*
28 Caledonia Golf & Fish Club, *Pawleys Island*
27 Sea Pines, Harbour Town, *Hilton Head*
　　Barefoot Resort, Fazio, *Myrtle Beach*
　　Tidewater, *Myrtle Beach*
　　Dunes Golf & Beach Club, *Myrtle Beach*
26 TPC of Myrtle Beach, *Myrtle Beach*
　　Wild Dunes, Links, *Charleston*
　　Heritage Club, *Pawleys Island*
25 Barefoot Resort, Love, *Myrtle Beach*

Charleston

Charleston National 🖾　　23 | 20 | 21 | 23 | $83
1360 National Dr., Mt. Pleasant; 843-884-4653;
www.charlestonnationalgolf.com; 7064/5086; 75.1/70.8; 142/126
"Since they cannot be disturbed", the "scenic" "wetlands make
for some interesting shots" at this "nifty" Lowcountry layout just
outside Charleston; luckily, "very fair" designer Rees Jones has
seen to it that "even average golfers can carry the marshes" –
unless you're playing "on a windy day" when "you'll go through a
dozen balls in no time" on the "rather challenging back side."

Dunes West 🖾　　▽ 22 | 22 | 21 | 20 | $85
3535 Wando Plantation Way, Mt. Pleasant; 843-856-9000;
www.golfduneswest.com; 6859/5208; 73.5/69.2; 138/118
"Stay out of the rough" and the Bermuda-covered dunes or pay the
price at this "great track" set "among a housing development"
just north of Charleston; the "excellent clubhouse" wrapped in
arches and furnished with a cupola tops off this "enjoyable
experience" that's "challenging" despite "wide holes", which
are "well maintained" for a "great value, especially in summer."

Kiawah Island, Cougar Point 🏌　　22 | 21 | 23 | 18 | $195
4394 Hope Dr., Kiawah Island; 843-768-2121; 800-576-1570;
www.kiawahgolf.com; 6887/4776; 73/67.6; 134/118
"Winding through the marshes and tidal basins" with "live oaks
and forced carries" over Kiawah River's "alligators", the island's
"easiest" spread sure is "beautiful" – if you turn a blind eye to the
"condos along many holes"; "newly redone" and "much, much
improved", its "traditional" layout offers "the Lowcountry game
without punishing lack of skill", leading "high-handicaps" to
proclaim "Gary Player has outdone himself with this gem of a
swamp", while "scratch players" simply "avoid the kiddie course."

Kiawah Island, Oak Point 🏌　　17 | 17 | 21 | 19 | $110
4255 Bohicket Rd., Johns Island; 843-768-2121; 800-576-1570;
www.kiawahgolf.com; 6759/4956; 73.8/69.8; 140/121
It might be the "least expensive" of the resort's options, but
this teenager "needs more time before it can be recommended"; a
couple of miles from the main facility where its "new clubhouse is a
much-needed addition", it's laid out in a "beautiful setting" of
marshlands and woods, but critics who call it "a relative dog track"
wonder "what it is doing even having Kiawah associated with it."

KIAWAH ISLAND, OCEAN 🏌   29 | 26 | 26 | 20 | $290

1000 Ocean Course Dr., Kiawah Island; 843-768-2121; 800-576-1570; www.kiawahgolf.com; 7937/5327; 79.6/72.7; 155/124

"Slightly easier than climbing Mt. Everest", the "merciless" "masterpiece of the Marquis de Sod" – and former Ryder Cup and future PGA and Senior PGA Championship host – is No. 1 in South Carolina for "spectacular ocean holes", "unreal bunkers", "forced carries" into a "constant gale", "slick greens" that "undulate to absurdity" and that trick that Pete Dye "plays with the sightlines leading you to believe there is no landing area when in fact the fairways are wide"; accompanied by a "helpful forecaddie", "getting your butt kicked was never so fun."

Kiawah Island, Osprey Point 🏌   24 | 25 | 25 | 21 | $195

700 Governors Dr., Kiawah Island; 843-768-2121; 800-576-1570; www.kiawahgolf.com; 6871/5023; 72.9/70; 137/121

"If you don't want a tough round at the Ocean", this is the Kiawah "favorite after the famed course"; Tom "Fazio has done a great job of creating an exciting" experience with "an abundance of pot bunkers" strewn around a "variety" of "pristine", "interesting holes" that "give mid-high-handicappers safer or go-for-broke options"; it's "a walk through a nature preserve" with "lovely views of the Lowcountry"; just "watch out for alligators on the greens" – "they make the putt really hard."

Kiawah Island, Turtle Point 🏌   23 | 25 | 24 | 20 | $195

1 Turtle Point Ln., Kiawah Island; 843-768-2121; 800-576-1570; www.kiawahgolf.com; 7054/5210; 74.2/71.5; 141/126

"When you get to the holes on the ocean" on the back, "beware! – the whole game changes" on this "elegant and challenging" "shotmaker's course"; even given "relatively tight fairways and lots of water" ("some right, some left, some just in front of the green"), this Nicklaus "gem" is "as fair as they come", leading masochists to label it "a big yawner, minus" the "stunning" "short stretch" along the Atlantic; still, with a "fabulous new clubhouse" and a "very nice teaching facility", most ball launchers believe it's "good stuff"

Links at Stono Ferry   ▽ 19 | 16 | 16 | 23 | $79

4812 Stono Links Dr., Hollywood; 843-763-1817; www.stonoferrygolf.com; 6700/4928; 72/69.2; 136/111

"Get through the pedestrian front nine and enjoy the scenic back, all the while learning a bit of history" on this "tight" march "with plenty of bunkers" on the site of a Revolutionary War battle and Civil War fortification; it's a "good course for the money", and with recent layout and clubhouse renovations, it's "getting better all the time", though the "swampy" spread is still "not where you want to play if it's rainy."

Wild Dunes, Harbor ⛳   22 | 22 | 23 | 20 | $120

5757 Palm Blvd., Isle of Palms; 843-886-2180; 800-845-8880; www.wilddunes.com; 6359/4774; 71.4/68.1; 131/117

It's "shorter than the signature Links" and "not as tough", but this "narrow" Fazio "target-golf" layout is "wonderful" in its own right; when "subject to the vagarities of the wind", it's "easy to score well or poorly", so "expect to lose some balls in the water" when it's blowing, and go ahead and lick the "vanilla course" when it's not; just "stay away on hot, humid days" and steer clear of the "waste package plant between holes", or despite "pretty surroundings", your round can be odious.

Wild Dunes, Links | 26 | 22 | 23 | 19 |$140|

5757 Palm Blvd., Isle of Palms; 843-886-2180; 800-845-8880; www.wilddunes.com; 6722/4849; 73.1/70.4; 132/120
The "oceanfront finishing holes" are "unbelievable" on the "better of the two at Wild Dunes", a "tough" and "narrow" Fazio links "with varied topography" "in excellent condition"; unfortunately, the rest of the track isn't as "picturesque": "the condos are so close, you can reach over and grab a doughnut off the guy's patio from the tee", or you can hit "floaters in a lake surrounded by high-rises" from the driving range; at least it's "near Charleston for great restaurants" after your round.

Hilton Head

Country Club of Hilton Head | 21 | 21 | 23 | 21 |$109|

70 Skull Creek Dr., Hilton Head Island; 843-681-4653; www.hiltonheadclub.com; 6919/5373; 73.6/71.3; 132/123
"Those who don't evacuate during hurricanes" can tell you that this "well-deserving" U.S. Open qualifier containing the "highest elevation point on Hilton Head" is "typical of a Rees Jones design": "attractive and fair", with a "better" back nine than the "plain" front; particularly in "great weather", the "wonderful staff" at its "friendly pro shop and cozy pub" helps make it "worth visiting."

Daufuskie Island, Bloody Point | 22 | 21 | 22 | 21 |$109|

1 Seabrook Dr., Hilton Head Island; 843-341-4875; 800-648-6778; www.daufuskieresort.com; 6900/5220; 72.7/69.7; 132/126
"Well worth the ferry ride" for its "old-fashioned Southern" flavor and "secluded private-club feel", this "very playable" and "well-maintained" Jay Morrish/Tom Weiskopf design at Daufuskie Island is "all the better without the big crowds" of the mainland; take in "great views of ocean and marshes", breathe in the "sea air" and scope out the eagle and osprey nests, but "make sure you don't play in bug season" lest you yourself end up bloody.

Daufuskie Island, Melrose | 25 | 25 | 24 | 22 |$129|

1 Seabrook Dr., Hilton Head Island; 843-341-4810; 800-648-6778; www.daufuskieresort.com; 7081/5575; 74.2/72.3; 138/126
Guys should "get a full-day pass from the wife for this one" because it's "worth the excursion" by boat from Hilton Head, if only for "one of the most memorable finishing holes in golf", featuring an "amazing", bunker-strewn split fairway ending in a peninsular green; Jack "Nicklaus forces you to think your way around" this "Lowcountry gem", so "if you like trees in the middle" of play, "this is for you" – "look for discount packages that include the ferry fee" over to the resort's "charming" island.

Golden Bear At Indigo Run | 22 | 21 | 21 | 20 |$105|

72 Golden Bear Way, Hilton Head Island; 843-689-2200; www.goldenbear-indigorun.com; 7014/6184; 73.7/70.1; 132/122
"Plenty of hazards and trees make it a bear of a day" even on a front nine that "leaves a little to be desired" at this "deceptively difficult" Nicklaus track; the "great people" at the pro shop provide a "top-rate reception", but the course itself is "generally

overcrowded and worn down", leaving golfers thirsting for a fine round making due with one that's more like "*vin ordinaire.*"

Hilton Head National ⌂
23 | 20 | 20 | 22 | $75

60 Hilton Head National Dr., Bluffton; 843-842-5900; 888-955-1234;
www.scratch-golf.com
National/Player: 6659/4563; 72.8/66.2; 135/106
Player/Weed: 6655/4631; 72.7/66; 135/111
Weed/National: 6718/4682; 72.7/66; 131/108

It's "core golf" on "27 very nice holes" "with none of the homes or villas that squeeze most Hilton Head tracks" at this Gary Player/Bobby Weed layout where three "very playable" nines offer "great variety" and "almost no waiting", particularly given a "friendly" and "knowledgeable staff" that "moves play along"; nonetheless, neat freaks "unimpressed" with "minimally kept grass" call it "nothing special."

May River at Palmetto Bluff 🏌 ⌂
– | – | – | – | $240

476 Mount Pelia Rd., Bluffton; 843-706-6580;
www.palmettobluffresort.com; 7171/5223; 75.4/70.4; 140/118

A "beautiful Jack Nicklaus course in a magical place", this "challenging and gorgeous", low-profile layout benefits from an "extraordinary environment" with "spectacular views" of massive, moss-drenched live oaks and freshwater wetlands; it's "first-class in every way", including service and facilities, so you can "walk with caddies and enjoy" the vista on the par-3 14th along the May River where oysters are harvested, then race to the finish "to get back to the club and resort and continue a decadent experience" that leaves wallopers whispering "it's a 'wow.'"

Old Carolina
19 | 18 | 21 | 22 | $80

89 Old Carolina Dr., Bluffton; 843-785-6363; 888-785-7274;
www.oldcarolinagolf.com; 6805/4725; 73.5/67; 145/121

"Where most others look the same" in Hilton Head, this "nice mix of holes" looks "different", with elevation changes, hazards and meadows not usually found in the Lowcountry; it offers "very good playability" in calm weather, but "with a little wind, it's tough" enough that you might be in danger of knocking shots into those "distracting" "homes built around the course."

Old South
20 | 17 | 19 | 21 | $92

50 Buckingham Plantation Dr., Bluffton; 843-785-5353; 800-257-8997;
www.oldsouthgolf.com; 6772/4776; 73.3/68.2; 141/116

"Look in *Webster's* for the term 'target golf', and this course will appear"; in other words, "placement is key" to avoid the live-oak forests and the "marshlands surrounding lily-pad fairways" and greens; set amid the natural landscape, it provides "a different look on every tee box" with "challenges for all levels of play" and "good value especially if you have kids", so bring the whole family "each time" to "discover something new" – like, alas, construction since "homes are still being built" here.

Oyster Reef
21 | 19 | 19 | 21 | $125

155 High Bluff Rd., Hilton Head Island; 843-681-7717; 800-234-6318;
www.heritagegolfgroup.com; 7005/5288; 74.7/71.1; 137/120

"Sleeping" in the "marshes" of Port Royal Sound is a club that has cultivated this "pearl of a course" with "gorgeous vistas" on "gems" like the "great 6th hole"; a "traditional Carolina" layout with "frequent doglegs" designed by Rees Jones, it's "well maintained" and "challenging from the tips", but it can also be "user-friendly" – if you "play early to avoid the heat" and make sure to tip the "uppity bag boys."

Palmetto Dunes, Arthur Hills 🏌 24 | 21 | 21 | 19 |$125

2 Lemington Ln., Hilton Head Island; 843-785-1140; 800-827-3006; www.palmettodunes.com; 6651/4999; 72.9/69.2; 129/119

"Where are the dunes?" – if this course "with no ocean views" is any indication, they're only in the "impressive facility's" name; still, this Palmetto is "primo", particularly in its "great finishing holes", which are "tight", so "be straight, accurate" and "patient" and "you will really enjoy" the "wonderful" woodland layout – especially "if you love nature" and "if you are a player"; in other words, hackers need not apply to this "challenge" that's "always in great shape."

Palmetto Dunes, George Fazio 21 | 21 | 22 | 19 |$125

2 Carnoustie Rd., Hilton Head Island; 843-785-1130; 800-827-3006; www.palmettodunes.com; 6873/5273; 73.9/70.8; 135/127

"Bring your sandpail and shovel" to this "target-golf" creation "with lots of traps", or pick up a wedge at the "well-stocked pro shop", but "go to the Jones course to hit practice balls", since there's "no driving range" on this Fazio formation; with "some long holes" and "a little water", it's "more difficult but not quite as pretty as its older brother", though with "pace officers who keep it moving even if crowded", it can still be a "joy to play."

Palmetto Dunes, Robert Trent Jones 20 | 20 | 21 | 19 |$125

7 Trent Jones Ln., Hilton Head Island; 843-785-1136; 800-827-3006; www.palmettodunes.com; 7005/5035; 74.3/64.6; 138/109

Pocket a hanky because the "spectacular" back nine "with ocean views and water on just about every hole" "can make a grown man cry" on this RTJ Sr. spread, a "great course that's even greater" following "major renovations"; they've set down "new fairways and irrigation", "improved the challenge", elevated the "sensational middle holes" for better vistas and added Hilton Head's only junior tees, making it a "nice place to play with the kids" – just try not to blubber in front of them.

Palmetto Hall, Arthur Hills 22 | 20 | 19 | 19 |$95

108 Fort Howell Dr., Hilton Head Island; 843-689-4100; www.palmettodunes.com; 6918/4956; 73.7/70.6; 136/123

"Off the beaten path but gorgeous all the way", this "good change of pace" from the other Palmettos is "a lot of fun" – if you "keep your tee ball out of the wooded areas surrounding" it; even big hitters need to crank it up at this "long, long, long" layout with "many forced carries" onto "tough, small greens", so "bring your A game", and try not to mind if the normally "great staff" is "having a bad day."

Palmetto Hall, Robert Cupp 20 | 19 | 20 | 18 |$95

108 Fort Howell Dr., Hilton Head Island; 843-689-4100; www.palmettodunes.com; 7079/5220; 75.6/71; 149/123

"'Unique' doesn't tell the half of it" at one of the more "interesting designs in golf" where everything seems as if it were "laid out with a protractor": "the mounds look like pyramids, the tee boxes are square" and even the woods appear non-organic, since "the pine trees need some needles"; though "near-misses are often severely punished", "if you like geometry", Robert Cupp's "tough" computer-generated course will be "enjoyable" for you; otherwise, you'll probably just think it's "silly."

SEA PINES, HARBOUR TOWN GOLF LINKS
27 | 25 | 24 | 17 | $250

11 Lighthouse Ln., Hilton Head Island; 843-363-4485; www.seapines.com; 6973/5208; 75.2/70.7; 146/124

"Playing a hole they've seen on TV and in mags for years" – the "paintinglike" "historic" 18th with a "beautiful lighthouse" as backdrop – adherents exclaim "this must be heaven" of this PGA Tour stop where "genuis" Pete Dye has made a "masterpiece" of "tiny, tough greens" and "killer par-3s"; "the pros love it, yadda, yadda", and so will you "as long as you hit it straight" and score a tee time when it's in "wonderful condition" for the MCI Heritage; otherwise, the "mystique" "isn't really worth" the "extremely expensive" fee.

Sea Pines, Ocean
23 | 21 | 21 | 20 | $115

100 N. Sea Pines Dr., Hilton Head Island; 843-842-8484; 800-955-8337; www.seapines.com; 6906/5325; 73.4/71.1; 142/124

"Bring plenty of balls and avoid the omnipresent lagoons" on this Sea Pines spread where the real water-based "thrill comes on the signature par-3 15th" "with magnificent ocean views"; "packaged with Harbour Town", it's "a real buy", but with "only one hole on the Atlantic", this "friendly" layout is "otherwise nothing too exciting" – perhaps its most "refreshing feature" is "the virtually constant presence of the drink girl in her cart."

Myrtle Beach

Arrowhead 🏌
22 | 21 | 21 | 20 | $106

1201 Burcale Rd.; 843-236-3243; 800-236-3243; www.arrowheadcc.com
Cypress/Lakes: 6666/4802; 71.6/67.8; 139/117
Lakes/Waterway: 6612/4688; 71.6/68.1; 140/118
Waterway/Cypress: 6644/4624; 71.6/69.1; 141/121

Pining "for a final pre-flight round" before leaving Myrtle?; tee off at this "surprisingly good" 27-holer "close to the airport", and the "friendly staff" might even "let you store your luggage in their back room" while you play; "all three nines are super", but "the Waterway is a must-play" if you like the wet stuff – just watch out for sometimes "patchy" conditions.

Barefoot Resort, Dye
25 | 25 | 24 | 18 | $155

4980 Barefooot Resort Bridge Rd., North Myrtle Beach; 843-399-7238; 877-237-3767; www.barefootgolf.com; 7343/5021; 75.3/69.1; 149/119

At once "gorgeous and gruesome", this "Dye-abolical" Barefooter contains "enough trouble to last a week", so "take notes and play it again" while you're still in South Carolina – unless "you're not a single-digit" golfer, in which case "don't waste money" and shots in the "ridiculous pot bunkers" on its "impossible par-3s"; as is the case with all its siblings, the track is kept in "excellent condition" with "top-notch facilities", so if you like to be tortured in style, succumb to it.

Barefoot Resort, Fazio ⛳   27 | 25 | 24 | 20 | $155
4980 Barefooot Resort Bridge Rd., North Myrtle Beach;
843-390-3200; 877-237-3767; www.barefootgolf.com;
6834/4820; 73.7/68; 139/115

"As good as it gets" in Myrtle Beach, this Fazio "favorite" offers "lots of different shots and looks" all the way through to the "great finishing hole", a sand-, water- and woods-laced par-4; the Lowcountry layout is just about the "best-maintained resort spread in the area", and its guests are some of the best maintained too, as the staff "treats them better than at any other course" around; it's an "expensive way to lose balls", "but it's worth it."

Barefoot Resort, Love ⛳   25 | 25 | 25 | 20 | $155
4980 Barefooot Resort Bridge Rd., North Myrtle Beach; 843-390-3200;
877-237-3767; www.barefootgolf.com; 7047/5346; 75.1/70.9; 138/118

"Interesting yet still immature", this young Love has besotted Barefooters swooning over its "creative touches" – after all, "where else can you kiss a ball off the ruins of a plantation house and land on a green that fronts it?"; its "tough hazards" are not without their "difficulty", but the resort's "easiest" layout "allows even average golfers to play some makeable shots" at a "first-class" facility where everything is "always in fine condition."

Barefoot Resort, Norman ⛳   23 | 24 | 24 | 19 | $155
4980 Barefoot Resort Bridge Rd., North Myrtle Beach; 843-390-3200;
877-237-3767; www.barefootgolf.com; 7035/4953; 73.9/68.6; 136/112

"Moss hanging from trees" and "an alligator or two" make for "picturesque" play at the "great Waterway holes" on the "most basic" of the Barefoot foursome; however, "outstanding views" from the clubhouse porch don't soothe Shark shooters who deem this "uninspired design" "too expensive for the way you are herded like a cow" across a layout that partially "had to be fitted between and behind condos" – "Norman's nearby restaurant is much better" than the course, they argue.

Blackmoor ⛳   21 | 18 | 20 | 21 | $95
6100 Longwood Rd., Murrells Inlet; 843-650-5555; 888-650-5566;
www.blackmoor.com; 6614/4807; 71.1/67.9; 126/115

"If you can look past" the "outdated" facilities and "the starter trying to sell you cigars", this "old course" can be "charming"; "risk-reward holes" include "a par-4 split fairway" where you can "drive for the green in one" or "play two short irons around the bend"; "considering the price, it's one of the area's best values", but "don't act like a tourist": "get the course book" "to stay out of trouble" and avoid it in summer when "conditions are poor."

Dunes Golf & Beach Club ⚲   27 | 23 | 23 | 21 | $160
9000 N. Ocean Blvd.; 843-449-5914; 866-386-3722;
www.dunesgolfandbeachclub.com; 7165/5345; 75.7/71.4; 144/131

"Grassy and classy", this "RTJ Sr. classic" is a "beauty" with "a great history" and a "solid" recent past, now that Rees Jones has redone its greens, leaving it in "pristine condition"; it "tempts you into trying shots you may not normally play", so note that there's "lots of water" here, and "you must be able to drive it off the tee", or else you're looking at a "tough par"; still, the "hardest thing may be finding your way on if you're not a member" – "stay at an affiliated hotel" for access.

Glen Dornoch Waterway
25 | 21 | 22 | 22 | $136

Hwy. 17 N., Little River; 843-249-2541; 800-717-8784;
www.glendornoch.com; 6850/5002; 73.2/69.8; 141/129

"Get ready for the three most beautiful and difficult finishing holes on the Grand Strand" at this "nice layout" where "16 is a brute, 17 is a beauty and 18 is a fitting finish", even if the "standard fare" before them "feels like the designer sometimes went to sleep"; nevertheless, "the whole package" is "well manicured" with "great views of the Intracoastal" and "deals on rounds if you play its sister courses", including Heather Glen and Possum Trot.

Grande Dunes
25 | 25 | 23 | 19 | $186

8700 Golf Village Ln.; 843-449-7070; 888-886-8877;
www.grandedunes.com; 7618/5353; 77.3/71.2; 142/123

"Lovely to look at but difficult to endure", this South Carolina Open host has "all you want with its length" and "scenic Intracoastal holes", particularly the 14th, which "has to be the Strand's most beautiful par-3" – "but you do pay a price" both wallet- and score-wise; "relax and you are dead" on the "huge" "three-putt" greens, while "all those bunker shots" might "make you want to take a plunge in the Atlantic to cool off and forget."

Heather Glen
24 | 20 | 21 | 22 | $102

Hwy. 17 N., Little River; 843-249-9000; 800-868-4536;
www.heatherglen.com
Blue/Red: 6783/5101; 72.4/69.3; 127/117
Red/White: 6771/5053; 72.4/69.3; 134/117
White/Blue: 6822/5082; 72.4/69.3; 137/117

"You feel like you are in Scotland" at this bonny "beach-corridor" 27 - it might not be the Highlands, but it's "the only course on the Strand with real elevation changes"; that plus "lots of water, monster sand traps and fairway bunkers" make this links "torture" for high-handicaps who should "bring lots of balls and a retriever to find 'em"; "the newest nine is not as satisfying", so "play the original 18, and you won't be disappointed."

Legends, Heathland
22 | 24 | 22 | 20 | $107

Hwy. 501; 843-236-9318; 800-552-2660; www.legendsgolf.com;
6785/5115; 72.3/71; 127/121

Woodsmen who wail "whaddya mean there are no trees?" are advised to "bring their game if the wind is up" on this links "landscape created by a bulldozer"; it's "well manicured" and "picturesque", but even "if you can stand six-hour rounds" due to "crowding", you might agree that this layout is "uninteresting" without "as many surprises as other area courses."

Legends, Moorland
22 | 23 | 22 | 20 | $107

Hwy. 501; 843-236-9318; 800-552-2660; www.legendsgolf.com;
6799/4905; 72.8/72.8; 135/118

It's "wacky golf time" on this recently renovated "favorite at Legends" where "twists on every hole" include "mounds, raised greens" and "two bunkers you don't want to be stuck in", Big Bertha on the 4th and Hell's Half Acre on the 16th; in other words, there are "lots of risk/reward shots", but "you must be accurate" – you'd also better "play very early or late in the afternoon in peak season", as the complex as a whole can be "overbooked", leading to "slow play."

Legends, Parkland ⛳

| 21 | 24 | 22 | 20 | $107 |

Hwy. 501; 843-236-9318; 800-552-2660; www.legendsgolf.com;
7170/5518; 74.9/71; 137/125

Legends' "only non-links", this "crafty" tree-lined parklander is also
"the toughest of the three", dishing out a "difficult target-golf" day
on "some tight holes"; it's in "fabulous condition" with fairly "new
greens", and the resort offers "nice lodging packages", but snobby
swingers say that, in a locale with so many courses to choose from,
this design is "solid" but "unremarkable."

Long Bay

| 23 | 22 | 21 | 19 | $94 |

350 Foxtail Dr., Longs; 843-399-2222; 800-344-5590; www.mbn.com;
7025/4944; 74.3/69.2; 140/115

"Do you cut the dogleg or not, do you play it too safe away from
the water and end up driving through the fairway" or not? – "no
boring holes" on this "solid" Nicklaus Signature where "every
tee shot presents something you have to consider before hitting";
for thinking thwackers, it's a "good overall experience", until you
get to the "painfully slow" greens where, even if you decide you
should, "you can't roll up" shots.

Myrtle Beach National, King's North

| 25 | 23 | 22 | 21 | $160 |

4900 National Dr.; 843-448-2308; 800-344-5590; www.mbn.com;
7017/4816; 72.6/67.4; 136/113

"The King rules" proclaim Palmer partisans playing their cards
with the "memorable" Gambler, the island-fairway 6th hole on
this "great layout" in "perfect condition" with "lots of water and
sand but lots of fair landing areas if you hit it right"; given "putt-
putt" touches like bunkers forming the state's initials, displeased
subjects dethrone it for its "bizarre, disjointed", "video-game"
feel, while the masses decry "crowding" and a "cafeteria-style
food court" that "adds to the feeling that you're just a number."

Myrtle Beach National, SouthCreek

| 21 | 23 | 22 | 20 | $99 |

4900 National Dr.; 843-448-2308; 800-344-5590; www.mbn.com;
6416/4723; 71/68; 128/117

"Prices are right" at this "very nice" slice of woods and wetlands,
which trusting tracksters are relieved is "not as tricked up as King's
North" – unless you count the "bandit squirrels" who might make
away with your lunch; "you'll enjoy" the little critters, though,
far more than the "nasty rangers and uninspired design" when
compared to the "many courses in Myrtle Beach that are better."

Pine Lakes International ⛳

| 20 | 23 | 28 | 21 | $99 |

5603 Woodside Ave.; 843-449-6459; 800-446-6817; www.pinelakes.com;
6701/5140; 73/70.5; 132/121

"Oh, The Grandaddy!" – the founding father of Myrtle Beach golf
and "birthplace of *Sports Illustrated*" is "still a great course",
"nice and traditional" with an "Augusta feel" and play that's
"easier to the newbie"; but the real deal here is the "impeccable
service": South Carolina's No. 1 staff "runs to your car to take
your bags", performs "great club cleaning and shoe polishing"
and serves you "chowder on the par-3 in wintertime" – and they
do it all in "fabu kilts", even if contemporary club wielders crab
that their employer is "living off its history."

Tidewater 🏌
27 | 23 | 23 | 21 | $186

1400 Tidewater Dr., North Myrtle Beach; 843-249-3829; 800-446-5363;
www.tide-water.com; 7078/4615; 74.8/67.1; 144/115
"Too green and too pretty to be true" "winding" through "the North
Carolina pines" and on "marshland with the sweet smell" of sea,
this "target-oriented" "challenge" is "for anyone who wants to
experience the best of nature" "while having a unique round of
golf"; it's "a tad pricey", but it's a Myrtle "must-play" "just for the
chance to aim for a par-3 green that's down the hill, over the
wetlands and probably into the water" at a club where even the
"gators" display "Southern hospitality and class at their best."

TPC of Myrtle Beach
26 | 25 | 24 | 18 | $185

1199 TPC Blvd., Murrells Inlet; 843-357-3399; 888-742-8721;
www.tpc-mb.com; 6950/5118; 74/70.3; 145/125
About the only thing folks can agree upon is that "quite a few
holes require long carries" on this "demanding driving course";
otherwise, the "hazard"-jumping jury is out: this former Senior
Tour host is either "the best TPC facility ever visited", where a
"great pro shop, practice facility and service" go with a "brilliant
design", or it's "a lot of hype over" "boring holes" on "an
overcrowded course" that "needs to mature"; guess you'll have
to play it yourself to decide if it "lives up" to its name.

Wachesaw Plantation East 🏌
21 | 20 | 22 | 20 | $128

911 Riverwood Dr., Murrells Inlet; 843-357-2090; 888-922-0027;
www.wachesaweast.com; 6933/4995; 74.1/68.8; 135/117
There are "lots of places to get in trouble" on this "challenging,
tight course", "including portions of the cart path" that "need
to be redone" along with the rest of the "sparse facilities"; as for
the layout itself, this former LPGA host set amid wetlands stays in
"good condition, even during poor weather periods", but amiable
aces say it's "average at best", while nastier linksters call it "a
large parking lot with golf flags."

Wild Wing Plantation, Avocet 🏌
22 | 24 | 22 | 22 | $130

Hwy. 501 N.; 843-347-9464; 800-736-9464; www.wildwing.com;
7127/5298; 74.6/70.4; 133/118
"They moved heaven and earth to carve out" the "moon-sized
bunkers" and "huge mounds" on this "links-style layout cut
through the marshes" "out in the wilderness" around the Wild
Wing resort; "stretching out long" with "sand everywhere", it
might "bring you to your knees", but it could also have you soaring,
since the "challenging but fair" layout is "doable" "for all levels",
at least compared to "most Myrtle Beach courses."

Wild Wing Plantation, Falcon 🏌
24 | 25 | 23 | 22 | $120

Hwy. 501 N.; 843-347-9464; 800-736-9464; www.wildwing.com;
7082/5190; 74.4/70.4; 134/118
The "best" of the resort's brood doesn't have "quite as much water
or wetlands" as its nestmates, yet it's still "very demanding on shot
selection", and on linksters' legs: "high mounds along edges" make
for "difficult" "climbing" on "cart-path-only days", huff hackers
not in as "great shape" as the course itself; short-stickers say
"you will not find any better greens to putt" than these, while
ironmen insist it's "beautiful" "in late fall when dormant grasses
frame the fairways."

Wild Wing Plantation, Hummingbird

23 | 25 | 24 | 21 | $99

Hwy. 501 N.; 843-347-9464; 800-736-9464; www.wildwing.com; 6853/5168; 73.6/69.5; 135/123

"Women generally do not like a forced carry", so lady lofters might not be pleased that they must beat their wings to fly over the soupy "natural areas" crossing the fairways on what is otherwise "the most forgiving of the quartet" at this resort; like its siblings, it's "in superb condition", but the buzz on this Byrd is that Willard made a spread that's "a little contrived."

Wild Wing Plantation, Wood Stork

▽ 21 | 26 | 22 | 21 | $112

Hwy. 501 N.; 843-347-9464; 800-736-9464; www.wildwing.com; 7044/5409; 74.1/70.7; 130/121

"Can you say 'wetland and water'?" – even if you can't, you'd "better be able to deal with those challenges" on two-thirds of the "original" layout at what some snide swingers call "a golf factory", a resort with a noteworthy pro shop and practice facilities and not a lot to offer non-sportsmen; this "good, solid test" can be "very playable", but it's "unspectacular" gulp golfers going fishing for balls on a spread they find "not as good as the others" here.

Witch, The

22 | 18 | 20 | 21 | $98

1900 Hwy. 544, Conway; 843-448-1300; www.mysticalgolf.com; 6702/4812; 71.2/69; 133/109

"Book your Halloween tee times early" at this "nice, secluded" "sleeper" that can get "a little creepy when you get away from the clubhouse", what with "all kinds of critters" joining your foursome; "lots of water throughout" bubbles and boils with trouble, giving you "plenty of chances to reload your shag bag", but the "quietest round you will ever play" does cast its spell, so "take in the bridges, swamps" and "occasional gator" and "bathe in the serenity."

Wizard, The

19 | 18 | 17 | 19 | $88

4601 Leeshire Blvd.; 843-236-9393; www.mysticalgolf.com; 6721/4972; 72/71.2; 125/121

"When the wind blows", "beware" the "par-3 with the island green" and the "par-5 with the island fairway" not far from the "old wizard's castle" of a clubhouse for this "nice links-style course" where "a lot of water results in lots of must-make shots"; believers under the influence of this "tricked-up track's" "awesome prices" "play it with The Witch on the same day and get half off one round", though disenchanted duffers say the "poorly managed" place "looks so much better in the brochure."

Pawleys Island

CALEDONIA GOLF & FISH CLUB

28 | 25 | 25 | 22 | $185

369 Caledonia Dr.; 843-237-3675; 800-483-6800; www.fishclub.com; 6526/4957; 72.1/68.7; 140/122

"The closest you'll get to playing Augusta" is this "outrageously beautiful", "flower"- and "gator"-graced "beast" on a nature preserve; a "tight, little" "Southern classic", it "lives up to" the comparison "with gusto", from the "evocative" magnolia-lined drive to the "massive amounts of sand" – just "start your round on the first hole, otherwise you'll finish on the stupid 9th", a piddling 118-yarder; later, "watch golfers take a splash in the pond at 18" while "sipping a cocktail at the clubhouse."

Heritage Club 🔙

26 | 23 | 22 | 22 | $112

478 Heritage Dr.; 843-237-3424; 800-552-2660; www.legendsgolf.com; 7005/5250; 74.8/67.4; 144/119

"You'll think you've died and gone to Southern heaven" at this "grand old course with oaks and pines overhanging many of the holes" "on a former rice plantation" with "wonderful grounds" along Waccamaw River; the "back nine rocks" on this "awesome layout" where "you don't need to be long, but you must make shots, or your score will fly"; just avoid it in the afternoon when "backup at the tees" results in "five- or six-hour rounds."

Pawleys Plantation 🔙 🕐

24 | 22 | 22 | 22 | $135

70 Tanglewood Dr.; 843-237-6200; 800-367-9959; www.pawleysplantation.com; 7026/5017; 75.3/70.5; 146/124

"Myrtle Beach's fastest greens" are found at this "unheralded Jack gem" that "shows Nicklaus' inclination for high shots" onto "mercilessly protected" dance floors, like the "13th where the putting surface is smaller than the 17th at Sawgrass, and the wind blows in off the marsh"; the front nine is "tougher", the wetlands-laced back is "prettier", but the whole course is surrounded by "too many condos" – escape to the "magnificent lodge" where the staff helps you "feel you're with friends."

Tradition Club, The 🔙

22 | 23 | 23 | 23 | $110

1027 Willbrook Blvd.; 843-237-5041; 877-599-0888; www.traditiongolfclub.com; 6875/4106; 72.6/63.9; 132/104

"A good, easy playing course that isn't too easy", this water-laced woodlander kept in "fine condition" on the site of an old plantation "won't disappoint" as a "warm-up" on a golf trip to the Pawleys Island/Myrtle Beach area; as for its particulars, players can't really tell you much more: it "has the curse of one hole blending into the next", so "you leave struggling to remember" your round.

True Blue

24 | 21 | 21 | 20 | $150

900 Blue Stem Dr.; 843-235-0900; 888-483-6801; www.truebluegolf.com; 7062/4995; 74.3/65.4; 145/109

This "links is on LSD" drawl drug-savvy duffers of Mark Strantz's "brutal", "bold, startling" spread; "everything is on a grand scale", from the "tons of sand" in the "loads of waste bunkers" to the "large fairways and humongous greens"; "long ball hitters" negotiating the "spectacular finishing holes" marvel this "must be what golf is like on the moon", at least compared to its more down-to-earth sister, Caledonia.

South Dakota

Sioux Falls

Prairie Green

– | – | – | – | $28

600 E. 69th St.; 605-367-6076; 800-585-6076; www.dakotagolf.com; 7179/5245; 74.2/70.2; 134/122

There's no little house on this links-style Dick Nugent design on the prairie, but there are generous fairways, stunning wetlands and well-bunkered greens; wide-open spaces and big skies team up with lakes in play on 14 holes to offer a good challenge on this Sioux Falls muni, the host of the state's 2005 Stroke Play Championship.

Vermillion

Bluffs, The　　　　　　　　– | – | – | – | $23
2021 E. Main St.; 605-677-7058; www.bluffsinfo.com; 6684/4926; 72.4/68.5; 123/113
Tucked in the southeast corner of South Dakota is a residential development with an incredibly affordable links layout shot through with lakes and wetlands; four holes sit in the Missouri River Valley with water views, while the others stand tall on the prairie highland, especially the 13th tee that's set 80 feet above the fairway.

Tennessee

Knoxville

Stonehenge at Fairfield Glade 🏌　▽ 26 | 23 | 23 | 23 | $79
222 Fairfield Blvd., Fairfield Glade; 931-484-3731; www.stonehengegolf.com; 6549/5000; 71.8/69.6; 135/124
Plan "a two- or three-day stay in the area with your buddies" in order to leave no stone unturned during an "enjoyable outing" on this "excellent" track in the Cumberland Mountains west of Knoxville; with rock outcroppings and walls dotting holes, it's especially "gorgeous in the early fall", but "check [conditions] before you tee off": "surprisingly, it stays a bit wet" and "soft", so "you can plug a ball" even "in the dead of summer."

Nashville

Bear Trace At Ross Creek Landing　– | – | – | – | $69
110 Airport Rd., Clifton; 931-676-3174; www.beartrace.com; 7131/5504; 74.8/67.4; 135/120
This final installment of Jack Nicklaus' Signature collection for the state is "hard to get to, but well worth it", say loyalists of the rugged layout halfway between Memphis and Nashville; it might be both the most demanding and the most dramatic of the five courses, thanks to holes such as the par-5 8th, which skirts the Tennessee River and the par-4 10th that forces an approach over a gorge.

Hermitage, General's Retreat　▽ 24 | 22 | 25 | 22 | $57
3939 Old Hickory Blvd., Old Hickory; 615-847-4001; www.hermitagegolf.com; 6773/5437; 72.3/70.8; 129/120
A tasty par-72 on the Cumberland River 20 minutes from Downtown Nashville, this Gary Baird design was the longtime venue for the LPGA's Sara Lee Classic; the 600-yd. 11th offers the toughest challenge with water in play on the second shot and the approach to the green, but you'll have no difficulty finding something tempting in the well-stocked pro shop before heading to the airport nearby.

Hermitage, President's Reserve　▽ 24 | 22 | 25 | 23 | $67
3939 Old Hickory Blvd., Old Hickory; 615-847-4001; www.hermitagegolf.com; 7157/5138; 74.2/69; 134/115
The "zoysia fairways make you envious when you're oftentimes in the rough" or sinking into the natural wetlands on this "strong" and

"beautiful" course at an "impressive facility"; still, even though it meanders along the banks of the Cumberland River with water in play on 11 holes, aesthetes argue it's "not as scenic as the General", its less "challenging" parkland sibling.

Springhouse ⌂
24 | 26 | 25 | 20 | $74

18 Springhouse Ln.; 615-871-7759; www.springhousegolfclub.com; 6842/5040; 74/70.2; 133/118

"Stay in the short stuff and bring lots of ammo" to battle "some of the most wicked, ball-eating rough you have ever seen" at this "extreme pleasure", a "challenging" links layout on the Cumberland River where the limestone cliffs, protected wetlands and turn-of-the-century namesake springhouse make for "very pretty holes"; "what's good enough" for the competitors in the Bell South Senior Classic "is more than good enough for me" drawl duffers.

Texas

★ Top Courses in State
28 Barton Creek, Fazio Canyons, *Austin*
27 Pine Dunes, *Tyler*
    Tribute, *Dallas*
26 La Cantera, Resort, *San Antonio*
    Cowboys, *Dallas*
    La Cantera, Palmer, *San Antonio*
    Texas Star, *Dallas*
25 Horseshoe Bay, Ram Rock, *Austin*
    Cliffs, *Dallas*
    Horseshoe Bay, Applerock, *Austin*

Austin

Barton Creek, Crenshaw Cliffside ⏱
23 | 26 | 26 | 19 | $165

8212 Barton Club Dr.; 512-329-4001; 800-336-6158; www.bartoncreek.com; 6553/4850; 71.1/67.2; 126/110

"High, low, bump-and-run" – you'll "love the number of shot options you can play" en route to the "larger-than-normal greens" on this design by Bill Coore and Ben Crenshaw that's "perfect" for both "a casual stroll among the deer or a hard-fought match between fierce competitors"; critics concede "the course has character", but it also has "too many blind shots where local knowledge is paramount" and too little of the "aesthetics of the other Barton Creek" offerings at too high a price.

BARTON CREEK, FAZIO CANYONS ⏱
28 | 26 | 26 | 21 | $180

8212 Barton Club Dr.; 512-329-4001; 800-336-6158; www.bartoncreek.com; 7153/5098; 75.4/70.6; 138/121

"Don't be misled by bland No. 1" – beyond it awaits a "magnificent" "mix" of "memorable holes"; Texas' Top Course "deserves nothing but an A+++ in every way" for its "challenge", "great condition" and "use of the natural landscape" in a setting so "serene" that you "feel you're alone" amid the "amazing Hill Country views"; "you have to be a billy goat" on cart-path-only days, and "you'll play better the second time around because of some blind shots", yet a couple of rounds are a "worthwhile splurge" at this "outstanding" resort.

Barton Creek, Fazio Foothills 🏌 ⛳   _ | _ | _ | _ |$205

8212 Barton Club Dr.; 512-329-4000; 800-336-6158; www.bartoncreek.com; 6956/5207; 74/70; 135/124

The current President's favorite layout is the original Barton Creek course, a fair design that won't leave you bushed after play on cliff-lined fairways amid natural limestone caves and waterfalls; following renovations, its new grass and spruced-up tees are already in stellar condition, and the length has been stretched 200 more yards to test the best, including Canadian Tour pros who stop here annually; the caddie program started in 2005 should help scores, while the luxurious spa can alleviate post-round sores.

Barton Creek, Palmer Lakeside ⊙   24 | 24 | 25 | 21 |$125

8212 Barton Club Dr.; 512-329-4001; 800-336-6158; www.bartoncreek.com; 6668/6007; 72.3/69.8; 135/121

"Give yourself a rest from the Fazio" on this "resort-type" sibling on "small hills" 25 minutes north of Barton Creek along "scenic" Lake Travis; the "vistas are good", Arnold Palmer's layout is "excellent" with its signature waterfall par-3 11th and the staff sure is "friendly" – they just might "open up the bar and grill" especially for you "on a slow day" so you can get a taste of that "great chicken-fried steak."

Circle C   21 | 21 | 21 | 20 | $65

7401 Hwy. 45; 512-288-4297; www.thegolfclubatcirclec.com; 6859/5236; 72.7/69.9; 122/120

"Puzzles" abound on the "ultimate setting for that country-club-for-a-day feel", this "secluded" Jay Morrish layout south of Austin that features tricky "holes in the woods" with "plenty of wildlife" and "greenery" but "no homes" surrounding them; nature lovers declare it "the best bang for your buck" (or doe) for "very good service" and a "well-maintained" course that's "getting better and better"; "bring your sticks and have a blast" – just "avoid it in spring when the trees can be worm-infested."

Forest Creek   21 | 15 | 15 | 22 | $59

99 Twin Ridge Pkwy., Round Rock; 512-388-2874; www.forestcreek.com; 7147/5394; 73.8/71.9; 136/124

"Every hole is a work of art" say intellectuals "thinking their way around" the narrow fairways and "undulating greens" sculpted out of the forest just north of Austin; there's "lots of trouble" amid the trees and water but "not too much traffic", so "bring plenty of balls" and take your time on the "well-groomed" course, even if it doesn't have masterpiece facilities.

Horseshoe Bay, Applerock 🏳 ⛳   25 | 24 | 22 | 18 |$149

1 Horseshoe Bay Blvd., Horseshoe Bay; 830-598-6561; 800-252-9363; www.horseshoebaytexas.com; 6999/5536; 74/73; 139/128

A "playable" layout and "outstanding views" of Lake LBJ mean "even bad shots" have a fruitful round at this "fantastic" formation at an "old-standby" resort in Texas Hill Country where facilities, including a private airport for jet-setting swingers, are "great"; "beautiful" No. 12, a par-3 "challenge" that leap-frogs across the water, is particularly "enjoyable" for diving drivers, but "course conditions have gone downhill over the years, which is truly unfortunate."

Horseshoe Bay, Ram Rock 🔥 ⚬━ | 25 | 25 | 24 | 19 | $149 |
1 Horseshoe Bay Blvd., Horseshoe Bay; 830-598-6561; 800-252-9363;
www.horseshoebaytexas.com; 6926/5306; 74.5/72.5; 140/129
"Tee off from the tips and hang on" or else this "fantastic but very
difficult course" will ram you, say "lower handicaps" taking
a test that's "not for less skilled golfers" by the horns; amid rock
gardens, meandering streams and dry creek beds, Robert Trent
Jones Sr. fashioned yet "another beautiful", well-bunkered layout
at this "great complement of courses" at the heart of a "true resort
experience that must be done."

Horseshoe Bay, Slick Rock 🔥 | 24 | 25 | 24 | 19 | $149 |
1 Horseshoe Bay Blvd., Horseshoe Bay; 830-598-6561;
800-252-9363; www.horseshoebaytexas.com;
6834/5438; 72.6/72.1; 127/1127
The original RTJ Sr. design here offers a "good break from other
Rock courses", but while it is "fun" even for foozlers, it still serves
up 71 bunkers and water in play on 12 holes; look out for granite
outcroppings and a variety of trees on the front before attacking
a wide-open back dressed in bamboo and pampas grass on this
"good" track at a resort that sports an elaborate putting course
and always delivers "great service", even if some city slickers
call it "overpriced."

Dallas

Buffalo Creek 🔥 | 22 | 15 | 16 | 22 | $59 |
624 Country Club Dr., Heath; 972-771-4003; www.americangolf.com;
7018/5209; 73.8/67; 133/113
"You can't go wrong with a Morrish/Weiskopf design", and indeed,
this "tough" spread was "fabulous when it opened" in 1992, with
"unusual holes" and "great elevation changes for around Dallas";
unfortunately, the lax "attitude" of the "inconsistent American
Golf operation" "is beginning to show" in "poor maintenance",
"practice facilities that leave a lot to be desired" and "houses
lining every fairway."

Chase Oaks, Blackjack 🔥 | ▽ 18 | 18 | 14 | 21 | $50 |
7201 Chase Oaks Blvd., Plano; 972-517-7777; www.chaseoaks.com;
6773/5132; 74.1/70; 139/122
Play your cards right on this "challenging" layout, and you'll have
an "enjoyable" game; "pretty good for a muni", this mid-1980s
creation by Robert Von Hagge and Bruce Devlin may be an "older
course", but it comes armed "with plenty of teeth", including
water on 10 holes and hilly, wooded fairways, so don't throw in all
your chips until you see what it's dealing you.

Cliffs, The 🔥 | 25 | 19 | 19 | 23 | $80 |
160 Cliffs Dr., Graford; 940-729-4520; 888-843-2543;
www.thecliffsresort.com; 6808/4876; 73.9/68.4; 143/124
"When the wind is not blowing anywhere else in Texas, it is"
whipping up a frenzy across the ravines, cedar groves and uneven
lies of this "good test", helping to make the cliffside course
"possibly the hardest" in the state; it's "not for the novice", but
aces agree that "some punitive holes are made up for by great
views" – both the panoramic vistas of Possum Kingdom Lake and
the close-ups of "abundant rattlesnakes."

Cowboys 🏌

26 | 26 | 26 | 21 | $150

1600 Fairway Dr., Grapevine; 817-481-7277; www.cowboysgolfclub.com;
7017/4702; 74.2/68.9; 140/114

"The Cowboys may be horrible, but their golf course is great", and the "friendly, courteous" "iced-towel girls", like the Cheerleaders, "are worth the trip" alone, say Lone Star State swingers of one of the "best upscale layouts in the area" where "you never know which athlete you'll see" hanging around the "neat clubhouse" filled with Dallas football "memorabilia"; "once you get used to the planes overhead, it's a real treat", particularly because the "delicious" "food is included."

Four Seasons at Las Colinas, Cottonwood Valley ⚡

24 | 26 | 26 | 17 | $185

4150 N. MacArthur Blvd., Irving; 972-717-2500;
www.thesportsclubfourseasons.com; 6927/5320; 74.3/70.4; 137/119

"One of the best staffs you'll ever encounter" "treats you like a king" at this "beautiful resort", and so does this course; "forgiving enough for novices but challenging for intermediates", the "rolling" layout "with lots of trees" makes everyone "feel like a champion, even though they're not on the TPC"; it's a "delight to play and always in great shape", but given its "bastard stepchild" status, penny-wise putters ponder "why am I paying so much?"

Four Seasons at Las Colinas, TPC ⚡

24 | 27 | 26 | 18 | $185

4150 N. MacArthur Blvd., Irving; 972-717-2500;
www.thesportsclubfourseasons.com; 6899/5340; 75.1/73.3; 140/134

"Everything you'd expect from a Four Seasons that hosts an annual PGA event", this "treasure" has seen "recent modifications that represent dedication to continuous improvement" of an "appropriately challenging" layout where the green on the 14th is guarded by water and a vigilant cedar elm; the state's Top Service "couldn't be better", nor could its Top Facilities: the "attentive" staff oversees "the best practice area", "a fabulous hotel", an "outstanding spa" and restaurants where the "food is wonderful" – but of course you "pay" "where the pros play."

Ridgeview Ranch

20 | 16 | 17 | 21 | $49

2701 Ridgeview Dr., Plano; 972-390-1039; www.americangolf.com;
7025/5335; 74.1/70.4; 130/117

You get "lots of bang for the buck" on this "nice course", a local "favorite" for its winning combination of "layout, playability and cost"; "conditioning is not always the best", the facilities are "nothing fancy or memorable" and the service is "inconsistent", but high-handicap history buffs "will not get bored on" the wide-open, forgiving layout or at the Civil War–era cemetery on-site, even if sweeter swingers swipe "'Ranch' says it all."

Tangle Ridge

21 | 18 | 21 | 23 | $49

818 Tangle Ridge Dr., Grand Prairie; 972-299-6837; www.tangleridge.com;
6835/5187; 72.2/70.2; 129/117

A "hidden gem of Dallas Metroplex", the "municipal course for Grand Prairie" is "fun, fair, challenging" and forested, with "nice elevation changes for North Texas"; it's "normally in good shape", though it "tends to get a little burnt in summer" and is "usually pretty busy" with locals scarfing up an "excellent value", but particularly if your sticks are a bit rusty, "you will enjoy" tangling with this track – with the help of the "great teaching staff."

Texas Star
26 | 19 | 18 | 23 | $75

1400 Texas Star Pkwy., Euless; 817-685-7888; 888-839-7827;
www.texasstargolf.com; 6936/4962; 73.6/69.7; 135/124
You "will lose lots of balls in the environmental protected areas" on this "awesome Keith Foster design", since it's best to let "those rattlers and cottonmouths" have 'em; "lost" amid "endless sprawl" and "daily-fee courses that spend a fortune on advertising", this Euless muni is a "good-value" "challenge" that "nicely pulls off" its "tough, tight and long" layout, while its Raven's Grille pulls off just about "the best breakfast burrito in the country."

Tour 18 Dallas 🖼
21 | 20 | 18 | 16 | $89

8718 Amen Corner, Flower Mound; 817-430-2000; 800-946-5310;
www.tour18-dallas.com; 7033/5493; 74.3/66.3; 138/119
"Try to beat your favorite pro's score" on each of these 18 "nice knockoffs" of "different famous holes from around the world"; "for those of us who will never get to play the originals", this "decent" "gimmick" brings back "memories of tournaments seen on TV" and allows you to "imagine yourself on those courses in pressure situations"; however, the layout "lacks true continuity because of its format", and the "size of the golfing herd" "flocking" to this "novelty" makes for "slow play" and "erratic conditions."

Tribute 🏌
27 | 23 | 21 | 22 | $95

1000 Boyd Rd., The Colony; 972-370-5465; www.thetributegolflinks.com;
7002/5352; 73.2/65.6; 128/111
"If you can't afford going across the big blue pond, then fly to Dallas/Ft. Worth and play this fantasy" "replica" of "great European holes"; complete with "wind off the lake", "nasty" "deep bunkers", "rough that is three feet tall", "great greens" and "service people who take care of you in the unique style" of the British Isles, this "classic redo" is "pretty authentic"; just "play it in the winter because Scotland does not reach 105 degrees."

Westin Stonebriar, Fazio 🖼 ⚬⚬
22 | 24 | 24 | 19 | $116

1549 Legacy Dr., Frisco; 972-668-8748; www.stonebriar.com;
7021/5208; 73.8/72.4; 133/105
It's only been around since 2000, so "give this course another three years for the trees to catch up to the beautifully conditioned fairways and greens, and it'll rank as one of the tops in Texas" testify tracksters taking in the "true roll" of the dance floors on this "pleasure" in Frisco; "forgiving landing areas" let you "go low" in your score, so "gamble" with your buddies on a "weekend stay" at the Westin where "rounds out your back door" are "worth the visit."

El Paso

Painted Dunes Desert
▽ 20 | 15 | 18 | 26 | $24

12000 McCombs St.; 915-821-2122; www.painteddunes.com
East/West: 6925/4781; 72.7/63.2; 134/114
North/East: 6904/4934; 72.3/63.5; 128/110
West/North: 6941/4917; 72.6/63.4; 131/114
On the "stark desert" of Western Texas, parched putters stumble onto this "oasis of fun"; "small green targets of fairways and putting

surfaces" and "views of the Franklin Mountains" make this "great test" feel "like Phoenix golf" at a "fantastic value", particularly if you play "the original 18", as "the new nine is just average."

Houston

Augusta Pines ☉   23 | 24 | 23 | 19 | $85

18 Augusta Pines Dr., Spring; 832-381-1010; www.tour18.com; 7041/5007; 73.6/68.5; 125/112

"The name says it all" at this "first-rate experience" with "different looks from different tees" and "water features that are prominent and a little sneaky"; the "killer hole" is the 18th, with "a narrow-waisted, long fairway" that has "water on the right" and a "fear-factor approach to an island green" that "slopes" – "par that one and you will feel well rewarded"; otherwise, the course is "very playable", but things "can get a little expensive", so hand-to-mouth hackers should hunt "for better values nearby."

BlackHorse, North   23 | 22 | 23 | 18 | $89

12205 Fry Rd., Cypress; 281-304-1747; www.blackhorsegolfclub.com; 7301/5065; 75/69.1; 130/115

"You can use every stick in your bag" – "it's just a question of how well you use them" on the "tougher of the two at BlackHorse", a "beautiful" parklander with "fair driving areas" leap-frogging over wetlands and a meandering creek; "one of the best-conditioned courses" northwest of Houston, its "greens are fab", and the "staff is par none" – if only "there wasn't so much construction around it."

BlackHorse, South   22 | 21 | 23 | 18 | $89

12205 Fry Rd., Cypress; 281-304-1747; www.blackhorsegolfclub.com; 7171/4946; 74.7/68.5; 138/123

Its "front nine starts humbly", but the "torturous approaches" and "horror forced carries" on Nos. 7, 8 and 9 at this spread give you a "taste of the difficulty to come" on "holes 14–17, four of the best in Houston" for their "interesting" routing through a sand quarry made into wetlands; with "great tee boxes" and a "staff that's a pleasure to work with", the "more picturesque" track here "could have been amazing had the developers not mixed and matched landscapes and surrounded it with (admittedly nice) housing."

Cypresswood, Tradition   24 | 17 | 19 | 20 | $65

21602 Cypresswood Dr., Spring; 281-821-6300; www.cypresswood.com; 7220/5255; 74.4/68.9; 134/122

This "classic" on the north side of Houston "rocks", trumpet traditionalists, even if the "woods and pine straw are constantly in play"; it's a "great" Keith Foster design "requiring patience, some skill and course management" to deal with the "prominent and dangerous water features and gullies", while a yardage book is "an investment that will produce lower scores immediately" here; aesthetes agree there are "no weak holes", but "conditions have lessened it recently", and as for the facilities, "eat elsewhere."

Falls, The   25 | 15 | 18 | 24 | $66

1750 N. Falls Dr., New Ulm; 979-992-3123; www.thefallsresort.com; 6765/5348; 72.5/70; 135/123

"Consider a day trip from the Big H" to "the big middle of nowhere" to play this "damn hard", "don't-miss jewel" where "some nice elevation changes" allow you to "experience terrain that is not normally found this close to Houston"; the "bent-grass greens are a pleasure", as are the "deer everywhere who sometimes eat right out of your hand" – while the namesake cascading waters might eat your balls.

Meadowbrook Farms
24 | 22 | 23 | 19 | $85

9595 S. Fry Rd., Katy; 281-693-4653; 7100/5000; 74.2/68; 137/108
A few years "short of excellent", this "interesting" Greg Norman layout is still a bit "rough around the edges"; but though it "needs to grow in and mature", it already has "plenty to offer" in terms of "challenges", since it's "well designed to play in the prevailing winds" and to "roll with the land and create difficulty through (mostly) natural features", such as "trees, gullies, native grass" and "wetlands"; unfortunately, in-the-works man-made features include "a vast sea of housing."

Memorial Park
22 | 16 | 15 | 24 | $32

1001 E. Memorial Loop; 713-862-4033; www.memorialparkgolf.com; 7164/5459; 73/70.7; 122/114
"In the heart of America's fourth largest city", ball beaters "crowd" this "cool, old muni that's been renovated" and returned to its original 1936 "beauty"; it's "a wonderful place to not only golf but to spend a day" – and spend it you will given the "slow play" caused by "tons" of "hackers" flubbing what should be "long, straight drives" (no wonder the "starters are grumpy"); while away the wait "peeking a view" at "some hotties jogging in the park."

Southwyck
18 | 15 | 16 | 17 | $49

2901 Clubhouse Dr., Pearland; 713-436-9999; 6914/5145; 66.2/73.2; 127/112
"Golfers at every level will find a challenge" – but not an impossible one – on this "very fair" "oldie but oft-overlooked goodie" with "a great links feel" to its mounds, pot bunkers and prairie knolls; "no two holes are alike" on this "interesting" layout that can "be a little windy", of course, but is still "easy to score" on; it's "unbearably hot in the summer" and "not walker friendly", so spring for the cart and don't expect much by way of facilities at a spread that "needs a better clubhouse."

Tour 18 Houston ⛳
22 | 20 | 19 | 18 | $89

3102 FM 1960 E., Humble; 281-540-1818; 800-856-8687; www.tour18golf.com; 6782/5380; 72.7/71.3; 129/129
"Hootie J. won't invite you to Augusta, so come here to play Amen Corner" say the unwashed masses sampling this "simulation" of a "variety of well-known" layouts; "18 great holes do not make a great course" rant rebels – "since each one is unique, it's hard to get a pace to your game", plus it's "built near some oil wells, and "at times you can't get them out of your view"; the people have spoken: "it's a neat concept", but the "novelty wears off" after you try it "once or twice."

Windrose
▽ 18 | 17 | 18 | 16 | $59

6235 Pinelakes Blvd., Spring; 281-370-8900; www.windrosegolfclub.com; 7203/5355; 73/69.3; 128/117
"Better have your A short game" with you to skate across "some of the best and fastest greens in Houston" at this "good course" northwest of the city incorporating woodlands, wetlands and open

links-style holes; "it can be difficult when the wind picks up", shrug
scratch players, but otherwise it's "nothing spectacular" with
maintenance that "used to be much better."

Lubbock

Rawls Course at　　　　　　　▽ 23 │ 19 │ 21 │ 25 │ $42
Texas Tech University, The
3720 Fourth St.; 806-742-4653; www.texastechgolf.ttu.edu;
7207/5373; 73.2/64.9; 126/112
Designed in 2003 by Tom Doak, this "great, new" parklander is home
to the Red Raiders golf teams; with 96 bunkers (including a 21-ft.-
deep gaping maw on the 8th) and wind-swept, expansive fairways,
it's "similar to a European course", but it's a far distance from
St. Andrews – "if only it were somewhere other than Lubbock"
lament lofters lost on the High Plains.

San Antonio

Canyon Springs 🏌　　　　　　22 │ 20 │ 21 │ 21 │ $100
24400 Wilderness Oak Rd.; 210-497-1770;
7077/5234; 72.8/70; 130/115
"The types of challenges vary" on this "fair balance" of "difficult"
and "forgiving" holes: the former sport "huge doglegs and blind
shots", while the "different tees allow all skill levels to enjoy"
the latter; "nestled in the beginning of Hill Country" with "great
waterfalls on the finish", its setting is "incredibly beautiful",
but "its rough is not well enough maintained to get it to the top
in the area."

Hyatt Hill Country　　　　　　22 │ 25 │ 24 │ 18 │ $125
9800 Hyatt Resort Dr.; 210-520-4040; 888-901-4653;
www.sanantonio.hyatt.com
Creeks/Oaks: 6867/4825; 73.7/68.2; 131/119
Lakes/Creeks: 6931/4939; 73.7/69.2; 132/118
Lakes/Oaks: 6940/4778; 73.7/67.8; 136/118
"Just because you're on the green doesn't mean you're in the cup
anytime soon" pout pooped putters on the "tricky" dance floors,
while other ball beaters "wear themselves out" "getting the rhythm
of the rolling hills" on this "great wandering layout" that's even
more meandering now that they've added a third nine as part of
a larger makeover to this resort near Sea World and Six Flags;
despite a "breeze at all times" in this "wonderful setting", the "huge
mosquitoes" linger, so "bring plenty of bug spray."

La Cantera, Palmer　　　　　　26 │ 26 │ 25 │ 20 │ $140
16641 La Cantera Pkwy.; 210-558-2365; 800-446-5387;
www.lacanteragolfclub.com; 6926/5066; 74.2/65.3; 142/116
"Wow, wow, wow" – Arnie's Army hails the heaps of "heroic holes"
with "ups and downs, ravines, doglegs", "blind shots", "majestic
elevations" and "gorgeous views" on this "stunning course" at
a "beautiful" Hill Country resort; "if the wind is blowing, bring
extra balls", or scavenge "dozens" of them from the "brush",
but "if you're a walker, forget about it" altogether; the course is
"not for the weak of heart", but you can calm yours with a "post-
round toddy at the quiet, classy clubhouse while spotting turkeys
and other wildlife."

La Cantera, Resort
26 | 27 | 25 | 20 | $140

16641 La Cantera Pkwy.; 210-558-4653; 800-446-5387;
www.lacanteragolfclub.com; 7021/4940; 72.5/67.1; 134/108

"Whoopee!" whoop wallopers riding this "awesome" "roller-coaster" track featuring "a few carnivallike holes with [Six Flags Fiesta Texas] amusement park right off the course"; "ever hit off a 180-ft. wall into an old rock quarry?" – "you will if you play here", so you'd better "like elevation changes and a lot of 'em"; the "first-class" resort's "accommodating staff" will help you "drop some pennies in one of the best-stocked pro shops in the U.S."

Pecan Valley
22 | 16 | 18 | 23 | $59

4700 Pecan Valley Dr.; 210-333-9018; www.pecanvalleygc.com;
7047/5310; 74.2/65.9; 128/118

Oh, the stories those "huge trees that line every fairway" of this "great, old-style course" could tell – the site of Arnold Palmer's historic one-stroke defeat in the 1968 PGA Championship "looks open", but "it gets tight when the pecans leaf out"; though the layout "has been restored to prominence" through a Bob Cupp redo, facilities including the "torn-up driving range" and carts that appear to be "from the '50s" still "need improvement" – "they're trying, but they have a way to go."

Quarry
23 | 21 | 21 | 20 | $90

444 E. Basse Rd.; 210-824-4500; 800-347-7759; www.quarrygolf.com;
6740/4897; 72.4/67.4; 128/115

"Close to the airport" and right "across from some fabulous shopping" is a "very unusual" Keith Foster design sporting two "totally different styles of layout"; the namesake "old stone quarry" and its "picturesque views" "get all the publicity" for the "really hot" "target-golf back", but the "links" front nine "is a good test", too, "with a lot of water" in play; "watch out" for both "the rattlers" and "the wall on the 17th – the hole is called 'Reload' for a reason."

SilverHorn
22 | 17 | 20 | 19 | $70

1100 W. Bitters Rd.; 210-545-5300; www.silverhorngolfclub.com;
6922/5271; 73.1/70.4; 129/116

"Live oaks on almost every fairway" plus strategic bunkers and water hazards make "accurate tee shots a must" on this "thinking person's course" with "lots of different hole layouts" to consider; in a location so "close" to the city that you can ponder your "dinner or flight plans" along with your putts, it's a "well-maintained" "fair test of golf" at a price that won't have your mind focused on the money.

Tyler

Pine Dunes
27 | 15 | 18 | 26 | $79

159 Private Rd. 7019, Frankston; 903-876-4336; www.pinedunes.com;
7117/5150; 74.4/71.3; 131/126

"Wow, what a layout" – "make the journey to east Texas" and discover "how nice" it is "to be in the country" amid "incredible peace and quiet" at this "hidden gem" set into the thick of the piney forest and draped over sand washes by Jay and Carter Morrish; this "pure-golf" "challenge" is "well worth the drive", but it's far from anywhere, so you might want to book your foursome in an on-site condo and stay awhile.

U.S. Virgin Islands

St. Croix

Carambola ▽ 23 | 21 | 21 | 21 | $104 |

72 Estate River, Kingshill; 340-778-5638; www.carambolabeach.com; 6865/5425; 74.3/66.3; 135/120

"Around par for the Caribbean", this Robert Trent Jones Sr. effort is a "nice, short course" in "decent shape" that divides opinions; fans say when "in St. Croix, don't miss" this "gem" with "many interesting holes" at a "lovely facility" in a "beautiful" inland valley location, while antsy aces dismiss it as "not terribly exciting", opting to "head to the Dominican Republic for some serious golf" instead.

St. Thomas

Mahogany Run 🏖 19 | 16 | 17 | 15 | $140 |

1 Mahogany Run Rd. N.; 340-777-6006; 800-253-7103; www.mahoganyrungolf.com; 6008/4873; 70.5/70.9; 133/134

You "don't come to St. Thomas to golf", but "when you're on a boat and you're dying to get to the links", this "solid but unspectacular" spread is "worth a visit" if only for its signature trio of holes "on the back nine"; if the Bermuda Triangle didn't swallow you when you were cruising the ocean, you might disappear here in the "awesome Devil's Triangle", a "gruelling" "Pebble Beach–type" "stretch" with "stunning views" "on a cliffside" "along the ocean"; otherwise, say critical clubwielders, this "expensive" course is a "mosquito"-ravaged "wasteland."

Utah

Salt Lake City

Homestead ▽ 22 | 18 | 21 | 20 | $60 |

700 Homestead Dr., Midway; 435-654-5588; 888-327-7220; www.homesteadresort.com; 7040/5091; 73/66.4; 135/125

"Prairie dogs abound", and as evidenced by the "aroma from the nearby grazing areas", so do lots of other animals on this "very hilly" track in a "mountain setting" "not far from Park City and Salt Lake City"; otherwise, it's "never crowded", perhaps because it's pricey "compared to other courses in the area"; nevertheless, it's "great to play in the fall" when you can "watch your ball fly in the high altitude" toward a "backdrop of wonderful foliage" followed by a meal at Simon's, the resort's highly recommended restaurant.

Thanksgiving Point 🏖 26 | 26 | 24 | 23 | $78 |

3300 W. Clubhouse Dr., Lehi; 801-768-7400; www.thanksgivingpoint.com; 7714/5838; 76.2/72.8; 140/135

The pros take "a real test from the tips" during the Champions Tour Challenge on this "long", "beautiful" "gem hidden" at a daytime resort 20 minutes south of Salt Lake City; "the course sits in a ravine", so "wind can be a factor", but "the views are unbelievable" and "shots are interesting throughout the round"; plus, with a working farm, a museum, botanical gardens, theaters and shops, there's "something for the family" to do "nearby while you play" (except on Sundays when the rest of the facility is closed).

Valley View　　　　　▽ 28 | 21 | 22 | 28 | $26
2501 E. Gentile St., Layton; 801-546-1630; 7147/5679; 73.5/71.1; 123/125
What the few flubbers who've found it call "the top public course in Utah" is also one of "the best values in the United States"; given "lots of changing elevation, water and mature trees" to "test shotmaking abilities" on a "fantastic" layout "nestled against the Wasatch Mountains with wonderful views of the Salt Lake Valley" all for a "hard-to-believe", rock-bottom fee, "low- and medium-handicaps" hail it as "a steal."

Wasatch Mountain, Lakes　　21 | 18 | 20 | 27 | $38
975 W. Golf Course Dr., Midway; 435-654-0532; www.stateparks.utah.gov; 6942/5573; 72/71.5; 128/123
"When it's too hot in the Valley, recharge your batteries" with a round at this "great getaway from the summer days" – or, better yet, tackle it "in the fall when the leaves are turning" and it's "pure heaven"; any season, "world-class Wasatch Mountains views" make this "must-play" one of the "most gorgeous courses in the state", at a "terrific" municipal value; just "beware" "wildlife galore", including "beer-drinking, denim-wearing rednecks" "crowding" the course on "Saturdays."

Wasatch Mountain, Mountain 🏌 24 | 18 | 19 | 28 | $38
975 W. Golf Course Dr., Midway; 435-654-0532; www.stateparks.utah.gov; 6459/5009; 70.4/67.4; 125/119
"The better 18 at Wasatch Mountain" is a "real favorite of locals and visitors alike" who play quickly since "rangers move along traffic", which includes "deer and moose on the fairways"; "it's easy to overlook the occasionally disease-laden greens because the rest of the course is so spectacular", and "oh, you can't beat the price"; eagle-eyed birdie-hunters might complain of "too many blind uphill approach shots", but "when the colors are at their peak" in autumn, "it's hard to watch your ball" anyway.

St. George

CORAL CANYON　　　　28 | 23 | 25 | 25 | $93
1925 Canyon Greens Dr., Washington; 435-688-1700; www.suncorgolf.com; 7029/4125; 73/69.1; 137/122
"Sign me up for another round" rave rooters of this "sublime" layout with "lush green fairways set against the red rock of southern Utah"; "the course is immaculate", "the service is excellent, the facilities are comfortable without being stuffy" and, with Zion and Pine Valley Mountain backdrops, there's "breathtaking scenery on almost every hole", making it a "blast to play."

Entrada at Snow Canyon　　25 | – | 22 | 22 | $120
2511 Entrada Trail; 435-674-7500; www.golfentrada.com; 7059/5200; 73.6/68.7; 131/115
"Is this heaven?" – if not quite that celestial, its "finishing holes are what golfing on the moon would be like" say aces as astrologically astute as the Anasazi Indians who once star-gazed in this "beautiful setting" in southwest Utah two hours north of Las Vegas; the back nine on this "phenomenal" semi-private "winds through a lava field that is target golf at its best", particularly given the "perfect 10 conditions"; with a "new clubhouse" just completed, the facilities are now as "awesome" as the layout and the views.

Vermont

Northern Vermont

Sugarbush ⛳
∇ 21 | 19 | 20 | 16 | $60

1804 Sugarbush Access Rd., Warren; 802-583-6725; 800-537-8427; www.sugarbush.com; 6464/5231; 71.7/70.5; 128/129

"Hmm, where the hell do you go now?" – "you might want to take a Sherpa with you as a guide to the location of some of the greens" on this "short but oh-so-tough" Robert Trent Jones Sr. layout that "optimizes" the "beauty" of the Mad River Valley; it's "not gimmicky" – it's just "very challenging", particularly to swingers with a "poor sense of direction"; "conditions can be rough after big rains", but if it's dry, it's a "pretty good value."

Southern Vermont

Gleneagles at The Equinox
22 | 19 | 22 | 17 | $99

108 Union St., Manchester; 802-362-3223; 800-362-4747; www.equinoxresort.com; 6423/5082; 70.8/69; 129/121

In southern Vermont is the "tranquil" but "magnificent" site of this "old-school course" that turns into "the most beautiful place on earth" come autumn; across the street from a historic hotel, the "rolling" layout is "short but tricky with challenging greens" and "breathtaking" views of Mount Equinox; "it's ridiculous there is no driving range", but the "outlet shopping", "great restaurant" and spa help "make it an enjoyable weekend with plenty" to do.

Green Mountain National
25 | 18 | 22 | 24 | $89

Barrows Towne Rd., Killington; 802-422-4653; 888-483-4653; www.greenmountainnational.com; 6589/4740; 72.1/63.9; 138/118

"Don't forget to hit your ball along the way" as you take "one of the greatest walks in the woods" on this "mountain" muni; "this course will make you work" with "blind shots over and around hills that increase difficulty"; still, given its "overwhelming beauty" especially "in October" when it's already starting to get nippy, really the "only problem is the season is way too short."

Okemo Valley
24 | 20 | 21 | 20 | $72

89 Fox Ln., Ludlow; 802-228-1396; www.okemo.com; 6400/5105; 71.1/70.1; 130/125

"You need to be a mountain goat to walk this" "little bit of Scotland" in Vermont, the state's only links-style layout; of course the "views are spectacular", but with a season that lasts only "five months per year" and an extensive indoor/outdoor practice facility, the course is "very popular" for vacationers and locals alike, so "play is slow on summer weekends" – perhaps the owners' acquisition of nearby Tater Hill Golf Club will help ease the congestion here.

Stratton Mountain
23 | 20 | 22 | 21 | $99

Stratton Mountain Rd., Stratton Mountain; 802-297-2200; 800-787-2886; www.stratton.com
Forest/Lake: 6526/5153; 71.2/69.8; 125/123
Lake/Mountain: 6602/5410; 72/71.1; 125/124
Mountain/Forest: 6478/5163; 71.2/69.9; 126/123

"What's not gorgeous about a course in the Green Mountains?" – "it even smells nice" on these "three different nines" "winding through the hilly forest on the approach to the Stratton ski area"; "each is challenging in its own way", but all offer "typically rugged" high-ridge play that "makes you work for par", and now that the layout is in "great shape", this "nice complement" to the teaching facility here "offers everything to the consumer" "looking for a golf-only vacation."

Woodstock Country Club
20 | 19 | 22 | 18 | $85

14 The Green, Woodstock; 802-457-6674; www.woodstockinn.com; 6052/4924; 69.7/69; 123/113

This "picturesque" "treasure" in a "flat-out beautiful", "pure New England village" with "a great hotel" is "short but difficult if you're not accurate"; "keep your woods in your bag here and bring your iron game", as well as "a ball retriever", since "a river truly runs through it" on 11 holes; while conceding that the course is "well-cared for", driver-happy drama queens dis "this flat rectangle is better suited for its winter use: cross-country skiing."

Virginia

★ **Top Courses in State**

27 Stonewall Golf Club, *Leesburg*
Golden Horseshoe, Gold, *Williamsburg*
Homestead, Cascades, *Roanoke*
Augustine, *DC Metro Area*
26 Royal New Kent, *Williamsburg*

Charlottesville

Birdwood
22 | 19 | 21 | 24 | $60

410 Golf Course Dr.; 434-293-4653; 800-476-1988; www.boarsheadinn.com; 6865/5041; 73.2/72.4; 132/122

It's "nestled in God's country", but the "18th hole is diabolical" on this "refreshing and interesting" university course; "I'd go to UVA just to play here" say rival collegians jealous of the "tremendous student value" available on the "awesome", "hilly" layout with "just-redone bunkers and greens complexes"; "try walking it for a truly life-changing experience", and stay at the "lovely" Boar's Head Inn where "old-world charm abounds."

Keswick Club ⚲
22 | 26 | 24 | 19 | $130

701 Club Dr., Keswick; 434-923-4363; www.keswick.com; 6525/4848; 71.8/68.5; 130/113

"Right in the heart of the area Thomas Jefferson called the 'Eden of America'" – the "rolling, hilly farmland of Virginia" – is this swath of "greenery in a gorgeous setting" at the "luxury" Keswick Club resort; the nation's third president probably "would have loved" the "tough-to-putt-on" sloping greens at this "delightful course", which is being "stretched" from the tips "during renovations" until early fall 2005 – check with the pro shop for new stats when the back nine is unveiled and re-rated.

Wintergreen, Devil's Knob
21 | 20 | 21 | 20 | $105

Rte. 151, Wintergreen; 434-325-8250; www.wintergreenresort.com; 6382/4392; 72.2/66.7; 138/128

"Let's see . . . 75-degree temperatures, 100-mile views of the Shenandoah and Rockfish valleys, really fast greens and a two-club advantage because of the altitude . . . yes, this course is a winner" assert aces adding up the assets of "VA's highest track"; it's "so tight, you need a ferret to get through it", but you'll be on "top of the world" literally and figuratively on this "mountain" "delight" that's "visually stunning" and "physically challenging."

Wintergreen, Stoney Creek   22 | 21 | 21 | 21 | $105
Rte. 151, Wintergreen; 434-325-8250; www.wintergreenresort.com
Monokan/Shamokin: 7005/5500; 74.2/71.8; 137/127
Shamokin/Tuckahoe: 6998/5594; 74.1/72.4; 135/128
Tuckahoe/Monokan: 6951/5462; 73.8/71.6; 136/129
"Breathtaking views" and a "really great layout" "offering varied challenges" "reward both the casual and serious golfer" on this "beautiful mountain course" at a "nice vacation spot" "in the foothills of the Blue Ridge"; "play the Monokan/Shamokin combo if you can", however, because the "incredible opening hole" on the Tuckahoe nine is "followed by mediocrity" and "sauna"-like humidity "in hot weather."

DC Metro Area

Augustine   27 | 21 | 21 | 21 | $79
76 Monument Dr., Stafford; 540-659-0566; www.augustinegolf.com;
6817/4838; 74.3/68; 142/117
"If you can hack the drive from DC, then you won't mind hacking out of the trees" on this "lush", "inspired" "mini-Augusta" en route to Richmond; "the first tee, with a choice of two fairways on either side" of "narrow" wetlands, "sets the tone for a scenic round", which winds through a subdivision, "yet you [almost] never see a house"; it's "worth the hefty price tag" if you "bring your A game" – otherwise, "stay home", but then you'd miss the "excellent food at the turn."

Gauntlet 🏌   20 | 18 | 19 | 19 | $45
18 Fairway Dr., Fredericksburg; 540-752-0963; 888-755-7888;
www.golfgauntlet.com; 6857/4955; 72.8/69.8; 137/126
Swinging soldiers "jump at the chance" to run this "narrow" gauntlet, a "devilishly difficult" P.B. Dye design "set in a forest preserve with lots of water" and "tough forced carries"; it holds loads of "surprises", so "spend the bucks to buy a course layout book" and take advantage of the "good practice facilities" beforehand, even if foozling foes say 'phooey' to a "tricked-up" "miniature golf"–like layout where the "sharply crowned greens are a bit of an overkill toward the end of the round."

Lansdowne Resort 🏌   21 | 23 | 20 | 15 | $115
44050 Woodridge Pkwy., Lansdowne; 703-729-4071;
800-541-4801; www.lansdowneresort.com;
7063/5165; 74.6/70.6; 139/124
"A straight-forward format" with "few blind shots" accompanied by "excellent practice facilities" makes for a "resort course" that's "good for corporate outings"; unfortunately, "conventioneers all over the place" "lead to a lot of long rounds" on "strange-type fairway grass" that always "turns yellow" "in the late fall"; hopefully after the summer 2005 completion of the new clubhouse and the autumn opening of the Greg Norman track here, the staff will have time to give the course "a little more TLC."

Meadows Farms
19 | 13 | 17 | 22 | $44

4300 Flat Run Rd., Locust Grove; 540-854-9890; www.meadowsfarms.com
Island Green/Longest Hole: 7014/4541; 73.3/65.3; 129/109
Island Green/Waterfall: 6067/4075; 68.4/62.8; 119/110
Longest Hole/Waterfall: 6871/4424; 72.7/65.1; 129/105

The record-breaking 841-yd. "par-6 will tax your ability to hit long and straight" at this "gimmicky" three-nine layout "with a few nice holes" not far from the Beltway; "die-hard golfers might not appreciate some of the designs" or the fact that "the track doesn't get exceptional care", but "the price is right for the only giant miniature golf course around" – no wonder it sees "very large crowds" of slaphappy hackers in "summer."

Westfields
25 | 22 | 23 | 19 | $99

13940 Balmoral Greens Ave., Clifton; 703-631-3300;
www.westfieldsgolf.com; 6897/4597; 73.1/65.9; 136/114

"Eighteen great holes from Freddy Couples" and "plenty of woods to lose balls in" "can be a lot of fun" on this "lush" layout; it's "still growing in" but is "nice" already, with "a reachable par-4 and a couple of short par-5s" augmented by the "interesting" "star power of the Boom-Boom tees" for the "brave"; "service is excellent, as are facilities and maintenance" at a course in a "decent location" near Dulles that's "not loaded with homes interfering with views."

Front Royal

Shenandoah Valley Golf Club
19 | 17 | 19 | 24 | $50

134 Golf Club Circle; 540-636-2641; www.svgcgolf.com
Blue/Red: 6399/4987; 71.1/67.8; 126/116
Red/White: 6121/4759; 69.6/66.3; 122/114
White/Blue: 6330/4838; 70.7/66.9; 122/113

"Worth the drive from DC just for the best hot dogs around", not to mention a "great deal" on a round, this 27-holer is "on the short side", but it offers "spectacular views" of the namesake valley and the Blue Ridge, and it sits high enough up that it "drains well when everything else in the area is wet"; a new set of tees for seniors has veterans vying for times, even if serious swingers label it a "goat track."

Leesburg

Bull Run
22 | 18 | 18 | 20 | $90

3520 James Madison Hwy., Haymarket; 703-753-7777; 866-285-5786;
www.bullrungolfclub.com; 7009/5069; 73.1/68.3; 134/110

"Go for No. 18 in two" to cap off this "nice blend of creative, fun and challenging" holes, urge bullish ball whackers, but watch "for the high brush right in front of the tees throughout"; this "wide-open" layout "without too many gimmicks" is "great for various abilities", but it's "starting to show a fair amount of wear" because the otherwise "really nice" staff "stacks the golfers up like planes on approach to nearby Dulles Airport."

Raspberry Falls
24 | 22 | 23 | 18 | $96

41601 Raspberry Dr.; 703-779-2555; www.raspberryfalls.com;
7191/4854; 74.3/68; 134/115

"If you're a masochist" (and there must be plenty of you in the state since this is Virginia's Most Popular), play "in peak season when the rough and tall grass are at their finest" and you'll need "an adding machine" for your score on this "great Gary Player course" in the rolling hills of horse country; "beautiful vistas from elevated tee boxes" have "diminished" due to "all the construction", but the layout still features an "excellent mix of holes" with "huge sand traps" and "some of the best greens in the area."

STONEWALL 🏕 | 27 | 25 | 24 | 20 | $110 |

15601 Turtle Point Dr., Gainesville; 703-753-5101;
www.stonewallgolfclub.com; 7002/4889; 74.1/67.9; 142/114
"Right around the corner from" – and "some say prettier than" – the private Robert Trent Jones Club, Virginia's Top Course is "pricey but gorgeous" with a layout kept in "top condition" along Lake Manassas; "the only flaw is the number and size of the homes surrounding holes" that are otherwise "wonderfully scenic" and "a lot of fun" to play, even if you spend the round "dreaming about" teeing off on its exclusive neighbor a stone's throw away.

Virginia National | 18 | 15 | 18 | 22 | $75 |

1400 Parker Ln., Bluemont; 540-955-2966; 888-283-4653;
www.virginianational.com; 6789/4981; 73.3/68.3; 137/116
"You can see God from the 14th tee" at this "best-kept secret" with a "to-die-for mountain" back nine in the foothills of the Blue Ridge Mountains; the "memorable track" and its "magnificent views" are "well worth the trip" to "the middle of nowhere", and it "will only improve with age"; just remember – on the "flat" front, "everything breaks toward the river."

Roanoke

Homestead, Cascades 🏌 | 27 | 24 | 24 | 20 | $240 |

Homestead Hotel, Rte. 220, Hot Springs; 540-839-7994; 800-838-1766;
www.thehomestead.com; 6679/4967; 73/70.3; 137/124
"What a treat!" – this 1923 "classic" with a "well-deserved rep as one of the world's top" peakside tracks is the place to "learn mountain golf"; it will "test every part of your game" with "rolling hills and sidehill lies" as it "winds" by "beautiful vistas" on grounds that, if "not manicured", are "naturally stunning"; "the clubhouse is a Sam Snead museum", and you might want to spend some time indoors checking out the old pro's memorabilia, as the "abundant ladybugs" outside are more "problem" than luck.

Homestead, Lower Cascades 🏌 | 22 | 23 | 23 | 18 | $130 |

Homestead Hotel, Rte. 220, Hot Springs; 540-839-7995; 800-838-1766;
www.thehomestead.com; 6752/4710; 72.6/66.2; 134/110
At the 239-year-old Homestead resort high up in the Alleghenys, Robert Trent Jones Sr. created a "very tight but lovely" track that's a "beautiful place to spend the day"; it's "a little chewed up" and "not as special as its older brother, Cascades", but it "does offer a great value for an outstanding layout" in a mountain setting that "feels like you're in Europe somewhere."

Homestead, Old 🏌 | 21 | 25 | 23 | 19 | $130 |

Homestead Hotel, Rte. 220, Hot Springs; 540-839-7739; 800-838-1766;
www.thehomestead.com; 6227/4877; 69/67.7; 129/116
With "the longest continuous use of a first tee in the USA", "history enhances an otherwise ordinary course", making this 1923 Donald

Ross design "a joy to play"; touched up by Rees Jones to provide both "tradition and challenge", it sports "six par-3s, six par-4s and six par-5s" with "many unexpected views of the Homestead's tower"; "long hitters can go low" on this "not-too-difficult but well-maintained" diversion to "the skeet range."

Virginia Beach

Bay Creek, Palmer 🖾   – | – | – | – | $85
1 Clubhouse Way, Cape Charles; 757-331-9000; www.baycreek.net; 7204/6922; 76/69.2; 141/123
Native hardwoods, loblolly pines and dogwoods frame many of the fairways and greens at this 2001 Arnold Palmer design, but as its name suggests, water is the dominant theme here, with four holes on the shores of the Chesapeake Bay and eight on Old Plantation Creek; from the noteworthy opening uphill par-5 through wetlands, beach bunkers and natural sand dunes, it's easy to understand why golfers take the long drive across the Bay Bridge Tunnel.

Williamsburg

Golden Horseshoe, Gold   27 | 24 | 25 | 20 | $155
401 S. England St.; 757-220-7696; 800-648-6653; www.goldenhorseshoegolf.com; 6817/5168; 73.6/66.2; 138/120
A "drop-dead gorgeous" "break from today's cookie-cutter" courses, this "masterpiece" by Robert Trent Jones Sr. is a "classic in every sense of the word", from its "picture-perfect" conditioning in a "botanical garden"–like setting to the "best set of par-3s on this side of the Atlantic", including "tremendous" No. 16 sporting the original "island green"; the "facilities are grand", and the "very courteous staff" "makes it a point to remember you and cater to your every wish", garnering the Top Service rating in Virginia.

Golden Horseshoe, Green   24 | 23 | 24 | 20 | $99
401 S. England St.; 757-220-7696; 800-648-6653; www.goldenhorseshoegolf.com; 7120/5348; 73.6/66.2; 138/120
"Not as majestic as the Gold", this "charmer" is nevertheless a "wonderful alternative to walking Colonial Williamsburg all day" say tracksters tired of tricornered hats; the Rees Jones design "winds its way through the woods beautifully" for a "challenging yet playable" round that "requires players to think", especially on the "great finishing hole", a par-5 off elevated tees with a forced carry over a pond to a green dressed in oval and pot bunkers.

Kingsmill, Plantation 🖾   ▽ 24 | 26 | 25 | 19 | $135
1010 Kingsmill Rd.; 757-253-3906; 800-832-5665; www.kingsmill.com; 6543/4880; 71.6/69; 124/119
Compared to its tourney-hosting sibling, this short layout with generous fairways might be "for beginners only", but the novices have it "very nice" in a "lovely", rolling setting "on the river" that's dotted with historical landmarks; so, even if you're greener than the greens here – "wow" – it's "worth it" to pony up for a round, after finding your bearings at the top-notch practice facilities and before a beer in one of the bars at this resort that Budweiser built.

Kingsmill, River 🏌
26 | 27 | 24 | 19 | $175

1010 Kingsmill Rd.; 757-253-3906; 800-832-5665; www.kingsmill.com;
6853/4646; 67.1/65.3; 137/113

"One of the best in the state" reopened in spring 2005 following a
multimillion-dollar renovation by original architect Pete Dye; the
home to the LPGA Tour's Michelob ULTRA Open is "perhaps no
longer as exotic a design as it was" when it was built in 1975, but its
newly recontoured greens, expanded tees, reshaped fairways and
rebuilt bunker complexes make for an "enjoyable and challenging"
round, particularly when you get to the "incredible finishing holes";
not only that but its "beautiful facilities" rank as Virginia's Top.

Kingsmill, Woods 🏌
25 | 24 | 24 | 19 | $125

1010 Kingsmill Rd.; 757-253-3906; 800-832-5665; www.kingsmill.com;
6784/5140; 72.7/68.7; 131/120

This "sleeper" of a beauty in the "woods without any homes in
sight" might not match the River for "popularity", but it provides a
"solid" "challenge" nonetheless on its "hilly" terrain; the "fairways
are well maintained and the greens are in very good condition",
including the one that's split by a bunker down its middle; follow up
the round with a beechwood-smoked steak at the resort's Eagles
chophouse or a special golfer's massage at the spa.

Kiskiack 🏌
20 | 19 | 19 | 21 | $79

8104 Club Dr.; 757-566-2200; www.traditionalclubs.com;
6775/4902; 72.5/67.8; 134/112

"Often overlooked and underappreciated", this "real surprise"
is one of the "best of the Williamsburg courses for playability"
on an "easy, mostly flat" layout, but it's also "tough from the
tips if you're looking for a challenge"; "water tests accuracy off
the tee", particularly on signature No. 11 with its peninsula green,
which is as "super-fast" as the other dance floors on a track laid
out on a natural bluff where "there are no houses."

Royal New Kent
26 | 23 | 23 | 23 | $99

10100 Kentland Trail, Providence Forge; 804-966-7023; 800-253-4363;
www.traditionalclubs.com; 6965/4971; 74.9/72; 144/130

"Hard doesn't even come close to describing this links-style
course" – "downright mean" is more like it, and "if the wind blows,
rename it Royal Pain"; late, great "evil genius" Mike Stranz
designed this "outrageously scenic" "gem", one of the "most
unique golf courses in the world", full of "very penal bunkers" and
"other hazards" that are "way too hard for the average golfer";
"the staff is great" and the "clubhouse is nice", but the "first time
you play it, expect a big number."

Tradition at Stonehouse 🏌
22 | 21 | 21 | 19 | $99

9700 Mill Pond Run, Toano; 757-566-1138; 888-825-3436;
www.traditionalclubs.com; 6963/5013; 75/69.1; 140/121

"Prepare to be humbled" at this "sister course to Royal New Kent",
"a truly great mountain" track for "strategic" play on "uneven lies"
in and out of ravines "without many bailout options" or "places to
miss greens"; the "distance between holes is sometimes mind-
blowing", and there are "way too many" "blind tee shots" for
traditionalists who call it "weird and contrived", but it's kept "in
very nice shape with some great views in the woodlands during
the early fall."

Washington

Bremerton

Gold Mountain, Cascade

▽ 22 | 18 | 19 | 27 | $32

7263 W. Belfair Valley Rd.; 360-415-5432; www.goldmt.com;
6707/5306; 72.1/70.3; 120/117

The "easier of the two courses" at Gold Mountain Golf Complex just a short drive north of Bremerton National Airport is a "gentle, older track with great turf" that's "fun and challenging for the average golfer" but rather "undemanding" for better sticks; "incredible value in a beautifully forested setting" earns putters' praise for everything but the "poor clubhouse", but you'll score almost the same bang for the buck here as at "its more publicized sister", Olympic, which means that this "city-owned course is a true bargain."

Gold Mountain, Olympic

27 | 18 | 19 | 27 | $50

7263 W. Belfair Valley Rd.; 360-415-5432; www.goldmt.com;
7140/5220; 74.1/70.2; 135/122

"Bremerton golfers are spoiled" by this "all-around great" muni where the "greens read true, the sand traps have just enough fluff and the staff is top-notch"; the site of the 2006 U.S. Public Links Championship features "amazing vistas to see while you contemplate your severe uphill and downhill lies" on a layout with "no two holes alike"; an "excellent option for reasonably priced golf", it's Washington's Top Value, so "get there early on the weekends" because the "staff can be overwhelmed by check-ins."

McCormick Woods

25 | 20 | 21 | 23 | $45

5155 McCormick Woods Dr., SW, Port Orchard; 360-895-0130;
800-323-0130; www.mccormickwoodsgolf.com;
7040/5299; 74.3/71; 134/127

"If only I could live in Port Orchard" pine players plotzing over "lush Northwest golf at its best" on this "subtle but tough" woodsy "challenge" "in a beautiful setting" amid cedars, firs and lots of lakes at the foot of Mt. Rainier; in fact, they *can* live in Port Orchard, which is part of the problem for putters pouting over "too many houses along the fairways for the price"; the "great restaurant on-site" helps deflect a "staff attitude" that hasn't "improved" as much as the course conditions.

Port Ludlow

26 | 17 | 20 | 20 | $55

751 Highland Dr., Port Ludlow; 360-437-0272; 800-455-0272;
www.portludlowresort.com
Tide/Timber: 6787/5598; 72.7/72.9; 131/126
Timber/Trail: 6756/5112; 73.6/70.8; 138/124
Trail/Tide: 6683/5192; 73.1/71.3; 138/124

"The nine holes of Trail are challengers", "like Spyglass cut out of a forest" with views of Puget Sound and Mt. Baker, but the whole of this "hilly, wooded" "gem" is a "don't-miss"; "a great place to play" at a bayside resort "away from noise and distractions" just 28 miles from Downtown Seattle, it's a walk "through nature" featuring "awesome trees and wildlife" at an "excellent value during off-peak season"; now if only they would "improve the clubhouse", it "would be a real destination."

Trophy Lake
25 | 22 | 23 | 19 | $60

3900 SW Lake Flora Rd., Port Orchard; 360-874-8337;
www.trophylakegolf.com; 7206/5342; 74.5/65.4; 135/118

"Bald eagle sightings are commonplace" at this "off-the-beaten-path gem" on the eponymous lake, so guard that "monstrous after-round lunker burger" lest the raptors swoop down and grab it on "one of best public courses in Washington"; if you're angling for a "challenging and beautiful track", this "golfer's golf course" "should be played at least once", particularly if you like to fly fish when not swinging.

Seattle

Apple Tree
▽ 19 | 18 | 16 | 20 | $60

8804 Occidental Ave., Yakima; 509-966-5877; www.appletreeresort.com;
6892/5428; 73.5/71.5; 135/127

"In the heart of Washington wine country" is a "beauty" themed not after the grape, but the original forbidden fruit; take a whack at the apple-shaped island green on the par-3 17th, and try to avoid all the century-old orchard namesakes, which might be tough given "too many blind shots"; coin-counting critics crab that the course is "overpriced" for the quality of its facilities, while the *pommes* the "caustic personnel" are eating must be sour.

Druids Glen
22 | 17 | 18 | 21 | $48

29925 207th Ave., SE, Covington; 253-638-1200; www.druidsglengolf.com;
7146/5354; 75.2/70.7; 140/129

"Awesome views of Mt. Rainier" and the "best par-3s in the area" – including the 12th, which "is like a Northwest version of the 7th at Pebble Beach" – make for a mystical round at this "terrific course" "worth the drive" from Seattle to just east of the Wenatchee National Forest; the "long" layout makes for "tough walking", but you can rest your sore dogs in the "excellent restaurant and bar" at the "new clubhouse that beats the old trailer" and probably outdates the Facilities score.

Golf Club at Newcastle, China Creek
22 | 28 | 26 | 14 | $100

15500 Six Penny Ln., Newcastle; 425-793-4653; www.newcastlegolf.com;
6416/4566; 71.4/66.1; 126/112

It "kicks your butt" and "plays with your mind" – in other words, this "steep" "challenge" is a "great overall experience", with "bunkers, banks and sand pits designed for the mighty", "an up-and-down layout with many hills" and "the best views of Seattle"; Washington's No. 1 Facilities include a "heated driving range that's great in winter" and a clubhouse that's "exceptional in the true old-world British sense" with a "first-rate restaurant and pro shop"; "but, oh, the cost!" lament local lofters accustomed to spending less.

Golf Club at Newcastle, Coal Creek
25 | 27 | 27 | 14 | $150

15500 Six Penny Ln., Newcastle; 425-793-4653; www.newcastlegolf.com;
7024/5153; 74.7/71; 142/123

Here's a "way to tear your hair out while having a good time": "watch your scores climb as high as this course" by Fred Couples; a "great view of the skyline" doesn't help on "narrow fairways" and "fast greens", so concentrate on "being accurate or pay a

dear price" – like the opportunity to "break an ankle looking for lost balls in the sidehill rough"; ease the pain by allowing the state's No. 1 staff to "treat you like a king" "over cocktails post-game" in the "tremendous" clubhouse.

Harbour Pointe
19 | 18 | 18 | 19 | $55

11817 Harbour Pointe Blvd., Mukilteo; 425-355-6060; 800-233-3128; www.harbourpointegolf.com; 6861/4836; 73/68.8; 137/118

Given "wildly varying conditions" and "a front and back as different from each other as Jekyll and Hyde", this "Northwest-style" track is a bit of an "enigma"; it seems "nice", but "it's tougher than you think", with water all over the first nine and tight, tall trees after the turn; "bring a few extra balls", don't play with "beginners [who] won't have a fun time" and avoid it during the "wet winter months."

Washington National
23 | 18 | 19 | 16 | $94

14330 SE Husky Way, Auburn; 253-333-5000; www.washingtonnationalgolfclub.com; 7304/5117; 75.5/70.3; 143/120

"Far from Seattle but close to excellence", the home course of the UW golf squads is an "amazing" "test for long-hitting" Huskies, who also warn "unless you have a bunker fetish, stay away", since there's "more sand here than on most beaches in the state"; the opposing team calls it an "over-hyped" "head-scratcher" with "not much in the clubhouse" but a lot of "purple and gold"; to deal with the weather, "wear a jacket", preferrably in you-know-what colors.

Tacoma

Classic Golf Club
∇ 19 | 13 | 18 | 23 | $40

4908 208th St. E., Spanaway; 253-847-4440; www.classicgolfclub.net; 6917/5656; 73.2/67; 134/122

This "better-than-average track" south of Seattle is "shorter" than most but "with deadly greens in summer" when "you can three-putt from four feet" away; amateur star and current PGA Tour pro Ryan Moore honed skills on this "fun layout", but it's now "in decline" dis duffers who warn "you get what you pay for in terms of course conditions" – that said, it's a "great price, especially for seniors."

Vancouver Area

Resort Semiahmoo, Loomis Trail ⊕
∇ 25 | 22 | 22 | 18 | $69

8720 Semiahmoo Pkwy., Blaine; 360-332-1725; www.semiahmoo.com; 7137/5399; 75.1/71.9; 145/125

"With water on every hole" and "not much" else "around the course except trees and wildlife", this "terrific" links is "worth a day trip from Seattle or a weekend with a stay at the resort"; "the better option of the two" courses at Semiahmoo's seaside hotel and spa, this "well-designed" canal- and lake-laced layout is "fun to play", and its "peaceful" location leaves lofters saying "wow."

Resort Semiahmoo, Semiahmoo Course ⊕
23 | 23 | 21 | 19 | $69

8720 Semiahmoo Pkwy., Blaine; 360-371-7005; www.semiahmoo.com; 7005/5288; 73.9/70.6; 137/124

"I wish I could go back now!" sigh swingers who've swooned over the "lush forests and great water views" on this "beautiful

Northwest" namesake; "even if it's pouring, it's worth the drive" for an "excellent" round on well-kept grounds with "deer usually somewhere in sight", but it's a "Palmer course and plays like one", so you've got to be a loyal subject of the King, or you might find it "good but not great."

Wenatchee

Desert Canyon 🏤   25 | 21 | 21 | 20 | $99
1201 Desert Canyon Blvd., Orondo; 509-784-1111; 800-258-4173; www.desertcanyon.com; 7285/5200; 75.3/70.2; 138/123
If you can imagine "desert golf in the state of Washington", you've conjured this "beautiful course high above the Columbia River with some gorgeous views" of the "surrounding mountains"; it's a "truly awesome golf experience", but the test is "long and hilly", so "bring your A game", and "combine the trip" with visits to "the local wineries springing up in the area, and your weekend will be memorable", though as "steep" in price as its altitude.

West Virginia

Elkins

Raven at Snowshoe Mountain   ▽ 24 | 21 | 23 | 22 | $69
10 Snowshoe Dr., Snowshoe; 304-572-1000; www.snowshoemtn.com; 7045/4363; 75.5/65.3; 142/120
Thanks to rolling terrain and elevation drops of up to 200 feet, this "very picturesque" Gary Player design in a "mountain setting" is "more difficult than your typical resort course"; it's also "hard to get to but worth the effort" to reach the Pocohontas County resort where the "prime time to play is October when fall foliage is awesome" and the deer, foxes and even bears are out foraging.

Weston

Stonewall Resort   ▽ 25 | 17 | 18 | 21 | $85
940 Resort Dr., Roanoke; 304-269-8885; www.stonewallresort.com; 7149/4921; 75.4/69.6; 143/127
It's "another Arnold Palmer masterpiece" according to all the King's men who select from six tees on each hole at this three-year-old woodlander two hours south of Pittsburgh on Stonewall Jackson Lake; though there's already plenty of challenge to forced carries over water and wetlands and sloping greens, less-loyal subjects say the test here "will be very good – once the property has had time to become more established."

White Sulphur Springs

Greenbrier, Greenbrier Course 🏌   26 | 28 | 28 | 21 |$350
300 W. Main St.; 304-536-1110; 800-624-6070; www.greenbrier.com; 6675/5095; 73.1/69; 135/120
Host to the 1979 Ryder Cup and 1994 Solheim Cup, this "awesome" nonagenarian steeped in international golf history in the hills of West Virginia "has aged well"; it leaves "no room for error" on "undulating fairways" that require "strategic shot placement" and "greens as well-manicured as the croquet court"; like "everything

at Greenbrier", "one of America's top resorts", it's "first-class in every respect", "but boy, do you pay."

Greenbrier, Meadows 🏌 | 25 | 29 | 29 | 21 | $350 |
300 W. Main St.; 304-536-1110; 800-624-6070; www.greenbrier.com; 6676/4979; 72.8/68.2; 129/114
"Now that this remake of the old Lakeside course has matured, it offers top-flight resort golf"; Bob Cupp enhanced this "very scenic" spread with Allegheny Mountain views and "many holes winding around Howards Creek" where you "can swing a golf club in the afternoon and catch a trout in the morning"; it's "supposed to be the least difficult of the three" at Greenbrier, but the water in play on a third of the layout is "not so easy."

Greenbrier, Old White 🏌 | 26 | 28 | 28 | 21 | $300 |
300 W. Main St.; 304-536-1110; 800-624-6070; www.greenbrier.com; 6735/5036; 71.8/68.3; 131/119
"It feels like you're playing in the 1920s" on this "time machine", albeit an "improved" one via "upgrades" that will continue through 2006 and likely result in changes to its stats; even given ongoing work, this links-style course's "condition is superb", as is the "Greenbrier hospitality", and there's "nothing like hitting off the elevated first tee at a time-tested beauty" originally taken to task by the likes of President Woodrow Wilson; just understand, there's "a lot of reputation here", and that's "what you are paying for."

Wisconsin

★ **Top Courses in State**
30 Whistling Straits, Straits, *Kohler*
29 Blackwolf Run, River, *Kohler*
27 Whistling Straits, Irish, *Kohler*
26 Blackwolf Run, Meadow Valleys, *Kohler*
   University Ridge, *Madison*

Kohler

Blackwolf Run, Meadow Valleys 🏌 | 26 | 28 | 27 | 21 | $141 |
1111 W. Riverside Dr.; 920-457-4446; 800-618-5535; www.blackwolfrun.com; 7142/5065; 74.6/70.2; 144/117
"Stay at the American Club and play all four courses" in "top-notch" Kohler, including this "tremendous" track "overshadowed by its well-known neighbors"; "while not as scenic" as its sister, River, it "doesn't get the credit it deserves" for designer Pete Dye's "interesting harmony of society and nature" on a "wonderfully varied layout without pretentiousness" but with plenty of pot bunkers, undulations and railroad ties rimming water; "challenging" yet "not overwhelming", it's "great for those intimidated by the other venues."

BLACKWOLF RUN, RIVER 🏌 ⏱ | 29 | 28 | 28 | 22 | $206 |
1111 W. Riverside Dr.; 920-457-4446; 800-618-5535; www.blackwolfrun.com; 6991/5115; 74.4/70.1; 148/124
"Risk/reward and drama define this" "fantastic" contradiction, a "beautiful stroll" along the "serene" Sheboygan as well as a "humbling test" that "never lets you catch your breath"; "leave the machismo at home and play off the tees for your handicap or you'll

be miserable" on 18 "stout challenges", including the water-girdled, "unbelievable" 9th; "bring extra balls" because the "river has an appetite" (and speaking of food, "don't miss the great brats at the halfway house"); good thing you're "pampered like a king" here, since "you need an icing down after the bruising you take."

Bull at Pinehurst Farms, The ▽ 22 | 23 | 20 | 16 |$145

1 Long Dr., Sheboygan; 920-467-1500; 800-584-3285;
www.golfthebull.com; 7332/5087; 76.4/70.9; 146/127

There's "not a bad hole to be found" on the Golden Bear's "great addition to golf in the Kohler region" an hour north of Milwaukee; a parkland/woodland mix on a former dairy farm where the dogleg bends on holes like No. 5, a 432-yd. cliffside par-4, it's "tough" and "more expensive than most" spreads elsewhere "but on par with others in the area"; less bullish ball hitters beef about "blind shot after blind shot" on a "penalizing" layout that's "not quite what one expects from a Nicklaus course."

Whistling Straits, Irish 🏌 27 | 28 | 28 | 20 |$141

N8501 County Rd. LS, Sheboygan; 920-565-6050; 800-618-5535;
www.whistlingstraits.com; 7201/5109; 75.6/65.6; 146/122

"Who needs to fly to Ireland" when you can play this "beautiful but lethal" layout in Kohler?; "maturing into a superb challenge that rivals the Straits, except for the views", this slice of "the British Isles in Wisconsin" ("watch out for sheep on the course") is "not for the timid", but wishful thinking makes all that sand "just a mental obstacle" anyway; "thank goodness the lodge has fantastic food" – "the potato-leek soup with a shot of sherry helped me forget that I lost so many balls" sighs one foodie foozler.

WHISTLING STRAITS, 30 | 29 | 29 | 22 |$297
STRAITS 🏌 ⏱

N8501 County Rd. LS, Sheboygan; 920-565-6050; 800-618-5535;
www.whistlingstraits.com; 7362/5396; 76.7/72.2; 151/132

Like an "amazing" fairy tale that "transports" you to "a faraway place where golf reigns supreme" and "everything is special" "from the moment you pull up to the stone castle and the caddie takes your bag", this *Survey*'s No. 1 Course, with Wisconsin's Top Facilities and Service, stars a "deadly" "wind" as villian – just "look at what it did to the world's best players at the [2004] PGA Championship" on this "incredible" "remaking of tabletop land that is a real tribute to architect Pete Dye's creativity"; you'll "spend your wad to be beaten up", but "the alternative is to fly to Scotland."

Lake Geneva

Geneva National, Gary Player 🏌⏱ 24 | 22 | 24 | 19 |$125

1221 Geneva National Ave. S.; 262-245-7000;
www.genevanationalresort.com; 7018/4823; 74.3/68.4; 141/120

Cheeseheads might be taken by surprise by the "great topography" of the back nine on the newest at Geneva National, as its many uphills and downhills are "unexpected for Wisconsin" – but they "like" it as a whole and "love the last par-5" with its bird's-eye Lake Como view; running through woods and parkland, it's a "nice layout in decent shape", but "too much traffic" has agoraphobic golfers grumping that it's "Gary Played-out."

Geneva National, Palmer 🏌⏱ 25 | 23 | 23 | 20 | $110

1221 Geneva National Ave. S.; 262-245-7000;
www.genevanationalresort.com; 7171/4904; 74.7/68.5; 140/122

"Well designed" on oak-, hickory- and walnut-dressed "rolling terrain" at a lakefront resort in the state's southeast, this "beautiful course" features sloping greens, wooded fairways, water vistas and an outstanding par-4 closing hole loaded with fairway bunkers; penny-pinching putters say the King's work is "too pricey for the common folk", but if you have some ducats left after your round, have a royal feast at the upscale Hunt Club.

Geneva National, Trevino 🏌⏱ 24 | 23 | 22 | 20 | $110

1221 Geneva National Ave. S.; 262-245-7000;
www.genevanationalresort.com; 7120/5193; 74.3/70.2; 136/124

This might be the "only Lee Trevino course you've played", but after playing it, you'll be looking for another"; "more trees" than its sisters make it "beautiful" but not any tighter – given generous fairways and a forgiving layout designed for all players (particularly practiced faders), it's the "least difficult of the three" at Geneva National, though a memorable collection of par-4s helps make it "still very fun."

Grand Geneva, Brute 🏌 24 | 23 | 20 | 17 | $139

7036 Grand Geneva Way; 262-248-2556; 800-558-3417;
www.grandgeneva.com; 7085/5244; 73.8/70; 136/129

Though its moniker might better refer to its "pushy starter", once you're on this "pristine" spread, you'll find it "very enjoyable"; "highly recommended" for its newly redone bunkering and "great variety" of holes including the watery par-4 17th, "the brutest of them all", it's a "grand golf experience" at an aptly named resort – "you will love (or hate) the challenges" here, but either way take advantage of the "outstanding health club and spa facilities."

Grand Geneva, Highlands 🏌 ▽ 21 | 21 | 18 | 15 | $125

7036 Grand Geneva Way; 262-248-2556; 800-558-3417;
www.grandgeneva.com; 6633/5038; 71.5/68.3; 125/115

Three top architects got their hands on this "solid" links: Pete Dye, Jack Nicklaus and, in a novice-friendly redesign, Bob Cupp – and some "resort golfers" call it "awesome"; you'd "better be prepared for a long day if you can't hit the ball straight", but otherwise, it's not so tough now that it's been "softened"; it "used to be fantastic" say scratch players scratching this "overpriced" track off their lists.

Madison

Lawsonia, Links 25 | 19 | 21 | 24 | $76

W2615 S. Valley View Dr., Green Lake; 920-294-3320; 800-529-4453;
www.lawsonia.com; 6764/5078; 72.8/65.2; 130/115

Welcome to "Whistling Straits without Lake Michigan and the mortgage requirement", this "grand links-style course" some 90 miles northwest of Milwaukee; "they don't build 'em anymore" like this, with "no trees, plenty of wind, lots of strategy and playing options" plus "some of the boldest green complexes you'll ever see", "just like at the British Open"; rumor has it they "beat Pete Dye to the freight yard by burying a boxcar as the foundation for the severely elevated 7th dance floor", while the par-5 13th hole is simply "unbelievable."

Lawsonia, Woodlands ▽ 24 | 20 | 19 | 22 | $99
W2615 N. Valley View Dr., Green Lake; 920-294-3320; 800-529-4453;
www.lawsonia.com; 6618/5106; 72.7/69.6; 132/125
"Carved through trees on most holes", this "great" "companion
to the Links course" is "extremely beautiful" and (despite "little
rough" and "quite generous fairways") "challenging to play",
especially on No. 3, the aptly named par-3 'Cliff Hole', where your
ball plummets 65 feet in 169 yards to the green; given these two
"totally different" courses, ball-launching boosters bellow "if
you're on a budget and can only play one resort in Wisconsin,
make it Lawsonia."

Sentryworld 衤 25 | 22 | 20 | 23 | $65
601 N. Michigan Ave., Stevens Point; 715-345-1600; 866-479-6753;
www.sentryworld.com; 6951/5108; 74.4/71; 142/126
Afloat on a sea of 90,000 blossoms, "the 'Flower Hole' itself makes
this course worth playing" say swinging sentries tiptoeing through
the annuals guarding the green on the famous and fragrant par-3
16th; Robert Trent Jones Jr. designed this "great course" that's
obviously "a must-play in spring" when it's "well worth the trip"
to a location west of Green Bay where the rest of the facilities are
so fine, "you'll want to return."

Trappers Turn 23 | 21 | 21 | 20 | $83
652 Trappers Turn Dr., Wisconsin Dells; 608-253-7000; 800-221-8876;
www.trappersturn.com
Arbor/Lake: 6738/5000; 73.3/69.7; 133/123
Canyon/Arbor: 6759/5017; 72.8/69.4; 133/122
Lake/Canyon: 6831/5000; 72.9/69.5; 133/122
The site of multiple Wisconsin PGA Championships, this "great"
27-hole track just north of Madison is "to be enjoyed by golfers of all
levels"; designed by U.S. Open champ Andy North and architect
Roger Packard on naturally varied terrain created by melting glacier
waters in the Wisconsin Dells, it features three different nines, one
lake-laced, one tree-lined and one undulating through a canyon;
it's a "nice course" lament locals, but "Chicago tourists drive the
price too high."

University Ridge 26 | 20 | 23 | 25 | $73
9002 County Rd. PD, Verona; 608-845-7700; 800-897-4343;
www.universityridge.com; 6888/5005; 73.2/68.9; 142/121
"Bucky knows how to lay out a challenge" cheer University of
Wisconsin fans who "never get tired of playing" this "outstanding"
and "beautifully maintained" collegiate where Robert Trent
Jones Jr. exercises your golf muscles while still providing "fun"
and fairness; "every hole is different", "every club in your bag
gets used" and you "need every part of the game to score", but
"trouble spots are in plain view" on a track that's "a tradition
during Badger football season – if you can get a tee time."

Milwaukee

Bog, The 24 | 24 | 22 | 20 | $135
3121 County Hwy. I, Saukville; 262-284-7075; 800-484-3264;
www.golfthebog.com; 7221/5110; 75.3/70.3; 143/124
Don't get bogged down on the few "really goofy", "gimmicky"
holes on this Arnold Palmer design – it's still the "best within 20

minutes of Milwaukee" for a layout spread over wetlands, woods and hills with greens that "always roll fast and true" and a "great practice facility"; however, at these "steep summer prices", the staff – "not the warmest in the world" – "could lighten up", since after all, golf is "a people business."

Bristlecone Pines ⛳　　　▽ 21 | 18 | 18 | 18 | $99

1500 E. Arlene Dr., Hartland; 262-367-7880; www.golfbristlecone.com; 7005/5033; 74.1/69.4; 138/120

If you're looking for a "way to see beautiful houses", this is it 20 minutes west of Milwaukee; the "golf is ok too" on the "well-maintained" "challenge" with water on 10 holes, but ball launchers bristle at some "blah" spots "bogged down by ever-increasing residences" and "construction noise"; N.B. public players can get in a "nice" round until the club goes private in the near future.

Brown Deer Park　　　24 | 15 | 15 | 23 | $79

7835 N. Green Bay Rd.; 414-352-8080; www.countygolf.com; 6759/5861; 72.9/73.8; 133/132

"One of the best munis in the country", this host of the PGA Tour U.S. Bank Championship "rivals Torrey Pines for a public, but it's much more playable for mortals"; a "classic" from 1929, it features tree-lined holes and an "excellent practice area", all for a fee that's a "great deal" – "if you're a Milwaukee resident" and "can get a tee time"; if you're lugging your clubs from outside the county, it's "way overpriced" for a "clubhouse facility that's not highly elaborate."

Fire Ridge　　　　　▽ 22 | 19 | 18 | 23 | $69

2241 Hwy. W., Grafton; 262-375-2252; www.fireridgegc.com; 7049/5463; 74.5/72.3; 136/126

Out in the northern boonies near Lake Michigan with a signature par-3 ringed in marshlands, this "nice layout and great value" "has the potential to rival The Bog" for the best of Milwaukee, but "ownership changes keep you guessing about its conditions" and routing; here's the skinny: it's "easier than in the past" now that they've "cut back the waste areas", making it "good" "for a tournament or outing" "if you can't play or afford" its competitor.

Naga-waukee　　　　▽ 19 | 10 | 12 | 25 | $37

1897 Maple Ave., Pewaukee; 262-367-2153; 6830/5817; 71.8/72.4; 125/125

"Good golf" can be had "for a pittance" at Wisconsin's Top Value, so of course it's "difficult to get on", particularly in fall when the "scenic views" of Pewaukee Lake and its surroundings are "beautiful"; "hills" "come into play often" on "rolling fairways", while "very large greens can cause a lot of three-putts" at this "challenging" muni "that competes with many private clubs" – and blows them away pricewise.

Wyoming

Jackson

Jackson Hole Golf & Tennis　▽ 23 | 17 | 20 | 18 | $155

5000 Spring Gulch Rd.; 307-733-3111; www.jhgtc.com; 7168/5492; 72.5/70.4; 123/123

"Your balls just soar" in the "clean" mountain air at this Big Sky Country layout that's "truly like a hike in the park"; "you just never know when" the "moose" or the "bison herd will be roaming the fairway", but you can always locate the mountains, given the "breathtaking views of the Grand Tetons as you tee off"; with ongoing renovations of the tees, bunkers, clubhouse and driving range to be completed in 2007, it's "beautifully maintained" – and "at these prices, it had better be."

Sheridan

Powder Horn    – | – | – | – | $71

23 Country Club Ln.; 307-672-5323; www.thepowderhorn.com
Eagle/Mountain: 7147/5292; 73.8/69.4; 136/128
Mountain/Stag: 6934/5161; 72.6/68.6; 132/124
Stag/Eagle: 7185/5321; 74.3/70; 139/129

Perched on the high plains backdropped by towering mountains is this 27-holer by Dick Bailed that opened in 1997 to rave reviews from the few who ventured to north-central Wyoming to experience the spacious front nine with holes framed by native grasses and a more wooded back tinged with wetlands; though the houses that have popped up detract a bit from the remarkable scenery, there's no denying that this is a more pleasant battlefield than the one 80 miles north known as Little Big Horn.

Private Courses

Access to play is limited to members and their guests.

Aronimink Golf Club
3600 Saint Davids Rd., Newtown Square, PA; 610-356-8000;
www.aronimink.org
Restored to its original Donald Ross design, this 1962 PGA
Championship host features rugged par-4s with elevated greens.

Atlanta Country Club
500 Atlanta Country Club Dr., Marietta, GA; 770-953-2100;
www.atlantacountryclub.org
The showstopper at the PGA Tour's 1967–1996 Atlanta home is
No. 13, with pines, wildflowers, a waterfall and covered bridge.

Atlantic Golf Club
1040 Scuttle Hole Rd., Bridgehampton, NY; 631-537-1818
Rees Jones' spiritual cousin to England's Royal Birkdale links is
buffeted by ocean breezes and framed in native grass mounds.

Augusta National Golf Club
2604 Washington Rd., Augusta, GA; 706-667-6000; www.masters.org
Home to the Masters Tournament, this hilly beauty at a men-only
club is rich in trees, flowers, creeks and ponds.

Baltimore Country Club, East
11500 Mays Chapel Rd., Timonium, MD; 410-561-3381;
www.bcc1898.com
A.W. Tillinghast crafted this host of the 1928 PGA Championship,
1932 U.S. Amateur, 1965 Walker Cup and 1988 U.S. Women's Open.

Baltusrol Golf Club, Lower
201 Shunpike Rd., Springfield, NJ; 973-376-1900;
www.baltusrol.org
An hour from Manhattan, this club has hosted seven U.S. Opens,
four on the Lower course, which closes with back-to-back par-5s.

Bel-Air Country Club
10768 Bellagio Rd., Los Angeles, CA; 310-472-9563
At this celeb-studded enclave, holes hopscotch barrancas, as at
the 10th, which golfers cross via the famed 'Swinging Bridge.'

Bellerive Country Club
12925 Ladue Rd., St. Louis, MO; 314-434-4400
The 1965 U.S. Open, 1992 PGA Championship and 2004 U.S. Senior
Open were played on RTJ Sr.'s elevated, fiercely trapped greens.

Black Diamond Ranch Golf & Country Club, Quarry
2600 W. Black Diamond Circle, Lecanto, FL; 352-746-3440;
www.blackdiamondranch.com
Holes that play up, down and around an old quarry make for a
striking back nine on this Tom Fazio design.

Camargo Club
8605 Shawnee Run Rd., Indian Hill, OH; 513-561-9292
Golden Age architect Seth Raynor crafted a wonderful variety of
ravine-skirting par-3s and par-4s on this 1926 course.

Canterbury Golf Club
22000 S. Woodland Rd., Beachwood, OH; 216-561-1000
Jack Nicklaus broke Bobby Jones' record for majors when he won the 1973 PGA Championship on this 1922 woodlander.

Castle Pines Golf Club
1000 Hummingbird Dr., Castle Rock, CO; 303-688-6000
At 7,559 yards, one of the PGA Tour's longest tracks is a 1982 Nicklaus design with sharp downhills framed in pines.

Cherry Hills Country Club
4125 S. University Blvd., Englewood, CO; 303-761-9900
President Eisenhower's home away from home in the Rockies has hosted numerous championships, including the 1960 U.S. Open.

Chicago Golf Club
25W253 Warrenville Rd., Wheaton, IL; 630-668-2000
American golf royalty, this 1892 classic was the first 18-holer in the country and hosted U.S. Opens in 1897, 1900 and 1911.

Colonial Country Club
3735 Country Club Circle, Ft. Worth, TX; 817-927-4200
Ben Hogan won the PGA Tour's Colonial National Invitational five times here, earning the track its nickname, "Hogan's Alley."

Congressional Country Club, Blue
8500 River Rd., Bethesda, MD; 301-469-2000
This host of the 1964 and 1997 U.S. Opens was redone by Robert Trent Jones Sr. and son Rees in 1960 and 1989, respectively.

Country Club, The, Clyde/Squirrel
191 Clyde St., Brookline, MA; 617-566-0240
A Boston Brahmin enclave for more than 100 years, this tree-lined layout has hosted three U.S. Opens and the 1999 Ryder Cup.

Country Club of Fairfield, The
936 Sasco Hill Rd., Fairfield, CT; 203-259-1601
Seth Raynor's 1914 breeze-fueled classic serves up a stout collection of par-4s and handsome views of Long Island Sound.

Creek Club
1 Horse Hollow Rd., Locust Valley, NY; 516-676-1405
Wooded and links holes, an island green and lovely views of Long Island Sound are on offer at this short but exciting 1923 layout.

Crooked Stick Golf Club
1964 Burning Tree Ln., Carmel, IN; 317-844-9938
This Dye design hosted John Daly's 1991 PGA Championship upset.

Crystal Downs Country Club
249 E. Crystal Downs Dr., Frankfort, MI; 231-352-9933
Atop a bluff between Lake Michigan and Crystal Lake, Alister MacKenzie's windswept gem is thick with native roughs.

Cypress Point Club
3150 17 Mile Dr., Pebble Beach, CA; 831-624-6444
Alister MacKenzie's seasider, five minutes from Pebble Beach Resort, hosted the PGA Tour's Bing Crosby National Pro-Am.

Desert Forest Golf Club
37207 N. Mule Train Rd., Carefree, AZ; 480-488-4589;
www.desertforestgolfclub.com
Fairways and back-to-front sloping greens hemmed in by cacti demand accuracy on this desert beauty with mountain views.

Double Eagle Club
6025 Cheshire Rd., Galena, OH; 740-548-4017
This Weiskopf/Morrish track boasts dual fairways and conditioning so superb that the tee boxes could double as greens.

East Lake Golf Club
2575 Alston Dr. SE, Atlanta, GA; 404-373-5722; www.eastlakegolfclub.com
Bobby Jones' boyhood playground is reborn with a Rees Jones redesign and a caddie program for local underserved youth.

Estancia Club
27998 N. 99th Pl., Scottsdale, AZ; 480-473-4400;
www.estanciaclub.com
Tom Fazio set tee boxes and greens on high desert outcroppings at this enclave that climbs Pinnacle Peak.

Eugene Country Club
255 Country Club Rd., Eugene, OR; 541-345-0181;
www.eugenecountryclub.com
In 1967, Robert Trent Jones Sr. reversed the tees and greens and enlarged the water hazards on this 1924 tree-laden track.

Firestone Country Club, South
452 E. Warner Rd., Akron, OH; 330-644-8441;
www.firestonecountryclub.com
RTJ Sr.'s redesign has hosted PGA Championships, the 2002 Senior PGA Championship and the World Series of Golf.

Fishers Island Club
Fishers Island, Fishers Island, NY; 631-788-7221
At a society retreat in Long Island Sound, this 1926 Seth Raynor links design is known for its Atlantic shore vistas.

Forest Highlands Golf Club, Canyon
657 Forest Highlands, Flagstaff, AZ; 928-525-5200; www.fhgc.com
Par-5s over 600 yards long are made more manageable by the 7,000-ft. altitude of this Weiskopf/Morrish design.

Friar's Head
3000 Sound Ave., Baiting Hollow, NY; 631-722-5200
Tree-lined dunes, open meadows and bluff-top views of CT and Long Island Sound spice the play on this Crenshaw/Coore design.

Garden City Golf Club
315 Stewart Ave., Garden City, NY; 516-747-2880
The 1902 U.S. Open host, Long Island's men-only institution plays like a British links, with tall fescues, bunkers and sea breezes.

Golf Club, The
4522 Kitzmiller Rd., New Albany, OH; 614-855-7326
Hidden at a men-only club, this early Pete Dye challenges with tall native roughs, clever bunkers and outstanding par-5s.

Grandfather Golf & Country Club, Grandfather
2120 Hwy. 105, Linville, NC; 828-898-4531;
www.grandfatherclub.org
In a high Blue Ridge valley next to the Linville River, this hilly design looks up through the pines at Grandfather Mountain.

Hazeltine National Golf Club
1900 Hazeltine Blvd., Chaska, MN; 952-448-4929; www.hngc.com
Designed by RTJ Sr. and reworked by son Rees, this farm/forest blend hosted the 1991 U.S. Open and 2002 PGA Championship.

Honors Course, The
9603 Lee Hwy., Ooltewah, TN; 423-238-4272
Tiger Woods' winning final-round 80 at the 1996 Men's NCAA Championship testifies to the difficulty of this Pete Dye design.

Interlachen Country Club
6200 Interlachen Blvd., Edina, MN; 952-929-1661;
www.interlachencc.org
Bobby Jones skipped his second shot across the pond at the 9th on this track to win the 1930 U.S. Open in his Grand Slam year.

Inverness Club
4601 Dorr St., Toledo, OH; 419-578-9000; www.invernessclub.com
Donald Ross' centenarian remains a superb test; just ask Bob Tway, who holed a sand shot to win the 1986 PGA Championship.

Jupiter Hills Club, Hills
11800 SE Hill Club Terrace, Tequesta, FL; 561-746-5228
Bob Hope and auto exec William Clay Ford were among the founders of this track with 70 feet of elevation changes.

Kinloch Golf Club
1100 Hockett Rd., Manakin-Sabot, VA; 804-784-8000;
www.kinlochgolfclub.com
Near Richmond, this millennial design from Lester George and Vinny Giles offers multiple avenues of play on nearly every hole.

Kittansett Club
11 Point Rd., Marion, MA; 508-748-0148; www.kittansett.org
Windy Buzzards Bay is home to the 1953 Walker Cup Match host, where No. 3 plays to an island green encircled by sand.

Laurel Valley Golf Club
175 Palmer Dr., Ligonier, PA; 724-238-9555
On an old pheasant-hunting preserve is this host of the 1965 PGA Championship, 1975 Ryder Cup Match and 1989 U.S. Senior Open.

Long Cove Club
399 Long Cove Dr., Hilton Head Island, SC; 843-686-1070;
www.longcoveclub.org
This 23-year-old is a stew of Pete Dye design with live oaks, palmettos, waste bunkers and an amazing variety of holes.

Los Angeles Country Club, North
10101 Wilshire Blvd., Los Angeles, CA; 310-276-6104
George Thomas' layout sits on pricey real estate at the meeting of Wilshire and Santa Monica Boulevards near Beverly Hills.

Maidstone Club
50 Old Beach Ln., East Hampton, NY; 631-324-0510
The 19th-century links design at this tony Hamptons club is washed in sea breezes that make it play longer than its yardage.

Medinah Country Club, No. 3
6N001 Medinah Rd., Medinah, IL; 630-773-1700; www.medinahcc.org
Site of the 1999 PGA Championship, this brute with par-3s playing over Lake Kadijah reopened in June 2003.

Merion Golf Club, East
450 Ardmore Ave., Ardmore, PA; 610-642-5600;
www.meriongolfclub.com
Bobby Jones clinched his Grand Slam in 1930 at the 'Babbling Brook' hole at this Mainline Philadelphia classic.

Milwaukee Country Club
8000 N. Range Line Rd., River Hills, WI; 414-362-5200
The host of the 1969 Walker Cup Match features a well-wooded back nine that tumbles down to the Milwaukee River.

Muirfield Village Golf Club
5750 Memorial Dr., Dublin, OH; 614-889-6700
Jack Nicklaus designed this track to host his own Memorial Tournament, won by Tiger Woods in 1999, 2000 and 2001.

Myopia Hunt Club
435 Bay Rd., South Hamilton, MA; 978-468-4433
The hilly host of four U.S. Opens 1898–1908 provides a solid, old-style test, thanks to bunkering and vexing putting surfaces.

Nantucket Golf Club
250 Milestone Rd., Siasconset, MA; 508-257-8520
Golfers maneuver in coastal gusts to avoid the numerous bunkers and tall rough on this British links–style Rees Jones design.

National Golf Links of America
Sebonac Inlet Rd., Southampton, NY; 631-283-0410
This nonagenarian on Great Peconic Bay is by Charles Blair Macdonald, who modeled creations after the British Isles' best.

NCR Country Club, South
4435 Dogwood Trail, Dayton, OH; 937-299-3571;
www.ncrcountryclub.com
Dick Wilson sculpted this boldly bunkered 1969 PGA Championship, 1986 U.S. Women's Open and 2005 U.S. Senior Open host.

Oak Hill Country Club, East
346 Kilbourn Rd., Rochester, NY; 585-586-1660;
www.oakhillcc.com
Host to three U.S. Opens and the 1995 Ryder Cup Match, Donald Ross' 1920s design calls for long, accurate shotmaking.

Oakland Hills Country Club, South
3951 W. Maple Rd., Bloomfield Hills, MI; 248-644-2500;
www.oaklandhillscc.com
Ben Hogan called this track a 'monster', but he tamed its undulating greens and many bunkers to win the 1951 U.S. Open.

Oakmont Country Club
1233 Hulton Rd., Oakmont, PA; 412-828-8000; www.oakmontcc.org
A seven-time U.S. Open site, this centenarian has the most bunkers and the largest, fastest greens in championship golf.

Oak Tree Golf Club
1515 W. Oak Tree Dr., Edmund, OK; 405-348-2004
Amid prairie gusts, Pete Dye dishes up undulations, moguls and superb variety for events like the 1988 PGA Championship.

Ocean Forest Golf Club
200 Ocean Rd., Sea Island, GA; 912-638-5834
On an Atlantic island, Rees Jones' fairly flat mix of wooded holes and windy, open links hosted the 2001 Walker Cup Match.

Olympia Fields Country Club, North
2800 Country Club Dr., Olympia Fields, IL; 708-748-0495;
www.ofcc.info
The North first hosted the U.S. Open in 1928 and was the site for it again in 2003.

Olympic Club, The Lake
524 Post St., San Francisco, CA; 415-587-4800; www.olyclub.com
You can see the Golden Gate Bridge from the 3rd tee of this pine-, cedar- and cypress-lined four-time U.S. Open site.

Peachtree Golf Club
4600 Peachtree Rd., NE, Atlanta, GA; 404-233-4428
A onetime-only Bobby Jones/RTJ Sr. co-design, this hilly, forested Southerner boasts broad fairways and huge greens.

Pete Dye Golf Club
801 Aaron Smith Dr., Bridgeport, WV; 304-842-2801; www.petedye.com
Routed over a former strip coal mine, this undulating namesake forces healthy carries across the Simpson Creek.

Pine Valley Golf Club
E. Atlantic Ave., Pine Valley, NJ; 856-783-3000
This brutal but beautiful favorite dishes out multiple forced carries on holes hopscotching from one island of turf to the next.

Piping Rock Club
150 Piping Rock Rd., Locust Valley, NY; 516-676-2332
Near where Matinecock Indians smoked peace pipes, this 1911 design retooled in the '80s pays homage to the British best.

Plainfield Country Club
1591 Woodland Ave., Edison, NJ; 908-757-1800; www.plainfieldcc.com
Host of the 1978 U.S. Amateur and 1987 U.S. Women's Open, this classic sports cross bunkers and contoured greens.

Point O'Woods Golf & Country Club
1516 Roslyn Rd., Benton Harbor, MI; 269-944-1433; www.pointowoods.com
Tom Weiskopf, Ben Crenshaw and Tiger Woods are among champs of the Western Amateur, played here since the '60s.

Prairie Dunes Country Club
4812 E. 30th Ave., Hutchinson, KS; 620-662-0581; www.prairiedunes.com
Amid sandhills, yucca and plum thickets, this rolling, windswept layout proved a formidable test at the 2002 U.S. Women's Open.

Pumpkin Ridge, Witch Hollow
12930 NW Old Pumpkin Ridge Rd., North Plains, OR; 503-647-9977; www.pumpkinridge.com
The 1996 site of Tiger Woods' third U.S. Amateur win hosted Nancy Lopez's heartbreaking loss at the '97 U.S. Women's Open.

Quaker Ridge Golf Club
146 Griffen Ave., Scarsdale, NY; 914-725-1100; www.quakerridgegc.org
Hidden next to Winged Foot, this A.W. Tillinghast design boasts outstanding par-4s and was host to the 1997 Walker Cup Match.

Quarry at La Quinta, The
1 Quarry Ln., La Quinta, CA; 760-777-1100; www.thequarrygc.com
Every hole offers scenic desert backdrops at this Palm Springs– area Tom Fazio course draped across mountain slopes.

Ridgewood Country Club, East/West
96 W. Midland Ave., Paramus, NJ; 201-599-3900; www.ridgewoodclub.com
A.W. Tillinghast's 27-holer hosted the 1935 Ryder Cup, 1990 U.S. Senior Open and 2001 Senior PGA Championship.

Rim Golf Club, The
300 S. Clubhouse Rd., Payson, AZ; 928-472-1480;
www.therimgolfclub.com
The boulder escarpment backdropping the par-5 13th is just one
high desert wonder on this final Weiskopf/Morrish design.

Riviera Country Club
1250 Capri Dr., Pacific Palisades, CA; 310-454-6591;
www.rccla.com
Host for the PGA Tour's Nissan LA Open, this eucalyptus-lined track
sits in a canyon south of Sunset Boulevard.

Robert Trent Jones Golf Club
1 Turtle Point Dr., Gainesville, VA; 703-754-4050; www.rtjgc.com
Named for the dean of U.S. golf architects, this Presidents Cup
host is chock-full of water hazards and puzzle-piece bunkers.

Sahalee Country Club, South/North
21200 NE Sahalee Country Club Dr., Sammamish, WA; 425-868-8800;
www.sahalee.com
Meaning "high, heavenly ground" in Chinook, this 1998 PGA
Championship site is bracketed by cedars, firs and hemlocks.

Salem Country Club
133 Forest St., Peabody, MA; 978-538-5400;
www.salemcountryclub.org
Amid maples, oaks and pines, this Donald Ross design has hosted
two U.S. Women's Opens and the 2001 U.S. Senior Open.

Sand Hills Golf Club
Hwy. 97, Mile Marker 55, Mullen, NE; 308-546-2237;
www.sandhillsgolfshop.com
This Ben Crenshaw/Bill Coore links, a noteworthy post–World
War II design, takes full advantage of sandy, rolling terrain.

Sand Ridge Golf Club
12150 Mayfield Rd., Chardon, OH; 440-285-8088;
www.sandridgegolf.com
A modern classic amid aged beauties, this 1998 Tom Fazio design
is dotted with strategically deployed, white sand bunkers.

San Francisco Golf Club
Brotherhood Way & Junipero Sierra Blvd., San Francisco, CA;
415-469-4100
A.W. Tillinghast designed this quiet beauty that features massive
cypresses, sensational bunkering, but nary a water hazard.

Scioto Country Club
2196 Riverside Dr., Columbus, OH; 614-486-4341;
www.sciotocc.com
Jack Nicklaus learned to play on this classic that's hosted the
U.S. Open, Ryder Cup, PGA Championship and U.S. Senior Open.

Seminole Golf Club
901 Seminole Blvd., Juno Beach, FL; 561-626-1331
At a posh retreat, this Donald Ross gem challenges with sea grape
bushes, palms, ocean breezes and close to 200 bunkers.

Shinnecock Hills Golf Club
200 Tuckahoe Rd., Southampton, NY; 631-283-1310
Wedged between the Atlantic Ocean and Great Peconic Bay, this
links was the site of the U.S. Open in 1986, 1995 and 2004.

Shoal Creek
100 New Williamsburg Dr., Shoal Creek, AL; 205-991-9000
The 1984 and 1990 PGA Championships were played on this Nicklaus course carved from dense forest.

Shoreacres
1601 Shore Acres Rd., Lake Bluff, IL; 847-234-1470
On Chicago's North Shore, this short but sweet 1921 Seth Raynor masterpiece offers several exciting shots over steep ravines.

Somerset Hills Country Club
180 Mine Mount Rd., Bernardsville, NJ; 908-766-0043
Near the USGA headquarters sits this A.W. Tillinghast design featuring a well-bunkered front nine and a heavily wooded back.

Southern Hills Country Club
2636 E. 61st St., Tulsa, OK; 918-492-3351; www.southernhillscc.com
Bermuda rough, prairie wind and challenging bunkers made this Perry Maxwell parklander a solid test for the 2001 U.S. Open.

Stanwich Club
888 North St., Greenwich, CT; 203-869-0555; www.stanwich.com
Fast greens, large bunkers, multiple water hazards and double-dogleg par-5s make this 1962 design the state's toughest course.

Troon Golf & Country Club
25000 N. Windy Walk Dr., Scottsdale, AZ; 480-585-4310; www.trooncc.com
This Weiskopf/Morrish debut is a desert target track sporting a 'Cliff' 14th amid boulders, with McDowell Mountain views.

Trump International Golf Club
1100 S. Ocean Blvd., West Palm Beach, FL; 561-682-0700; www.trumpnational.com
The host to the LPGA's ADT Championship features risk/reward holes designed by Jim Fazio, with input from The Donald himself.

Trump National Golf Club
339 Pine Rd., Briarcliff Manor, NY; 914-944-0900; www.trumpnational.com
A celebrity-laden membership enjoys this Jim Fazio/Donald Trump design with a spectacular 'waterfall' par-3 13th hole.

Trump National Golf Club
567 Lamington Rd., Bedminster, NJ; 908-470-4400; www.trumpnational.com
Hewn from John DeLorean's former estate in rolling horse country is this sleek, gull-winged Tom Fazio beauty.

Valhalla Golf Club
15503 Shelbyville Rd., Louisville, KY; 502-245-4475
This Kentucky thoroughbred's bluegrass rough and split fairways hosted Tiger Woods' 2000 PGA Championship win.

Valley Club of Montecito
1901 E. Valley Rd., Santa Barbara, CA; 805-969-2215; www.valleyclub.org
Amid sycamore and eucalyptus groves, this 1929 Alister MacKenzie design offers stylish bunkering and superior par-3s.

Victoria National Golf Club
2000 Victoria National Blvd., Newburgh, IN; 812-858-8230; www.victorianational.com
Tom Fazio transformed an old strip mine into a gorgeous layout with lush mounding weaving through small ponds.

Wade Hampton Golf Club
Hwy. 107 S., Cashiers, NC; 828-743-5465; www.wadehamptongc.com
In the Smoky Mountains, Tom Fazio's 1987 design winds through
a valley heavy with pines and crisscrossed by clear streams.

Wannamoisett Country Club
96 Hoyt Ave., Rumford, RI; 401-434-1200; www.wannamoisett.com
Donald Ross' rare par 69 is crammed into 104 acres yet still packs
a wallop with long, strong par-4s and speedy, undulating greens.

Whisper Rock Golf Club, Lower
32002 N. Old Bridge Rd., Scottsdale, AZ; 480-575-8700;
www.whisperrockgolf.com
Lined in saguaro, prickly pear and ocotillo, Phil Mickelson's debut
offers superb par-4s and risk/reward par-5s.

Winged Foot Golf Club, East
Fennimore Rd., Mamaroneck, NY; 914-698-8400; www.wfgc.org
West's shorter sister sports handsome par-3s and a tournament
pedigree, including the inaugural U.S. Senior Open in 1980.

Winged Foot Golf Club, West
Fennimore Rd., Mamaroneck, NY; 914-698-8400; www.wfgc.org
A.W. Tillinghast designed this four-time U.S. Open test with pear-
shaped greens and deep bunkers on rolling parkland.

Yeamans Hall Club
900 Yeamans Hall Rd., Hanahan, SC; 843-744-5555
Tom Doak restored this layout to its 1925 glory with huge square
greens and yawning traps amid aged oaks and magnolias.

Urban Driving Ranges

Within a short ride from a major business district

Atlanta

Blue Heron Golf Club
460 Morgan Falls Rd.; 770-390-0424;
www.blueherongolfclub.com

Charlie Yates Golf Course
10 Lakeside Village Dr., SE; 404-373-4655;
www.charlieyatesgolfcourse.com

Boston

Boston Golf Driving Range at The Radisson Hotel
200 Stuart St.; 617-457-2699; www.bostongolfacademy.com

City Golf Boston
38 Bromfield St.; 617-357-4653; www.citygolfboston.com

Chicago

Diversey Driving Range
141 W. Diversey Pkwy.; 312-742-7929; www.diverseygolf.com

Dallas

Hank Haney City Place Golf Center
3636 McKinney Ave.; 214-520-7275; www.hankhaney.com

North Texas Golf Center
2101 Walnut Hill Ln.; 972-247-4653; www.northtexasgolf.com

Denver

All Golf at Overland
1801 S. Huron St.; 303-777-7331; www.allgolf.com

Kennedy Golf Center
10500 E. Hampden Ave.; 303-755-0105; www.allgolf.com

Honolulu

Coral Creek Golf Club
1111 Geiger Rd.; 808-441-4653;
www.coralcreekgolfhawaii.com

Houston

Clear Creek Golf Club
3902 Fellows Rd.; 713-738-8000; www.clearcreekgolfclub.com

Las Vegas

Badlands Golf Club
9119 Alta Dr.; 702-242-4653; www.troongolf.com

Callaway Golf Center
6730 S. Las Vegas Blvd.; 702-896-4100

Los Angeles

Griffith Park Golf Courses
4900 Griffith Park Dr.; 323-663-2555; www.laparks.org

John Wells Golf Driving Range
11501 Strathern St.; 818-767-1954

Lakes at El Segundo, The
400 S. Sepulveda Blvd.; 310-322-0202; www.premiergolfcenters.com

Rancho Park Golf Course
10460 W. Pico Blvd.; 310-838-7373; www.laparks.org

New Orleans

Bayou Oaks Golf Facility
1 Palm Dr.; 504-483-9396; www.neworleanscitypark.com

New York City

Alley Pond Golf Center
232-01 Northern Blvd.; 718-225-9187;
www.golfandsportsinfo.com/alleypond

Chelsea Piers Golf Club
Pier 59; 212-336-6400; www.chelseapiers.com

Randall's Island Golf Center
1 Randall's Island; 212-427-5689

Philadelphia

FDR Golf Club
Pattison Ave. & 20th St.; 215-462-8997; www.golfphilly.com

Karakung at Cobb's Creek Golf Club
7200 Lansdowne Ave.; 215-877-8707; www.golfphilly.com

San Diego

Bonita Driving Range
3631 Bonita Rd.; 619-426-2069

Stadium Golf Center
29-90 Murphy Canyon Rd.; 858-277-6667;
www.stadiumgolfcenter.com

Seattle

Interbay Golf Center
2501 15th Ave. W.; 206-285-2200; www.jeffersonparkgolf.com

Jefferson Park Golf Course
4101 Beacon Ave. S.; 206-762-4513; www.jeffersonparkgolf.com

Washington, DC

East Potomac Park Golf Course & Driving Range
972 Ohio Dr., SW; 202-554-7660; www.golfdc.com

Indexes

Properties in indexes are followed by nearest major city.
Indexes list the best of many within each category.

Budget

(\$40 and under)

Bunkering

Indexes

Celebrity Designs

Arnold Palmer

Arthur Hills

Shadow Creek, *Las Vegas, NV*

TPC of Myrtle Beach, *Myrtle Beach, SC*

Treetops, Tom Fazio Premier, *Gaylord, MI*

Turning Stone, Atunyote, *Finger Lakes, NY*

Ventana Canyon, Canyon, *Tucson, AZ*

Ventana Canyon, Mountain, *Tucson, AZ*

Walt Disney World, Osprey Ridge, *Orlando, FL*

Westin Rio Mar, Ocean, *Rio Grande, PR*

Wild Dunes, Harbor, *Charleston, SC*

Wild Dunes, Links, *Charleston, SC*

World Woods, Pine Barrens, *Tampa, FL*

World Woods, Rolling Oaks, *Tampa, FL*

Wynn Las Vegas, *Las Vegas, NV*

Tom Weiskopf/ Jay Morrish

Buffalo Creek, *Dallas, TX*

Daufuskie Island, Bloody Point, *Hilton Head, SC*

Harbor Club, *Lake Oconee, GA*

La Cantera, Resort, *San Antonio, TX*

TPC of Scottsdale, Desert, *Scottsdale, AZ*

TPC of Scottsdale, Stadium, *Scottsdale, AZ*

Troon North, Monument, *Scottsdale, AZ*

Troon North, Pinnacle, *Scottsdale, AZ*

Waikoloa Beach, Kings, *Big Island, HI*

Wilds, *Minneapolis, MN*

Conditioning

Arizona Nat'l, *Tucson, AZ*

Arnold Palmer's Bay Hill, *Orlando, FL*

Augustine, *DC Metro Area, VA*

Aviara, *San Diego, CA*

Bandon Dunes, Bandon Dunes Course, *Coos Bay, OR*

Bandon Dunes, Pacific Dunes, *Coos Bay, OR*

Barton Creek, Fazio Foothills, *Austin, TX*

Baywood Greens, *Rehoboth Beach, DE*

Bear's Best Vegas, *Las Vegas, NV*

Belgrade Lakes, *Central Maine, ME*

Bethpage, Black, *Long Island, NY*

Blackwolf Run, River, *Kohler, WI*

Boulders, North, *Scottsdale, AZ*

Boulders, South, *Scottsdale, AZ*

Brickyard Crossing, *Indianapolis, IN*

Broadmoor, East, *Colorado Springs, CO*

Broadmoor, West, *Colorado Springs, CO*

Bulle Rock, *Baltimore, MD*

Caledonia Golf & Fish, *Pawleys Island, SC*

Cascata, *Las Vegas, NV*

Challenge/Manele, *Lanai, HI*

Club/Old Kinderhook, *Lake of the Ozarks, MO*

Coeur d'Alene Resort, *Coeur d'Alene, ID*

CordeValle, *San Francisco Bay Area, CA*

Crooked Creek, *Atlanta, GA*

Crystal Springs, Ballyowen, *NYC Metro, NJ*

Desert Willow, Firecliff, *Palm Springs, CA*

Diablo Grande, Legends West, *Sacramento, CA*

Duke Univ. Golf, *Raleigh-Durham, NC*

Dunes/Mauni Lai, *Maui, HI*

Eaglesticks, *Columbus, OH*

Indexes

Exceptional Clubhouses

Expense Account
(\$200 and over)

Indexes

TPC of Scottsdale, Stadium, *Scottsdale, AZ*
Troon North, Monument, *Scottsdale, AZ*
Troon North, Pinnacle, *Scottsdale, AZ*
Turning Stone, Atunyote, *Finger Lakes, NY*
Ventana Canyon, Canyon, *Tucson, AZ*
Ventana Canyon, Mountain, *Tucson, AZ*
Westin Innisbrook, Copperhead, *Tampa, FL*
Westin Innisbrook, Island, *Tampa, FL*
Whistling Straits, Straits, *Kohler, WI*
Wynn Las Vegas, *Las Vegas, NV*

Fine Food Too

Arizona Biltmore, *Phoenix, AZ*
Aviara, *San Diego, CA*
Bali Hai, *Las Vegas, NV*
Balsams Panorama, *Colebrook, NH*
Bandon Dunes, *Coos Bay, OR*
Barnsley Gardens, *Atlanta, GA*
Biltmore, *Miami, FL*
Blackwolf Run, *Kohler, WI*
Boca Raton Resort, *Palm Beach, FL*
Boulders, *Scottsdale, AZ*
Breakers, *Palm Beach, FL*
Bridges, *Gettysburg, PA*
Broadmoor, *Colorado Springs, CO*
Caledonia Golf & Fish, *Pawleys Island, SC*
Camelback, *Scottsdale, AZ*
Carmel Valley Ranch, *Monterey Peninsula, CA*
Cascata, *Las Vegas, NV*
Château Élan, *Atlanta, GA*
CordeValle, *San Francisco Bay Area, CA*
Cordillera, *Vail, CO*

Crumpin-Fox, *Berkshires, MA*
Edgewood Tahoe, *Reno, NV*
Farm Neck, *Martha's Vineyard, MA*
Four Seasons/Las Colinas, *Dallas, TX*
Fox Hopyard, *East Haddam, CT*
Geneva Nat'l, *Lake Geneva, WI*
Grand Cypress, *Orlando, FL*
Grayhawk, *Scottsdale, AZ*
Great River, *Danbury, CT*
Greenbrier, *White Sulphur Springs, WV*
Half Moon Bay, *San Francisco Bay Area, CA*
Harvester, *Des Moines, IA*
Homestead, *Roanoke, VA*
Homestead, *Salt Lake City, UT*
Kapolei, *Oahu, HI*
Keswick Club, *Charlottesville, VA*
Keystone Ranch, *Vail, CO*
Kiawah Island, *Charleston, SC*
La Costa, *San Diego, CA*
La Paloma, *Tucson, AZ*
La Quinta, *Palm Springs, CA*
Legends Club, *Minneapolis, MN*
Links/Lighthouse Sound, *Ocean City, MD*
Lodge/Four Seasons, *Lake of the Ozarks, MO*
Marriott Des. Springs, *Palm Springs, CA*
Mauna Lani, *Big Island, HI*
May River/Palmetto Bluff, *Hilton Head, SC*
Mid Pines Inn, *Pinehurst, NC*
Mission Inn, *Orlando, FL*
Nemacolin Woodlands, *Pittsburgh, PA*
Ocotillo, *Phoenix, AZ*
Ojai Valley Inn, *Los Angeles, CA*
Oyster Bay Town Golf, *Long Island, NY*
Pebble Beach, *Monterey Peninsula, CA*
Pelican Hill, *Orange County, CA*

Finishing Holes

Instruction

Junior-Friendly

Cape May Nat'l, *Cape May, NJ*
Carmel Valley Ranch, *Monterey Peninsula, CA*
Center Valley Club, *Allentown, PA*
Cinnabar Hills, *San Francisco Bay Area, CA*
Cobblestone, *Atlanta, GA*
Colbert Hills, *Topeka, KS*
Crumpin-Fox, *Berkshires, MA*
Eagle Mountain, *Scottsdale, AZ*
Eagle Vail, *Vail, CO*
Golden Bear/Indigo Run, *Hilton Head, SC*
Gray Plantation, *Lake Charles, LA*
Grossinger, Big G, *Catskills, NY*
Harbor Pines, *Atlantic City, NJ*
Harding Park, *San Francisco Bay Area, CA*
Heather Glen, *Myrtle Beach, SC*
Heritage Palms, *Palm Springs, CA*
Hershey, Parkview, *Harrisburg, PA*
Hog Neck, *Easton, MD*
Howell Park, *Freehold, NJ*
Hyatt Hill Country, *San Antonio, TX*
Indian Peaks, *Boulder, CO*
Kebo Valley, *Central Maine, ME*
Kiva Dunes, *Mobile, AL*
Kona Country Club, Ocean, *Big Island, HI*
Legacy Ridge, *Denver, CO*
Longbow, *Phoenix, AZ*
Makaha, *Oahu, HI*
Meadows Farms, *DC Metro Area, VA*
Memorial Park, *Houston, TX*
Murphy Creek, *Denver, CO*
Myrtle Beach Nat'l, SouthCreek, *Myrtle Beach, SC*
Naperbrook, *Chicago, IL*
Oyster Bay Town Golf, *Long Island, NY*

Pacific Grove, *Monterey Peninsula, CA*
Palmetto Dunes, Robert Trent Jones, *Hilton Head, SC*
Penn Nat'l, Founders, *Gettysburg, PA*
PGA Golf Club, North, *Port St. Lucie, FL*
Pinehurst, No. 1, *Pinehurst, NC*
Pinehurst, No. 3, *Pinehurst, NC*
Poipu Bay, *Kauai, HI*
Royce Brook, East, *Bridgewater, NJ*
Smithtown Landing, *Long Island, NY*
SouthWood, *Panhandle, FL*
Spencer T. Olin, *St. Louis Area, IL*
Sterling Farms, *Danbury, CT*
Stow Acres, South, *Worcester, MA*
Sycuan, Oak Glen, *San Diego, CA*
Sycuan, Willow Glen, *San Diego, CA*
Tahquitz Creek, Legend, *Palm Springs, CA*
Tan-Tar-A, The Oaks, *Lake of the Ozarks, MO*
TPC at Valencia, *Los Angeles, CA*
TPC of Scottsdale, Desert, *Scottsdale, AZ*
Trilogy at Vistancia, *Phoenix, AZ*
Valley View, *Salt Lake City, UT*
World Woods, Pine Barrens, *Tampa, FL*
World Woods, Rolling Oaks, *Tampa, FL*

Links-Style

Amelia Island, Ocean Links, *Jacksonville, FL*
Arcadia Bluffs, *Traverse City, MI*
Bandon Dunes, Bandon Dunes Course, *Coos Bay, OR*

Indexes

Noteworthy Newcomers

Opening Holes

Pace of Play

Par-4s

Practice Facilities

TPC at Sawgrass, *Jacksonville, FL*
TPC of Scottsdale, *Scottsdale, AZ*
TPC of Tampa Bay, *Tampa, FL*
Treetops, *Gaylord, MI*
Troon North, *Scottsdale, AZ*
Univ. of NM Championship, *Albuquerque, NM*
Univ. Ridge, *Madison, WI*
Victoria Hills, *Daytona Beach, FL*
Whistling Straits, *Kohler, WI*
World Golf Village, *Jacksonville, FL*
World Woods, *Tampa, FL*

Private Functions

Aldeen, *Rockford, IL*
Angeles National, *Los Angeles, CA*
Angel Park, *Las Vegas, NV*
Arizona Biltmore, *Phoenix, AZ*
Aviara, *San Diego, CA*
Bald Head Island, *Myrtle Beach Area, NC*
Barnsley Gardens, *Atlanta, GA*
Barton Creek, *Austin, TX*
Boca Raton Resort, *Palm Beach, FL*
Boulders, *Scottsdale, AZ*
Boyne Highlands, *Petoskey, MI*
Breakers, *Palm Beach, FL*
Brickyard Crossing, *Indianapolis, IN*
Broadmoor, *Colorado Springs, CO*
Callaway Gardens, *Columbus, GA*
Carambola, *St. Croix, USVI*
Challenge/Manele, *Lanai, HI*
Coeur d'Alene Resort, *Coeur d'Alene, ID*
DarkHorse, *Sacramento, CA*
Dragon/Gold Mtn., *Lake Tahoe, CA*
Druids Glen, *Seattle, WA*

En-Joie, *Finger Lakes, NY*
Experience/Koele, *Lanai, HI*
Four Seasons/Las Colinas, *Dallas, TX*
Gleneagles/Equinox, *Southern Vermont, VT*
Gold Canyon, *Phoenix, AZ*
Grand Cypress, *Orlando, FL*
Grande Dunes, *Myrtle Beach, SC*
Grand Geneva, *Lake Geneva, WI*
Grayhawk, *Scottsdale, AZ*
Greenbrier, *White Sulphur Springs, WV*
Homestead, *Roanoke, VA*
Horseshoe Bay, *Austin, TX*
Hualalai, *Big Island, HI*
Hyatt Dorado, *Dorado, PR*
Hyatt Hill Country, *San Antonio, TX*
Kapalua, *Maui, HI*
Kauai Lagoons, *Kauai, HI*
Keswick Club, *Charlottesville, VA*
Keystone Ranch, *Vail, CO*
Kiawah Island, *Charleston, SC*
Kierland, *Scottsdale, AZ*
Kingsmill, *Williamsburg, VA*
La Costa, *San Diego, CA*
La Quinta, *Palm Springs, CA*
Las Vegas Paiute, *Las Vegas, NV*
Little Mountain, *Cleveland, OH*
Longbow, *Phoenix, AZ*
Mahogany Run, *St. Thomas, USVI*
Marriott Des. Springs, *Palm Springs, CA*
Marriott's Wildfire, *Phoenix, AZ*
Mauna Kea, *Big Island, HI*
Mauna Lani, *Big Island, HI*
May River/Palmetto Bluff, *Hilton Head, SC*
Mission Inn, *Orlando, FL*
Missouri Bluffs, *St. Louis, MO*

Indexes

Nemacolin Woodlands, *Pittsburgh, PA*

Neshanic Valley, *Bridgewater, NJ*

Old Silo, *Lexington, KY*

Pebble Beach, *Monterey Peninsula, CA*

Phoenician, *Scottsdale, AZ*

Pine Needles Lodge, *Pinehurst, NC*

Piper Glen, *St. Louis Area, IL*

Princeville, *Kauai, HI*

Raven at Three Peaks, *Vail, CO*

Reflection Bay/Lake Las Vegas, *Las Vegas, NV*

Reynolds, *Lake Oconee, GA*

Ritz-Carlton Orlando, *Orlando, FL*

Samoset, *Southern Maine, ME*

Sand Barrens, *Cape May, NJ*

Sea Island, *Lowcountry, GA*

Sea Pines, *Hilton Head, SC*

Seaview Marriott, *Atlantic City, NJ*

Sedona Golf, *Sedona, AZ*

Shennecossett, *New London, CT*

Shepherd's Crook, *Chicago, IL*

Spanish Bay, *Monterey Peninsula, CA*

Starr Pass, *Tucson, AZ*

Sunriver, *Bend, OR*

Sun Valley Resort, *Sun Valley, ID*

Tot Hill Farm, *Greensboro, NC*

TPC at Heron Bay, *Ft. Lauderdale, FL*

TPC at Sawgrass, *Jacksonville, FL*

TPC at The Canyons, *Las Vegas, NV*

TPC of Myrtle Beach, *Myrtle Beach, SC*

TPC of Tampa Bay, *Tampa, FL*

Troon North, *Scottsdale, AZ*

Vineyard Golf/Renault, *Atlantic City, NJ*

Wailea, *Maui, HI*

We-Ko-Pa, *Scottsdale, AZ*

Wente Vineyards, *San Francisco Bay Area, CA*

Whistling Straits, *Kohler, WI*

Wigwam, *Phoenix, AZ*

Wild Dunes, *Charleston, SC*

World Golf Village, *Jacksonville, FL*

Wynn Las Vegas, *Las Vegas, NV*

Pro-Event Hosts

Arnold Palmer's Bay Hill, *Orlando, FL*

Augusta Pines, *Houston, TX*

Barton Creek, Fazio Foothills, *Austin, TX*

Bayonet Blackhorse, Bayonet, *Monterey Peninsula, CA*

Bethpage, Black, *Long Island, NY*

Breakers, Rees Jones Course, *Palm Beach, FL*

Broadmoor, East, *Colorado Springs, CO*

Brown Deer Park, *Milwaukee, WI*

Bulle Rock, *Baltimore, MD*

Capitol Hill, Senator, *Montgomery, AL*

Club/Savannah Harbor, *Savannah, GA*

Cog Hill, No. 4 (Dubsdread), *Chicago, IL*

Crandon Park, *Miami, FL*

Doral, Blue Monster, *Miami, FL*

Doral, Great White, *Miami, FL*

Dunes Golf & Beach, *Myrtle Beach, SC*

Edgewood Tahoe, *Reno, NV*

En-Joie, *Finger Lakes, NY*

Four Seasons/Las Colinas, Cottonwood Valley, *Dallas, TX*

Pro Shops

Apache Stronghold, *San Carlos, AZ*
Arizona Nat'l, *Tucson, AZ*
Arnold Palmer's Bay Hill, *Orlando, FL*
ASU Karsten, *Tempe, AZ*
Aviara, *San Diego, CA*
Bald Head Island, *Myrtle Beach Area, NC*
Bandon Dunes, *Coos Bay, OR*
Barton Creek, *Austin, TX*
Bay Harbor, *Petoskey, MI*
Black Butte Ranch, *Bend, OR*
Boulders, *Scottsdale, AZ*
Breckenridge, *Vail, CO*
Broadmoor, *Colorado Springs, CO*
Callaway Gardens, *Columbus, GA*
Cambrian Ridge, *Montgomery, AL*
Camelback, *Scottsdale, AZ*
Cantigny, *Chicago, IL*
Capitol Hill, *Montgomery, AL*
Carmel Valley Ranch, *Monterey Peninsula, CA*
Carter Plantation, *Baton Rouge, LA*
Challenge/Manele, *Lanai, HI*
ChampionsGate, *Orlando, FL*
Club/Savannah Harbor, *Savannah, GA*
Cordillera, *Vail, CO*
Coyote Hills, *Orange County, CA*
Crystal Springs, Great Gorge, *NYC Metro, NJ*
Deer Creek, *Kansas City, KS*
Desert Dunes, *Palm Springs, CA*
Desert Willow, *Palm Springs, CA*
Diablo Grande, *Sacramento, CA*
Doral, *Miami, FL*
Dragon/Gold Mtn., *Lake Tahoe, CA*
Eagle Ranch, *Vail, CO*

Falcon's Fire, *Orlando, FL*
Forest Akers MSU, *Lansing, MI*
Fox Hollow, *Tampa, FL*
Glen Annie, *Santa Barbara, CA*
Golf Club/Newcastle, *Seattle, WA*
Grand Cypress, *Orlando, FL*
Grand Nat'l, *Auburn, AL*
Grand View Lodge, *Brainerd, MN*
Grayhawk, *Scottsdale, AZ*
Great River, *Danbury, CT*
Greenbrier, *White Sulphur Springs, WV*
Half Moon Bay, *San Francisco Bay Area, CA*
Hampton Cove, *Huntsville, AL*
Harborside Int'l, *Chicago, IL*
Indian Peaks, *Boulder, CO*
Industry Hills, *Los Angeles, CA*
Kiawah Island, *Charleston, SC*
Kierland, *Scottsdale, AZ*
Ko Olina, *Oahu, HI*
La Cantera, *San Antonio, TX*
La Costa, *San Diego, CA*
Lake Jovita, *Tampa, FL*
La Paloma, *Tucson, AZ*
La Quinta, *Palm Springs, CA*
Legacy Ridge, *Denver, CO*
Little Bennett, *Frederick, MD*
Lockeford Springs, *Stockton, CA*
Longaberger, *Columbus, OH*
Los Caballeros, *Phoenix, AZ*
Lost Canyons, *Los Angeles, CA*
LPGA Int'l, *Daytona Beach, FL*
Lyman Orchards, *Danbury, CT*
Maderas, *San Diego, CA*
Marriott Des. Springs, *Palm Springs, CA*
Mission Inn, *Orlando, FL*
Monarch Beach, *Orange County, CA*
Montauk Downs, *Long Island, NY*
Murphy Creek, *Denver, CO*
Oak Creek, *Orange County, CA*

Putting Courses

Angel Park, *Las Vegas, NV*
Arizona Biltmore, *Phoenix, AZ*
Camelback, *Scottsdale, AZ*
Hawk Hollow, *Lansing, MI*
Horseshoe Bay, *Austin, TX*
Legend Trail, *Scottsdale, AZ*
Marriott Des. Springs, *Palm Springs, CA*
Orange County Nat'l, *Orlando, FL*
Quail Lodge, *Monterey Peninsula, CA*
Ravines, *Jacksonville, FL*
RedHawk, *San Diego, CA*
Running Y Ranch, *Klamath Falls, OR*
Sunriver, *Bend, OR*
Turtle Creek, *Philadelphia, PA*
World Golf Village, *Jacksonville, FL*
World Woods, *Tampa, FL*

Replicas

Bear's Best Atlanta, *Atlanta, GA*
Bear's Best Vegas, *Las Vegas, NV*
Boyne Highlands, Donald Ross Memorial, *Petoskey, MI*
Grand Cypress, New, *Orlando, FL*
McCullough's Emerald, *Atlantic City, NJ*
Royal Links, *Las Vegas, NV*
Tour 18 Dallas, *Dallas, TX*
Tour 18 Houston, *Houston, TX*
Tribute, *Dallas, TX*

Resort

Amelia Island Plant., *Jacksonville, FL*
Arizona Biltmore, *Phoenix, AZ*
Arnold Palmer's Bay Hill, *Orlando, FL*
Aviara, *San Diego, CA*

Bald Head Island, *Myrtle Beach Area, NC*
Balsams Panorama, *Colebrook, NH*
Bandon Dunes, *Coos Bay, OR*
Barefoot Resort, *Myrtle Beach, SC*
Barnsley Gardens, *Atlanta, GA*
Barton Creek, *Austin, TX*
Bay Harbor, *Petoskey, MI*
Beaver Creek, *Vail, CO*
Black Butte Ranch, *Bend, OR*
Blackwolf Run, *Kohler, WI*
Boca Raton Resort, *Palm Beach, FL*
Boulders, *Scottsdale, AZ*
Boyne Highlands, *Petoskey, MI*
Brasstown Valley, *Atlanta, GA*
Breakers, *Palm Beach, FL*
Bristol Harbour, *Finger Lakes, NY*
Broadmoor, *Colorado Springs, CO*
Callaway Gardens, *Columbus, GA*
Carmel Valley Ranch, *Monterey Peninsula, CA*
Carroll Valley, *Gettysburg, PA*
Challenge/Manele, *Lanai, HI*
Château Élan, *Atlanta, GA*
Circling Raven, *Coeur d'Alene, ID*
Club/Savannah Harbor, *Savannah, GA*
Coeur d'Alene Resort, *Coeur d'Alene, ID*
Concord Resort, *Catskills, NY*
CordeValle, *San Francisco Bay Area, CA*
Cordillera, *Vail, CO*
Craft Farms, *Mobile, AL*
Cranwell, *Berkshires, MA*
Dancing Rabbit, *Jackson, MS*
Daufuskie Island, *Hilton Head, SC*

Scenic

Indexes

Storied

Toughest

(Courses with the highest slope ratings from the back tees)

Indexes

University

Walking Only

Women-Friendly

Amelia Island, Ocean Links, *Jacksonville, FL*

Bay Creek, Palmer, *Virginia Beach, VA*

Baywood Greens, *Rehoboth Beach, DE*

Bear Trace/Ross Creek, *Nashville, TN*

Big Mountain, *Kalispell, MT*

Big Run, *Chicago, IL*

Birdwood, *Charlottesville, VA*

Black Lake, *Traverse City, MI*

Boca Raton Resort, Resort Course, *Palm Beach, FL*

Boulders, South, *Scottsdale, AZ*

Boyne Highlands, Heather, *Petoskey, MI*

Breakers, Ocean Course, *Palm Beach, FL*

Broadmoor, East, *Colorado Springs, CO*

Bulle Rock, *Baltimore, MD*

Camelback, Club, *Scottsdale, AZ*

Camelback, Resort, *Scottsdale, AZ*

Carmel Valley Ranch, *Monterey Peninsula, CA*

Challenge/Manele, *Lanai, HI*

Château Élan, Château, *Atlanta, GA*

Château Élan, Woodlands, *Atlanta, GA*

Coeur d'Alene Resort, *Coeur d'Alene, ID*

Coral Canyon, *St. George, UT*

Cowboys, *Dallas, TX*

Coyote Hills, *Orange County, CA*

Desert Willow, Mountain View, *Palm Springs, CA*

Dragon/Gold Mtn., *Lake Tahoe, CA*

Eagle Ridge, *Freehold, NJ*

Eaglesticks, *Columbus, OH*

Farm Neck, *Martha's Vineyard, MA*

Four Seasons/Las Colinas, Cottonwood Valley, *Dallas, TX*

Glen Annie, *Santa Barbara, CA*

Golf Club/Newcastle, China Creek, *Seattle, WA*

Grand Cypress, *Orlando, FL*

Greenbrier, Meadows, *White Sulphur Springs, WV*

Greenbrier, Old White, *White Sulphur Springs, WV*

Half Moon Bay, Ocean, *San Francisco Bay Area, CA*

Harvester, *Des Moines, IA*

Hershey, West, *Harrisburg, PA*

Homestead, Old, *Roanoke, VA*

Keystone Ranch, River, *Vail, CO*

Kiawah Island, Osprey Point, *Charleston, SC*

Kierland, *Scottsdale, AZ*

Kingsmill, Plantation, *Williamsburg, VA*

La Cantera, Palmer, *San Antonio, TX*

Linville, *Asheville, NC*

Longaberger, *Columbus, OH*

Los Caballeros, *Phoenix, AZ*

Lost Canyons, Shadow, *Los Angeles, CA*

LPGA Int'l, Champions, *Daytona Beach, FL*

LPGA Int'l, Legends, *Daytona Beach, FL*

Marriott Desert Springs, Palm, *Palm Springs, CA*

Mauna Lani, South, *Big Island, HI*

Mission Inn, Las Colinas, *Orlando, FL*

Monarch Beach, *Orange County, CA*

Murphy Creek, *Denver, CO*

Myrtle Beach Nat'l, SouthCreek, *Myrtle Beach, SC*

Alphabetical Page Index

Alphabetical Page Index

Alphabetical Page Index

subscribe to zagat.com

Alphabetical Page Index

Alphabetical Page Index

Alphabetical Page Index

Alphabetical Page Index

Alphabetical Page Index

Alphabetical Page Index

Alphabetical Page Index

Alphabetical Page Index

Alphabetical Page Index

Alphabetical Page Index

Alphabetical Page Index

Alphabetical Page Index

Alphabetical Page Index

Alphabetical Page Index